Byzantium's Balkan Frontier is the first narrative history in English of the northern Balkans in the tenth to twelfth centuries. Where previous histories have been concerned principally with the medieval history of distinct and autonomous Balkan nations, this study regards Byzantine political authority as a unifying factor in the various lands which formed the empire's frontier in the north and west.

It takes as its central concern Byzantine relations with all Slavic and non-Slavic peoples – including the Serbs, Croats, Bulgarians and Hungarians – in and beyond the Balkan Peninsula, and explores in detail imperial responses, first to the migrations of nomadic peoples, and subsequently to the expansion of Latin Christendom. It also examines the changing conception of the frontier in Byzantine thought and literature through the middle Byzantine period.

PAUL STEPHENSON is British Academy Postdoctoral Fellow, Keble College, Oxford

BYZANTIUM'S
BALKAN FRONTIER

A Political Study of the
Northern Balkans, 900–1204

PAUL STEPHENSON

British Academy Postdoctoral Fellow
Keble College, Oxford

CAMBRIDGE
UNIVERSITY PRESS

PUBLISHED BY THE PRESS SYNDICATE OF THE UNIVERSITY OF CAMBRIDGE
The Pitt Building, Trumpington Street, Cambridge, United Kingdom

CAMBRIDGE UNIVERSITY PRESS
The Edinburgh Building, Cambridge CB2 2RU, UK http://www.cup.cam.ac.uk
40 West 20th Street, New York, NY 10011-4211, USA http://www.cup.org
10 Stamford Road, Oakleigh, Melbourne 3166, Australia
Ruiz de Alarcón 13, 28014 Madrid, Spain

First published 2000

Printed in the United Kingdom at the University Press, Cambridge

Typeface Monotype Baskerville 11/12½ pt.   *System* QuarkXPress™ [SE]

A catalogue record for this book is available from the British Library

Library of Congress cataloguing in publication data

Stephenson, Paul.
  Byzantium's Balkan Frontier: a political study of the Northern
Balkans, 900–1204 / Paul Stephenson.
    p.   cm.
  Includes bibliographical references and index.
  ISBN 0 521 77017 3 (hardback)
    1. Balkan Peninsula – Politics and government.   2. Byzantine
Empire – Politics and government – 527–1081.   3. Byzantine Empire –
 – Politics and government – 1081–1453.   4. Byzantine Empire – Ethnic
relations.   I. Title.
DR39.S76   2000
949.6′0144 – dc21   00-42114   CIP

ISBN 0 521 77017 3 hardback

Contents

Maps and figures

Preface

This book began as a refinement of my doctoral dissertation which I defended at the University of Cambridge in April 1996. My thesis presents a distillation, in the form of four regional surveys, of the written and archaeological evidence pertaining to the Byzantine frontier in the northern Balkans in the period 971–1180. The refinement, I thought, should have a narrative structure, since no synthetic narrative political history of the northern Balkans exists in English for this period. I also decided to increase its chronological and geographical range to allow a cursory treatment of Bulgaria before the imposition of the 'Byzantine Yoke', and a fuller exploration of how the 'yoke' was cast off by Bulgarians, Vlachs, Serbs and others. In the end the refinement bears no resemblance whatever to the thesis. It takes as its central concern Byzantine responses, first to the migrations of nomadic peoples, and subsequently to the expansion of Latin Christendom. It also examines the changing conception of the frontier in Byzantine thought and literature through the Middle Byzantine Period.

In the course of writing the thesis and book I have enjoyed the support of a number of institutions. St John's College, Cambridge awarded me a Benefactors' Scholarship and travel funds sufficient to take me around Turkey and the Balkans more than once. The British Academy funded my Ph.D. I was honoured to be appointed to a British Academy Postdoctoral Fellowship, and privileged to hold this at Keble College, Oxford. The Warden and Fellows of Keble have provided intellectual and other sustenance.

I have benefited from the instruction, advice and criticism of many friends and scholars. My greatest debt is to Jonathan Shepard, who supervised the thesis, read drafts of papers published separately and reworked for the book, read the book in two drafts, allowed me to make use of his forthcoming works, supplied me with offprints of his published papers, provided bibliographical information and assistance with tricky texts, and saved me from many errors of fact and judgement. Simon Franklin and Elizabeth Jeffreys examined the thesis, and encouraged me to produce the refinement. Elizabeth has continued to provide encouragement and advice during my time in Oxford. Averil Cameron brought me to Oxford, and provided a home at Keble where I have been able to complete this project, and begin another. As my 'mentor', appointed by the British Academy, she has supervised my fellowship, and as a friend and critic she has improved my scholarship considerably. Other Byzantinists have helped: James Howard-Johnston provided the most insightful historical instruction at an early stage; Michael Metcalf taught me numismatics; Cyril Mango taught me sigillography, and inspired with his wit and erudition; Paul Magdalino offered welcome advice at a late stage. Ned Goy taught me Serbo-Croat in Cambridge, and David Raeburn improved my Greek in Oxford. Neven Budak and Mladen Ančić welcomed me in Zagreb and Zadar. Csanád Bálint and József Laslovszky welcomed me in Budapest. Despina Christodoulou argued with me in Cambridge and Athens. Dean Kolbas made me think about what I was doing and why I was doing it. My sisters and grandmother, Ian Stewart and Jennifer Lambert, Kristen Laakso and Brian Didier, Graham Stewart and Caroline Humfress have taken a keen and welcome interest. Clare lost interest years ago, but this book is still dedicated to her, and now also to Jack Jolly.

Oxford, March 1999

A note on citation and transliteration

In citation, more for reasons of length than style, I have employed a modified author-date system similar to that used in *The New Cambridge Medieval History*. Primary sources are referred to, according to common practice, by the name of the author, or by an abbreviation of the title of the work. Thus, I refer to Cinnamus (not *The Deeds of John and Manuel Comnenus*), but the *Alexiad* (by Anna Comnena). Most abbreviated titles are self-evident, for example *Codex Diplomaticus* refers to the *Codex Diplomaticus regni Croatiae, Dalmatiae et Slavoniae*. However, some sources have a more cryptic abbreviation which is in common use, for example *DAI*, the *De Administrando Imperio*, or *PVL*, *Povest' Vremennych Let* (*Russian Primary Chronicle*). In each such case the work is listed in the bibliography after the abbreviation, and is also included in the list of abbreviations which precedes the text. Where an author has produced multiple works, both name and title are used, for example Theophylact [of Ohrid], *Lettres*, and Theophylact, *Discours*. Where a work exists, and is commonly cited, in more than one standard edition, the name of the editor has been included, for example Cecaumenus, ed. Litavrin (not ed. Wassiliewsky and Jernstedt). Secondary works are cited in notes (and occasionally within the text) according to the simple formula author, date, page, and (where necessary), column (col.), ep. (letter), number (nr.) or note (n.). Thus Michael Angold, *The Byzantine Empire, 1025–1204: a Political History*, 2nd edn., London and New York 1997, page 176, note 3, is cited as: Angold 1997: 176, n. 3.

In transliterating from Cyrillic I have used, I hope consistently, the Library of Congress system. This has led to my occasionally emending an author's chosen transliteration of a work, or even her or his own name. Thus, I refer to I. Dujčev as Duichev, and V. Šandrovskaya as Shandrovskaia. I have been less consistent in my transliteration from Greek. On the various methods for transliterating Greek I refer the reader, for once, to Treadgold 1997: xxi–xxiii, and to the criticism of

Treadgold by George Dennis, in *BMGS* 21 (1997): 283, 'Latinisation . . . is contrary to th[e practice] of most serious Byzantinists today, and is especially unwarranted now that the *Oxford Dictionary of Byzantium* has provided writers in English with a standard system of representing Byzantine terminology. To continue with Latinisation is simply a foppish affectation, with a touch of arrogance.' This is correct, and for specific Greek terms I have employed a Greek transliteration italicized, so *strategos* not strategus, and *doux* not dux or duke. However, with just a hint of foppish affectation, I have employed a Latin transliteration for each proper name except where a common English variant exists, for example Alexius Comnenus not Alexios Komnenos, and John not Ioannes nor Ioannis. In my defence I cite precedent not principle, and skulk behind the authority of a serious Byzantinist: Angold 1995: ix, 'I have come to favour far more than in the past a Latin transliteration of Byzantine proper names: so Comnenus not Komnenos.'

Abbreviations

B	*Byzantion*, Brussels and Paris 1924–
BF	*Byzantinische Forschungen*, Amsterdam 1966–
BMGS	*Byzantine and Modern Greek Studies*, Oxford 1975–83, Birmingham 1984–
BS	*Byzantinoslavica*, Prague 1929–
BZ	*Byzantinische Zeitschrift*, Leipzig and Munich 1892–
CFHB	*Corpus Fontium Historiae Byzantinae*, Washington, DC *et al.* 1969–
Choniates	All references to Choniates are to Nicetas' *History* unless otherwise specified
CMH	*The Cambridge Medieval History*, IV, ed. J. M. Hussey, Cambridge 1966
CSHB	*Corpus Scriptorum Historiae Byzantinae*, Bonn 1828–97
DAI	*Constantine Porphyrogenitus De Administrando Imperio*, ed. G. Moravcsik, trans. R. J. H. Jenkins, Washington, DC 1967
DOP	*Dumbarton Oaks Papers*, Cambridge, MA and Washington, DC 1941–
FRB	*Fontes Rerum Byzantinarum*, eds. V. E. Regel and N. I. Novosadskii, St Petersburg 1892–1917, reprinted Leipzig 1982
JÖB	*Jahrbuch der Österreichischen Byzantinistik*, Vienna, Cologne and Graz 1969–
LPD	*Letopis Popa Dukljanina*, ed. F. Šišić, Belgrade and Zagreb 1928
MGH	*Monumenta Germaniae Historica*, Hanover et al. 1824–1934
MGH SS	*MGH Scriptores*, in folio, 30 vols., Hanover 1824–1924
ODB	*The Oxford Dictionary of Byzantium*, ed. A. Kazhdan, A.-M. Talbot, A. Cutler, T. E. Gregory and N. P. Ševčenko, 3 vols., Oxford and New York 1991

PG	*Patrologia Cursus Completus, series Graeco-Latina*, ed. J. P. Migne, Paris 1857–66, 1880–1903
PL	*Patrologia Cursus Completus, series Latina*, ed. J. P. Migne, Paris 1844–1974
PVL	*Povest' Vremennynkh Let*, ed. D. S. Likhachev and V. P. Adrianova-Perrets, 2 vols., Moscow and Leningrad 1950
REB	*Revue des Etudes Byzantines*, Bucharest and Paris 1944–
RESEE	*Revue des Etudes Sud-Est Européennes*, Bucharest 1963–
RHC	*Recueil des Historiens des Croisades*, Paris 1844–95, 1872–1906
SBS	*Studies in Byzantine Sigillography*, ed. N. Oikonomides, Washington, DC 1987–
SEER	*The Slavonic and East European Review*, London 1922–
SRH	*Scriptores Rerum Hungaricarum*, ed. E. Szentpétery, 2 vols., Budapest 1937–8
TM	*Travaux et Mémoires*, Paris 1965–
ZRVI	*Zbornik Radova Vizantološkog Instituta*, Belgrade 1952–

Introduction

Byzantium's Balkan Frontier seems a straightforward title, but it is ambiguous: the meanings conveyed by the three words to a modern reader would not have been recognized in medieval south-eastern Europe. The Byzantines called themselves *Rhomaioi*, Romans, and their capital 'New Rome'. Byzantium – from Byzantion, the site on the Bosphorus refounded as Constantinople – was a neologism of the sixteenth century, and its use was essentially pejorative, intended to distinguish the decadent Christian successor from its predecessor, the Enlightenment ideal of Rome. Balkan is a Turkish word for mountain, first applied by the Ottomans to the range known to classical and Byzantine authors as Haemus, and today as the Stara Planina. Balkan was first applied to the whole mountainous peninsula in the nineteenth century.[1] There was no Byzantine collective word for all the lands beween the Danube and the Mediterranean, except as part of a greater whole: Europe, as defined by Herodotus, or – in contexts we will explore further – *oikoumene*, 'the civilized world'. The word 'frontière', from the Latin 'frons', emerged in French to signify the facade of a church, or the front line of troops disposed in battle formation. It came to be used as an alternative to 'limite', from the Latin 'limes', and by the sixteenth century had absorbed the meaning of the latter; that is, it contained the notion of limitation. However, 'frontière' also retained its own connotations of facing and moving forward.[2] The English derivation is still used in such contexts as 'advancing (or pushing back) the frontiers of knowledge', which while positing outward expansion at the same time implies a delimited, finite body.

---

[1] Obolensky 1971: 20. See now more expansively Todorova 1997: 21–37.
[2] Febvre 1973: 208–11.

0.1 The Balkans, 900–1204

MAPS AND FRONTIERS

A full historical articulation of the concept of the frontier was integral
to the creation of nation states with their profoundly politicized borders.
The geopolitical developments of the eighteenth and nineteenth centuries heralded, indeed required, the rise of cartography as a method for
representing graphically the extent and limits of nations. It remains to
be seen whether there existed an equivalent Byzantine conception of the
frontier, but we can be fairly certain that they did not articulate the
notion cartographically. Byzantium, an empire which endured for over
a millennium, has left us no maps.[3] Three Byzantine portolans have survived which list ports and the distances between them, but these were
not accompanied by maps.[4] Maritime charts of the twelfth century and
later show the Dalmatian coast, but nothing of the peninsula's interior.
The earliest known map of the whole of the northern Balkans was produced in Bulgaria between 1430 and 1453, probably in 1444.[5] This was
a military map, and might lead us to suppose that Byzantine emperors
and generals who fought so often in the northern Balkans between 900
and 1204 would have benefited from the production of similar charts.
But there is no indication that they ever did, and accounts of campaigns
and journeys through the highlands and passes refer most often to local
guides, for example the Vlachs, whose geographical knowledge gave
them a remarkable advantage in dealings with the empire. Nevertheless,
historians of Byzantium frequently produce maps which show the extent
of the empire at a stated point in time. Their maps will generally include
clear indications of where they believe the empire's borders, the political limits of imperial authority, should be located. Sequential maps
might illustrate clearly, indeed far more clearly than text alone, how the
empire's limits, and by implication political fortunes, fluctuated through
time. For example, the second edition of Michael Angold's excellent
political history of the empire between 1025 and 1204, has maps with the
straightforward titles 'The Byzantine Empire *c.* 1025', and 'The Empire

[3] *ODB*: ii, 385–6. Of course, the Byzantines preserved ancient cartographic wonders, such as
Ptolemy's world map, which are on a quite different scale to the charts with which we are concerned. It is to these that Eustathius of Thessalonica was referring when he wrote of 'the image
of the earthly chart drawn by the hand of the craftsman', cited at Zafiropoulou 1997: 41. See
also Dilke 1985: 72–86, 154–82.
[4] Zafiropoulou 1997: 42–3. The relationship between portolans and navigational charts is analogous to that between itineraries and terrestrial maps. Itineraries were used effectively without the
need for graphical representation of the locations, distances and key sights *en route*, throughout
the medieval period.   [5] Nikolić 1982–3: 63–75.

under the Comneni'.[6] Such illustrations do not reveal that Byzantine authors rarely provide details to help a reader locate a place, and it has taken considerable effort on the part of modern scholars to locate some of the more familiar sites or regions in space and time. Examples which we will encounter in the following chapters are Presthlavitza, 'Little Preslav' (a fortified town), Dendra (a region), and Paradounavon (a Byzantine administrative district).

The maps which accompany this text, like all maps of the Byzantine Balkans, are the creation of a modern author which do not, since they cannot, illustrate medieval perceptions of the empire or of its frontiers. And to that extent they are little different from the text itself, which is a work of synthesis and interpretation with a particular perspective. Many historians now believe it is impossible to produce an objective historical narrative from the often highly subjective data with which they must work. Historians of medieval Byzantium have better reason than many to despair of ever divining 'truths', for the limited written sources on which all interpretations rely are remarkably difficult to handle, still less decipher. The most eminent commentators have written of 'distortion' and condemned Byzantine literature as derivative. Prejudice in the selection and arrangement of information is ubiquitous, and the usual 'solution' – employing Rankean rules to compare contemporary sources – is frequently impossible: there are simply too few texts. Nevertheless, there are pertinent questions that we can ask of our texts and expect answers, starting with 'How did Byzantines in the tenth to twelfth centuries conceive of the empire's frontiers?'

The medieval Byzantine dictionary, the *Souda*, states that 'the zones near the edges (*termasi*) of the lands are called *eschatia*', which might be translated as 'the extremities', 'the periphery' or 'the borders'.[7] The *Souda* is a compilation of excerpts from earlier sources, and this definition appears to date from the third century.[8] Further specific terms appear to have been formulated on the empire's eastern front in the seventh and eighth centuries, a period of significant retrenchment.[9] By the mid-tenth century, the *De Administrando Imperio* – a source to which I will devote considerable attention in chapter one – uses three terms. The first, *sunoros*, means 'bordering on'.[10] The second, *akra*, is most simply translated as 'the extremity', although it can also mean the top of a hill,

[6] Angold 1997: 352–3 (map 1), 356–7 (map 3). An alternative to Angold's map of the Comnenian empire may be found at Magdalino 1993: xxi, where borders are not indicated. See also *ODB*: i, 354–5.   [7] *Suidae Lexicon*: i, 432.   [8] Isaac 1988: 125–47.
[9] Haldon and Kennedy 1980: 79–116; Kaegi 1986: 279–305.   [10] *DAI*: 140, 144, 154, 212, 214.

and hence came to mean 'citadel'.[11] The third term, *horos* (alternatively *horion* or *horismos*) is a fixed linear border, often defined by the setting up of boundary stones: a process known as *horothesia*.[12] Documents preserved in the archives of monasteries on Mount Athos refer frequently to the *horion* or *horismos* of monastic lands, since it was imperative to establish the exact extent and limits of lands granted to or possessed by foundations which were subject to or exempt from taxation.[13] The same principles and terms applied to the empire as a whole. In the twelfth century Anna Comnena uses *horos*, *horion* and *horismos* to refer to linear borders, for example to refer to a river established as the border in a peace treaty.[14]

Such fixed linear borders are often regarded as the empire's natural frontiers, and for both medieval and modern authors the Danube is the empire's natural frontier in the northern Balkans.[15] But as with all natural frontiers, 'nature only serves as a mask; it is the mask worn by long-standing historical and political facts, the memories of which men retained over centuries' (Febvre 1973: 215). The notion of the natural frontier is profoundly politicized, and culturally proscriptive: it marks the barrier and point of transition between 'self' and 'other' in many historical contexts. In medieval Byzantium the frontier delimited the *oikoumene*, and marked the point of transition from the civilized world to the barbarian. The notion of the barbarian was an invention of fifth-century Athens. The barbarian was the universal anti-Greek defined in opposition to Hellenic culture. The two identities were polarities and together were universal: all that was Greek was civilized; all that was barbarian was uncivilized. Byzantine authors, through their classical education, inherited this way of seeing other peoples.

Barbarism did not only threaten the political borders, it constantly circled the conceptual limits of the Christian Roman empire, and threatened to fall suddenly and swiftly upon those not standing vigilant guard. Thus, in the early 1080s in his capacity of Master of Rhetors, Theophylact Hephaistus delivered an oration in which he praised the weather in Constantinople where 'winter does not rebel, nor does he rush the frontiers and fall upon us in Scythian fashion, freezing the blood of living creatures and laying crystalline fetters upon the rivers' (Theophylact, *Discours*, ed. Gautier: 181.5–8). His chosen subject is

[11] *DAI*: 228, 236, 238.   [12] *DAI*: 266, 270.
[13] For example, *Actes de Lavra*: 263–9, especially 268.69 (*horion*), 269.87 (*horismos*).
[14] *Alexiad*: i, 138; ii, 43 (trans.: 130, 182).
[15] One medieval scholar is Michael Psellus, *Scripta Minora*: ii, 239, which is translated below at p. 112; a modern scholar is Alexander Kazhdan, *ODB*: ii, 1797.

prophetic, for he would later write often and at length of his exile from Constantinople, and his choice of imagery is fascinating. The winter outside the most civilized of cities is personified as the archetypal barbarian, the Scythian, launching sudden raids across the limits of the *oikoumene*. As we will see below (at pp. 107–14, 153) Byzantine authors refer to numerous northern peoples as Scythians, alluding both to their origins (as far as the Byzantines were concerned) in ancient Scythia, and to their way of life, which resembled that of Herodotus' Scythians.

The barbarian beyond the frontier has been a constant feature of attempts by various peoples to define their own brand of 'civilization'. The seminal frontier thesis in modern historiography, expounded in 1893 by Frederick Jackson Turner, historian of the American west, considers the frontier as 'the meeting point between savagery and civilization'.[16] Turner saw the frontier as crucial to the creation of a distinctly American identity, where the American was self-reliant, innovative and ruggedly individualistic. This 'pioneer spirit' facilitated the westward expansion of a peculiar form of 'civilization' across lands previously occupied by native American 'savages'. Turner's thoughts on the significance of the frontier were a statement of a prevailing ideology which we can now contextualize and criticize. Similarly, we can contextualize and criticize Byzantine perceptions of frontiers and barbarians. There can be no barbarian except in the mind of the self-consciously civilized person, and just as Turner's Indians were savages in the minds of his European-American frontiersmen, so northern peoples were considered by Byzantine authors to be Scythians.

Already it will be clear that few frontiers are purely political or military, and to place such emphasis on the linear border side-steps many concerns addressed in recent frontier studies.[17] Wherever sufficient data allows, I will be concerned with the place of the frontier in Byzantine thought, rhetoric and ideology. However, and in spite of my earlier statements, the main body of my text will comprise a narrative of Byzantine activity in the northern Balkans through three centuries with emphasis on political and military matters. I believe this is still a valuable exercise, and one which will hopefully facilitate further discussion of the significance of the frontier in Byzantine history. Moreover, even a political approach raises interesting conceptual questions. First, for example, what did the political border signify for the peoples living on either side of it? Can we even know that they were aware of the border, or exactly

---

[16] Turner 1920: 3.   [17] Mathisen and Sivan 1996: 1–7.

where it ran? Occasionally these questions can be answered, for example by the discovery of boundary stones. More frequently they cannot. Second, by drawing a simple line on a map we are obliged to consider the nature of political authority within and beyond that line. If we accept that Basil II extended the political borders of the empire as far as the Danube (see below at pp. 62–77), we cannot assume that political authority in every region south of the Danube was exercised in the same way. Nor can we assume that this way was (or these ways were) different to those beyond the frontier. If, as I argue, Byzantine authority was almost always exercised through existing local power structures, how does Byzantine government in Raška (in Serbia, within the frontier) differ from Byzantine influence in southern Hungary (beyond the frontier)? Or how do both differ from government in the highly developed *thema* (administrative district) of Thrace, or the new *thema* of Bulgaria established by Basil II? Can we identify both an internal and external frontier? And where then do we cross from domestic policy into foreign policy, or from provincial administration into frontier policy?

CONTENTS AND CONTEXTS

In the following chapters we will explore the nature of Byzantine influence and authority in each of the frontier regions in the northern Balkans: Paristrion, the lands beside the Ister (Danube) in modern Romania and Bulgaria; Sirmium, from the Danube-Sava to Niš (in Serbia); Dalmatia and Croatia; Dyrrachium and Duklja, Zahumlje and Travunija which comprise most of modern Albania, Montenegro and Hercegovina. We will also consider regions of the interior highlands: Bosna and Raška, which stretched across the regions known today in English as Bosnia, Kosovo and the Sandžak; the *thema* of Bulgaria, with its centre in the modern Republic of Macedonia; and lands beyond the frontier, principally medieval Hungary (including modern Vojvodina), but also Italy. Each region was of interest to various Byzantine emperors between 900 and 1204, but certain areas were of greater interest at certain times.

The chronological limits of this study were chosen with maps in mind. It begins when Bulgaria dominated the northern Balkans, and her political borders ran along the Danube to the north, in the south-west within miles of the great Byzantine cities of Thessalonica and Dyrrachium, and in the south stopped at the Great Fence of Thrace. A suitable modern illustration of this can be found in *The Cambridge Medieval History*

(*CMH*), or alternatively Dimitri Obolensky's *Byzantine Commonwealth*, which is still the best analysis of Byzantine concerns in the northern Balkans and beyond.[18] My text becomes fuller when the empire's border is restored to the lower Danube by John I Tzimisces (969–76), and again by Basil II (976–1025). However, the period 900–1025 is treated as an introduction to lands, peoples, and *themata* which will be developed in considering the subsequent period. Thus the text becomes fuller still in the later eleventh century, and is at its fullest in the reign of Manuel I Comnenus (1143–80) when the imperial frontier was advanced, for the first time in centuries, beyond the rivers Danube and Sava following the annexation of Sirmium and Dalmatia.

The eleventh and twelfth centuries have received a great deal of scholarly attention in recent years, particularly in Britain and France, which has done much to revise the dominant interpretation established by George Ostrogorsky. Ostrogorsky's political *History of the Byzantine State* posits the thesis that the empire achieved its medieval apogee under Basil II. One of the few maps in the second English edition of his book illustrates the extent of the First Bulgarian Empire, inviting the reader to consider the scale of the reconquest masterminded by the 'military' emperors of the late tenth and early eleventh centuries, and to contrast this with the ineffectual 'civilian' emperors of the mid-eleventh century.[19] He states unambiguously: 'The death of Basil II marked a turning point in Byzantine history. It was followed by a period of decline in which in its foreign policy Byzantium lived on the prestige won in the previous age and at home gave play to all the forces making for disintegration' (Ostrogorsky 1968: 320). In the first chapter of this work I present my own interpretation of imperial foreign policy in 'the previous age', the tenth century. In chapter two I offer my assessment of John I's and Basil II's campaigns in the Balkans. It will be clear that my judgement of their achievements differs considerably from Ostrogorsky's, and sets the scene for a fuller analysis of imperial foreign and frontier policy in the western half of the empire in the period after Basil II's death.

Paul Lemerle mounted the first powerful defence of imperial policy in the period of 'civilian' government. He called for Byzantine policy to be considered in relation to the wider historical picture, for attention to be paid to the forces and changes affecting northern and western Europe at this time, and for credit to be given for the enlightened and sensitive

---

[18] *CMH*: iv.1, 512; Obolensky 1971: 100. Alternatively, see Runciman 1963 [1929]: 80.

[19] Ostrogorsky 1968: 289. The maps in the third German edition are better. See Ostrogorsky 1963: 256–7 (Karte IV: 'Das Reich Basileios II. um 1025'), 320–1 (Karte V: 'Das Reich der Komnenen').

manner with which successive emperors responded. Lemerle also demanded that less attention be paid to individual agency, and maintained that emphasis placed on the emperors and their personal roles obscured appreciation of processes. It led, he stressed, to the inevitable and obfuscatory juxtaposition of strong and weak, 'civilian' and 'military', good and bad. Nevertheless, Lemerle had his own champions. He praised Constantine IX Monomachus (1042–55) for widening access to the senate, promoting education, and instituting a more meritocratic system of government. Another of his heroes was Nicephoritzes, chief minister in the reign of Michael VII Ducas (1071–8), who attempted to restore central control over the empire's economy and rebuild her armies, albeit with a great reliance on mercenaries.[20] In effect Lemerle credited a 'civilian' emperor and chief minister with creating a 'New Society'.

Lemerle, with his French disciples and colleagues, took discussion of the eleventh century onto a different level, and his ideas have been embraced in Britain and the USA. As Angold (1997: 16–17) put it: 'The old notion . . . that the eleventh-century crisis received political expression in the shape of a struggle between the civil and military aristocracy . . . has been quietly shelved.' However, Angold questioned Lemerle's upbeat interpretation of the eleventh century, and his shifting all the blame onto Alexius I. He stressed the poisoned legacy of Basil II, which his successors struggled to master, but ultimately failed to control. For this reason, like Lemerle, he dealt more sympathetically with Constantine IX, who attempted to 'face up to the state's predicament', 'to put the empire on a peacetime footing', and 'to ease the state's financial difficulties by cutting military expenditure'. Such an analysis has been made possible by the great advances in our understanding of the medieval Byzantine economy. Much of the seminal work was undertaken by Alexander Kazhdan, whose studies in Russian have gradually been made more widely accessible through his collaborative projects with English-speaking colleagues. Others have made substantial contributions, and there is now no doubt that the Byzantine economy was growing rapidly throughout the eleventh century and into the twelfth. An issue with which scholars now must grapple is how the imperial government managed the wealth, how it controlled and distributed resources. In chapters three and four I offer a particular perspective on the empire's predicament as it was bequeathed by Basil II, on the methods employed to deal with subject

---

[20] Lemerle 1977: *passim*, especially 249–312.

peoples and neighbours on a peacetime footing, and on the relations between centre and periphery and the flow of resources. I do not intend for these chapters to constitute a full political history of the northern Balkans in the eleventh century, still less solve the problems of the relationship between Byzantine orthodox culture and the nascent Slavic orthodox culture, or cultures, in the peninsula; so much will be apparent from the lack of attention I have devoted to the emergence of Slavic literary culture in exactly this period. However, I hope that my contribution adds something to a continuing discussion, and provides an impetus to further explorations of processes of cultural transmission and change in the medieval Balkans.

The twelfth century, the age of the Comneni, has followed the eleventh into vogue, with corresponding criticism of Ostrogorsky's approval for the revival of triumphal militarism. Once again Lemerle was in the vanguard of those who valued John Zonaras' highly critical account of the reign of Alexius I Comnenus (1081–1118) more highly than the *Alexiad*, the biography produced by Alexius' daughter Anna. A recent collection of essays restores the balance between the two accounts, and advances our knowledge of diverse aspects of Alexius' reign, and of the government and society at the beginning of the twelfth century. The most valuable contribution for this work is Jonathan Shepard's study of Alexius' diplomacy, which, when placed alongside his many other detailed papers, establishes a new context for any analysis of relations between east and west.[21] The rise of the Latin Christendom, and its most obvious confrontation with the eastern empire in the form of the First Crusade have deservedly received significant attention from Byzantine scholars, following the eloquent lead of Steven Runciman.[22] Similarly, the Norman achievement has generated interest, but too few useful studies by Byzantinists. My brief contribution, in chapter five, must be read in this context. However, my emphasis, naturally, is on the frontier lands where Normans and Crusaders first entered the empire. The Norman invasion of Dyrrachium in 1081 gives the first, and best documented opportunity to study how the frontier system in the western Balkans functioned. The advent of the First Crusade, and its successes in the east, presages a new era when Byzantine eastern and western policy, always related, can no longer be regarded as wholly distinct.

Venice played a central role in the Latin expansion into Outremer, and her merchant fleet was essential for supplying Frankish colonists trapped

[21] Shepard 1996: 68–132.
[22] Runciman 1951: *passim*; Shepard 1988b: 185–277; Shepard 1997: 107–29.

between the Syrian frontier and the Mediterranean. Simultaneously Venice was expanding her interests in the west, most notably into Dalmatia. There she competed with the new sedentary Christian kingdom of Hungary. Some attention has been paid to Byzantine relations with Venice, although much has focused on the cultural rather than the political. Far less attention has been devoted to Byzantine dealings with Hungary. A notable exception is the enormously detailed study by Ferenc Makk of relations between *The Árpáds and the Comneni* (1989). In chapter six I address both Hungary and Venice in the appropriate context for this study: the eastern littoral of the northern Adriatic. The expansion of Venetian and Hungarian interests into the northern Balkans occurred without substantial Byzantine interference. Consequently it received very little coverage in Greek sources, and we are reliant on the written testimonies of Latin chroniclers. Fortunately, however, the maritime cities of Dalmatia, over whom the powers competed to extend their authority, have archives where many documents relating to the process have been preserved.

The general neglect by Byzantine authors of the northern Balkans at this time relents only to allow an analysis of John II Comnenus' (1118–43) confrontation with the Hungarians in 1127–29. While it may appear odd to devote disproportionate space to an episode which, I argue, is inconsequential, I do so in order to highlight a common problem in the written sources on which we rely: the gulf between 'rhetoric' and 'reality' in Byzantine literature. I will not offer here any substantial comment on individual written sources, but will do so where appropriate in the body of the narrative. (The interested reader should also consult the introductory accounts offered by Angold and Magdalino in works already cited.) However, I will remark briefly on the nature of Byzantine historiography, and its intimate link with court panegyric (*enkomia*), in the era of the Comneni. All genres of Byzantine literature were written for and by a highly educated elite according to prescribed rules. The rules which governed the composition of *enkomia* make the extraction of reliable historical information a peculiarly difficult task. Panegyrists were concerned primarily with presenting those being praised in a certain manner, and saw mere historical events as opportunities to allude to familiar models and draw from a corpus of imagery and motifs that are only now being deciphered.[23] Historians attributed greater import to recording events in

---

[23] The forthcoming edition and translation of the *enkomia* of the anonymous twelfth-century panegyrist, called Manganeius Prodromus, by Elizabeth and Michael Jeffreys, will contain an appendix of key words and motifs. I am grateful to them for encouraging me to make use of their work in its draft form.

the correct order – if not always the most appropriate context – and, for want of a better term, accurately. The objective of historiography, as Byzantine historians often remarked in their proemia, was the pursuit of 'truth' (or, alternatively, 'plausibility'). However, they certainly did not strive for objectivity or clarity, and for the period under scrutiny they were obliged to compose in Attic Greek, which had been a dead language for over a millennium.[24]

The gulf between rhetoric and reality is at its widest in the reign of Manuel I Comnenus (1143–80), when the fullest corpus of written material is court panegyric. Our understanding of the empire during the reign of Manuel I has been revolutionized by Paul Magdalino's recent study, which makes the fullest use of panegyric. Tellingly, Magdalino chose to set the scene for his analysis of political culture and the imperial system with a lengthy treatment of Manuel's foreign policy.[25] We no longer believe that Manuel was, from the unexpected death of his father during a hunting expedition until his own death thirty-seven years later, driven by a desire to extend the limits of his empire to Justinianic proportions, and chapters seven and eight of this study reflect the view that Manuel's reign must be divided into two distinct periods: pre- and post-1156. In the earlier period Manuel seemed set to pursue his father's policy of controlled aggression in the east, facilitated by a solid alliance with Germany, which was based on a mutual antipathy towards the Normans who had established themselves in southern Italy and Sicily. Chapter seven traces Manuel's early attempts to bolster the German alliance against the resurgence of the Norman threat to the Byzantine position in the western Balkans. This is the first instance of Manuel's supposed preoccupation with western affairs, and there are clear indications that it stemmed from John II's neglect of the west during a period of rapid development. John's failure effectively to check the consolidation of Norman power, and, as importantly, to prevent the expansion of Venice and Hungary into the northern Balkans, was a result of his deal with Germany. The new powers expanded into the vacuum between the two 'empires', and, in the protracted aftermath of the Second Crusade, revealed quite how hollow and superficial the imperial entente had been.

After 1156 Manuel was obliged to confront, and attempt to solve the problems he had inherited. He determined to consolidate his authority in the northern Balkans, and to annex the frontier regions that had fallen under Hungarian and Venetian influence: Sirmium and Dalmatia.

---

[24] Mango 1975: *passim*; 'Historiography', *ODB*: ii, 937–8.   [25] Magdalino 1993: 27–108.

Chapter eight is a close examination of this undertaking, which was successful but ephemeral. The end of Manuel's reign signalled the collapse of Byzantine authority throughout the northern Balkans, and the emergence (or re-emergence) of autonomous polities in Serbia and Bulgaria. This will be the subject of chapter nine. Accessible and objective studies of this period are few. Charles Brand's *Byzantium Confronts the West 1180–1204* is still unsurpassed, thirty years after publication. He built on earlier work, still often cited, by Robert Lee Wolff, who went as far as was possible using the then published narrative and documentary sources.[26]

An alternative perspective on the lands and peoples here considered is offered by John Fine in his excellent critical surveys *The Early Medieval Balkans* (1983), and *The Late Medieval Balkans* (1987). Fine's coverage considerably surpasses the chronological and geographical scope of the present study, and is the essential starting point for any English speaker interested in the medieval Balkans. However, Fine quite deliberately diminishes the role of Byzantium to balance studies which have treated the Balkan lands as a footnote to imperial history. He is similarly critical of the myriad histories which treat the Balkan lands as so many embryonic nation states.[27] If one must criticize Fine's approach, which he explains fully and honestly, his relegation of Byzantium leads to a type of fragmentation which, contrarily, supports the vision of the medieval Balkans offered by the nationally prescribed and ethnocentric texts he does so much to discredit.

ARCHAEOLOGICAL EVIDENCE

Fine is surely right to warn against drawing firm conclusions from the incredibly meagre written material that he surveys. The current work would have suffered similarly, and perhaps taken the format of a critical survey, had there not been a vast new body of evidence on which I was able to draw: the wealth of archaeological material uncovered by extensive programmes of excavations in Albania, Bulgaria, Romania, former Yugoslavia, and Hungary. From the first chapter it will be apparent that material evidence can transform our interpretation of even the most familiar topics and themes. In chapter two it will be stressed that particular pieces of material evidence, Byzantine lead seals, can be used to provide information of a type and volume sufficient to revolutionize our

---

[26] Wolff 1947: 187–236; Wolff, 1949: 167–206.   [27] Fine 1983: vii.

understanding of the Byzantine occupation and reorganization of Bulgaria. In chapter three it will be apparent that an entirely novel hypothesis – that the 'civilian' successors of Basil II introduced an enlightened trade policy at the lower Danube to discourage nomad raids – can be formulated using numismatic and ceramic evidence where previously it was felt little could be said. In chapters four, five and six, excavation reports from towns and castles throughout the frontier lands will be used to illustrate and develop the narrative. Finally, in chapters seven, eight and nine, detailed treatment of the evidence from particular sites will demonstrate how and where resources were deployed in, or withdrawn from, the northern Balkans in the second half of the twelfth century.

Very little of the information I utilize has been noticed, and even less remarked upon, by the majority of Byzantine historians, and I hope that my presentation is sufficiently plain so as to make this 'new evidence' more accessible. Therefore, it seems sensible here to offer some indications of how I have interpreted archaeological material, which may not always be apparent in the distilled form presented in the narrative. I have not been greatly concerned with Byzantine ecclesiastical architecture. This is a highly developed field of study with which I am familiar, but in which I am far from expert. Of more use for the present work has been recent research on Byzantine military architecture and fortifications. The seminal study by Foss and Winfield, *Byzantine Fortifications* (1986), has a vast chronological range, but a correspondingly narrow geographical focus: Asia Minor. The basic conclusions which Foss and Winfield advanced have been developed by British scholars who have conducted a survey of eleventh- and twelfth-century Byzantine castles, again in Asia Minor. I have used their insights in my study of the fortifications in the western part of the empire, and where appropriate I have made reference to construction and masonry techniques which are also found in contemporary fortifications in Asia Minor.

I have made greater use of Byzantine coins and lead seals. The enormous potential of coins as a source for Byzantine history has long been known, but only recently has a coherent framework for the interpretation of numismatic evidence been constructed, principally by Cécile Morrisson, Philip Grierson, Michael Metcalf and Michael Hendy. Morrisson's catalogue of the Byzantine coins in the Bibliothèque Nationale in Paris has provided a system of classification to replace the outdated British Museum scheme. Morrisson has made substantial contributions beyond classification which I will address at appropriate junctures in the text. Further work continues, not least the ongoing publication of the Dumbarton Oaks Collection in Washington under the guidance of Grierson. Metcalf has demonstrated that the Byzantine monetary system must be viewed in the wider context of south-eastern European systems which developed from and alongside the imperial model. Hendy has explained the developments in the imperial system of the eleventh and twelfth centuries, identifying the reformed coinage produced by Alexius I Comnenus, probably in or shortly after 1092.

Despite these advances, Byzantine historians, with few exceptions, have continued to neglect numismatic evidence. I have attempted to make full and appropriate use of coins, observing two of Hendy's dicta. First, 'the study of coins, while justified and necessary, is (or should be) merely a means to an end, and the end is the contribution they can make . . . towards the study of the civilization that produced and used them.'[28] Second, 'coinage was essentially a fiscal phenomenon: produced and distributed, that is, in order to provide the state with a standard medium in which to collect public revenue and distribute public expenditure. It would be absurd to suggest that it did not circulate freely and perform the function of mediating private exchange; but this was not its primary function, only its secondary.'[29] While the introduction of a more flexible system of coinage after 1092 suggests a greater awareness of the importance of a range of values for private exchange, I will maintain that coinage remained essentially a fiscal phenomenon, and played a role in a series of initiatives of economic importance which were implemented for political reasons.

Coins are found in three contexts: as stray losses (or casual finds), site finds (during excavations), and as deliberately concealed parcels (or hoards). Stray finds and site finds are generally low value coins, since these, if lost, are less likely to be missed, or if they are will not always inspire the user or others to search. Moreover, coins of low value are more likely to be lost, since they have a more vigorous currency than those of higher value; that is, they change hands more frequently. For the same reason they are likely to show greater signs of wear. Both the lack of reason or purpose for their loss, and their vigorous currency, make stray finds particularly valuable for assessing the numbers and types of coins in circulation at a given site, and during a particular period. Therefore, statistical differences in total numbers of stray finds between sites will in principle reflect varying intensities of coin use (provided the same level of effort has been spent in searching for them – for example

---

[28] Hendy 1985: 10.   [29] Hendy 1989: xi–xii.

by conducting systematic excavations). This consideration has been of
particular use in my exploration of trade and diplomacy at the lower
Danube in the eleventh century (see below at pp. 81–9, 97–100). Hoards
are more problematic; we can assume that a hoard was concealed for a
purpose, and therefore that the owner of the coins intended to recover
his parcel at a later date, but we cannot ever know completely the reasons
for concealment or for non-recovery. The most likely reason for concealment is generally assumed to be the desire for security, and this desire is
manifested most frequently at times of unrest. Thus a series of contemporary hoards can often be associated with a rebellion or an invasion.
Such episodes also provide possible, or probable reasons for non-recovery: either a tragedy befalling the hoarder, or – a lesser tragedy – his or
her forgetting where the hoard was concealed.

Lead seals (or more properly sealings) have a variety of characteristics
which resemble those of coins, but differentiate them from other artefacts. Like coins, they are material evidence but with a vital documentary component. However, unlike coins, which are struck only by
emperors (or imitative authorities), seals are inscribed with information
pertaining to individuals (including emperors), including their name
and, very frequently, their imperial rank and office. The second charac-
teristic that seals share with coins is their official nature. Seals not only
gave a degree of security to despatches, but also seem to have conferred
authority or legitimacy to the documents attached. It might be too bold
to suggest that a document had no legal validity unless it bore an appropriate lead sealing. However, seals appear to have been struck most often,
if not exclusively, by individuals operating in an official capacity. The
survival of inscribed signet rings for all periods suggests that wax persisted as a means for sealing private communications. This is not to
suggest that we can hope to distinguish entirely between private and
public correspondence, still less to suggest that such a distinction would
be helpful. Nevertheless, in the majority of cases the discovery of
Byzantine lead seals can be taken to suggest a degree of official imperial
interest in a particular site or area. They may also provide very
significant details as to the nature of that interest.

It would be of immense interest for studying the administration of
Byzantium's Balkan frontier if we could ascertain the direction and
volume of sealed communications reaching particular sites. Unfortunately, most seals do not bear an indication of the location where they
were struck. We can, however, narrow the range of possible provenances
considerably by observing some simple rules. First, Constantinople was

without question the source of and destination for the vast majority of sealed communications. The testimony of the letters themselves, and the contents of treatises and other works of literature is confirmed sigillographically: by far the greatest number of seals now in private and museum collections were discovered in Constantinople (Istanbul); and many seals discovered elsewhere were struck by officials known to have been resident in the capital. Second, most other sealed despatches remained within a region. Margaret Mullett's study of the letters of Theophylact of Ohrid contains a map of the archbishop's 'letter network', as well as a reproduction of his unpretentious seal.[30] It is clear that this ecclesiastical prelate of the later eleventh century corresponded principally with his colleagues and friends in Constantinople, but also maintained a web of contacts in Bulgaria and the northern Balkans. The evidence for communication between Ohrid and Skopje, and Prespa and Debar, supports the hypothesis proposed by Cheynet and Morrisson that most seals discovered at provincial sites (and not from Constantinople) will have come from nearby.[31] The 'principle of territoriality' rests on the entirely plausible premise that the majority of sealed documents will have circulated within the area of jurisdiction of the issuing authority. It is supported by the discovery of an archive of seals (but not the documents they once sealed) at Preslav, which further supports the notion that seals served the function of validating as well as securing documents. (Why else would archived copies bear seals?) These issues will be addressed, and the greatest use of seals will be made, in considering the Preslav archive and the numerous seals discovered at sites on the lower Danube (below at pp. 55–61, 78, 87, 104–5).

And so back to the maps. If all has gone to plan, the diligent reader should find that by the end of this book she or he will have an idea – my idea, if it is sufficiently clear – of how and why the line of the Byzantine frontier in the northern Balkans changed so dramatically between 900 and 1204. She or he should also be familiar with the probable ramifications of those changes for the peoples settled beyond or within the shifting frontiers. The sensible scholar will then want to take a longer look at the eastern frontier, for the situation of the empire was ever a balancing act. The most obvious limitation of the present study is that it prioritizes one half of the empire: a flaw also attributed to the last great Byzantine emperor, Manuel Comnenus. And Manuel was great by default: Constantinople fell to the Latins just twenty-four years after his death. That is where I will end.

---

[30] Mullett 1997: xv–xvi.   [31] Cheynet and Morrisson 1990: 105–36.

CHAPTER ONE

Bulgaria and beyond: the Northern Balkans (c. 900–963)

For most of the tenth century Byzantium was the second power in the Balkans. The Bulgarian empire reached it fullest extent during the reign of Tsar Symeon (894–927), when its borders ran within miles of Thessalonica, in this period Byzantium's second city, and Dyrrachium (modern Durrës), the Adriatic port and gateway to the great land route called the Via Egnatia. Byzantine authority in the Balkans was restricted to Greece, Thrace, and a strip of land between the Rhodope mountains and the Aegean coast, including the administrative district (*thema*) of Macedonia. The border of Symeon's empire was marked by the erection of inscribed boundary stones.[1] This frontier, as a line of political demarcation, was recognized by both Bulgaria and Byzantium in bilateral treaties.[2]

SYMEON'S BULGARIA, 894–927

It has generally been maintained, not least in the excellent histories written in English of tenth-century Byzantium and Bulgaria,[3] that for most of his reign, and certainly from 913, Symeon was intent on establishing himself in Constantinople, from which he would rule a combined empire as emperor of the Romans and Bulgarians. However, his efforts to establish a new capital at Preslav, and the extensive and expensive building projects therein, suggest that his principal interests lay north of the Haemus (Balkan) mountains. Distancing himself from the former Bulgarian capital, Pliska, and its pagan past, Symeon expanded the stone walls of his fortress at Preslav and constructed within a palace

---

[1] Beshevliev 1963: 215–19, nr. 46 a-b, for the inscribed boundary stones discovered 22 km north of Thessalonica dated 904. See also Shepard 1989 [1994]: 12.

[2] Theodore Daphnopates, *Correspondance*: 65.129–30.

[3] The classic political history is by Steven Runciman 1963 [1929]. English speakers also have fine studies by Obolensky 1971; Browning 1975 and Fine 1983. The latest important scholarship in English is by Jonathan Shepard.

complex surrounded by stone residences for his nobles (*boyars*) arranged along straight limestone-paved streets. He ensured a fresh water supply reached the citadel with the construction of a limestone aqueduct, and placed massive gate towers beside the apertures in the crenellated ramparts. The town's outlying suburbs grew markedly, and there were developments beyond the walls.[4] The development, its churches and tall palaces 'remarkably richly decorated with stone, wood, and colours', was celebrated by John the Exarch, who urged visitors to witness for themselves the wonders of Preslav, and to contrast the wonders with their own 'wretched straw huts'.[5]

The rich colours upon which John remarks were polychrome wall and floor tiles, produced in monasteries in the vicinity of Preslav from the later ninth century.[6] Excavations at the monasteries of Tuzlal'ka and Patleina have uncovered many fragments of polychrome tiles, and, most importantly, the workshops where they were made. The tiles at Tuzlal'ka were fashioned from rich white clay scooped from a local deposit, and clumps have been discovered within the workshop which still bear the impression of the fingers of a tenth-century artisan. Eight tiles have been discovered in a nearby debris pit. Each tile, measuring 16×15.5 cm, is painted with an icon and an identifying legend written in Greek. Other fragments from other sites bear Cyrillic letters. At Patleina the most remarkable find has been the unique composite icon of St Theodore, fashioned from twenty-one terracotta tiles, three of which bear his name in Greek letters.[7] More than 2,000 whole or fragmented painted tiles have been discovered at the royal monastery in Preslav, mostly produced from locally available white clay and of various shapes and sizes bearing numerous designs. Most common are zoomorphic or vegetal motifs, but around fifty bear painted icons of the highest quality.[8] Such abundant production at numerous workshops must have served to line walls and floors in the monasteries themselves, and the many public and private buildings constructed during Symeon's reign.

In expending such effort creating his own Constantinople north of the Haemus, Symeon gave no indication that his true desire was to move his court wholesale to the city on the Bosphorus. In fact, Symeon sought

[4] Shepard 1999a: 573.   [5] John the Exarch: vi, 3–5; Obolensky 1971: 144.
[6] For an illustrated introduction in English see now Alchermes 1997: 320–35. For comparison with tile production in Constantinople and its hinterland see Mason and Mango 1995: 313–31.
[7] Totev 1979: 65–73; Schwartz 1982: 45–50; Alchermes 1997: 329–31. The latest research by R. Kostova (for her Ph.D. dissertation at the Central European University, Budapest) questions whether Patleina and Tuzlal'ka were monasteries at all, and suggests that they were secular complexes.   [8] Totev 1987: 65–80; Vogt and Bouquillon 1996: 105–16.

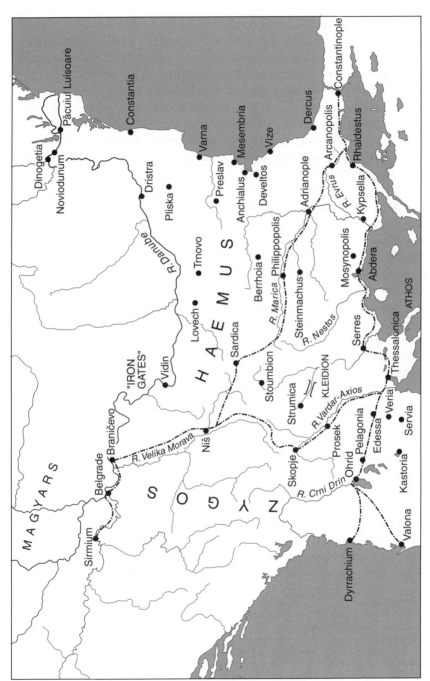

1.1 The northern Balkans

three things from Byzantium: trade, tribute, and recognition of his imperial title. The first time Symeon went to war with Byzantium, in 894, was in response to the capricious decision to transfer the designated commercial centre where Bulgarian traders met with Byzantines from Constantinople to Thessalonica, and to impose a customs levy. The trade routes, by land and sea, from the lower Danube to the capital of East Rome, passed through the centre of Symeon's realm, whereas Thessalonica lay at the south-western fringe of Bulgaria, far from the heartland around Pliska and Preslav. It is not surprising that the new ruler, seeking to consolidate his hold on power, should react strongly to the arbitrary Byzantine decision, and the subsequent curt dismissal of his protests.[9] Symeon's actions saw trade diverted back to Constantinople. Moreover, in a treaty negotiated by the envoy of Leo VI (886–912), Leo Choerosphactes, probably in 897, the Byzantine emperor undertook to pay Symeon annual tribute.[10] Many prisoners were ransomed, although probably not the 120,000 Choerosphactes claimed in a letter written years later when seeking to return from exile.[11]

After 897 Bulgarian relations with Byzantium were generally peaceful. Thus, in Philotheus' *Kleterologion*, produced in 899, much is made of the reception of a Bulgarian embassy in Constantinople.[12] Symeon advanced into Byzantine lands only once in the 900s, inspired by the depredations of Arab pirates along the coast of Thessaly and the Peloponnese, and their remarkable, cataclysmic sack of Thessalonica in 904. Shortly afterwards a second mission by Leo Choerosphactes secured Byzantine control over thirty fortresses in the *thema* of Dyrrachium.[13] The tribute payments continued. Then, in 912 the Byzantine emperor Leo VI died. His brother and successor Alexander determined to end the tribute payments to Bulgaria, and dismissed an embassy from Symeon that came seeking to continue the peace that had endured under Leo.[14] There is no justification for Runciman's claim that Symeon would have been well pleased with the rebuke.[15] It seems clear that the tribute was essential to Symeon as a symbol of his prestige, but also as a means of acquiring cash for his own coffers and to distribute as

---

[9] Theophanes Continuatus: 357.
[10] Fine 1983: 139–40. Tougher 1997: 179–80, prefers the date 896.
[11] Leo Choerosphactes: 112–13; Shepard 1989 [1994]: 11–12; Fine 1983: 140. Tougher 1997: 180, posits 25,000 ransomed prisoners.
[12] *Listes de préséance*: 163, 167, 169, 177, 181, 203, 207. See also Tougher 1997: 180.
[13] Leo Choeresphactes: 113; Shepard 1989 [1994]: 11–12; Tougher 1997: 181, dates this mission to 902–3. On the fortresses of Dyrrachium see below at pp. 160–4.
[14] Theophanes Continuatus: 380.   [15] Runciman 1963 [1929]: 46.

largesse to his *boyars*. Despite the increased political stability of his reign, and the flourishing of trade in and through his realm, Symeon struck no coinage of his own. Therefore, in 913 he prepared for war. But by the time he appeared before the walls of Constantinople Alexander had died, and the patriarch Nicholas I Mysticus had secured for himself the role of regent for the seven-year-old emperor, the *porphyrogennetos* ('born in the purple chamber' in the imperial palace; that is, born to a ruling emperor) Constantine VII (913–59).

What followed has been obscured by the deliberate rewriting of the episode by Byzantine historians. It seems certain that in a meeting at the Hebdomon outside the City the patriarch agreed to the restoration of tribute payments. He also performed a ceremony involving a crown (*stephos*) and a public acclamation (*anarresis*), and arranged for the emperor Constantine to marry Symeon's daughter.[16] Thereafter, Symeon withdrew his forces and began to use the title 'emperor of the Bulgarians'. It seems likely that the patriarch had crowned him thus, and he departed from Constantinople believing that he had secured recognition of his status from the highest authorities in the Orthodox world: the emperor and the patriarch. Moreover, he had the promise of an enduring bond between Constantinople and Preslav through the union of his daughter and the son and heir of Leo VI, the *porphyrogennetos* Constantine. To mark both achievements Symeon changed his seals to include the acclamation he had received in Constantinople. Henceforth they read 'Symeon, *eirenopoios basileus po*[l]*la* [e]*t* [e], 'Symeon, peacemaking emperor, [may you reign for] many years'.[17]

The continued recognition of Symeon's imperial title and the fulfilment of the marriage agreement depended entirely on the continued ascendancy of Nicholas Mysticus and his regency council. As early as 914 this was threatened, and Symeon returned in force to Thrace. The Byzantine stronghold of Adrianople (modern Edirne) was opened to him, but he satisfied himself with devastating the rich cultivated lands which supplied Constantinople before returning to Preslav. Clearly, he had secured the concessions he required from the new regent, Constantine's mother Zoe. There are no reported incidents of hostilities before the unprovoked Byzantine assault of 917, which resulted in a

---

[16] Jenkins 1966a: 291, 295.
[17] Gerasimov 1960: 67–70; Beshevliev 1963: 331–2, nr. 90; Bozhilov 1986: 81; Shepard 1989 [1994]: 32–3, 47, n. 205; Shepard 1999a: 574. Symeon's claiming the title 'emperor of the Romans' was condemned by Romanus I's secretary, Theodore Daphnopates, *Correspondance*: 56–85. See Jenkins 1966a: 291, 295. For the acclamation see *De Cerimoniis*: 373.

great Bulgarian victory at Anchialus. Letters exchanged between Nicholas Mysticus and Symeon present the background to the events of 917, and the patriarch acknowledges that the Byzantine attack had been unjustified. Clearly, Symeon was greatly aggrieved by the episode, and when next he met the patriarch he rode the warhorse which bore a scar inflicted at Anchialus seven years before.[18]

Symeon's hopes for continued Byzantine recognition of his imperial title, and for the fulfilment of the marriage agreement of 913 were dashed by the usurpation of Romanus I Lecapenus (920–44). The new emperor sealed his coup by marrying his own daughter to the *porphyro-gennetos*. Symeon returned to the offensive, invading Serbia and penetrating Greece as far as the Gulf of Corinth, before he returned in full force to Thrace in 920. He installed garrisons in Bizye (modern Vize) and other Thracian towns, and for the following four years his forces ravaged as far as the suburbs of Constantinople. He twice, unsuccessfully, attempted to secure naval assistance to effect a blockade. But his regular appearances before the city's walls did not result in Symeon entering Constantinople in triumph. Instead, the tsar was forced to accept Lecapenus' accession, and to renegotiate the agreement of 913.

At a reception outside Constantinople in 924, Symeon received the recognition of his imperial title by Romanus I, and the further concession that he would be regarded as Lecapenus' imperial brother, that is his equal, and no longer his son (see below at pp. 37–8). The continued annual payment of tribute is also alluded to in letters to the tsar drafted by the imperial secretary Theodore Daphnopates (*Correspondance*: 56–85). However, Symeon had failed to engineer the imperial marriage he had once desired, and satisfied himself thereafter with hollow claims. Thus, soon after 924 he began to style himself 'emperor of the Bulgarians and Romans', and his seals depicted him for the first time in full imperial dress with the accompanying inscription *basileus Romaion*.[19]

PETER'S BULGARIA, 927–967

Symeon died on 27 May 927, and his successor Peter (d. 967) immediately launched a major invasion of the Byzantine administrative district of Macedonia. As one of four sons such a show of strength would have been necessary to secure the support of his father's *boyars*. However, the

[18] Nicholas Mysticus, *Letters*: 74–6, 96–8, 122–6, 208–10; Shepard 1989 [1994]: 25–8.
[19] Gerasimov 1934: 350–1; Beshevliev 1963: 330–1, nr. 89; Shepard 1989 [1994]: 22–4; Shepard 1999: 574.

Bulgarian troops withdrew swiftly, at the same time razing the fortresses that they had held until then in Thrace, and this early performance was not repeated. Instead, it heralded forty years of harmony and cooperation between the two major powers in the northern Balkans. The reason for the withdrawal, and the centrepiece of the enduring Bulgarian-Byzantine accord, was the marriage in 927 of Peter to Maria Lecapena, granddaughter of the (senior) ruling emperor Romanus I Lecapenus.

As we have already noted, the Lecapeni were usurpers, exploiting the youth and weakness of the legitimate emperor Constantine VII Porphyrogenitus. They were anxious to portray the Bulgarian marriage in the best possible light, and to use it to further their own interests. Our knowledge of the stage-managed event and its consequences derives mostly from sources sympathetic to, or commissioned by the usurping family. The account provided by the author of the continuation of Theophanes' chronicle (Theophanes Continuatus) is very much the official version. It seeks to portray the marriage as an achievement rather than a dreadful necessity provoked by the invasion of Macedonia, and fits with a series of contemporary sources that stress the benefits of peace brought about by Romanus' actions.[20] Furthermore, Theophanes Continuatus (414) maintains that 'the Bulgarians vehemently insisted that Christopher should be acclaimed first, that is before Constantine; the emperor acceded to their request'. In this way the author seeks to attribute to the Bulgarians the initiative for having Romanus' son Christopher recognized as the heir to the imperial throne before Constantine Porphyrogenitus.

Given the bias of the Byzantine sources we should be wary of placing faith in the notion that the marriage immediately cemented good relations between the two courts. However, it has recently been argued that Maria may have come to wield a degree of authority in Preslav. Indeed, Peter's imperial seal depicted the married couple together in a manner identical to the contemporary Byzantine method of representing joint rulership, and it seems impossible that the Bulgarian ruler would have been unfamiliar with both the iconography and the relationship it implied.[21] Still, we must not leap from this observation to the conclusion that Byzantium had nothing more to fear from Bulgaria.

Just as Symeon has been portrayed (falsely) as desiring more than anything to become emperor in Constantinople, so Peter has generally been held to have presided over the dramatic decline of Bulgaria. Thus

---

[20] Shepard 1995a: 128–33.   [21] Gerasimov 1938: 359–64; Shepard 1995a: 142–7.

Browning (1975: 194–5) concludes his stimulating comparative study with the observation 'the grandiose dreams of . . . Symeon ended in the dreary reality of Peter's long reign, when Bulgaria became a harmless Byzantine protectorate'. Such interpretations focus on Bulgaria's military prowess, comparing Symeon's successes with his son's inactivity, and draw heavily on Byzantine narrative sources. If we examine the material evidence the indications are entirely different, suggesting a period of political consolidation and economic expansion under Peter.[22] Once again Preslav may serve as an indicator. The north wall of the citadel was demolished to create space for further construction; new churches were built. Large new private structures bear witness to the wealth of Peter's *boyars*.[23]

THE *DE ADMINISTRANDO IMPERIO*

Byzantine sources, as much by their silences as their occasional references to the tsar's irenic disposition, bear testimony to the relative peace, if not the prosperity of Peter's reign and his good relations with Constantinople. This is not to suggest that Bulgaria was no longer considered a potential threat in Constantinople, for as we will see shortly many other peoples were considered suitable allies against Peter. Nevertheless, in the mid-tenth century the productive hinterland of Constantinople was no longer trampled under the boots of Bulgarian troops. Perhaps the most significant indication of the new *status quo* is the absence of any substantive chapter on the Bulgarians in the treatise known as the *De Administrando Imperio* (*DAI*). Compiled on the instruction of Constantine VII, to whom it is generally attributed, it comprises fifty-three chapters of advice addressed to his son and heir Romanus II (959–63). Some chapters are culled directly from earlier histories to provide antiquarian information on peoples and places of contemporary concern to the imperial court. However, the chapters of greatest interest are those based on dossiers of information on the empire's neighbours compiled in the century before the work was completed *c.* 952–4.[24] Virtually all that we know of Byzantine diplomatic procedure is based on the *DAI*, and it is possible to construct a detailed picture of imperial policy in the Balkans and beyond from a close examination of

---

[22] The revisionist view was first proposed by Fine 1978: 88–95; reprised in Fine 1983: 160–71. For proof that the new interpretation has been incorporated into broader literature, see Whittow 1996: 292–4.   [23] Shepard 1999a: 572.

[24] Lemerle 1986: 320–1; *ODB*: i, 593.

the text. It is worth dwelling awhile on the *DAI* for the light it sheds on early tenth-century history, and on peoples and themes that will be central to the following chapters.

First, Constantine directly refutes the testimony of our principal written source for the period of his minority. In chapter thirteen (72.147–53) Constantine addresses the matter of Maria Lecapena's marriage, hoping thereby to rewrite the official history of that union. "'How then", he asks "did the lord Romanus, the emperor, ally himself in marriage with the Bulgarians . . .?" This must be the defence: "The lord Romanus, the emperor, was a common, illiterate fellow, and not from among those who have been bred up in the palace . . . nor was he of imperial and noble stock, and for this reason in most of his actions he was too arrogant and despotic"'. He concludes that the union was 'contrary to the canon, and ecclesiastical tradition and the ordinance and commandment of the great and holy emperor Constantine [the Great, d. 337]' (74.167–9). We are fortunate indeed to have this commentary to place against the account in Theophanes Continuatus (see above at p. 24). We are reminded that the sources on which we base our interpretations of Byzantine and Balkan history in this period are far from objective statements of fact, and this is a theme to which we will return frequently.

BEYOND BULGARIA: THE SERBS

Although it fails to treat Bulgaria fully, the *DAI* contains much information on the schemes and strategies that might be employed against the empire's nearest neighbour. We can discern in its pages the growing importance of the peoples beyond Bulgaria: the sedentary southern Slavs within the Balkans, and the nomads and warrior-merchants of the south Russian steppe whose activities would, within thirty years of the *DAI*'s completion, both allow and oblige Byzantium to occupy Bulgaria.

We know from the *DAI* that it was established Byzantine practice to buy the loyalty and services of the peoples beyond Bulgaria. Chapter thirty-two dwells at some length on Bulgarian relations with the Serbs. It is apparent that in 917 the Byzantine commander of Dyrrachium, Leo Rhabduchus, was charged with securing Serbian assistance for the assault on Bulgaria. The ruler of the Serbs, Peter son of Goinikos, was persuaded to march against Symeon, taking with him the *Tourkoi*. (The *Tourkoi* can only have been the Magyars, to whom we will return at length below.) However, Symeon's generals, Marmaim and Sigritzes

Theodore, persuaded him otherwise, 'tricked him into coming out to them, and then on the instant bound him and carried him off to Bulgaria, where he died in captivity' (156.97–158.99). Paul, a Serbian princeling whom Peter had blinded, was put in charge of Serbia for three years until he too was bought by the Byzantine emperor. When Marmaim and Sigritzes Theodore returned to Serbia, Paul defeated them and 'sent their heads and their armour from the battle to the emperor of the Romans as tokens of his victory' (158.112–14).

The cycle was then repeated. Bulgarian generals arrived in Serbia with a princeling, Zacharias (also known as Zaharije, son of Prvoslav), whom, once he had replaced Paul, was bought by the Byzantines. Despairing of this inevitable pattern of war, bribery and defection, Symeon sent his final candidate to the border of Serbia: a certain Tzeeslav (Chaslav) whose father had been a Serbian prince, but who had been born in Bulgaria of a Bulgarian mother.

The Bulgarians sent a message to the *zoupanoi* [*župans*, regional leaders] that they should come to them and should receive Tzeeslav as their ruler; and having tricked them by an oath and brought them out as far as the first village, they instantly bound them, and entered Serbia and took away with them the entire population, both old and young, and carried them into Bulgaria, though a few escaped and entered Croatia; and the country was left deserted. (*DAI*: 158.120–6)

Only after Symeon's death could Tzeeslav leave Preslav and return to the depopulated region. He secured Byzantine support, and 'the emperor of the Romans continually benefited him, so that the Serbs living in Croatia and Bulgaria and the rest of the lands whom Symeon had scattered, rallied to him when they heard of it. Moreover, many had escaped from Bulgaria and entered Constantinople, and these the emperor of the Romans clad and comforted and sent to Tzeeslav. And from the rich gifts of the emperor of the Romans he organized and populated the country' (160.135–41).

The chapter is of enormous interest for all it reveals about early Serbian history, Byzantine diplomacy, and Bulgarian policy towards her Balkan neighbours. The problems encountered in dealing with recalcitrant regional rulers in the lands of the southern Slavs would persist throughout the eleventh and twelfth centuries. However, when the *DAI* was written the matter of greatest import was the conclusion that, despite Symeon's pretensions, 'the ruler of Serbia has from the beginning, that is ever since the reign of Heraclius the emperor, been in servitude and subjection to the emperor of the Romans, and was never subject to the ruler of

Bulgaria.' (160.146–8). This sentiment is repeated in chapter thirty-one, which deals with the Croats. Indeed, exactly the same words are used, substituting only the *archon Chrobatias* (ruler of the Croatians) for *archon Serblias*.

THE CROATS AND *ROMANI*

Chapters twenty-nine, thirty and thirty-one of the *DAI* provide unique information on the early history of the Croats. Great pains are taken to distinguish the Slav peoples (*ethne Sklabike*) from the inhabitants of the maritime cities in Dalmatia, who are known as *Romani* (not *Rhomaioi*, as the Byzantine called themselves). Romans had been settled in Dalmatia since the days of the Republic. Zadar was an attractive site for Roman emigrants as early as the first century BC, and before 27 BC colonies of army veterans were settled at Salona (Solin) near Split, Narona on the river Neretva, and Epidaurum near Dubrovnik. The emperor Diocletian settled many more families at Split and Dioclea (near modern Podgorica).[25] Then, in the reign of Heraclius, Avars invaded and took possession of Salona, from which 'they began to make plundering raids and destroyed the *Romani* who dwelt in the plains and on the higher ground'. Thus 'the remnant of the *Romani* escaped to the cities of the coast and possess them still, namely Kotor, Dubrovnik, Split, Trogir, Zadar, Rab, Krk and Osor' (*DAI*: 124.44–52).

According to the *DAI* the fundamental division of Dalmatia was between mountainous uplands settled by the Slavs and the narrow coastal plain studded with cities occupied principally by 'Romans' (see below at pp. 117–23). This distinction was recognized a century earlier in Einhard's *Life of Charlemagne* (trans. Thorpe: 69), where we are told that Charles conquered 'both provinces of Pannonia, the part of Dacia which is beyond the Danube, Istria, Liburnia and Dalmatia, with the exception of the maritime cities which he allowed the emperor of Constantinople to keep in view of his friendship with him and the treaty that he had made.' The coastal mountain ranges afforded the maritime cities some protection from Slavic incursions, and their access to the sea and Italy beyond ensured that they survived through the 'Dark Ages'. The production of elaborately carved sarcophagi and pilasters in the eighth and ninth centuries supports the contention that city life recovered swiftly after the turmoil of the seventh century, and indicates that a certain level of prosperity was restored.

[25] Wilkes 1969: 207, 220–6, 245–54.

We will see in later chapters that the maritime cities remained distinct from the Slav hinterland well into the twelfth century, although much immigration took place, and Croatian magnates became significant patrons within the cities. The interchange, or symbiosis between cities and hinterland must have been a powerful factor in the acceptance by the Croats of Latin Christianity. By the later eleventh century more than forty Benedictine monasteries had been founded in Dalmatia, with the oldest possibly dating from 839.[26] However, political arrangements were also made to ensure the *status quo*. During the reign of Basil I (867–86), the cities of Dalmatia paid an annual sum to a Byzantine governor (*strategos*) of Dalmatia. Among the governor's principal tasks was to arrange for the cities to pay a substantially larger annual tribute to the Croats. The arrangement was essentially practical: for a nominal sum, as recognition of Byzantine suzerainty, the *strategos* coordinated relations between the numerous autonomous cities and their equally fragmented Slav neighbours. Several lead seals have survived which confirm the existence of rulers (*archontes*), who were natives of the cities with Byzantine titles carrying out duties in Dalmatia in the mid- to late ninth century.[27] However, the Croats did not strike such seals. A single, weakly impressed seal from the Fogg Collection is the only evidence that Byzantine authority was ever exercised in Croatia, and that is very likely to have been struck by a native lord who recognized Basil II.[28] Nevertheless, as we have already seen, Constantine VII was adamant that the whole of Dalmatia, and therefore the peoples settled there, was subject to the emperor in Constantinople and not the tsar of Bulgaria. Therefore, the Croats were potential allies against the Bulgarians. The major drawback, to which Constantine VII draws his son's attention, was that the 'baptized Croats will not leave their own lands to make war on others' (*DAI*: 148.31–2). Other peoples would.

THE PECHENEGS

The river Danube was no barrier to imperial diplomacy, and agents often sought to acquire the services of the Pechenegs, fierce steppe nomads who occupied the grasslands of southern Russia either side of the river Dnieper. Marvazi, an Arabic author of the twelfth century who preserved passages from earlier accounts, described the Pechenegs as 'a

---

[26] Ostojić 1973: ii, 583–4.   [27] Nesbitt and Oikonomides 1991: i, 46–8.
[28] Nesbitt and Oikonomides 1991: i, 48–9. See below at pp. 74–5.

wandering people following the rainfalls and pasturage', and noted that they were 'a wealthy people', grown rich by controlling the trade routes across the region they dominated, and from selling goods such as hides and wax, and also slaves. Marvazi also provided details of the location and extent of their lands in the ninth century.

Their territory extends a distance of thirty days, and they are bordered on all sides by many people . . . between the Pechenegs and [their neighbours, a people known as the] Chazars there is a distance of ten days, the country being steppes and forest. There is no beaten track between the two territories, and they travel over the distance by means of the stars, landmarks, or at random. (Marvazi, ed. & trans. Minorsky 1942: 20–1, 32–3)

The Pechenegs' desire for large tracts of suitable pasturage for their livestock, and their ability to move rapidly across vast tracts by day or night would later prove a considerable menace to Byzantine lands. However, in the mid-tenth century their nomadic inclinations were a considerable asset to the empire. All nomadic peoples display a keen sense of monetary wealth and commodity circulation 'because all their worldly goods consist of movable objects and are therefore directly alienable; and because their mode of life, by continually bringing them into contact with foreign communities, solicits the exchange of products' (Marx, *Capital*: i, 88).[29] Their greed for Byzantine gold and prestige wares made the Pechenegs ideal allies, and once secured their martial skills could be turned against any potential enemy. Moreover, their social structure was typical for a nomadic people, being a confederation of clans arranged hierarchically but free, for the most part, to operate independently. This enabled interested parties to strike deals with the leaders of smaller independent bands of nomads without having to deal directly with the highest ranking chieftain.

The *DAI* begins with eight chapters dedicated to the Pechenegs, and in chapter five Constantine observes:

To the Bulgarians the emperor of the Romans will appear more formidable, and can impose on them the need for tranquility, if he is at peace with the Pechenegs, because the said Pechenegs are neighbours to these Bulgarians also, and when they wish, either for private gain or to do a favour to the emperor of the Romans, they can easily march against Bulgaria, and with their preponderating multitude and their strength overwhelm and defeat them. And so the Bulgarians also continually struggle and strive to maintain peace and harmony with the Pechenegs. For from having frequently been crushingly defeated by

---

[29] Quoted by Anderson 1974: 223.

them, they have learned by experience the value of being always at peace with them. (*DAI*: 52.3–13)

The reference to nomads attacking Bulgaria as 'a favour to the emperor' is telling. In 917 the Pechenegs had been incited to do just that, but were prevented when the Byzantine *droungarios* (admiral of the fleet) Romanus Lecapenus (the future emperor) failed to transport them across the river Danube.[30] In 924 Nicholas Mysticus wrote to Symeon warning him that a grand alliance of northern peoples including 'Pechenegs, Alans and many other Scythians' was being constructed. In a contemporary letter to Prince George of Abasgia, a region in the northern Caucasus, Nicholas answered George's enquiry regarding the Bulgarian war, and reminded him to 'be steadfast in your readiness to fight with us'.[31]

The methods by which the Pechenegs' services were acquired are also detailed in the *DAI*. They must be won over by 'letters and gifts' (chapter four; 50.10). They must also be offered the opportunity to avail themselves of the luxury goods produced within the empire. The groups living nearest to Cherson, a city to the north of the Black Sea that recognized Byzantine authority, would be encouraged to provide their services in exchange for 'a prearranged remuneration . . . in the form of pieces of purple cloth, ribbons, loosely woven cloths, gold brocade, pepper, scarlet *or* "Parthian" leather, and other commodities that they desire, according to a contract each Chersonite may make or agree with an individual Pecheneg' (chapter six; 53.6–11). The Pechenegs were thus encouraged to acquire by peaceful means what they might otherwise have taken by force, and their services, once bought, could be directed against the empire's enemies.

Besides 'struggling and striving to maintain peace and harmony with the Pechenegs', the Bulgarians could also use the nomads as a threat to Byzantium. Symeon was intent upon reaching a lasting agreement with the Pechenegs, spurring Nicholas Mysticus to write that the Byzantines were aware of his diplomatic exchanges 'not just once or twice, but again and again', even proposing a marriage alliance.[32] However, Bulgaria itself sat between Byzantium and the steppe lands of southern Russia, so the tsar would have been disinclined to allow nomads through his territory to strike at Byzantine lands beyond.

---

[30] Theophanes Continuatus: 389–90; Scylitzes: 201. The incident is also recorded in the *Russian Primary Chronicle* under the year 915 (*PVL*: 31; trans.: 71).
[31] Nicholas Mysticus, *Letters*: 160–1, 486–7.   [32] Nicholas Mysticus, *Letters*: 59.

The Rus, like the Pechenegs, were warrior-merchants, whose power rested on their ability to dominate their neighbours. But the Rus were not nomads. Instead, they established permanent settlements beside the great rivers that flowed into the Black and Caspian seas. From around 800 they had transported goods from the Russian forest belt along the Don and Volga to the markets of Chazaria and the Muslim lands beyond. Numismatic evidence suggests that this trade was peculiarly lucrative for the first part of the ninth century, but that after *c.* 870 it slowed considerably. By this time the Abbāsid Caliphate was in decline, and while mint output continued at similar levels, Arab coins (dirhams) no longer reached Russia. The traditional route, always hazardous, had become far less profitable. The Rus began to look for alternative markets for their wares. Their preferred eastern market became the Samanid realm in Transoxania, whence significant volumes of dirhams arrived after *c.* 870.[33] The Rus also looked south to Byzantium as a further market. It has recently been demonstrated that from 911, if not 907, the Rus made annual journeys to Constantinople. The volume of trade on this route had increased dramatically by 944, when a detailed trade agreement specified various restrictions absent from earlier arrangements. There is evidence for the rapid development at this time of a riverside development at Podol in Kiev, where abundant finds attest to an intensification of economic activity.[34]

It has been suggested that the Rus specialized in the slave trade, and that human cargo was especially suited to the arduous journey along the river Dnieper to Constantinople, since they could not only propel the boats, but also carry them at the numerous portages *en route*.[35] Indeed, slaves are the only 'commodity' specifically mentioned in the account of the Russians' journey to Constantinople contained in the *DAI* (60.50–6), although there are allusions to other unspecified goods (*loipa pragmata*: 58.32). (This clearly parallels Byzantium's earliest dealings with the Magyars at Kerch, to which we will turn shortly.) The intensification of trade in the first part of the tenth century must be interpreted in the light of the increased threat the Rus posed to Byzantium. As Shepard (1995b: 259) has maintained, the explanation 'lies less in the realm of trade or the provisioning of Constantinople than in Byzantine diplomacy'.

---

[33] Noonan 1985: 179–204.
[34] Shepard 1995b: 243–60; Franklin and Shepard 1996: 91–111, 117–20.
[35] Shepard 1995b: 255–7.

THE *DE CERIMONIIS: TAXIS* AND HIERARCHY

The *DAI*, therefore, provides invaluable information on numerous peoples in and beyond the northern Balkans, and outlines pragmatic methods for influencing their behaviour. Overall, the world beyond Constantinople is portrayed as unstable, even turbulent, and the peoples threatening. In this light it is worth emphasizing that the *DAI* was a work of the greatest secrecy, intended only for the eyes of the emperors Constantine VII and Romanus II, and their closest advisors. A quite different view of the empire and its neighbours is given by a second contemporary work of compilation, also attributed to the emperor Constantine VII Porphyrogenitus: the *De Cerimoniis*.

The *De Cerimoniis* is a compilation of religious and secular ceremonial procedures which took place in Constantinople, and other matters of concern insofar as they affected the rhythm of life in the city. The attention paid in the *De Cerimoniis* to foreign affairs is minimal, and to some extent this can be explained by the existence of a distinct treatise devoted to such matters. Nevertheless, it most clearly reflects the fact that domestic matters, and particularly affairs in and between the Great Palace and St Sophia, dominated imperial thought in the mid-tenth century. Since the retrenchment of the seventh century Constantinople had played an increasingly large role in the articulation of the imperial ideology. Olster (1996: 100) has noted that 'as the borders ceased to define the extent of Roman authority [from the seventh century], the *oikoumene* was reduced to a central point from which Romanity radiated', and imperial rhetoric focused largely on the 'head', which, so long as it survived, would keep the body alive. Thus pseudo-Methodius asked 'what other place could be named the navel of the world except the city where God has set the imperial residence of the Christians, and that he has created by its central location even that it might serve as the intermediary between east and west?'[36]

Foreign affairs, therefore, played a limited role in Byzantine imperial thought and ceremony between the seventh and tenth centuries, and chapters in the *De Cerimoniis* are devoted to such matters only where they affected life in the city, such as the reception and treatment of ambassadors from various lands in Constantinople. Moreover, much of this tiny percentage of the large compilation is of purely antiquarian interest: for example the four chapters (Book I, chapters eighty-seven to ninety; ed.

---

[36] Cited with translation by Olster 1996: 101.

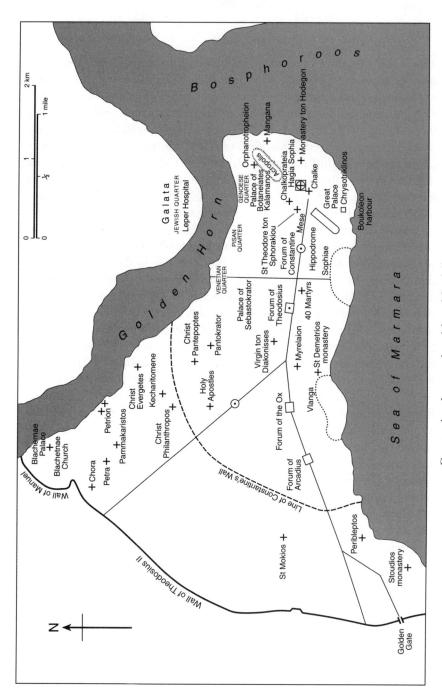

1.2 Constantinople, reproduced from Magdalino 1993

Reiske: 393–410) devoted to the reception of envoys from Persia and of ambassadors announcing the promotion of an Ostrogothic emperor in Rome are copied from a sixth-century text by Peter the Patrician. Nevertheless, the information on other peoples contained in the *De Cerimoniis* has been of concern for those seeking to reconstruct the Byzantine world view, for the manuscript has been transmitted with a separate document, incorporated as chapters forty-six to forty-eight of the second book, which lists the correct protocols to be observed in despatches from the emperor to foreign rulers.[37] The central theme in this document, as it is of the whole compilation, is *taxis*.

Taxis, or correct order, within Byzantine society produced the 'harmonious hierarchy of institutions that constituted the state'.[38] *Taxis* in human society mirrored that of heaven, and systems of precedence mirrored the divine hierarchy. Thus the Byzantine empire was rigidly structured, and the opposite of the world beyond the empire, the barbarian world where *ataxia* (disorder) reigned. However, the late antique concept of universality had been reinstituted as a principal component of imperial ideology before the tenth century, and this required that the empire introduce order to other human societies, to correct *ataxia*. (In this context we might understand the ideological rationale behind the missions to the Slavs in the ninth century, which saw the extension of the spiritual frontiers of Orthodoxy even as the political frontiers of the Orthodox empire were in abeyance.)

The extension of order to the non-Byzantine world led to the creation of what has been dubbed 'the hierarchy of states'.[39] At the top of the hierarchy, after Byzantium, came the Sassanian Persians, then the Arabs and later the sultan of Egypt, with whom the emperor negotiated on terms of quasi-equality. Next came the chagan of the Chazars, and after this various western potentates, including the king of the Franks.[40] The order of precedence is illustrated in the *De Cerimoniis*, which contains protocols for letters despatched to the rulers of independent peoples, and also those deemed to be subject to the emperor. Independent rulers received letters (*grammata*), subject peoples received commands (*keleusis*). Each was sealed with a golden sealing, or bull, with a specified value in Byzantine *solidi*. Thus the 'Emir of the Faithful' received a letter with a golden bull of four *solidi*, while the 'Pope of Rome' received either a one-*solidus* or two-*solidi* bull. The peoples in and

---

[37] *De Cerimoniis*: 679–92. On the 'diplomatic style sheet', see Bury 1907: 223, 227; *ODB*: i, 597.
[38] *ODB*: iii, 2018.   [39] Ostrogorsky 1956: 1–14; *ODB*: iii, 1945.
[40] Brehier 1949: 282–6; *ODB*: i, 634–5.

beyond the northern Balkans were integral to this system, and the protocols for correspondence are recorded in the *De Cerimoniis*:

To the *archontes* of the Pechenegs, a golden bull of two *solidi*: 'Letter (*grammata*) of the Christ-loving emperors Constantine and Romanus to the *archontes* of the Pechenegs.' To the *archon* of the Croats; to the *archon* of the Serbs; to the archon of [the people of] Zahumlje; to the *archon* of Kanali; to the *archon* of [the people of] Travunija; to the *archon* of Duklja; to the *archon* of Moravia. The protocol for them: 'Command (*keleusis*) from the Christ-loving despots to that person *archon* of there.' A golden bull of two *solidi*. (*De Cerimoniis*: 691.4–13)

The treatment of the Pechenegs is in agreement with that outlined in the *DAI*; there is no single *archon*, but the leaders of distinct confederate groups each receive the same honour. Moreover, each is accorded the status of an independent ruler, who receives a letter from the emperors. In contrast, and also in accordance with the claims advanced in the *DAI* – where as we have seen it is stated that the Croats and Serbs have never been subject to the ruler of the Bulgarians – the *archontes* of the Croats and the Serbs are considered dependent peoples of the empire, and are issued with imperial commands. So are the rulers of the Slavic regions of Zahumlje, Kanali, Travunija, Duklja and Moravia. We will consider each of these regions (except Moravia) in greater detail in chapter four (below at pp. 117–55).

The inclusion of Moravia suggests that the protocols for the Balkan peoples, as they have been preserved, date from before the Magyars arrived in the Carpathian Basin in *c.* 895. Bury (1907: 223), suggests the Isaurian period (i.e. before 802), but the later ninth century seems more likely. Received opinion holds that Moravia fell to the Magyars before *c.* 906, although if we believe recent attempts to relocate Moravia we might accept an earlier date. However, the impossibility of identifying the date of the protocol precisely is not a hindrance to our understanding of the *De Cerimoniis*; rather it reveals to us the essence of the document, for although much of the information it contains is clearly antiquarian, and many of the ceremonies redundant, they are included to bolster the image of continuity and immutability that is central to the notion of *taxis*, and to impose a framework of idealized relations within the overarching hierarchy which has persisted from antiquity to the present. And in its accumulation of principles and precedents from the pool of Roman and Late Antique ideology, the *De Cerimoniis* was dynamic because it facilitated the invention of traditions suited to conditions in the mid-tenth century, and gave them solid pseudo-historical roots.

Averil Cameron (1987) has noted that the vulnerability of emperors in the century preceding Constantine VII contradicts the image of strength and continuity in the imperial office as it is enshrined in the *De Cerimoniis*. Usurpation was a constant threat: Constantine's grandfather, Basil I, had seized power from a murdered predecessor, and Constantine's own ascendancy had been interrupted by the accession of Romanus Lecapenus and his promotion of his sons over the *porphyrogennetos*. As Cameron states: 'This is exactly the kind of situation which the [*De Cerimoniis*] entirely conceals, in its bland assumption that all is well if only the due forms are preserved' (124). The same can be said of imperial foreign and frontier policy, where continuous development drove the need for an image of solidity. From the *De Cerimoniis* we might believe that the Byzantines considered the world around them was stable and that it could be controlled merely by the observance of appropriate protocols in Constantinople. Fortunately we have the *DAI* which demonstrates that the emperor and his functionaries were well aware of the turbulence beyond the walls of Constantinople, and were willing and able to engage with it. However, such activity could not be seen to interfere with the slow and apparently changeless world of ritual, where emphasis was placed on hieratic calm.[41]

Nevertheless, the fluidity and dynamism of foreign affairs have left marks in the *De Cerimoniis*. For example, ambiguity and confusion is evident in the various entries which record the correct form of address for the ruler of the Bulgarians. The first form given in the *De Cerimoniis* considers the Bulgarian ruler as *archon* and spiritual grandson of the emperor, but it is noted that this changed 'when the name [of the *archon*] was changed and he entered into sonship'.[42] However, we also know that for a period Tsar Symeon had been acknowledged as a spiritual brother, and therefore an equal to the emperor. In several letters to Symeon drafted by his secretary Theodore Daphnopates, Romanus I addresses the tsar as his spiritual brother (*pneumatikos adelphos*).[43] He even warns the tsar that '[when] you freed yourself of spiritual sonship, and at the same time of your natural subordination, you turned order (*taxis*) on its head and brought trouble on our two peoples' (Theodore Daphnopates, *Correspondance*: 73.55–7). Order was restored when Peter once again acknowledged Romanus I as his spiritual father.

---

[41] Cameron 1987: 107–8, on the virtue of hieratic calm (Gr. *galene*; L. *tranquilitas*).

[42] *De Cerimoniis*: 681–2.

[43] For example, Theodore Daphnopates, *Correspondance*: 57.3, 59.38, 61.51, 69.2, 81.9–10. See also Westerink's index entry *adelphos*: *pneumatikos*.

While he was entitled to refer to himself as emperor of the Bulgarians, Peter was once again subordinate to the *basileus* in Constantinople. Moreover, in Book II, chapter forty-eight of *De Cerimoniis* the correct form for addressing the Bulgarian ruler is revised as follows:

To the God-appointed ruler (*archon*) of Bulgaria. 'In the name of Father and the Son and the Holy Spirit, our one and only true God. Constantine [VII] and Romanus [II], emperors of the Romans, whose faith is in God, to our sought-after spiritual son, the God-appointed ruler (*archon*) of the most Christian people (*ethnos*) of the Bulgarians.' The recent formulation. 'Constantine and Romanus, pious *autokratores*, emperors of the Romans in Christ who is God, to our sought-after spiritual son, the lord, emperor (*basileus*) of Bulgaria.' (*De Cerimoniis*: 690.6–16)[44]

So, the *De Cerimoniis* preserves the rhetoric of the empire: an accumulated, and not always even patina on the *Realpolitik* observable in the *DAI*. But the conceptual world is no less real for being a veneer created in Constantinople, nor is it inherently contradictory to the world of the *DAI*. It illustrates the broader picture which diplomacy on all levels was intended to preserve, and underlines the pacific and ecumenical vision which Constantine VII made central to his imperial image. As we will shortly see, Constantine's successors drew different ideas from the pool of Late Roman ideology, placing greater emphasis on military expansion and advancing the empire's frontiers.

THE MAGYARS

Byzantine dealings with a newly arrived people, the Magyars, demonstrates clearly the close and dynamic relationship between ideology, ceremony and *Realpolitik* in the tenth century. Known almost invariably in Byzantine sources of this period as *Tourkoi*, the Magyars were another confederation of nomadic clans who arrived at the Danube from across the south Russian steppe. According to the list of protocols, like the rulers of the Pechenegs the *archontes* of the *Tourkoi* received a two-*solidi* gold bull and an imperial letter (*grammata*).[45] They were, therefore, not considered a subject people, and recognition was given to their having more than one ruler. Constantine provides further details of the

---

[44] *ODB*: i, 595–7, suggests that the revision of titles applied to the Bulgarian ruler was written *c.* 945–59, but refers to a change most probably effected in 927.

[45] *De Cerimoniis*: 691.2–4. The date of this protocol is once again controversial, although I believe it must date before *c.* 948, for reasons advanced below. See also Antonopoulos 1993: 263.

Magyars' sociopolitical organization in chapter forty of the *DAI*, entitled 'of the clans of the *Kabaroi* and the *Tourkoi*'.

> The first is the aforesaid clan of the *Kabaroi* [which consisted of three distinct clans, and] which split off from the Chazars; the second, of *Nekis*, the third, of *Megeris* [hence the name Magyar]; the fourth of *Kourtougermatos*; the fifth of *Tarianos*; the sixth, *Genach*; the seventh, *Kari*; the eighth, *Kasi*. Having thus combined with one another, the *Kabaroi* dwelt with the *Tourkoi* in the land of the Pechenegs. (*DAI*: 174.1–7).

The Magyars were driven from that region by the Pechenegs, and settled permanently in the Carpathian basin in 895 or 896. However, they had already played a part in Byzantine-Bulgarian affairs when, in 894, the Byzantine emperor Leo VI had despatched an envoy to persuade the newest arrivals north of the Danube to cross into Bulgaria. Several sources (Greek, Latin and Slavonic) report the subsequent invasion, although they present alternative accounts. The *Russian Primary Chronicle*, probably drawing on extant Byzantine accounts, reports starkly that 'the emperor Leo employed the Magyars against the Bulgarians', who were defeated and 'Symeon barely escaped to Dristra', a fortified city on the lower Danube. The *Fulda Annals* report that several battles took place, two of which were won by the Magyars, but according to a reliable Greek source, Leo VI's own *Taktika*, they 'totally destroyed the army of the Bulgars in three battles'. Perhaps the most interesting account is preserved in a nearly contemporary Slavic source, the *Miracles of St George in Bulgaria*. Supposedly the eye-witness account of a Bulgarian soldier, it relates that after Symeon took the Bulgarian throne he was attacked by Magyars who defeated him in battle. The author reports of his own participation: 'fifty of us were escaping in one direction. But the Magyars gave chase, and my horse began to weaken and tire'. At this point Saint George intervened, his horse recovered, and the soldier-author escaped through a hail of arrows. If it is impossible to construct a coherent composite picture, it is nevertheless clear that the Bulgarians at the height of their power and military prowess under Symeon were routed at least twice by these nomads in the paid service of the Byzantine emperor.[46]

For some years thereafter the Magyars were concerned principally with the lands to their west. However, they launched raids deep into the Balkans as far as Byzantine Thrace in 934, and again in 943. The nomads came in search of booty. The wealth had to be movable, and for

---

[46] References to all sources here mentioned, and translations of some excerpts, can be found in Kristó 1996: 183–90.

that reason the greatest prizes were *psyche*, living creatures, including humans whom the emperor was obliged to ransom, or whom might be sold as slaves.[47] The devastation and widespread fear caused by the raids obliged Byzantium to make arrangements with the Magyars over and above their accord with Bulgaria. After the second Magyar raid of 943 the Byzantine *patrikios* Theophanes was responsible for negotiating a five-year peace accord. Antonopoulos (1993: 260) has correctly maintained that the use of the terms *eirene* and *spondai* in the Greek sources point to a formal treaty with the Magyars. Hostages were secured who resided thereafter in Constantinople. When the treaty was up for renewal in 948, the emperor employed a far more potent device: the conversion to the Orthodox Christian faith of the third-ranked Magyar chieftain, the Karhas named Boultzous (Bulcsu).[48] In 948, or shortly after, a baptism was carried out in Constantinople, and the emperor himself became Boultzous' godfather. A miniature in the illustrated manuscript of Scylitzes' chronicle shows Constantine VII raising his spiritual son from the baptismal font.[49] The ceremony was repeated in *c.* 952 for the second-ranked Magyar chieftain, the Gylas. Both were raised to the rank of *patrikios*.

These are the first examples we have encountered of the emperor taking a personal role in securing loyalty of regional chieftains. Of course, there are exact historical precedents, for example Heraclius' becoming baptismal godfather to 'the chieftain of the Hunnic people', and investing him with the rank of *patrikios*;[50] and just as in the seventh century, the ceremonial aspects of the Magyars' receptions were designed to impress and intimidate. All visitors to Constantinople could be expected to feel such emotions. However, the personal ceremony, involving baptism and elevation to a lofty rank, was deemed to be particularly effective in forging links where political authority was fragmented. It augmented the authority of the individual in the eyes of his peers and competitors, and he would return to his own lands bearing symbols of his new authority and great wealth to distribute as he saw fit. In the case of the Gylas he also took a bishop of *Tourkia* with him who 'converted many from their barbarous delusions. And the Gylas remained firm in the faith and undertook no raids against Byzantine territory and cared for Christian prisoners' (Scylitzes: 239; trans.:

---

[47] Excerpts from Byzantine sources on the Magyar raids have recently been compiled by Antonopoulos 1993: 254–67 (258–9 on *psyche*).   [48] Scylitzes: 239; *DAI*: 178.51–2, 63–8.

[49] Cirac Estopañan 1965: 141–2, 337, fig. 338; Grabar and Manoussacas 1979: 79, nr. 331.

[50] Nicephorus, *Short History*: 48–50, 177–8.

Obolensky 1971: 207). At least one seal struck by a subsequent bishop attests to the continuation of this office based at Bács (Bač, north of the river Drava on the east bank of the Danube) into the eleventh century.[51]

It has been remarked that the ceremonies of *c.* 948 and *c.* 952 were extraordinary since the senior Magyar, the prince of the Árpád clan, was neglected in favour of subordinates. In fact, the treaties and conversions must be seen as pragmatic responses to the problems encountered in dealing with a confederate nomadic people whose distinct tribes had settled distinct regions. The *DAI* lists the lands known as *Tourkia*, that is settled by the *Tourkoi*, at exactly this time. The list includes only those lands immediately bordering Bulgaria, north of the Danube and east of the river Tisza; that is, the lands of greatest strategic interest to the empire. In marked contrast, the *Hungarian Chronicle* (255–60) fails to mention this region in a list of the lands conquered by the Magyars. It is clear that the *Hungarian Chronicle* is concerned with the lands around the middle Danube, settled by the ruling Árpád clan, while the *DAI* is concerned with lands settled by the Árpáds' confederates, principally the second- and third-ranked tribes ruled by the Gylas and Karhas.[52]

While the provision of annual stipends appropriate to the rank of *patrikios* may have quenched the Gylas' and Karhas' immediate thirst for plunder, it did not remove the incentive for other semi-autonomous war bands to launch booty raids. Indeed, in 959, the final year of Constantine VII's reign, the Magyar raids recommenced. The return of the nomad threat should not be considered a reversal for Byzantine diplomacy; the arrangement with certain chieftains would have had little effect on other distinct groups. Nor can the raids be cited as proof that Bulgaria was in decline, unable to defend her borders. Lightning raids were practically impossible to police, as the marcher lords of Saxony and Bavaria had long appreciated. The shift in Magyar attention to lands to the south followed on from their defeat at the battle of Lech in Bavaria in 955. It would then have been even more apparent that a way had to be found to provide all elements in the loosely-knit confederate structure with access to the products and wealth of the sedentary world. The natural answer was to encourage peaceful processes of exchange with the Magyars, and to provide incentives for them to trade rather than to

---

[51] Nesbitt and Oikonomides 1991: i, 103.

[52] In fact this is a highly contentious issue which I can only gloss here. There is a strong case for the regions of greatest interest to Byzantium being occupied by a tribe of Chazar extraction known as the *Kabaroi* (Kavars). The best synthesis in support of this is Göckenjan 1972. See now also Tóth 1999: 23–33.

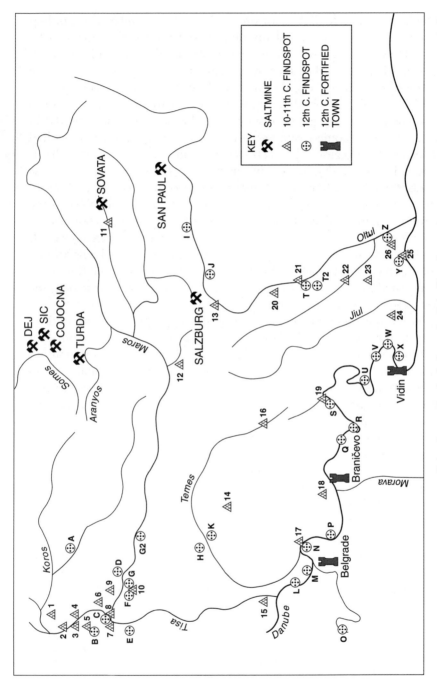

1.3 Salt mines and coin finds north of the Danube, 900–1204

raid. This was an idea familiar to the Byzantines when dealing with the Magyars in their former home north of the Black Sea. The Arab author Ibn Rusteh, writing between 903 and 913, reported that it was the practice of the nomads of al-Majgariya to live in tents, to tax their neighbours heavily, and to take those whom they seize in raids 'along the sea shore to one of the ports of Byzantium (ar-Rūm) which is called Kerch . . . where the Byzantines meet them to trade. The Magyars sell them their slaves and buy in return Byzantine brocade, woollen cloaks and other products of the empire'.[53]

Further documentary references to trade between Byzantium and the Magyars are absent before the twelfth century, and even then are rare. The *Itinerary of Benjamin of Tudela* (ed. Adler: 12) records that Magyar merchants regularly travelled as far as Constantinople to sell their wares. Abū Hāmid reveals that the slave trade between the two peoples still existed in the mid-twelfth century, recording that he personally owned a ten-year-old Turkic slave boy.[54] But slaves cannot have been all that the Magyars sold. Indeed, it would have been self-defeating for Byzantium to promote slave-trading, since this would encourage the Magyars to continue to launch raids. What then did the Byzantines and Magyars exchange in the second half of the tenth century? We can find some indications in the distribution of artefacts produced in Byzantium that have been discovered north of the Danube.

Many pieces of Byzantine jewellery, especially earrings, have been discovered by chance or in excavations in modern Hungary and Transylvania. Recently, a comprehensive summary has been produced in Hungarian by Mesterházy, who has dismissed the notion that such a volume and distribution of finds could have resulted from Magyar raids. The maps he has produced illustrate a concentration of finds around Szeged, at the confluence of the rivers Tisza and Maros, and north along the Tisza as far as the river Körös. Smaller concentrations have been found further along the Tisza, and also on the middle Danube beyond Esztergom.[55] The latter is the region occupied by the princely Árpád clan; the former regions were settled by their confederates, including the Gylas, and possibly the Karhas. Therefore, we can conclude provisionally that Byzantine precious jewellery was a commodity which reached the lands north of the Danube through a process of exchange from the mid-tenth century; and that there was

[53] Ibn Rusteh: 160–1. We only have one volume of Ibn Rusteh's large work 'on precious objects', and he cannot be considered (as he often is) a 'geographer'.   [54] Hrbek 1955: 208–9.
[55] Mesterházy 1990: 87–115 (especially the map at 106); Mesterházy 1991: 145–74 (map at 164).

greater activity along the river Tisza than the Danube, serving the region settled by the Árpáds' confederates rather than the princely tribe.

A remarkably similar pattern is evident when we plot the findspots of Byzantine coins north of the Danube (see map 1.3). The greatest number of coins struck and circulating in the second half of the tenth and eleventh centuries have been found in the environs of Szeged. Far fewer have been found on the middle Danube.[56] Once again, the coins cannot simply be the fruits of booty raids, or even tribute payments. There are coins of all denominations, both precious metals and bronze issues, and finds represent both individual stray losses and deliberately interred hoards. The volume and distribution of the finds clearly support the thesis that Byzantine goods were being exchanged with those who dominated the region around Szeged. What then were Magyars at Szeged exchanging for Byzantine jewels and coins? The answer must be salt.

The seven salt mines of Transylvania, which give the region its German name Siebenbürgen, had operated for centuries before the Magyars' arrival there. During their migration westward the nomads took control of the mines. The eminent Hungarian historian Györffy (1975: 20–1) has maintained that before this, when the Magyars were settled in Etelköz (Atelkouzou) they had access to sea salt in quantities sufficient for export, and that 'only the possession of salt mines could secure for the Magyars this prime necessity'. It is harder to accept his further claim that each of the seven Magyar tribes took control of one salt mine after the migration into Transylvania. However, the established link between the Magyars and the salt trade is sufficient to suggest that they knew the value of the commodity, and were experienced in bringing it to markets. We have documentary evidence that control over the salt routes and the tolls levied on its transportation was an issue in the disputes between the Árpád ruler Stephen I and the confederate chieftain Ajtony in the early eleventh century.[57] Ajtony dominated the region along the river Maros, and his power base was in the vicinity of Szeged.

Therefore, numismatic and documentary evidence both indicate that Szeged was the regional centre for storage and sale of Transylvanian salt, and that much of this was exchanged for Byzantine coin and luxury goods. And yet what need did Byzantium have for Transylvanian salt? We know that salt was expensive and in great demand throughout the

---

[56] Kovács 1989: fig. 40 (insert map: 'Byzantinische Münzen vom Karpatenbecken aus der Landnahmezeit').   [57] *Vita Gerardi Maioris*: 489–90.

empire at this time. A ninth-century letter composed by the deacon Ignatius of Nicaea begins with 'a trite statement concerning the necessity of salt for humans (even bread, says he, cannot be eaten without salt)'.[58] He then offers the enormous sum of twelve gold coins for an unspecified contractual quantity of salt. But Ignatius' salt was to be supplied from established salt pans (*halyke*). Whatever the level of demand, salt at an appropriate price could be supplied from within the empire; there was no need to look as far as Transylvania.[59] Clearly, the Byzantine desire was not for the Magyars' salt *per se*, but to establish a process of peaceful exchange with the nomads. Political considerations overrode any economic concerns, and business was conducted according to the principle that trading prevented raiding.

So, Byzantine dealings with the Magyars and their confederates in the first part of the tenth century involved a combination of utilitarian and ceremonial devices, both intended to neutralize the threat the empire's newest neighbours posed to the integrity of her Balkan lands, and to secure support against the other peoples who might threaten the empire, including the Bulgarians. Like various 'barbarian' *archontes* before and after them, the Magyar chieftains benefited from their relationship with the empire by the receipt of titles, with associated stipends and prestige, tribute payments, and trade which guaranteed risk-free access to the products of a 'civilized' sedentary society. If the protocols preserved with the *De Cerimoniis* had been updated, we might expect the Gylas and Karhas to be deemed dependents and subject to the emperor's command (*keleusis*) in the manner of the *archontes* of the Serbs and Croats, while the Árpád ruler of the Magyars remained independent and would still receive an imperial letter (*grammata*).

BEYOND BULGARIA

Thus far we have progressed some way into the northern Balkans by some well trodden avenues, and some less familiar paths only recently cleared. We have encountered many of the peoples with whom we will be concerned, and placed some names on the Byzantine map of the medieval Balkans (and beyond). We have explored a variety of diplomatic techniques that Byzantium employed to secure the cooperation of various *ethne*, and observed that the principal weapons in the Byzantine diplomatic armoury were tribute, trade and titles. Tribute payments

---

[58] Ignatius the Deacon: 50–3 (ep. 13); Kazhdan 1992: 198–9.   [59] *ODB*: iii, 1832–3.

underlay most Byzantine relations with 'barbarian' peoples. Trade was already used to enhance stability in volatile regions, and routes and contacts were expanded to encompass new peoples and products – for example Magyars and salt. The ultimate weapon, which our sources deal with an obfuscatory manner, was the recognition of the Bulgarian ruler's right to use the imperial title. However, equally important was the manner in which Magyar chieftains were involved in personal ceremonies where baptism and oaths of loyalty were integral and integrated elements. Thus *ethne* who lay far beyond the geographical frontiers of the Byzantine empire were brought within its ecumenical orbit, absorbed into the *oikoumene*, the civilized world. This was wholly distinct from any attempt at the political absorption of Bulgaria, which cannot have been contemplated by Constantine VII and his son Romanus II. However, even before the end of Constantine's reign imperial troops were taking the offensive in the east, and imperial ceremonial had begun to move from the palace and cathedral back to the streets of Constantinople, the Forum of Constantine and the Hippodrome, in the form of triumphal military processions.[60] This triumphal militarism soon found expression in the northern Balkans, and in the next half-century Byzantium's Balkan frontier was twice advanced to the Danube.

---

[60] McCormick 1986: 159–78 characterizes the period 956–72 as the 'high tide of triumph'. For the locations of the Forum and Hippodrome in Constantinople see map 1.2.

CHAPTER TWO

The Byzantine occupation of Bulgaria (963–1025)

The *status quo* that prevailed between Byzantium and Bulgaria in the period 927–59 was based on a mutual desire to ensure continued stability in each empire, and to eliminate the nomad threat to both. The arrangement was underpinned by the marriage alliance of 927, where the emperor undertook to recognize the tsar's imperial status, and to continue annual tribute payments. In return the tsar promised to defend the Byzantine empire's Balkan lands. Tribute payments continued to be paid until the death of Tsarina Maria Lecapena, some time in 963. However, through this period the Byzantine emperor had subtly altered his attitude to the Bulgarian tsar, and the tsar had acquiesced in this.

During the same period the Byzantine emperor had significantly improved his contacts with the various peoples settled beyond Bulgaria. The increased frequency of Magyar raids had alarmed the Byzantines, and a series of arrangements were made with powerful Magyar chieftains over and above the Bulgarian accord. To stabilize the situation in the lands immediately bordering the Danube trade was encouraged, Byzantine coins and jewellery made available, and salt from the Transylvanian mines purchased. A similar system for distributing goods had long been established to deal with the Pechenegs around Cherson. New contacts with the Rus of Kiev sought to exploit the northern peoples' greed for precious goods and metals. Slaves and the products of the Russian forest belt were brought to Constantinople annually according to stipulations laid down in increasingly detailed agreements. South of the Danube, the Croats remained within their own lands, and the previously turbulent situation in Serbia had calmed. For many years the various local rulers had recognized Byzantine overlordship. It is therefore explicable that soon after his accession the militant emperor Nicephorus II Phocas (963–9) decided that he was in a position to renegotiate the arrangement with Tsar Peter.

NICEPHORUS II PHOCAS' NORTHERN POLICY

Returning victorious from Tarsus, Nicephorus received the regular Bulgarian embassy in Constantinople contemptuously, probably in 966.[1] He refused them the annual tribute payment, maintaining that any obligation had ended with the death of Maria Lecapena; he drew Peter's attention to the Bulgarian failure to prevent nomad raids reaching Byzantine lands; and he set out for the 'great ditch' in Thrace to parade his troops and shore up his border defences. Anxious to appease Nicephorus, Peter arranged for his two sons, Boris and Romanus, to be conveyed to Constantinople as hostages. This did not satisfy Nicephorus, but despite his bravura in dealing with Peter, he was committed to an aggressive campaign of reconquest in the east and could ill afford to open a second front. More than this, he was reluctant to lead his own forces into Bulgaria, 'where caverns and ridges succeed the dense, overgrown country, and then are followed by swamps and marshes'. He knew the country to be 'extraordinarily wet, and heavily wooded, everywhere enclosed by impassable mountains . . . and surrounded by very large rivers.'[2] He therefore determined to avoid a military confrontation with the Bulgarians by inciting the leader of the Rus of Kiev, Svyatoslav Igorevich, to lead a punitive raid on the cities of the lower Danube.

The exact sequence and chronology of events that follows is confused by inconsistencies in our main sources. However, the key strands of Nicephorus' plan, and their consequences are fairly clear. Probably in 967 he raised a certain Calocyras to the rank of *patrikios*, and despatched him to bribe the Rus with the promise of 'gifts and honours in abundance'.[3] Leo the Deacon (63) claims that the sum concerned was 1,500 pounds of gold. The plan proceeded well enough, and in August 968 the Rus arrived at the lower Danube where they wrought great destruction. Soon after this a Bulgarian embassy arrived in Constantinople. We can date this to before 2 October, when the ambassador Liutprand of Cremona who records the incident, left the city. Liutprand, offended to be shown less courtesy than they, was informed that 'Bulgarian envoys

---

[1] Scylitzes: 55; Leo the Deacon: 61–2. The date of the Bulgarian embassy is disputed, and is integral to any attempt to establish the chronology of subsequent events. See, for example, the recent account by Whittow 1996: 294–5. For the illustration of the embassy in the Madrid Scylitzes (fol. 148 v (a)), see Cirac Estopañan 1965: 156, 353, fig. 387; Grabar and Manoussacas 1979: fig. 189.

[2] Leo the Deacon: 62–3; McGeer 1995: 328.

[3] Scylitzes: 277. For further commentary see Ivanov 1981: 88–101. Among the latest contributions in English, Hanak 1995: 138–51, has excellent coverage of recent scholarship in Russian. However, I disagree with him on many points of detail.

should be preferred, honoured and cherished above all others' (*Legatio*: 540; trans.: 246). Nicephorus' treatment of the Bulgarian embassy was this time exemplary. Holding all the cards, he was able to demand the deposition of Peter (who shortly afterwards retired to a monastery) and his replacement with Boris, who was despatched forthwith from Constantinople where he had recently been held. Moreover, according to Nicephorus' wishes, the Rus withdrew to Kiev, hastened by the news that the Pechenegs had invaded their lands 'for the first time. [Svyatoslav's mother] Olga shut herself up in the city of Kiev with her grandsons . . . while the nomads besieged the city with great force' (*PVL*: 47 trans.: 85). In winter 968 Nicephorus could be delighted with the success of his scheme. However, he had not reckoned with the attraction that the flourishing markets on the lower Danube would hold for the Rus, nor anticipated the treachery of his envoy Calocyras.

Svyatoslav, we are told 'marvelled at the fertility' of the region bordering the lower Danube. According to the *Russian Primary Chronicle* he announced 'it is not my pleasure to be in Kiev, but I will live in Pereyaslavets on the Danube. That shall be the centre of my land; for there all good things flow: gold from the Greeks [Byzantines], precious cloths, wines and fruits of many kinds; silver and horses from the Czechs and Magyars; and from the Rus furs, wax, honey and slaves'.[4] He determined to return in full force, and secured the assistance of Calocyras, whom the Byzantine sources accused of aspiring to the imperial throne; a topos, but perhaps with some basis. Calocyras was the son of the leading man (*proteuon*) in Cherson, and had almost certainly been kept as a guest (or dignified hostage) in Constantinople until 967.[5] His defection would have been all the more worrying in that it threw into question the loyalty of the Chersonites, upon whom much of the empire's northern policy depended. Calocyras may even have assisted Svyatoslav in constructing a grand alliance of northern peoples. Svyatoslav arrived at the lower Danube in autumn 969 with a mighty allied force of Pechenegs and Magyars.[6] Bulgarian resistance was initially solid; the *Russian Primary Chronicle* relates that when:

Svyatoslav arrived before Pereyaslavets, the Bulgarians fortified themselves within the city. They made one sally against Svyatoslav. There was great carnage and the Bulgarians came off victors. But Svyatoslav cried to his soldiers 'Here is where we fall! Let us fight boldly, brothers and companions!' Toward

---

[4] *PVL*: 48 (trans.: 86); Franklin and Shepard 1996: 145. For the location of Pereyaslavets (modern Nufǎrul), and its association with Presthlavitza, see below at pp. 56–7. See also Scylitzes: 288.
[5] Scylitzes: 277.   [6] Scylitzes: 288; Leo the Deacon: 108.

2.1 Paristrion

Legend:

1 Dristra
2 Păcuiul lui Soare & Dervent
3 Cernavoda
4 Capidava
5 Hîrsova
6 Igliţa
7 Dinogetia
8 Novio dunum
9 Niculiţel
10 Tulcea
11 Nufărul
12 Kilia
13 Constantia
14 Varna
15 Mesembria
16 Anchialus
17 Preslav

Chilia
Sulina
St. George

Prut

Ialomiţa

DOBRUDJA

MOESIAN PLAIN

BLACK SEA

evening Svyatoslav finally gained the upper hand and took the city by storm. (*PVL*: 49; trans.: 87)

Thereafter, Peter's sons swiftly capitulated, and the Rus established their hegemony over the other towns on the lower Danube without further bloodshed. Garrisons were installed in Dristra (modern Silistra) and Preslav, where Boris remained titular leader retaining the trappings of his imperial status. Only Philippopolis (modern Plovdiv) seems to have resisted, and some 20,000 captives were impaled as an example when the city eventually fell.

The reversal in Byzantine fortunes was astonishing. The loyalty of the Chersonites was in doubt; Nicephorus' agents had failed to prevent an alliance of steppe peoples; the leader of the fierce warrior merchants from Kiev had successfully shifted the centre of his operations from the middle Dnieper to the mouth of the Danube; and the young ruler whom the emperor had despatched to Bulgaria, far from being his puppet, now acknowledged Russian authority. In a final, desperate attempt to inspire the Bulgarians to return to the offensive Nicephorus proposed an unprecedented marriage agreement: the two young emperors, Basil and Constantine (the grandsons of Constantine VII), were offered as husbands to unspecified Bulgarian princesses.[7] The rejection of this offer signalled the collapse of his entire northern policy. Shortly afterwards, on 11 December 969, Nicephorus was murdered by a small band of his confidants led by his nephew, the general John Tzimisces.[8]

JOHN I TZIMISCES AND THE RESTORATION OF THE DANUBE FRONTIER

John I Tzimisces (969–76) spent the first year of his reign dealing with the irate Phocas family, whose lands and power were concentrated in Anatolia. He delegated the war against the Rus to his brother-in-law, Bardas Sclerus, who achieved a significant victory at Arcadiopolis near Philippopolis in March 970.[9] The Rus withdrew north of the Haemus, satisfied with their control of Preslav and the major strongholds on the lower Danube. However, they failed to secure the mountain passes, and fell victim to a classic Byzantine ruse: John Tzimisces chose Easter week

---

[7] Leo the Deacon: 79.   [8] Scylitzes: 279.

[9] Scylitzes: 288–91; Leo the Deacon: 108–11. McGeer 1995: 294–9 provides a translation of, and commentary on, Sclerus' tactics, which conform to the paradigms in Nicephorus Phocas' military manual, now called the *praecepta militaria*.

in the following spring to lead his troops across the Haemus mountains, and thus advanced swiftly and without resistance as far as Preslav. The commander of the Russian garrison, Sphangel, could not withstand the Byzantine assault, and the Bulgarian ruler Boris was captured with his entire family. They were taken back to Constantinople along with the Bulgarian imperial regalia. Tzimisces pressed on to Dristra to confront Svyatoslav himself. The Russian feared a local uprising, and had 300 leading Bulgarians executed. He also feared a long siege, and was aware that the imperial fleet was on its way to the lower Danube. Arraying his forces, Svyatoslav forced an indecisive pitched battle, before withdrawing within Dristra's strong walls. The siege persisted for three months, and envoys from nearby Constantia and other *phrouria* approached the emperor with offers of submission.[10] However a Byzantine victory was in no way certain; John Tzimisces even challenged Svyatoslav to decide the outcome by single combat. The Russian refused, but consulted with his officers and decided to chance all on battle.

Leo the Deacon and Scylitzes provide detailed battle narratives which show remarkable similarities.[11] It is clear that both authors have drawn from a common source, and it is safe to assume that this was an official account of the episode which was produced for Tzimisces on his triumphant return to Constantinople. Leo, writing shortly after the events he describes, places greater emphasis on Tzimisces' abilities as a general, recounting how he rallied his troops after the heroic death of a certain Anemas, and personally led a renewed assault on the Rus.[12] Scylitzes omits the emperor's final charge, but emulates Leo in recounting how suddenly a wind storm, divinely-inspired, heralded the appearance of St Theodore the Stratelate mounted on a white steed. This *deus ex machina* signals the defeat of the Rus, and brings an end to the narrative for both Leo and Scylitzes. As McGrath (1995: 163) has observed, 'If the Byzantine[s] . . . had any doubt of the validity of the reasons and motives that led to the war with the Rus, the divine presence, verified by the appearance of the martyr, confirmed the soundness of the Byzantine cause.' More than this, it confirmed the legitimacy of Tzimisces' protracted campaign in Bulgaria, and was seen to absolve him for his role in the murder of Nicephorus Phocas, and to confirm the legitimacy of his usurpation. God was on Tzimisces' side, and the turmoil that Nicephorus Phocas had produced by his complicated northern policy

---

[10] Scylitzes: 301; Cirac Estopañan 1965: 171–2, 370, fig. 439. See also Zonaras: iii, 530.

[11] McGrath 1995: 152–64, provides an intelligent commentary on the two passages.

[12] Leo the Deacon: 153–4; McGrath 1995: 161–2.

was resolved by the new emperor's strong right arm and the aid of a military saint and martyr.

A few days later peace terms were negotiated. The treaty, which is recorded in the *Russian Primary Chronicle*, was, as Shepard has recently pointed out, in no way a capitulation by Svyatoslav.[13] Russian trading privileges were confirmed in exchange for his undertaking never again to 'contemplate an attack on [Byzantine] territory, nor collect an army of foreign mercenaries for this purpose, nor incite any other foe against your realm' (*PVL*: 52; trans.: 89–90). However, Svyatoslav did not live to benefit from the terms he had negotiated. On the return journey to Kiev the Pechenegs attacked at the Dnieper rapids. According to nomad custom, Svyatoslav's head was gilded and used as a drinking vessel. Before returning to Constantinople John Tzimisces took precautions against further Russian attacks. He placed commanders from his field-army in Preslav and in key strongholds on the lower Danube.[14] Lead seals discovered during excavations in Preslav prove that the city was renamed Ioannopolis, in honour of the victorious emperor, and placed under the command of Catacalon '*protospatharios* and *strategos*'.[15] Leo Saracenopoulos, who had been Domestic of the *Hikanatoi* (the commander of a regiment of the standing army), was placed in charge of Dristra.[16] A certain Sisinios was appointed as *strategos* of Presthlavitza, which was renamed Theodoropolis after St Theodore.[17]

The act of renaming cities confirms that Tzimisces had determined to use his victory to maximum political advantage in Constantinople. Upon his reentry into the city, the emperor enjoyed splendid triumphal victory celebrations. We might surmise that orators produced verses to mark his victories, and to propagate the notion that it was divinely-inspired. Their poems may have been based on official victory bulletins which recorded the details of the battles – the heroic death of Anemas, the emperor's final charge, and the martyr's intervention – and which were later reproduced by Leo the Deacon and John Scylitzes.[18] In this way the defeat of the Rus and the conquest of Bulgaria became central to the legitimation of Tzimisces. Small wonder then that his triumphal

[13] Franklin and Shepard 1996: 149–50; *pace* Hanak 1995: 148–51.
[14] Yahya of Antioch: 827–9. [15] Iordanov 1993a: 134–5. [16] Iordanov 1993a: 94–7, 105.
[17] Iordanov 1993a: 124–5. The identification of Theodoropolis with Pereyaslavets (which was also known as Presthlavitza, or Little Preslav) has been debated. For an introduction see Oikonomides 1983: 1–9.
[18] On the composition, content and public delivery of official victory bulletins see McCormick 1986: 190–6. For the possible influence of a victory bulletin in forging the image of Basil the Bulgar-slayer, see below at p. 72.

celebrations culminated with the ritual subordination of the Bulgarian ruler. Once again Leo and Scylitzes provide interlocking accounts. Tzimisces rode a white horse behind a wagon containing an icon of the Virgin and the Bulgarian imperial regalia. Behind the emperor rode Boris, the deposed Bulgarian tsar.[19] Upon reaching the Forum of Constantine, the emperor was acclaimed before Boris was symbolically divested of his imperial regalia: the intimate link between John's victory and his legitimacy was thus made explicit.[20] Then the procession moved on to the Great Church of Holy Wisdom (*Hagia Sophia*) where Boris' crown was given to God, and the former tsar was given the Byzantine rank of *magistros*.[21] Thus, his authority and the symbols of it were absorbed within the imperial hierarchy, and the independent realm of Bulgaria was absorbed into the Byzantine *oikoumene*, brought back within the limits of 'the civilized world'.

Tzimisces' victory at the Danube brought to culmination a number of developments which saw the pacific ecumenical world view propagated by Constantine VII transformed into an ideology which linked imperial fortunes with military conquest and advancing the frontiers. The change in emphasis had already been clear to the aforementioned Liutprand of Cremona during his sojourn at Nicephorus Phocas' court. Liutprand contrasted Constantine, 'a mild man . . . [who] made other peoples friendly to him with things of this nature' (referring thus to the silks he was trying to smuggle out of Constantinople), with Nicephorus, 'a man devoted to warfare [who] does not win the friendship of peoples by offering them money, but subjugates them by terror and the sword'.[22] Phocas himself had stressed his duty to expand the empire during his campaigns of conquest, and had been thus praised by John Geometres (*PG* 106: 902) for stretching out 'both hands, the right bringing victory (*nikephoros*) in the east, and the left to western lands, so that you marked out the limits of the land and at the same time extended the five frontiers (*pente tous horous*) of the Romans'. But Nicephorus had achieved little

---

[19] The scene is depicted in the Madrid Scylitzes, fol. 172v (a). See Cirac Estopañan 1965: 174, 374, fig. 450; Grabar and Manoussacas 1979: plate 34 and fig. 221. See also Evans and Wixom 1997: 15.

[20] Scylitzes: 310. Leo the Deacon: 158 omits this episode and appears to imply that the highly symbolic divestiture took place in the palace. This is highly unlikely. For further comment see McCormick 1986: 174.

[21] Scylitzes: 297, 310–11; Leo the Deacon: 138, 159; John Geometres: cols. 919–20; Zonaras: iii, 535–6. The emphasis placed on the Bulgarian crown makes one wonder whether it was not in fact the same crown with which Nicholas Mysticus honoured Symeon in 913. See above at p. 22, and for the significance of crowns, see below at pp. 188–9, 259, 311, 323.

[22] Liutprand, *Legatio*: 205–6 (trans.: 269); Shepard 1992a: 41.

in western lands, and consequently the annexation of Bulgaria became central to Tzimisces' imperial image. Shortly after his return from Dristra, Tzimisces issued the first in the series of so-called anonymous *folles*, bronze coins which bore an image of Christ in place of the emperor, with the reverse inscription 'Jesus Christ, emperor of emperors'.[23] The emperor was thus seen to be only the agent of his divine master, and his duty to extend Christ's earthly domain. But there was a world of difference between the Bulgarian ruler recognizing the emperor's authority, and the annexation of the lands between the Haemus mountains and the lower Danube. As we will see, the rhetorical absorption of Bulgaria was far more complete than the reality.

THE REORGANIZATION OF NORTHERN BULGARIA, 971–976

John Tzimisces' victory in Bulgaria required the creation of a new type of organization between the Haemus mountains and the lower Danube. The form which this took has been the subject of a protracted, and often acrimonious academic debate. Scholars from Romania and Bulgaria have failed to agree on whether Paristrion (the lands beside the lower Danube in general, but in particular the region that today comprises the Dobrudja) was ever part of Bulgaria, or whether it remained ethnically, culturally, and politically distinct. They have also clashed over the nature and type of administrative structure introduced into the region in the period of Byzantine domination. The significance of the alternate (indeed diametrically opposed) interpretations for the distinct national histories of both modern states cannot be ignored. However, much of the discussion can be put aside if we focus exclusively on the rather meagre evidence. If it is impossible to answer the 'Paristrion Question' without becoming enmeshed in highly contentious and subjective analyses, it is possible to approach the 'Question' differently.

Svyatoslav Igorevich had demonstrated that it was possible to dominate the whole of Paristrion and northern Bulgaria from a few strongholds, which the emperor now held. The Russian had also eradicated the potential leaders of Bulgarian resistance to Byzantine hegemony by his slaughter of 300 *boyars*, and Peter's sons were hostages in Constantinople. Tzimisces' agents could therefore proceed with the 'absorption' of Bulgaria without major distractions. However, there was much to do, and the sheer numbers of lead seals that have come to light

---

[23] Scylitzes: 311; McCormick 1986: 175.

which date from the period immediately after 971 attest to the volume of communications that passed between Constantinople and the region, and between the officers within the region. They also reveal stages in the evolution of military commands.[24]

Before 975, the aforementioned Leo Saracenopoulos' jurisdiction was extended to embrace both Dristra and Ioannopolis (Preslav). Eighteen seals bearing the legend 'Leo *protospatharios* and *strategos* of Ioannopolis and Dristra' have been discovered in what must have been an archive at Preslav.[25] They are most likely to represent sealed copies of his own despatches kept on file in his headquarters. We know that Leo was now based in Preslav because his former role, as garrison commander at Dristra, had been taken by either Peter or Arcadius. Seals of both these *strategoi* have been discovered, but we cannot tell in which order they held the position.[26] Peter was also garrison commander at Preslav (before or after his tenure at Dristra).[27]

The *Escorial Taktikon* (or *Taktikon Oikonomides*) – the modern name given to a precedence list drawn up in Constantinople between 975 and 979 – reveals that the coupling of Dristra and Preslav was swiftly superseded by a new command of Thrace and Ioannopolis.[28] Once again Leo Saracenopoulos held the command, and the discovery of five seals in his archive prove that he was still based in Preslav.[29] At the same time a command known as 'Mesopotamia of the West' was created in the lands of the Danube delta; however, the lowly position of the *strategos* in the precedence list suggests that he was merely a garrison commander, and certainly was not in charge of a whole frontier theme.[30]

As supreme commander Leo Saracenopoulos oversaw the reconstruction of fortifications at several locations beside, and islands in the lower Danube (see map 2.1). The selection of sites, and the nature of the renovations demonstrate that the Byzantines' greatest fear was the return of the Rus. As we have seen, the site that Svyatoslav declared he desired most of all was Pereyaslavets on the Danube (*na dunaj*). A continuing discussion over the site of Pereyaslavets must surely have been resolved by the extensive excavations at Nufărul on the St George arm of the Danube delta. The material evidence uncovered there confirms Oikonomides' observation that the site is indeed Presthlavitza, 'Little

---

[24] For general comments on the interpretation of Byzantine lead seals, see above at pp. 16–17.

[25] Iordanov 1993a: 136–7. The reform is also recorded by Scylitzes: 298.

[26] Iordanov 1993a: 118–19.   [27] Iordanov 1993a: 135–6.   [28] *Listes de préséance*: 264–5.

[29] Iordanov 1993a: 128–9. Another seal in the Hermitage collection in St Petersburg has been published by Shandrovskaia 1981: 460–1.

[30] *Listes de préséance*: 268–9; Oikonomides 1965: 57–79.

Preslav', the rich trading city whither wealth from all regions flowed. Excavation has uncovered the foundations of ramparts on a promontory overlooking the river which measure between 1.8 and 2.4 metres in thickness. At the eastern end of the promontory archaeologists have identified a semi-circular tower. The adjacent site is littered with fragments of pottery – glazed and unglazed, local and imported – and other everyday utensils. If further proof were needed, more than 700 stray finds of coins have been discovered at Nufǎrul which date from Tzimisces' reign until soon after 1092.[31]

Upstream from Presthlavitza, the *kastron* (fortified town) of Noviodunum dominated the Danube at one of its principal fords. It had been the base of the Roman fleet of the Danube (*Classis Flavia Moesica*), and shows signs of substantial renovations in the period after 971. Similarly, at Dinogetia (modern Garvǎn) the original walls of the *kastron*, which were destroyed by an invasion of Koutrigours in around 560, were rebuilt and a whole new gate complex was added.[32] Capidava was also a fortified naval base constructed under the emperor Trajan (d. 117). Finds of copper *folles* struck by Tzimisces, the first coins for many centuries, prove that it was rebuilt after 971. They also suggest that it was home to a small garrison, since low value coins in such isolated outlying sites tend to represent troops' wages.[33] There are similar signs of activity at nearby Dervent, where the seal of a certain 'John Maleses, *patrikios* and *strategos*' has been discovered.[34]

The most impressive Byzantine project was the construction of a naval complex on an island opposite Dervent and just a few miles downstream from Dristra.[35] It is known today as Pǎcuiul lui Soare (the Island of the Sun). A huge landing stage was fashioned from massive rocks in the south-east corner of the complex. Above this rose a tower gateway which formed the fortress' principal entrance. The walls were constructed of huge carved blocks, and it has been argued that the monumental structure and the extensive use of marble was intended to

---

[31] For collected references to the ongoing excavations see Baraschi and Damian 1993: 237, n.1.
[32] Barnea 1971: 343–59.
[33] For introductory comments on the interpretation of coin evidence see above at pp. 14–16.
[34] Barnea 1964: 245–7. This dates from the period *c*. 1000–36.
[35] In fact, as with almost every other aspect of the history of this region, there is a heated discussion between Romanian and Bulgarian scholars. Since the Island of the Sun falls within modern Romania the excavations and subsequent monograph stress the novelty (i.e. absence of any Bulgarian influence in the construction) of the fortress. Bulgarians have argued that the site was already home to a fortress under Tsar Peter. However, its naval function, the novelty of the Russian threat, and the absence of any mention of the site (which would have been the front line of defence in 969) support the Romanian interpretation.

symbolize an age of reconquest, but it probably signalled little more than
the site's proximity to several quarries and an abundance of readily
available late antique spolia. The use of spolia even extended to the
mortar which bound many of the irregularly shaped blocks. Of the three
types of mortar analysed, two contained fragments of pulverized late
antique brick.[36]

As well as consolidating Byzantine military control over Bulgaria,
Tzimisces reestablished control over the independent Bulgarian church.
Recognition of the Bulgarian patriarchate was rescinded, and a metropolitan subject to the patriarch of Constantinople was instituted. Two
seals of 'Stephen, metropolitan of Ioannopolis' have been discovered at
Preslav and Pliska.[37] We have no other firm information on ecclesiastical matters, except for an inscription which records the restoration of a
church in Dristra and attributes the work to the joint reign of the emperors Basil II and Constantine VIII. The epigraphy confirms that it dates
from early in Basil's reign (976–1025).[38]

THE REVOLT OF THE COMETOPULI[39]

The development of Byzantine military organization in Bulgaria was
well underway by 976, despite the emperor having taken very little personal interest. Tzimisces was preoccupied after 972 with protracted campaigns in the east whence he returned to Constantinople victorious, but
fatally ill, and died on 10 January 976. Immediately a civil war erupted
in Byzantium between the young emperors, Basil and Constantine, and
several aristocratic families led by Bardas Phocas, the nephew of the
emperor Nicephorus. The struggle for mastery of the empire took place
in Anatolia, where the aristocrats had their vast estates. Bulgaria and the
lands beyond were neglected, and in the absence of any firm imperial
interest a revolt by the four sons of Nicholas, a regional commander in
Macedonia, secured control over certain lands east of Thrace. At the
same time the Bulgarian imperial brothers, Boris and Romanus, were

---

[36] Diaconu and Vîlceanu 1972: 27–46. On quarries, Diaconu and Zah 1971: 289–306.
[37] Iordanov 1993a: 187; Diaconu 1991: 73–89; Diaconu 1994–5: 449–52, argues that two metropolitan sees were established at this time, at Preslav (Ioannopolis) and Tomis (Constantia), and a
bishopric at Dristra which was initially subject to Preslav. On the metropolitan of Tomis, see
below at p. 64.
[38] Salamon 1971: 487–96, which corrects Ševčenko 1969: 591–8.
[39] Jonathan Shepard's forthcoming book, *Byzantium Between Neighbours*, will contain a fuller narrative treatment of the revolt and its consequences. I am grateful to him for allowing me to read
and use several draft chapters. The fullest published interpretation in English remains Antoljak
1985.

allowed to flee Constantinople. Boris was killed by a Bulgarian sentry, supposedly by mistake, but Romanus reached the four brothers, who were known as the Cometopuli. Although the sources are silent about his role or title until 1004 (when he reappears as governor of Skopje), it seems clear that Romanus gained the brothers local support when they turned their attention to the lands between the Haemus and the lower Danube.[40]

As resident commander, Leo Saracenopoulos was responsible for resisting the encroachments of the brothers. It is probably in this period that Leo's command in Ioannopolis was linked to Thrace. However, he failed to prevent the advance of the Cometopuli, and was withdrawn shortly after 979. Promoted to the rank of *patrikios* as a palliative, he was appointed Count of the Stable, an honourable military rank which saw him retire to Constantinople. A seal discovered at Preslav inscribed with his new credentials must have been attached to a letter he sent from the capital and attests to his continued interest in affairs north of the Haemus.[41] His successors, Theophanes and Stauracius, both struck seals as *strategos* of Thrace and Ioannopolis. The final commander was Nicephorus Xiphias, who could not prevent Preslav falling to the brothers in 986.[42] Thereafter, a form of jurisdiction in Thrace was granted to other commanders. A seal discovered at Dristra bears the inscription 'D[avid], *protospatharios* and *strategos* of Thrace and Dristra'.[43] Wasilewski (1975: 641–5) has suggested that such joint commands facilitated recruitment of troops from south of the Haemus to bolster defences in the north. It is equally likely that they reflected the *de iure* claims of field commanders charged with the recovery of lost territory.

With the fall of Preslav affairs beyond the Haemus had reached a critical juncture. Basil II was forced to tear his attention away from the domestic disputes, and, in 986, launched his first campaign in the Balkans. However, his march to Sardica ended in a humiliating retreat, and worse still defeat at the hands of Samuel's forces who waited in ambush near the so-called 'Trajan's Gates'. Encouraged by the emperor's defeat, his opponents in the east renewed their efforts. In the following years the Byzantine civil war reached its climax, when the two

---

[40] On the civil war see Whittow 1996: 361–73. On the Cometopuli see Fine 1983: 188–97. As Ostrogorsky 1968: 302, n.1, maintains, contra Antoljak 1985: 15–17, there is no indication in the sources that the Cometopuli had established control of 'western Bulgaria' between 969 and 976, still less during Peter's reign.

[41] Iordanov 1993a: 104–5. Shandrovskaia 1982: 167 reports that a similar seal exists in the Dumbarton Oaks collection.   [42] Iordanov 1993a: 129–32.

[43] Iordanov 1985: 101–2, nr. 6.

most powerful aristocratic families, led by Bardas Phocas and Bardas Sclerus, made common cause against the young emperor. In a desperate move Basil forged an alliance with the Rus. Knowing of Nicephorus Phocas' dealings with Svyatoslav, Basil must have been wary of seeking the assistance of his son Vladimir. Furthermore, the latter had taken advantage of Byzantine preoccupations to seize Cherson. Basil was obliged to offer the greatest prize at his disposal to secure the return of Cherson and a detachment of 6,000 Russian warriors. He offered his sister, the *porphyrogennete* (a daughter born to a ruling emperor), in marriage to Vladimir.[44] Basil's Russian troops, known to modern scholars as the Varangian Guard, proved to be crucial in securing his victories at Chrysopolis in spring 988, and at Abydos on 13 April 989, where Bardas Phocas was killed. Sclerus retired to his Anatolian estates with the palliative rank of *kouropalates*, and died shortly after. With the civil wars finally over, the victorious Basil turned his attention to the northern Balkans.

Basil was clearly familiar with precedents for dealing with a recalcitrant ruler in Bulgaria, and promptly entered into negotiations with the Serbs. A document dated September 993 from the Lavra monastery contains a reference to a subsequent Serbian embassy which was forced to travel to Constantinople by sea to avoid the lands dominated by Samuel. Consequently the envoys were captured and taken prisoner on the island of Lemnos by Arab pirates.[45] At the same time, spring 991, the emperor led an army into Macedonia. We know practically nothing of what ensued, and are totally reliant on the meagre testimony of Scylitzes, from whom we also learn that a Fatimid attack on Antioch and Aleppo in 994 forced the emperor to march east, leaving his confidant Nicephorus Ouranus in command. If Basil had made significant progress in the Balkans, the position was soon reversed by Samuel Cometopulos. With his three brothers dead, one killed by his own hand, Samuel ruled alone. From his base at Prespa, near Ohrid (in modern Macedonia) he launched regular attacks on surrounding lands, focusing his attention on Thessalonica, the great Byzantine stronghold and rich trading centre, and Larissa, the metropolitan see of Thessaly. Repeated raiding saw the destruction of the nearby Athonite monastery of Hierissos.[46]

Samuel's invasions, which reached as far south as the Isthmus of Corinth, engendered great fear among the populations of Hellas and

[44] Franklin and Shepard 1996: 162–4. It has been suggested that Cherson was occupied subsequently.

[45] *Actes de Lavra*, ed. Lemerle et al.: 124, nr. 12; Ostrogorsky 1949: 187–94; Ostrogorsky 1968: 307.

[46] *Actes de Lavra*, ed. Lemerle et al.: 117, nr. 8; Duichev 1949: 129.

Peloponnesus, and so much is reflected in the *Life of St Nikon*, which was written within living memory of Samuel's campaigns. The saint is credited with alleviating the suffering and anxiety of the *praitor* and *strategos* of Corinth, Basil Apocaucus, who faced Samuel's advance, and with prophesying the eventual elimination of the Bulgarian menace. But this was for the future, and in the mid-990s Samuel was considered 'invincible in power and unsurpassed in strength'.[47] Samuel's great coup was gaining control of Dyrrachium, the gateway to the Via Egnatia which passed through his lands as far as Thessalonica, and from there ran on to Constantinople. He did so by marrying a daughter of the leading man, Chryselius.[48] By 997 he held most of the lands that had pertained to Tsar Symeon at the height of his power, from the lower Danube to Dyrrachium, and in that year had himself crowned as tsar of Bulgaria.

We cannot underestimate the significance of Samuel's coronation as tsar of the Bulgarians. The exact meaning of the title and his right to bear it have been questioned by Balkan scholars. However, much debate has centred rather unfortunately on Samuel's ethnicity, and thus whether his empire was Macedonian or Bulgarian.[49] The true significance of the title must surely be that his exact ethnicity, his place of birth and his chosen residence (in today's Republic of Macedonia), were less important than the existence of a precedent. Symeon, his son Peter, and his grandson Boris had all been recognized by the Byzantine emperor to have a right to use the imperial style and, in 927 and *c.* 968 had been offered Byzantine imperial brides. Through the tenth century this style had become engrained in the public consciousness – of both Slavs and Byzantines – as the title held by the most powerful ruler among the peoples in the northern Balkans. It is only to be expected that Samuel would seek that title to give legitimacy to his broad geographical powers. It is also no surprise that he sought to use the eunuch Romanus, Peter's youngest son, to bolster his claim. (As a eunuch Romanus was not entitled to hold the imperial office himself.) The practice of claiming the title emperor of the Bulgarians, therefore, had no ethnic significance. We will see below that competitors for authority in the western Balkans in the early 1040s sought to associate themselves with Samuel, and thus to inherit his claims to be emperor of the Bulgarians (at pp. 130–2).

---

[47] *Life of St Nikon*, ed. and trans. Sullivan: 2–7 (for the date of composition, shortly after 1042), 141–2 (Basil Apocaucus), 149 (judgement on Samuel).   [48] Scylitzes: 349.

[49] It has also been argued, quite convincingly, that Samuel was Armenian. See the seminal work by Adontz 1938 [1965]: 347–407; Antoljak 1985: 17–21 agreed; Ostrogorsky 1968: 301, n.1 was unconvinced.

BASIL II AND BULGARIA

Received opinion holds that between 1001, when he reappeared in the
northern Balkans, and 1018 Basil II masterminded a prolonged, systematic and bloody recovery of strongholds and territory which earned him
the epithet *Boulgaroktonos*, 'the Bulgar-slayer'. Basil certainly sought to
cultivate his image as a conquering hero in his later years. The much
reproduced illumination in Basil's psalter, now in the library of St Mark
in Venice, shows the emperor holding a spear and sword, surrounded by
military saints, and standing over the defeated Bulgarians. Similarly, his
epitaph claims that no one saw his spear lie still during his fifty-year
reign.[50] Between 1072 and 1079 the Armenian historian, Aristakes
Lastivert (trans. Bedrosian: 31), remembered Basil as 'mighty among
rulers and always victorious in battle, who had trampled underfoot many
lands'. But the epithet *Boulgaroktonos* did not gain currency until the late
twelfth century, when Basil's exploits were rewritten and contrasted with
the weakness of his 'civilian' successors.[51] The references to Basil's
Bulgarian campaigns written nearest, geographically and chronologi-
cally, to the events described are contained in the *Life of St Nikon* (ed.
Sullivan: 140–3, 148–51). Here Basil is not called *Boulgaroktonos*, but he is
considered (148–9) 'the most fortunate of all emperors . . . [whose] life
was famous and time of his rule the longest, and his trophies over opponents quite numerous'. It is further noted that by his hand 'the nation of
the numberless Bulgarian phalanx was struck down and humbled, *as the
story about him shows in fuller detail*' (my italics). Already, it seems, the story
of the Battle of Kleidion, to which we will turn shortly, was known and
Basil's image in the process of posthumous reconstruction.

Recent scholarship has drawn attention to the inadequacy of the traditional accounts of Basil's reign, which have conflated the meagre testimony of Scylitzes and Yahya of Antioch, and been misled by the
pointed biography by Psellus. Basil can no longer be considered a boor
who despised things cultural and kept the company only of soldiers. The
emperor was, in his youth, a patron of the arts. And while later he certainly preferred the company of military men, they too were men of
letters: Nicephorus Ouranus, his most intimate confidant for many years
was both a general and a writer (inevitably his works included military
manuals).[52] In this revisionist vein, it is possible to demonstrate that

[50] Mercati 1970: ii, 230–1. I am indebted to Jonathan Shepard for this reference.
[51] *ODB*: i, 261–2, with an illustration of Basil from the Venice psalter.
[52] Crostini 1996: 55–80; Angold 1997: 101.

Basil's Balkan campaigns were far shorter and his intentions far more limited than has generally been supposed. Moreover, although he did wage successful campaigns against Samuel, it is clear that Basil also regularly employed familiar diplomatic devices in pursuit of stability in the northern Balkans and beyond.

Basil's Balkan campaigns were facilitated by the remarkable stability of the empire's eastern frontier. The collapse of the Buyid position in Baghdad after 983 meant, for the first time since the seventh century, no great power sat beyond Armenia and the Transcaucasus. An alliance with the Fatimid Caliph al-Hakim in 1001 (renewed in 1011 and 1023) thus freed Basil to look west. Basil also benefited from a change in the situation north of the Black Sea. Whereas Tzimisces' campaigns north of the Haemus, and subsequent imperial activities there had been inspired by the threat of Russian attacks along the lower Danube, Basil's closer relationship with the Rus after 988 limited this threat, and the Russian conversion to Orthodox Christianity in this period must also have been a pacifying influence. However, a greater boon to Basil's expansion into the northern Balkans was the intensification in hostilities between the Rus and Pechenegs recorded in the *Russian Primary Chronicle* (*PVL*: 83; trans.: 119). Constant warfare between Russians and Pechenegs during Vladimir's reign prevented either people from harbouring designs towards the lower Danube. Excavations have confirmed the *Chronicle's* testimony that the Russian ruler, Vladimir, undertook extensive construction work to defend Kiev. He constructed long lines of earthworks known as the 'Snake Ramparts' to the south and west of the city, including a continuous wall on the left bank of the Dnieper. Fortifications were erected along the Dnieper's tributaries, which Vladimir garrisoned with the best men from local Slav tribes.[53]

Basil's first advance towards Sardica (modern Sofia) in 1001 divided Samuel's realm in two, and we will return to his actions in the western portion later. Success in Paristrion (the lands 'beside the Ister', another name for the Danube) was swift. His generals Theodorocan and Nicephorus Xiphias recovered Preslav, Little Preslav (Presthlavitza), and Pliska with remarkable alacrity, indicating that Samuel's support in the heartland of the former Bulgarian realm was patchy.[54] Their success also illustrates once again how control of the whole region rested with a few familiar strongholds. Following John I's example, officers from the Byzantine field army were installed as garrison commanders. The first

---

[53] Franklin and Shepard 1996: 169–80; Shepard 1979a: 218–37.   [54] Scylitzes: 343–4.

strategoi of Preslav (no longer called Ioannopolis) were a certain *protospath-arios* named John, and the more senior *protospatharios epi tou Chrysotrikliniou* Constantine Carantinus.[55] The commander appointed at Dristra was the *primikerios* Theodore.[56] Contemporary *strategoi* at Presthlavitza were Leo Pegonites,[57] and John Maleses, also known as Malesius (and possibly Melias).[58]

Basil also took measures to restore ecclesiastical administration in the region. In 1020 he issued three sealed judgements (*sigillia*) which placed former Bulgarian bishoprics and new sees that he created in the northern Balkans under the jurisdiction of an autocephalous archbishop of Bulgaria based in Ohrid (see below at p. 75). However, certain measures were taken before 1020 (possibly in 1005). First, a certain George 'monk and *synkellos*' was appointed to the vacant archbishopric of Bulgaria. We have five of his seals discovered at both Dristra and Preslav.[59] Second, the ancient metropolitanate of Tomis (modern Constantia) was revived. The port on the Black Sea had been a metropolitan see in the sixth century, but is only mentioned thereafter as the archbishopric of Scythia Minora in an episcopal list of the ninth century. At the start of the eleventh century lead seals were struck by two metropolitans, Anicetus and Basil.[60] Attempts have been made by Romanian scholars to prove that Constantia remained free of Bulgarian influence between the late antique period and the Byzantine recovery. However, they place far too much emphasis on the discovery of single bronze *folles* of Leo IV (775–80), Nicephorus I (802–11) and Michael III (842–67). Moreover, the *DAI* (chapter nine; 62.99) clearly states that Constantia was within Bulgarian territory, and as we have seen, both Scylitzes (301) and Zonaras (iii, 530) report that envoys from Constantia and other *phrouria* approached Tzimisces as he besieged Dristra to offer him pledges of loyalty. We can say with certainty that the city's fortunes revived with the return of Byzantine authority: stray finds of low value coins increase dramatically after 971, and the discovery of a seal of one 'Papastephanus, *protospatharios* and *kommerkiarios*' demonstrate that mer-

[55] Iordanov 1993a: 146–9; Iordanov 1985: 102, nr. 6.   [56] Iordanov 1983: 109, nr. 16.
[57] Iordanov 1983: 104–5, nr. 10 (from Silistra); Iordanov 1993a: 153–4 (from Preslav); Bănescu and Papahagi 1935: 601–6 (from Silistra); Shandrovskaia 1981: 462 (now in St Petersburg).
[58] Shandrovskaia 1981: 463–4 (now in St Petersburg); Iordanov 1992: 232 (from Silistra); Iordanov 1993a: 152–3 (from Preslav ('Melias'): 154); Barnea 1964: 245 (from Dervent).
[59] Seibt 1975: 55–9, who dates the seals to the reign of John I. See also Georgiev 1987: 146–58; Diaconu 1991: 73–89.
[60] Nesbitt and Oikonomides 1991: i, 180–1; Popescu 1986: 121–48. See also Diaconu 1994–5: 449–52.

chants passed through the town and trade was monitored by a Byzantine agent charged with collecting the ubiquitous sales tax, the *kommerkion*.[61]

Basil also cast his gaze upon the upper paristrian lands, west of Dristra as far as Sirmium (modern Sremska Mitrovica) beyond the confluence of the rivers Danube and Sava. In 1002 he personally conducted an eight-month siege of Vidin.[62] Shortly afterwards a Magyar chieftain known as Ajtony (or Achtum), whose lands stretched north to the river Körös, was received by imperial officials at the recently recovered *kastron*. He was baptized according to the Orthodox rite, and subsequently founded a monastery in honour of St John the Baptist at Marosvár, on the river Maros.[63] There is evidence for the promotion of Orthodoxy in and around Szeged in the first quarter of the eleventh century, and we know from a rare charter that the monastery of St Demetrius at Sirmium owned land in that district.[64] The fullest account of Ajtony's activities is contained in the *Vita Gerardi Maioris* which reveals further (490) that he controlled the passage of salt along the Maros and Tisza to Szeged. There can be little doubt that he would have enjoyed the fruits of established and peaceful trade with the empire. Here, then, we have evidence that the archetypal military emperor employed exactly the same policy as his irenic grandfather, promoting the Orthodox faith and established patterns of trade across the Danube in pursuit of stability.

Basil's efforts to consolidate his authority, ecclesiastical and military, in upper Paristrion have left clear traces in the archaeological record. Excavations show that a new episcopal church, the third on the site, was built opposite Sirmium (modern Mačvanska Mitrovica).[65] At Sirmium renovations were undertaken on the walls, and a garrison installed. Occupation was limited to a small area near the southern ramparts, where twenty-six class A2 anonymous bronze *folles* have been discovered. These coins probably reached the site in the purses of troops before 1020.[66] Similarly, a sixth-century church was renovated alongside the antique fortress of Taliata, known as Veliki Gradac (and today as Donji Milanovac).[67] The restoration of ramparts, and relatively large number of class A2 coins found, suggest that Basil also installed garrisons at Belgrade and Margum; both had been Roman fortresses.[68] The principal Byzantine stronghold besides Sirmium was at Braničevo, at the confluence of the rivers Danube and Mlava. Coins now in the national

---

[61] Barnea 1985: 299; Mănucu-Adameşteanu 1991: 522–5.   [62] Scylitzes: 346.
[63] Kristó 1981: 129–35.   [64] Kubinyi 1980: 427; Györffy 1959: 47.
[65] V. Popović 1980: i–iv. See map 6.1.   [66] V. Popović 1978: 189–93.
[67] Janković 1981: 21–3, 41–2; 75–8.   [68] Ivanešević 1993: 79–92; M. Popović 1982: 42–3.

museum at Požerevac suggest a brief Byzantine military presence associated with Basil's campaigns.[69]

In 1018 the *patrikios* Constantine Diogenes was designated commander in Sirmium and the neighbouring territories. The geographical range of Constantine Diogenes' powers is remarkable, and he seems to have enjoyed *de iure* authority across a wide, if poorly defined region which stretched from Sirmium at least as far as Vidin, and then south into the mountains of Raška (modern Serbia) and Bosna (Bosnia). A seal in the Dumbarton Oaks collection bearing the legend 'Constantine Diogenes, [. . .] *strategos* of Ser*b*ia' can only be attributed to this character.[70] However, the reconstruction of the reverse inscription suggested by the editors assumes that the command was created after he reached the rank of *patrikios*. It is more likely that the position was the command of the *kastron* of Ser*v*ia recovered in the campaign of 1001.[71] Constantine was then promoted to the rank of *patrikios* with command in the empire's second city Thessalonica, and was second-in-command to his fellow patrician David Arianites, the *strategos autokrator*, who was based in Skopje. Constantine was, therefore, a key figure in the Byzantine struggle with Samuel, which was fought mainly in the lands immediately north of Thessalonica, and to which we will now turn.

BASIL 'THE PEACEMAKER'?

A decade before the battle of Kleidion (1014), on which his later reputation as 'Bulgar-slayer' was founded, Basil fought a series of campaigns against Samuel. However, the inadequate narrative sources do not support Ostrogorsky's suggestion (1968: 309) that the result was a foregone conclusion, nor do they prove, as Scylitzes (348) claims, that Basil was engaged in continuous warfare against Samuel until 1014. The first major Byzantine offensive in Macedonia began auspiciously with the recovery of Veria and Servia.[72] Control of these *kastra* consolidated the Byzantine position north and east of Sardica, and allowed Basil to further into western Macedonia and Thessaly. Further victories secured the recovery of Vodena (modern Edessa), and then, in 1004, Skopje. There can be no

[69] Ivanešević 1988: 87–99; Popović and Ivanešević 1988: 130.
[70] Nesbitt and Oikonomides 1991: i, 102.
[71] Nesbitt and Oikonomides 1991: i, 88 for the seals of two bishops of Servia. I cannot agree with Wasilewski 1964: 465–82, that a *thema* of Serbia was constituted at this time; see below at p. 123.
[72] Scylitzes: 344, notes the capture of 'Berrhoia'. This must surely be Veria, between Servia and Vodena, not Berrhoia to the north-east of Philippopolis. For the common confusion see *ODB*: i, 283.

doubt that Basil's achievements between 1001 and 1004 were significant, and that to a great extent they restored the faith of regional magnates in the empire. It is evident from reading Scylitzes' account of these campaigns that control was achieved by securing the support of the leading man (*proteuon*) in a *kastron*, and the ruler (*archon*) of a district. And in this struggle Basil's greatest weapon was his capacity to award lofty imperial titles, with their associated insignia, stipends and prestige. Thus, Veria came with the loyalty of Dobromir, who was a relative of Samuel by marriage, and who received the rank of *anthypatos*. He is almost certainly the character granted a roving command in Thrace and 'Mesopotamia' known from a seal discovered at Preslav, and thus he was both rewarded for this defection, and removed from his centre of power.[73] Similarly, Servia was handed over by the commander Nicolitzas, who was taken to Constantinople and given the rank of *patrikios*. Unlike Dobromir, he proved fickle, and fled back to Samuel. A further prize, Skopje, came with Romanus, the son of the former Tsar Peter, whom Samuel had installed there as governor. Romanus, who had taken the name Symeon, was promoted to the rank of *patrikios praipositos* (the latter a title reserved for eunuchs) and given an imperial command in the city of Abydos on the Hellespont. Basil was able to install his own man as *strategos* in Skopje, which became the military headquarters of the district of Bulgaria (see below at pp. 77–9). Then, and crucially, in 1005 Dyrrachium, the great stronghold on the Adriatic, was returned to Byzantine suzerainty by the leading family, the Chryselioi, who had previously acknowledged Samuel. Since, as Scylitzes (349) recounts, Samuel was married to a daughter of John Chryselius, the leading citizen (*proteuon*) of Dyrrachium, the change in loyalty was even more remarkable. Chryselius did so in exchange for imperial recognition for himself and his two sons as *patrikioi*.

The *patrikios* Eustathius Daphnomeles received the city on the emperor's behalf, but the first recorded commander there was another patrician, Nicetas Pegonites.[74] An inscription in the Istanbul archaeological museum almost certainly records this appointment, noting that before the arrival of a certain '[Peg]onites', Epidamnus (the ancient name for Dyrrachium) had been entrusted to a series of incompetent *strategoi*, allowing the previously accessible city to become isolated, and her riches lost. This can only refer to the city's capture by Samuel, and the consequent demise in trade with the empire along the Via Egnatia.[75] The recovery of Dyrrachium secured the land route to Thessalonica,

---

[73] Iordanov 1993a: 127–8.   [74] Scylitzes: 343, 357.   [75] Mango 1966: 410–14.

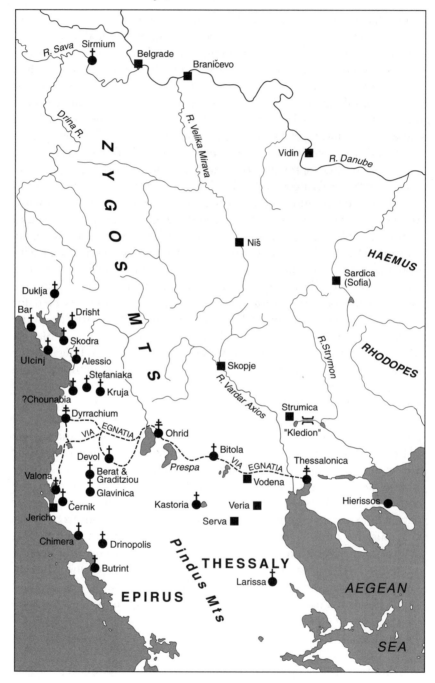

2.2 Dyrrachium – Ohrid – Thessalonica

allowing regular communications between the two major centres of trade, and ensuring mutual support against Samuel.

We have no information on any campaigns between the recovery of Dyrrachium and the fateful campaign of 1014.[76] Whittow has recently noted that Scylitzes may have exaggerated when he claimed that warfare was continuous, and he draws attention to the statement by Yahya of Antioch that after *four* years of fighting Basil had won a 'complete victory'.[77] This corresponds exactly with the notion that the campaigns which began in 1001 were brought to an end by the events of 1005. It seems clear that Basil was satisfied with his achievements to date, which included the recovery of the key coastal stronghold of Dyrrachium, the reopening of the Via Egnatia, and consolidation of control north of Thessalonica. Therefore, he was content to leave Samuel with a realm based around Prespa and Ohrid, from which he could dominate the southern Slavs in Duklja and southern Dalmatia (known as Dalmatia Superior), but was denied access to the lands north and east of Sardica. Samuel must also have kept his imperial title. Indeed, the fact that Basil's agreement with Samuel has been erased from the documentary record suggests very strongly that the 'Bulgar-slayer' had previously been a 'peacemaker'. Once again, as with our earlier concern for Symeon's imperial title and his acknowledged spiritual fraternity with the emperor, reliance on a few subjectively written histories has obscured our understanding of Byzantine policy towards Bulgaria. Indeed, it has recently been suggested that Scylitzes wrote his account in order to inspire military aristocrats to rally to Alexius I's protracted campaigns in the northern Balkans between 1081 and 1091. It is also clear that they might otherwise have felt disinclined to campaign at length in western lands when their estates in the east had been overrun or were threatened by the Seljuk Turks.[78]

---

[76] Runciman 1930: 240 maintained that Basil fought Samuel at a village called Kreta, somewhere in the vicinity of Thessalonica, in 1009. His claim is based on his reading of a sixteenth-century Latin translation of the *Life of St Nikon*, by one Sirmondo. This, in turn, is based on the version of the *vita* contained in the fifteenth-century Barberini Codex, which is unique in referring to an epsiode 'en Krete'; there is no reference to this taking place 'in anno 1009', which Sirmondo has interpolated. Moreover, it has been convincingly demonstrated that 'en Krete' was a simple misreading. Cf. *Life of St Nikon*, ed. and trans. Sullivan: 290, 'with the date [1009] removed from consideration, it seems more likely that the passage is a reference to . . . 1014 in a general panegyric of Basil as victor over the Bulgarians.' Antoljak 1985: 78–81 errs considerably further than Runciman in maintaining that Basil fought Samuel on the island of Crete in 1009, and further suggests Samuel had secured Arab assistance to transport his army!

[77] Whittow 1996: 389, 423. See also Jenkins 1966b: 317 for a translation of the Yahya quotation.

[78] The ideas were presented in an unpublished seminar paper by Catherine Holmes, and will appear in her forthcoming Oxford doctoral thesis. We will return to Alexius' Balkan campaigns below at pp. 101–3, 165–73, 179–83.

There may also be further evidence that Basil reached an agreement with Tsar Samuel. A suggestion that Basil was satisfied with the new *status quo*, and regarded it as a lasting solution in the western Balkans, can be detected in the *notitiae episcopatuum*, lists of bishops and sees subject to the patriarch of Constantinople. Although these notices are notoriously difficult to date, making an absolute chronology impossible to construct, a firm relative chronology has been established. According to *notitia* 7, compiled at the beginning of the tenth century, Dyrrachium had slipped to forty-second in the precedence list of metropolitan sees subject to Constantinople. The list of bishops suffragan to Dyrrachium had been reduced to just four: Stefaniaka (near Valona in Albania), Chounabia (between Dyrrachium and the river Mat), Kruja, and Alessio (both of which we will visit later).[79] According to *notitia* 9 (which was first completed in 946, and revised between 970 and 976) the status of Dyrrachium remained the same throughout the tenth century. However, its standing improved suddenly in *notitia* 10, when it was granted eleven more suffragan sees, bringing the total under the metropolitan to fifteen. These were Stefaniaka, Chounabia, Kruja, Alessio, Duklja, Skodra, Drisht, Polatum, Glavinica, Valona, Likinida (Ulcinj), Bar, Tzernikos (Chernik, near Valona), and Pulcheropolis (Berat) with Graditzion (see map 2.2).[80] The date of *notitia* 10 cannot be ascertained precisely, but it certainly post-dates *notitia* 9, and must pre-date the *sigillia* issued by Basil II in 1020 (see below at p. 75). Therefore, it must date from the final years of the tenth, or – in my opinion more likely – the first years of the eleventh century.[81] The reasons for the short-lived promotion of the metropolitanate of Dyrrachium has been the subject of much speculation. However, if we accept that between 1005 and 1014 Basil acknowledged Samuel's control over Ohrid, the brief promotion of Dyrrachium makes perfect sense: it was to serve as the centre of Byzantine ecclesiastical authority in the lands to the west of Samuel's realm, and a check to further encroachments from Ohrid. Moreover, the geographical distri-

[79] *Notitiae episcopatuum*: 272, 286. This seventh extant list is generally attributed to Patriarch Nicholas I Mysticus.
[80] *Notitiae episcopatuum*: 113–14, 330. The additional sees are recorded in two of the four recensions of *notitia* 10, being *a* (the oldest) and *c* (the most numerous). They are not recorded in recensions *b* and *d*. According to Darrouzès (117) contradictions between *ac* and *bd* are the most historically significant, and therefore one must choose which version is to be preferred. In coming to the choice presented here I have followed his advice that one must regard *a* as the 'conservateur' and the other recensions as 'évolutif'.
[81] *Notitiae episcopatuum*: 103, 116–17, where Darrouzès suggests in or after the later years of the tenth century, but sees no grounds to be more precise. The context for compilation suggested here would allow greater precision.

bution of the sees is a fine illustration of the limits of Basil's political authority, which was concentrated in the coastal lands north and south of Dyrrachium and in the mountains to the west of Prespa and Ohrid.[82]

BASIL THE 'BULGAR-SLAYER'?

Basil only returned to the western Balkans in force in 1014, when, with his generals Nicephorus Xiphias and Constantine Diogenes, he engaged Samuel's forces in a mighty battle at Kleidion. It is on this episode that the myth of the *Boulgaroktonos*, the Bulgar-slayer, is founded. Scylitzes provides the following description, which owing to the notoriety of the episode, deserves to be presented in full.

The emperor did not relent, but every year he marched into Bulgaria and laid waste and ravaged all before him. Samuel was not able to resist openly, nor to face the emperor in open warfare, so, weakened from all sides, he came down from his lofty lair to fortify the entrance to Bulgaria with ditches and fences. Knowing that the emperor always made his incursions through the [plain] known as Campu Lungu and [the pass known as] Kleidion ('the key'), he undertook to fortify the difficult terrain to deny the emperor access. A wall was built across the whole width [of the pass] and worthy defenders were committed to it to stand against the emperor. When he arrived and made an attempt to enter [Bulgaria], the guards defended the wall manfully and bombarded and wounded the attackers from above. When the emperor had thus despaired of gaining passage, Nicephorus Xiphias, the *strategos* of Philippopolis, met with the emperor and urged him to stay put and continue to assault the wall, while, as he explained, he turned back with his men and, heading round to the south of Kleidion through rough and trackless country, crossed the very high mountain known as Belasica. On 29 July, in the twelfth indiction [1014, Xiphias and his men] descended suddenly on the Bulgarians, from behind and screaming battle cries. Panic stricken by the sudden assault [the Bulgarians] turned to flee, while the emperor broke through the abandoned wall. Many [Bulgarians] fell and many more were captured; Samuel barely escaped from danger with the aid of his son, who fought nobly against his attackers, placed him on a horse, and

---

[82] Falkenhausen 1997: 173, 'the organization of the ecclesiastical geography and hierarchy [was] almost inevitably, a reflection of secular organization'. A complementary, but equally controversial feature of *notitia* 10, recension *a* (but not *c*) is the apparent consolidation of the authority of the bishop of Larissa in Thessaly. Larissa temporarily acquired five additional sees: Vesaine, Gardikion, Lestinos and Charmenoi. These are also recorded as suffragans of Larissa in a separate manuscript of the fifteenth century (Parisinus 1362), which, Darrouzès suggests, was conflating information from several earlier documents. Samuel's influence had certainly stretched as far as Larissa, and for that reason the temporary extension of that see's authority in the early eleventh century would have acted as a complement to that of Dyrrachium, guarding against possible encroachments to the south from Ohrid. See *Notitiae episcopatuum*: 110–11, 326–7, 339.

made for the fortress known as Prilep. The emperor blinded the Bulgarian captives – around 15,000 they say (*phasi*) – and he ordered every hundred to be led
back to Samuel by a one-eyed man. And when [Samuel] saw the equal and
ordered detachments returning he could not bear it manfully nor with courage,
but was himself struck blind and fell in a faint to the ground. His companions
revived him for a short time with water and smelling salts, and somewhat recovered he asked for a sip of cold water. Taking a gulp he had a heart attack and
died two days later *on 6 October*.[83] (Scylitzes: 348–9)

Two points deserve immediate comment. First, Scylitzes adduces no
supporting information for the statement that Basil invaded Bulgaria
each year before 1014. Therefore, it is possible that this is the author's
invention to fill an obvious gap in his coverage, and to do so in a sentence that agrees with his general portrait of Basil's reign. An alternative view, which complements the deafening silence of our sources, is
that Basil's invasion followed ten years of relative harmony, and his
return to the field may indicate that the peace treaty – which we have
proposed above – had simply expired.[84] If this were the case, we might
further suggest that Basil took the field intending only to accumulate bargaining chips for renegotiating the treaty. This would then explain his
first reaction on meeting solid resistance, which was to return home:
hardly the actions of a man bent on the annihilation of an independent
Bulgarian realm. Second, the suggestion that such a huge number of
Samuel's troops were captured and blinded has to be questioned.[85] The
figure 15,000 is also noted by Zonaras (iii, 564), who has presumably
copied from Scylitzes, or a common source (perhaps Basil's victory bulletin, see above at p. 53), and the approximate figure is independently
confirmed by Cecaumenus (ed. Litavrin: 152), who prefers 14,000 men.
However, Scylitzes qualifies his own account with the aside 'they say'
(*phasi*). This is an indication that the huge figure was subject to scrutiny
even by contemporaries. Taking these two points together, we must question the veracity of Scylitzes' account, just as the chronicler seems to
question the source upon which it was based. If this source was a victory
bulletin despatched to the capital by the emperor we would expect some
exaggeration and hyperbole. Furthermore, we cannot ignore the fact
that Scylitzes' may have had his own agenda. It has recently been sug-

---

[83] The date, in italics, is supplied in a gloss on one of the extant manuscripts of Scylitzes, attributed to a certain Michael of Devol.
[84] Treaties were often reckoned in multiples of ten years. See *ODB*: iii, 2111, for general comments.
[85] For modern scepticism, see Obolensky in *CMH*; Ostrogorsky 1968: 310, n. 1; most recently,
Whittow 1996: 388.

gested that the author wished to promote the protracted campaigns conducted in the Balkans by Alexius I Comnenus between 1081 and 1091 (to
which we will turn below, pp. 101–3, 165–73, 179–83). If Scylitzes wrote
his account in order to inspire military aristocrats to rally to Alexius'
cause, we might better understand the chronicler's copious references to
aristocrats – here praising Xiphias far more highly than Basil himself –
and his use of family names whenever possible. Basil's generals were the
ancestors of Alexius' nobles, and the latter might thereby be inspired to
emulate the prolonged efforts of their forebears.[86]

It has been maintained that after Samuel's death, the Bulgarians were
forced into humiliating submission, and their independent realm swiftly
annexed. Adontz (1965 [1938]: 374–5) long ago pointed out obvious fal-
lacies in this account. First, one detachment of the Byzantine forces
under Theophylact Botaneiates was heavily defeated, and Basil himself
retreated to his established base. This defeat was not recorded by
Zonaras who wrote about the 'Bulgar-slayer' in the later twelfth century.
Second, Scylitzes continues with an account of continued Bulgarian
resistance in 1015. Clearly, despite the mutilations at Kleidion, however
numerous they were, hostilities continued for several years after Samuel's
death in 1014. Moreover, they were all the more vigorous for the emergence of competing claims to Samuel's legacy. We might remember that
Peter, one of four sons of Symeon, went to war with Byzantium in 927
to secure his hold on power and won major concessions from the
emperor. The *Chronicle of the Priest of Duklja*, although hardly the most reliable source, provides the only detailed description of affairs, much of it
convincing:[87]

Not long after Samuel died his son [Gabriel] Radomir succeeded to his realm.
This brave and courageous man waged numerous wars against the Greeks
during the reign of the Greek emperor Basil, conquering all the lands as far as
Constantinople. Therefore, fearing the loss of his authority (*imperium*), the
emperor secretly sent ambassadors to Vladislav, Radomir's cousin, who asked:
'Why do you not avenge the blood of your father? Take our gold and silver, as
much as you desire to be at peace with us, and take Samuel's realm because he

---

[86] It is also clear that many aristocrats might otherwise have felt disinclined to campaign at length
in western lands when their estates in the east had been overrun or were threatened by the Seljuk
Turks. These ideas were presented in an unpublished seminar paper by Catherine Holmes, and
will appear in her forthcoming Oxford doctoral thesis. An obvious parallel is Michael Attaleiates'
copious praise for the ancestors of Nicephorus Botaneiates.

[87] This section of the *LPD* incorporates an independent life of St Vladimir, and is generally
afforded greater credibility than the rest of the text. For further commentary on the *LPD* see
below at pp. 118–21.

killed your father, his own brother. If you get the upper hand, kill his son Radomir, who now rules the realm'. Vladislav agreed to this, and on an appointed day while Radomir was out hunting, he rode out with him and struck him dead. (*LPD*: 336)

Here we have independent verification that the battle of Kleidion, far from being conclusive, was merely the prelude to a new period of unrest in the western Balkans, and that Samuel's son Gabriel Radomir achieved some significant successes against the emperor. Basil's solution was to have Gabriel Radomir murdered by his cousin. Besides gold and silver, Basil appears to have offered Vladislav control over Dyrrachium.[88] The emperor reneged on this promise, forcing Vladislav into a siege of the city. It is here that the Byzantine chroniclers Scylitzes (357) and Zonaras (iii, 565) once again take up the story, relating how the heroic commander Pegonites met and defeated Vladislav in single combat before the city's walls. We should prefer these accounts to the Priest of Duklja's (*LPD*: 341) suggestion that Vladislav was struck down by a vision of St Vladimir (whom he had also murdered).

The *LPD* (344) then informs us that 'after the death of Vladislav, emperor of the Bulgars, the emperor Basil mustered a mighty army and a powerful fleet, which he set to attacking the land until he captured the whole of Bulgaria, Raška and Bosna, and the whole of Dalmatia and the maritime cities as far as the border of Dalmatia Inferior'. This is entirely supported by the appointments of the *patrikios* Eustathius Daphnomeles as *strategos* in Dyrrachium, of Constantine Diogenes to a position of authority in Sirmium which extended over Raška, and of the *patrikios* David Arianites as *strategos autokrator* in Skopje. This last command was surely the senior position in all the lands north of Thessalonica and Dyrrachium, with authority over the *strategoi* of numerous *kastra* and districts once subject to Samuel.[89] These included Slav warlords, for once again Basil secured his victory by acquiring the loyalty of regional magnates. According to Scylitzes (357, 365) a certain Drogomouzus ceded Serres and the region of Strumica in exchange for the title *patrikios*, and *archontes* as far away as Croatia submitted to Basil's authority. The veracity of the last claim is confirmed by the discovery of a seal bearing the legend 'Leo, imperial *spatharokandidatos* and [. . .] of

---

[88] *LPD*: 341.

[89] Scylitzes: 358. That David had overall authority in Bulgaria is confirmed by the interpolation by Michael of Devol in Scylitzes' chronicle which names David as '*katepano Boulgarias*'. See Ahrweiler 1960: 85–6, n. 13 for the fragmentation of Bulgaria and existence of numerous commands, or 'small *themata*'. See also Mullett 1997: 60–1.

Croatia', where the most likely reconstruction of the missing section is *archon*.[90] Thereafter Basil set about the reorganization of the lands annexed from Samuel, centred on his capital at Prespa and nearby Ohrid.

In 1020, Basil issued a *sigillion* which outlined the rights and possessions that pertained to the autocephalous archbishop of Bulgaria, now based in Ohrid. It confirmed the suffragan status of sees in Macedonia, eastern Bulgaria, and Sirmium, listed as: Kastoria, Glavinica, Moglena, Bitola (including Pelagonia), Strumica, Morobisdos, Belebusda (Köstendil), Triaditsa (Sardica, or Sofia), Niš, Braničevo, Belgrade, Sirmium, Skopje, Prizren, Lipljan and Serbia (see maps 4.1, 4.2 below at pp. 118, 120). Soon afterwards Basil issued a second sealed ruling in which he extended these rights to Dristra, Triaditsa (repeated), Vidin, Rassa (Raška), Horaia, Chernik, Chimara, Drinopolis, Butrinto, Ioannina, Kozila and Petra, as well as jurisdiction over the Vlachs and the *Tourkoi* of the Vardar. The last must be Magyars settled within the empire. A third *sigillion* added Serbia (repeated), Stagoi and Berrhoia.[91] The series of revisions probably reflect the piecemeal nature of Basil's reconquest, as he established his authority over regions and magnates who had previously recognized Samuel, and gradually instituted administrative reforms. It is an ecclesiastical equivalent of the rapid development of the military command structure in Paristrion after 971, which was illustrated by the telescoped *cursus honorum* of Leo Saracenopoulos (see above at pp. 56–9).

A telling detail of the second *sigillion* is that Basil explicitly commanded the metropolitan of Dyrrachium to abide by his decision, to be satisfied with his own property and possessions, and not to encroach upon the bishoprics which pertained to the archbishop of Bulgaria. Clearly, the metropolitan was distressed at having lost sees so soon after his promotion, and was obliged to acknowledge Ohrid's authority over those which previously had been his suffragans such as Glavinica and Chernik. Once again the distribution of sees is an illustration of the extent of Basil's political authority, which in contrast to the situation in 1005 stretched across the whole of the northern Balkans. The only significant omission was northern Dalmatia, where Latin Christianity dominated. We will return to this in later chapters (below at pp. 117–21, 261–4).

---

[90] Nesbitt and Oikonomides 1991: i, 48–9. See above at p. 29.
[91] Gelzer 1893: 42–6. The list can be compared to an appendix to *notitia* 13 (*Notitiae episcopatuum*: 371–2): Kastoria, Skopje, Köstendil, Sofia, Morobisdos, Moglena, Pelagonia (Bitola), Prisdianon, Strumica, Niš, Glavinica, Braničevo, Belgrade, Vidin, Sirmium, Lipljan, Raška, Selasphoros, Slanitses, Kanina, Grevena, Bebar, and the Vlachs. See now Mullett 1997: 64–6.

THE RHETORIC AND REALITY OF BASIL'S BULGARIAN WARS

There is no doubt that Basil II was a successful general who personally led his forces into battle and had a reputation for individual valour. He placed military success at the top of his list of imperial qualities, and towards the end of his reign issued an edict which recorded that 'among the many and great benefits which God has lavished upon Our Majesty . . . the one preferred above all else is that there should be addition to the Roman empire'.[92] This was addition by conquest, and the greatest addition in recent years had been the annexation of Bulgaria. Similarly, his epitaph declared him to have been a tireless defender of 'the children of New Rome' who marched 'bravely to the west and to the very frontiers (*autous tous horous*) in the east', repeating the sentiments expressed in John Geometres' epitaph to Nicephorus Phocas.[93] Clearly, the conquest of Bulgaria was central to the image Basil sought to propagate in his later years.

Like his immediate predecessors Basil made full use of triumphal processions, but this was not limited to Constantinople. After his final victory of 1018 he proceeded through the conquered lands to Athens, where he celebrated with special services in the Parthenon to thank the Virgin for her aid. The triumphal procession through Constantinople in spring 1019 saw Basil enter the city through the Golden Gate, driving before him Bulgarian nobles including the wife of John Vladislav.[94] However, Basil was not the unassailable conqueror he wished to appear, and it is noteworthy that shortly after the final victory in Bulgaria, while he was in Georgia in 1021–2, the emperor's authority was challenged by the rebellion of his once trusted generals Xiphias and Phocas. David Arianites, the *strategos autokrator* in Bulgaria may also have been involved, for when Basil heard of the rebellion he took as a hostage the son of a certain *patrikios* named David.[95] It is possible that Basil was far more vulnerable than the historians of his reign would have us believe, and like many before him he saw the cultivation of a strong martial image as both a deterrent to potential rebels in the provinces, and as a means to secure popular support in Constantinople and other major cities like Athens.

---

[92] Zepos and Zepos 1931–62: i, 272. I am grateful to Jonathan Shepard for this reference.
[93] Mercati 1970: ii, 230. See above at p. 54.
[94] Scylitzes: 364–5; McCormick 1986: 178. Cyril Mango (in a paper delivered to the Oxford Byzantine Seminar, May 1998) has argued that the gate was decorated at this time with carved reliefs so that it resembled a Roman triumphal arch (although the subject matter had little bearing on the triumph). The carvings were taken down in the nineteenth century.
[95] Duichev 1949: 129–30.

Basil cultivated the image of the 'Bulgar-slayer' for both urban populace and provincial elites; and Bulgaria, like every other province, had its own elite who were potential leaders of rebellions. While he had won over many with court titles and stipends during his campaigns, Basil wished to ensure their continued support. Therefore, as we have seen, his policy in Bulgaria was sensible and measured, indeed hardly that of a 'Bulgar-slayer'. He secured support by granting elevated court ranks and titles, with associated stipends. In several instances he moved magnates he had honoured along with their retinues to different regions within the empire to discourage them from rebellion – for example Romanus to Abydos, and Dobromir to 'Mesopotamia of the West' – but only rarely did he transfer whole populations.[96] Basil notoriously levied taxes in kind rather than cash, which was exceptionally scarce. Similarly, the promotion of Ohrid was central to his sensitive approach. By allowing the Bulgarian Church to remain independent, and extending its rights across lands that had been Samuel's, he granted the empire's newest subjects a degree of autonomy and removed a potential focus for native unrest. Although he retained the right to appoint the prelate himself, Basil's first appointee was a Slav. Overall, it seems that we can believe our one contemporary observer, Yahya of Antioch, who described Basil's conquest of Bulgaria from the eastern frontier in the following terms:

All the Bulgarian chieftains came to meet Basil, and brought with them the wife and children of the Bulgarian tsar 'Haroun'. The emperor took possession of their fortresses, but showed himself to be well disposed towards them by awarding each an appropriate title. He preserved intact powerful fortresses, installing in them Greek governors, and razed others. He reestablished order in Bulgaria, naming *basilikoi*, functionaries charged with the administration of finances and state revenues. In this way the kingdom of Bulgaria was annexed to the empire and transformed into a *katepanate*. (Yahya of Antioch: iii, 217).[97]

A NEW 'BULGARIA'

By including within the remit of the archbishop of Ohrid lands such as Dristra that had previously belonged to Symeon and Peter, but only

---

[96] *Pace* Charanis 1961: 148–51.

[97] A partial French translation is provided by Cheynet 1990: 387–8. See Scylitzes Continuatus: 162 for the revelation that 'when Bulgaria was annexed [Basil] was not willing to make innovations in government or customs, but let them rule over their own lands and customs'. See also 164, for an important *kastron* which was razed (Ohrid). We will return to this below at p. 138.

briefly to Samuel, Basil acknowledged that 'Bulgarian' sentiment was distributed widely in the northern Balkans.[98] However, Basil's 'Bulgarian' wars had been fought mainly in the lands immediately to the north of Thessalonica, and south of Prespa and Ohrid where Samuel had made his base. Samuel's chief concern was to control the territory between Thessalonica and Dyrrachium, and to benefit from the trade which passed between those two rich cities along the Via Egnatia. These were the lands which, during the course of Basil's campaigns were referred to as Bulgaria, and were controlled by a man who claimed to be the tsar of the Bulgarians. Therefore, after Basil's victory in 1018, the usual Byzantine application of the term 'Bulgaria' was to the lands around Ohrid, Prespa and Skopje, recreated as an administrative and military district, and not to those around Preslav and Pliska, nor yet Dristra and Presthlavitza. The latter were called 'the lands beside the Danube' (either Paristrion, or from the mid-eleventh century as an administrative district called Paradounavon). However, there are occasional references to 'the whole of Bulgaria' (*pases Boulgarias*) in ecclesiastical and administrative contexts, and here we must consider the sphere of influence to have included Paristrion. Thus, according to Basil's reorganization, the prelate in Ohrid might claim to be archbishop of *all* Bulgaria. See for example seals of 'John, monk and archbishop of all Bulgaria'. Exceptionally we also have the seal of the financial doyen 'Constantine, *patrikios, anthypatos, vestes, logariastes*, and *anagrapheus* of all Bulgaria'.[99]

The term 'Bulgaria' was, therefore, both closely and loosely defined after Basil's wars. It might be used to refer quite exactly to the region centred on Skopje, the headquarters of the *strategos autokrator* who was the senior military administrator and superior to the numerous *strategoi* in sundry scattered *kastra*. Or it might refer more loosely to any of the lands which had previously recognized the Bulgarian tsar, including those between the Haemus mountains and the lower Danube. In the same way, the peoples who occupied the various lands might be called 'Bulgarians' (*Boulgaroi*), although other names were used more frequently, and with little concern for contemporary accuracy. Thus the Bulgarians are often called *Mysoi*, Mysians (but not Moesians) because they occupied the lands of the former Roman province of Moesia. Rarely is this qualified, as for example in the *Short life of St Clement* where

---

[98] Psellus, *Chronographia*: i, 76, later refers to an undefined 'Bulgarian sentiment' (*to sympan ethnos*). See below at pp. 154–5.   [99] Nesbitt and Oikonomides 1991: i, 93, 95–6.

it is remarked that the saint 'drew his origins from the European Mysians, who were also known to most people as Bulgarians'.[100]

One thing we can say for certain is that the use of the ethnonym 'Bulgarian' and the toponym 'Bulgaria' in the medieval sources does not correspond with the modern usage. The emotive force which the name has today is quite distinct from that which inspired the emperors John I and Basil II to celebrate their victories with elaborate ceremony. Their achievement, which they heralded for the residents of Constantinople and for posterity, was to restore the empire to her ancient limits, and eliminate the distinct, independent empire that had been established and recognized within those limits. But the elimination of a distinct Bulgarian empire did not amount to the elimination of Bulgarians, or any other non-Romans in the northern Balkans. Where peoples and local power structures had been brought within the empire's borders, they had to be made to work for the Byzantines, since they remained the empire's buffer between the turbulent northern peoples and the rich lands of Thrace, Macedonia and Constantinople. Many of the peoples that we met in the previous chapter now owed allegiance to the emperor by virtue of the extension of the empire's political frontier; others who had been distant relations were now next-door neighbours. Similarly, much that had been foreign policy became domestic, and diplomatic techniques employed to ensure stability across the empire's borders became techniques of accommodation within them. Imperial relations with various peoples and frontier policy during the eleventh century will be the subject of the following chapters.

---

[100] *Short Life of St Clement*: 127; Obolensky 1988: 12. We will return to 'Mysians' below at pp. 109, 289.

CHAPTER THREE

Northern nomads (1025–1100)

Basil's annexation of Bulgaria established Byzantium's Balkan frontier at the Danube. However, there are no signs that he established a civilian or financial administration at the lower Danube, nor is there proof that Basil II organized a distinct theme of Paristrion. Instead, he relied, as Tzimisces had, on military commanders in far-flung citadels. His control of Bulgaria – in all its constituent parts – rested on his ability to ensure the support of the local elites, and to operate through existing power structures. This was not essentially different to the methods of government employed elsewhere in the expansive and ethnically diverse empire. However, in Bulgaria local and regional support was guaranteed, at least initially, by the presence of large numbers of Byzantine troops in strategic citadels and watchtowers, and the forbidding presence of a large standing army some way to the south, in Philippopolis and Adrianople. For this reason, despite the revised picture of his reign that is emerging, there is a great deal of truth in the characterization of Basil II as a 'military' emperor.

As we have noted in the introduction, George Ostrogorsky believed the period of Basil's military conquests marked the apogee of the medieval empire. Consequently, he considered the weakness of Basil's 'civilian' successors to have been instrumental in the empire's supposed 'disintegration' after 1025, with the denouement in 1071: the year that Bari fell to the Normans, and Romanus IV lost the infamous battle at Mantzikert. We no longer believe Ostrogorsky's interpretation of Byzantine decline in the eleventh century. Abundant scholarship has proven that the economy of the Byzantine empire was growing rapidly at this time, and this has to be related to the social and political developments Ostrogorsky did so much to elucidate. As Michael Angold recently reiterated: 'The old notion . . . that the eleventh-century crisis received political expression in the shape of a struggle between the civil

80

and military aristocracy . . . has been quietly shelved.'[1] Angold posits, instead, the thesis that Basil II left his successors a poisoned legacy which they struggled to master, but ultimately failed to control. The major problem was the aforementioned standing army, which had been mobilized frequently during the period of military conquest and expansion, but would prove cumbersome and costly as the empire entered a period of relative peace and security. Moreover, there are indications that the large infantry divisions Basil bequeathed his successors were ill-suited to meet the new threats which appeared beyond the empire's frontiers. Nevertheless, any attempts at military reform would meet resistance from the empire's generals, the doyens of the great Anatolian families.

FRONTIER POLICY IN PARISTRION AFTER BASIL II

Towards the end of Basil II's long reign the emperor's attention was drawn back to the lands bordering the Danube. The struggles between the Rus and Pechenegs had reached a juncture, and the improved Russian defences around Kiev had driven some Pechenegs to look elsewhere for booty (see above at p. 63). The lower Danube proved to be an attractive target, and in 1017, Scylitzes (356) relates that Tzotzicius the Iberian was despatched to Dristra to direct negotiations with a group of nomads who had departed from the main body of their confederates and settled north of the river. The nomad threat was contained for some years, but it erupted violently in 1027 when a force of Pechenegs invaded and massacred many troops in Bulgaria. Constantine Diogenes was appointed to command the army that drove them back across the Danube. Then, between 1032 and 1036, a series of raids penetrated the empire as far as Thessalonica, laid waste much of Thrace and Macedonia, and sacked a number of the smaller fortified *kastra* on the lower Danube. Excavations at two such fortresses, Dervent and Capidava, have revealed destruction levels dated by coins of Michael IV (1034–41). At Capidava archaeologists have uncovered a pit full of dismembered bodies and burnt debris.[2]

The towers had been rebuilt initially in the 970s by John I Tzimisces, whose greatest fear, as we have seen, had been a further Russian invasion along the lower Danube. That threat had not materialized, and the isolated outposts and watchtowers had proven

[1] Angold 1997: 16–17.   [2] Diaconu 1970: 48–9.

inadequate against raids by the small bands of highly mobile warriors; indeed the towers themselves provided incentives on account of the booty within. Therefore, Michael IV, or rather his brother and chief minister John the Orphanotrophus, was faced with a choice: he could commit greater military resources to the frontier, rebuilding and manning extensive fortifications and maintaining regular patrols by land and river; or he could withdraw completely to the easily defensible Haemus, or Balkan mountains where a concentration of resources and manpower in the passes would prevent nomad incursions into the rich lands of Thrace. (A similar policy was adopted in the western Balkans, where, as we will see in the following chapter (at pp. 123–30), a withdrawal to Niš and Skopje was effected to defend the access route into Macedonia.) However, there are several reasons why this would not have been possible in Paristrion. First, we can identify a very real concern for the welfare of the native population. This involved providing for their security in times of crisis, and a degree of order and prosperity at other times. Second, we cannot ignore the notion, which we have already seen expressed, that the 'Mighty Ister' was the appropriate frontier for the 'Roman Empire'. Writers of the late tenth and early eleventh centuries made much of the empire's return to her 'natural limits', and any emperor would have to expect a strong popular reaction to ceding so much, and such ideologically significant territory.[3] Third, and most significantly, there was a fear that the Pechenegs would migrate into Paristrion and settle there, as the nomadic Bulgars had several centuries before. The Mysian plains were eminently suitable for herding, and were within easy striking distance of the empire's riches. Michael IV could not risk the establishment of an independent Pecheneg realm where Bulgaria had only recently been eliminated.

Therefore, the emperor and chief minister chose what seemed a rational and reasonable middle course. First, they made a treaty with the Pechenegs.[4] Having secured respite from immediate assaults, the brothers determined to minimize exposure by removing potential targets for nomad raids and concentrating resources at fewer, more heavily fortified sites. Capidava and Dervent were not rebuilt; instead, their displaced populations were relocated at the larger, more heavily fortified towns.

---

[3] John Geometres: cols. 902, 919–20, for which see above at p. 54. And in the twelfth century, see Manganeius Prodromus: poems 1.91–100; 2.21–30, 171–80; 7.147–154, 217–18, treated below at pp. 235–6.   [4] Diaconu 1970: 52.

One such town was Dinogetia. Although the suburbs of Dinogetia show signs of a devastating nomad assault, dated to spring 1036 by over one hundred coins of Michael IV, the population was afforded protection within the fortress. The absence of contemporary signs of destruction indicate that the ramparts could not be breached, although the fear caused by the assault inspired numerous well-to-do occupants to bury their gold and silver coins and jewellery.[5] A new level of houses was placed directly on the suburban destruction level of 1036. Unlike earlier dwellings, which were semi-subterranean, these were surface-level structures erected on a foundation of small stones and twigs. They were built rapidly, and the regular pattern of construction across the site suggests further that it was not a series of independent actions, but rather an imperial enterprise to facilitate the site's colonization by immigrants. A contemporary project saw the construction of similar surface-level houses at Păcuiul lui Soare.[6]

The decision to concentrate resources was the first element in an integrated frontier policy to discourage further nomad raids. The second element was the vast uncultivated and uninhabited Mysian plain which stretched south of the river. In the twelfth century the historian Cinnamus (93; trans.: 76) noted that the emperor Manuel I could hunt on this plain 'for a great quantity of wild beasts dwell in herds there, since it has been entirely deserted for many years'. Not long afterwards, Nicetas Choniates (373; trans.: 206) wrote of the emperor Isaac Angelus being 'hindered by the vast wilderness from making his way through Mysia'. The plain remained poorly cultivated and sparsely settled until the advent of widespread irrigation in the nineteenth century. It presented a powerful physical and psychological deterrent to potential raiders, who, once they had crossed the river Danube, faced a long trek and the prospect of crossing the Haemus mountains before they reached lands rich in plunder. Since they could not live off the land *en route* they would have to carry sufficient provisions for the outward journey, and faced hardship on the return leg if their enterprise failed. This presupposes that the raiders intended to return across the Danube, and before 1036 they had shown no desire to settle on the plains.

The third element in John the Orphanotrophus' frontier policy was to allow the nomads controlled access to the goods they desired.

---

[5] Ştefan et al. 1967: 22–50. [6] Diaconu 1978: 62.

Coins per year of reign

	Dristra	Păcuiul	Dinogetia	N'dnum	Nufărul
John I, Basil II & Constantine VIII (969–1028)	0.92	1.18	2.39	2.05	1.63
Romanus III (1028–34)	0.16	15.5	6	10.66	10
Michael IV (1034–41)	3.29	26.14	5.14	16.28	13.28
Constantine IX (1042–55)	2.39	23.07	9.1	7.52	10.75
Constantine X (1059–67)	2.9	20.87	5.25	7.75	15
Romanus IV (1067–71)	3	28	1.66	15	16.25
Michael VII (1071–8)	4.9	12	3.85	5.05	6.42
Nicephorus III (1078–81)	4.3	15	7	19.66	15.66
Alexius I – pre-reform coins (1081–92)	0.01	3.45	0.01	4.63	4.9

3.1 Table of coin finds in Paristrion

EMPORIA ON THE LOWER DANUBE: INCENTIVES TO TRADE

A remarkable growth in trade between Constantinople and the lower Danube coincided exactly with the intensification of the Pecheneg threat in Paristrion. Written references to this phenomenon are scarce. The *Life of St Cyril the Phileote* (63; trans.: 284–5) reveals that in the mid-eleventh century the saint was employed as a navigator on board a ship that traded along the Black Sea coast and at the *phrouria* (watchtowers) of the lower Danube. Attaleiates (204) provides a brief description of these veritable Babels, where a myriad languages could be heard. However, archaeological evidence provides far more and greater insights. Finds of amphorae, used to transport a variety of goods including olive oil and wine, have been abundant within the frontier *phrouria*. These may now be compared with the comprehensive classification and chronology established by Hayes, working on the finds from Saraçhane in Istanbul (Constantinople), and such a comparison demonstrates that trade between the imperial capital and the lower Danube picked up significantly at the start of the eleventh century. The first type of amphora discovered at Dinogetia (Ștefan et al. 1967: 249–57; fig. 154) corresponds to Saraçhane type 54 (Hayes 1992: 73–4). These short spheroidal vessels represented 30–50 per cent of all early eleventh-century amphora finds at Saraçhane, and were among the most widely exported of all Byzantine amphorae. Dinogetia type 2a (Ștefan et al. 1967: 257–60;

Isolated finds of low-value Byzantine coins at the lower Danube (coins per year of each reign).

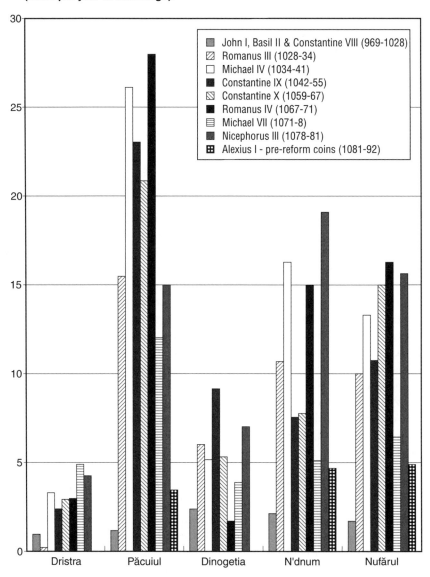

3.2 Graph of coin finds in Paristrion

fig. 159) of the twelfth century correspond to Saraçhane type 60 (Hayes 1992: 75), being slighter larger and more elongated than type 1=54. There have been many similar finds at Dristra and Păcuiul lui Soare.[7] The trade in other ceramics produced in Constantinople also grew rapidly. The most common finds are olive green glazed wares, classified by Hayes (1992: 18–29) as 'Glazed White Ware II', known from many Constantinopolitan deposits of the eleventh century.[8] If further evidence were needed for contacts with the imperial capital, a seal discovered at Noviodunum bears the legend 'Nicetas, *notarios* and *boullotes*'. The *boullotes* was an official based in Constantinople responsible for the exchange of controlled merchandise.[9]

Large numbers of coins were made available to facilitate trade at the lower Danube, most of which were struck in Constantinople. Total numbers of coins discovered at each of the major fortified settlements have been calculated in figure 3.1. It clearly illustrates sudden and dramatic increases in the number of coins in circulation in the mid-eleventh century. At Dristra, where excavations have been limited by the topography of the modern city of Silistra, only 200 coins have been discovered. Over 1,000 eleventh-century Byzantine bronze coins have been discovered at Păcuiul lui Soare, with a peak under Michael IV (183 coins) and Constantine IX (300 coins). Over 700 copper coins have been discovered at Noviodunum. Once again finds are most abundant for the years 1025–55, peaking with 114 coins for the eight-year reign of Michael IV. Nufărul (Presthlavitza) shows a remarkably similar numismatic profile. Of the 600–plus bronze coins discovered at Dinogetia, 100 represent a single hoard of class C anonymous *folles* struck by Michael IV. Two rare hoards of precious coins have also been discovered at Dinogetia. The first, uncovered in 1939, comprised 103 gold *tetartera* of Basil II, and three gold *solidi* of Romanus III and Constantine IX. The second, found in 1954, contained seven of Basil's gold *tetartera* and four silver *miliaresia*.[10]

The fortified entrepôts with their well-stocked markets provided the Pechenegs with a peaceful way of acquiring Byzantine goods and gold. Just as the nomads had traded with the Chersonites when they were settled north of the Black Sea, now they would travel to Dinogetia or Păcuiul lui Soare to acquire the trappings of distinction, 'purple cloth, . . . gold brocade, pepper, scarlet or "Parthian" leather' (see above at

---

[7] Angelova 1987: 106–14; Diaconu and Vîlceanu 1972: 71–119. See now Stephenson 1999a: 43–66.
[8] Diaconu and Vîlceanu 1972: 71–119; Ştefan et al. 1967: 229–49.
[9] Barnea 1983: 265, nr. 3; *Listes de préséance*: 21.   [10] Metcalf 1979: 75.

p. 31). Moreover, as we will see shortly, their leaders received cash to spend in the form of annual stipends associated with their court titles. In effect they were paid a form of tribute, completing the familiar set of diplomatic devices employed to secure stability on the empire's northern frontier: trade, titles and tribute.

Having said this, the boom in trade on the lower Danube did not only benefit the Pechenegs. Russian merchants were still frequent visitors to Paristrion. Various examples of carved bone, including combs and boxes fashioned from narwhal horn have been discovered in excavations. Obolensky (1994 [1965]: 167) has drawn attention to the testimony of a fourteenth-century historian, Gregoras, who notes that 'in the oceans neighbouring [Russia] fishes are caught, some of whose bones [once carved] provide useful enjoyments to satraps, princes, emperors and nearly all those who lead a refined life and are distinguished men.' Both Russian and Pecheneg merchants travelled on along the Black Sea coast to Constantinople, visiting several further commercial centres *en route*. We have seen that Constantia was a minor market at this time (above at p. 64), with coin finds and the seal of a *kommerkiarios*, an officer charged with the collection of the imperial sales tax (*kommerkion*). Contemporary seals reveal a Byzantine presence in Mesembria (modern Nesebăr) and Develtos (Debelt, near Burgas), the towns where the controlled exchanges between Bulgarian and Byzantine merchants had taken place in the ninth and tenth centuries. A seal in the Dumbarton Oaks collection was struck by a certain 'Theodore, *protospatharios, exaktor, chartoularios* of the *genikos logothetes* and *kommerkiarios* of Develtos'. Three others, discovered at Silistra (Dristra) and Anchialus bear the legend 'Constantine Syropoulos, *spatharokandidatos* and *kommerkiarios* of Develtos'.[11] Both groups of merchants were then given access to the empire's greatest commercial centre. Scylitzes (430) identified competition between 'Scythian' merchants in Constantinople as the catalyst for the Russian attack of 1043.

The other major beneficiaries of the booming regional economy in Paristrion were the local population, predominantly settled by Bulgarians (that is, Slavs who were formerly subjects of the Bulgarian tsars), and Vlachs (not proto-Romanians). We will return to these peoples, who were both called Mysians (*Mysoi*) by Byzantine authors, in chapter nine (below at pp. 288ff.). Locals certainly produced wares for sale in the emporia, predominantly ceramics (simple hand-moulded coarse

---

[11] Nesbitt and Oikonomides 1991: i, 172; Iordanov 1993b: nr. 5.

wares) and essential tools such as harpoons and fishhooks.[12] Excavations
have uncovered many examples of locally-produced bone carvings.
Modelled on the Russian and/or steppe nomad art, the local artisans
replaced narwhal horn with the bleached bones of cattle.[13] There would
also have been regular employment for local sailors and port workers.
Except for its lowest reaches, the Danube was not navigable by the
largest transport ships. In the fifth century Zosimus (ed. Paschoud: iv,
272–3) noted that supplies were loaded onto river barges from the
Roman transports (*holkades*) that plied the Black Sea route from
Constantinople. Although medieval ships were certainly smaller, it is
likely that anything larger than the Russian *monoxyla* would have trouble
sailing fully laden beyond Noviodunum and Dinogetia, where the river
becomes significantly shallower (from seven to only two metres deep).[14]

The growth in trade at the lower Danube outlined above was in
keeping with a general expansion throughout the empire which has been
explored at greatest length by Alexander Kazhdan, Alan Harvey and
Michael Hendy. However, I have argued further that Byzantine currency
was made available to facilitate trade at the lower Danube, and this
deserves further comment. On first glance this statement appears to
contradict Michael Hendy's dictum that Byzantine coinage was essentially a fiscal phenomenon, produced and distributed to provide a
medium for collecting public revenue and distributing public expenditure (cited above at p. 15). While Hendy does not deny that coinage also
facilitated private exchanges, he stresses that this is a secondary function.
The argument for deliberate provision of low value coinage from
Constantinople to support the process of exchange in the emporia
appears to run contrary to this. However, we must interpret the provision of cash subsidies and low value coins as a political rather than an
economic measure, and therefore it does not contradict the main thrust
of Hendy's thesis. Coins were produced and distributed for both the
reasons Hendy stated, but also to facilitate private exchange, where that
exchange were essential to ensure political stability.

By whatever means the money arrived at the lower Danube, it did so
in vastly greater quantities than during the reign of Basil II, and this
must have had implications elsewhere in the empire. All evidence suggests that the money supply was fairly inelastic, and it has been argued
that the demands placed on it by the economic boom throughout the

[12] Diaconu and Vîlceanu 1972: 174–7.
[13] Ştefan et al. 1967: 84–94; Diaconu and Vîlceanu 1972: 163–79.   [14] Bulgaru 1977: 87–101.

empire placed such a strain on mints that emperors were obliged to debase the high value coinage.[15] It is perhaps significant that Michael IV was the first to reduce the gold content of the imperial *nomisma*, although the reasons for his move have been the subject of a discussion which we cannot reprise here. In dealing with low value coinage it seems safe to state that a huge leap in the volume of copper coins required in one region would require far more to be struck in Constantinople, if the bullion were available, or for a greater proportion of the *folles* struck to be directed towards Paristrion at the expense of other regions. Furthermore, the shift occurred at the same time as a push to increase the fiscalization of taxation in the new administrative district of Bulgaria, which we will address in greater detail in the following chapter (below at pp. 135–8). For now it is important to note that the prioritization of Paristrion, and the large numbers of coins, both low and high value denominations, which were pumped into the region from Constantinople to facilitate the process of exchange and payments of stipends, appear to have had consequences in lands in the western Balkans during the reign of Michael IV and the administration of John the Orphanotrophus.

THE PECHENEG WARS, 1046–1053

Shortly after the Russian attack on Constantinople in 1043 Catacalon Cecaumenus, whom Scylitzes (433) described as '*archon* of the towns and lands along the Ister', sent news that a very large group of Pechenegs had departed their established lands, and were pressing towards the empire's Danube frontier. The Pecheneg migration was the result of pressure from a further nomad people, the Oghuz or Ouzes. Scylitzes provides a remarkably detailed account of northern affairs at this time, and documents a feud which erupted between the Pechenegs' supreme chieftain, Tyrach, and his subordinate Kegen.[16] The latter had gained distinction in the Pechenegs' wars with the Ouzes, and decided to challenge Tyrach for supreme command. A battle was fought, but Kegen was routed and fled with his followers to an island near Dristra. He was received by the Byzantine commander, Michael, son of Anastasius the

---

[15] Although as Angold 1997: 84 has pointed out, the argument which relates an inelastic money supply to debasement is circular and based on the assumption that debasement proves inelasticity.

[16] Shepard 1992b: 171–81 maintains that Scylitzes is drawing here on a source written by the aforementioned Catacalon Cecaumenus, who had first-hand knowledge of the Pechenegs in question, and may even have befriended Kegen.

Logothete, who had by then replaced Catacalon Cecaumenus. Michael informed the emperor of his arrival, and swiftly arranged for Kegen to be conveyed to Constantinople, where he was baptized, awarded the rank of *patrikios* and given command of three frontier *kastra*. Subsequently many of his followers were allowed to settle within imperial territory. However, from the southern banks of the Danube, Kegen continued to harry Tyrach, who appealed to the emperor to control his newest patrician. When his protests were ignored, Tyrach took matters into his own hands, and in winter 1047 he launched an invasion of Paristrion across the frozen river.[17] The nomads pillaged widely, before an outbreak of pestilence forced Tyrach to surrender to a joint army of Kegen's Pechenegs and Byzantine troops. The captives were not massacred, as Kegen demanded, but instead settled along the main road that ran from Niš to Sardica. Tyrach and others were taken to Constantinople, baptized and given high ranks.[18]

This episode is treated at greater length by others, but several features deserve further comment here. The promotion and exploitation of divisions among the confederate peoples settled beyond the Danube is a practice we have met before. It is a corollary to the policy of promoting dissension between rival peoples that we have seen explained fully in the *DAI*, and one employed by the author of that treatise, the emperor Constantine VII who promoted links with the second- and third-ranked Magyar chieftains over the ruling Árpád clan. As Obolensky (1994 [1963]: 6) observed in his seminal article on Byzantine diplomatic techniques, this was less a process of 'divide and rule', and more one of 'weaken and watch'. Constantine IX's implementation of this strategy, promoting and directing the interests of a minor nomad chieftain, had many familiar characteristics, not least his swift reaction to changed circumstances and opportunism in deploying Kegen's followers as border patrols. Moreover, in granting Kegen control over three *kastra*, the emperor may have found a novel way of reviving redundant watchtowers abandoned after the nomad assaults of 1032–6. However, in this instance the rifts between rival Pecheneg chieftains were disadvantageous for Byzantium, being the reason for the instability that affected the Danube frontier after a decade of relative peace.

Constantine IX was making the best of a bad job, and in doing so he used time-honoured techniques of accommodation. We have encoun-

---

[17] The date is now fairly certain. See Kazhdan 1977: 65–77.
[18] Scylitzes: 455–7, 465. See also Shepard 1975: 61–89; Malamut 1995: 118–22.

tered several instances where native leaders were baptized and promoted to an esteemed imperial rank (usually that of *patrikios*) by Constantine IX's predecessors, including Constantine VII and Basil II. Similarly, the implantation of ethnic groups within the empire has many precedents, and the settlement of nomads on the flat lands south of the Danube was perspicacious, allowing them to persist in their traditional way of life, or in Attaleiates' words 'lead a Scythian lifestyle'.[19] He is clearly alluding to their nomadic ways, and we will expand upon this chacterization later (at pp. 107–10). The settlement of Pechenegs between Niš and Sardica was less appropriate to their 'Scythian lifestyle', and may well represent a concerted imperial attempt to have them adopt sedentary practices. Nevertheless, the nomads had been established within the empire in distinct groups and according to imperial wishes. Constantine IX could be happy that he had prevented an independent colonization of Paristrion by the massed groups of nomads under their own leaders, and had thus prevented the establishment of an embryonic 'Patzinakia' – the contemporary Greek term for Pecheneg was *Patzinakos* – where previously there had been an independent 'Bulgaria', and at the same time bolstered the empire's northern defences.[20]

Although Constantine IX must have been satisfied with his arrangements with the Pechenegs, an attack on the eastern frontier by the newly arrived Seljuk Turks inspired the emperor to raise a force of 15,000 from among the colonists. Despatched to the east under their own chiefs, the nomads rebelled as soon as they had crossed the Bosphorus. They made their way back into the Balkans, crossed the Haemus and settled in the vicinity of Preslav. Kegen's Pechenegs, previously loyal to the emperor, subsequently joined the rebellion, and the emperor's arrangements lay in ruins.

The bitter struggles that ensued between 1048 and 1053 contradict the oversimplified characterization of Constantine IX's frontier policy as pacific and money-grubbing. Ostrogorsky (1968: 334) glossed over Constantine IX's dealings with the Pechenegs in a paragraph, and his brevity brings to mind Aristakes Lastivert's (trans. Bedrosian: 107–8) summary dismissal of Constantine, who neglected the cavalry to squander his money on whores 'and was in no way troubled by the ruin of the land'. However, the contemporary Greek accounts devote significantly more space to these campaigns, and suggest that the emperor prosecuted a vigorous, protracted and innovative military strategy; they do not

[19] Attaleiates: 30–1, 205; Kazhdan and Epstein 1985: 205.
[20] For the rhetorical manner in which this settlement was portrayed see below at pp. 111–12.

support Ostrogorsky's blanket assertion that Constantine, more than any other 'civilian', presided over the decay of the Byzantine army. For example, much has been made of Constantine's well-documented decision to disband the empire's army in the eastern frontier region of Iberia. Cecaumenus (ed. Litavrin: 152–4) records that a certain Serblias was despatched to raise taxes in the region. Scylitzes (476) states that Serblias allowed 50,000 men to pay taxes rather than do military service. The twelfth-century historian Zonaras (iii, 647) also condemns the change in policy, explaining that these 'were lands which, in lieu of payments to the emperors, ensured the defence of invasion routes, and denied the barbarians access to Greek lands'. This was a clear example of a civilian emperor reversing Basil's frontier strategy with disastrous consequences: Turkish razzias into the region recommenced after many years in abeyance. But in fact, as Paul Lemerle noted, the recommencement of razzias had more to do with the changed situation beyond the frontier, and there is no indication that a large standing army could effectively have monitored or prevented the incursions by small Turcoman warbands.[21] It became equally apparent that the large standing army Constantine IX had inherited was wholly inadequate to confront and control the mobile warbands of Pechenegs who had established themselves across the vast Mysian plain.

The first Byzantine commander to confront the nomads at the head of the Byzantine field army, the eunuch Constantine *rektor* and *praepositos*, suffered a humiliating defeat. There was an 'indescribable massacre of Roman troops, and the survivors of the rout threw down their arms, dismounted from their horses, and fled into the dense woodlands and mountain fastnesses'.[22] A second pitched battle near Adrianople ended similarly, despite the bravery of the *magistros* Arianites, and the *vestarches* Michael Doceianus. Constantine IX thus determined to reorganize his forces, and the field army was broken up and dispersed through various fortified camps. From these they launched surprise attacks on the Pechenegs' camps, seizing booty and prisoners. Employing such guerrila tactics the Byzantines gained significant successes, driving the nomads back as far as the so-called 'Iron Gates' near Vidin. Byzantine successes continued, inspiring the emperor to consider a joint assault by forces from Bulgaria and Paristrion. However, the jealousy of the governor (*pronoetes*) of Bulgaria, the eunuch and monk Basil, precluded his cooperation with the commander in Paristrion, and reversed Byzantine for-

---

[21] Lemerle 1977: 268.   [22] Attaleiates: 33.

tunes. The great Byzantine army was forced to take refuge in Preslav without adequate provisions and endure the taunts of the nomads, who harangued them with war-cries and lewd dances.[23] This debacle and further defeats saw Constantine IX's martial spirit waver. Public reaction to the series of defeats and the cruel massacre of Byzantine youth was strong, and the emperor was left with no option but to recognize the settlement of an independent group of nomads between the Haemus and lower Danube, in a region called the 'hundred hills'.[24] In 1053 he agreed a thirty-year peace treaty, and with 'gifts and imperial titles soothed the ferocity and barbarity' of the Pechenegs.[25] Henceforth, the soothed 'Scythians' were allowed to remain within the frontiers of the *oikoumene*.

Great care was also taken to maintain good relations with the native *proteuontes* who now lived alongside the Pechenegs. Thus, Attaleiates also tells us, the citizens of the 'paristrian' cities were granted honours with annual stipends (*philotimiai*) to guarantee their loyalty and support a substantial native army, largely of so-called 'Bulgarians'.[26] This was not a radical departure from earlier policy, since Byzantine control in the peripheral cities always depended upon securing local cooperation, and we have seen how in the case of Calocyras of Cherson the defection of a leading figure could lead to disaster in one of the empire's semi-autonomous outposts (above at p. 49). Nevertheless, we should note that the locals came to rely upon the stipends, and this would have consequences later.

PECHENEGS IN PARISTRION 1053–1072

Throughout the war and afterwards the major *kastra* on the lower Danube remained in Byzantine hands. Besides the emporia, however, other measures were taken which hint at reforms. Oikonomides (1966: 413–17) saw Constantine's installation of guerilla units in fortified encampments as a shift towards a permanent defensive strategy based around numerous small castles. The *kastrophylakes*, guardians of the castles, were later the subject of a law, a 'constitution of the emperor Michel VII Ducas, decreeing that anybody receiving castles in any way must possess them for life.'[27] That is, the grant was for life only, and the castle did not become the private property of the *kastrophylax*, nor was it

---

[23] Cecaumenus, ed. Litavrin: 164.   [24] Scylitzes: 465, 467; Diaconu 1970: 66–9.

[25] Attaleiates: 37–8; Diaconu 1970: 75–6; Dölger 1925: ii, nr. 909; Dölger, ed. Wirth 1977: ii, 30, nr. 909.   [26] Attaleiates: 83, 204–5.

[27] Dölger 1925: ii, nr. 1012; Dölger, ed. Wirth 1977: ii, 68, nr. 1012.

heritable or alienable. However, he was entitled to a military levy, the *kastroktisia*, which was earmarked for the construction and upkeep of castles. Most often the *kastroktisia* was an exemption granted to a powerful individual or institution charged with local defence duties.[28] We will see in the next chapter that the *kastroktisia* was common in the western Balkans, where the archbishop of Ohrid complained of the wickedness of the *kastrophylakes*.[29] It would certainly make sense to operate the system in Paristrion, where, as we have seen, the *kastra* provided refuge for locals. Furthermore, increased reliance on *kastrophylakes* is unremarkable in a region which was dominated and administered from a few scattered strongholds.

Constantine IX also sought to create a coordinating authority in the district beside the lower Danube. In effect, we may credit him with the creation of a unified theme of Paristrion, which was known for the first time as Paradounavon, and the commander known as the *katepano*. A seal of one Michael *vestarches*, surely the aforementioned Michael Doceianus, proves that he held the command of *katepano* of Paradounavon before he was killed by his Scythian captors.[30] Several seals struck by the *katepano* of Paradounavon, Demetrius Catacalon, *patrikios*, *anthypatos* and *vestes* have been discovered at Dristra. This character may be the court dignitary not named by Attaleiates who achieved significant victories over the Pechenegs at Arcadiopolis and Rentakion before the dispute with the *pronoetes* of Bulgaria.[31] However, the historian may also be referring to a contemporary commander in the region, the *vestes* Symeon, who is known from seals with the legend '*vestes* and *katepano* of Paradounavon'. (With such a title, he cannot have held this command in the 1020s as Bǎnescu (1946: 70) claimed.) A subsequent commander of Paradounavon, the *magistros* and *doux* Basil Apocapes was probably appointed during the brief reign of Isaac I Comnenus (1057–9).[32] Bǎnescu (1946: 84–8) was the first to make the connection between Apocapes and Basil, *magistros tou Paradounabi*, mentioned in the manuscript *Paris. Coisl.* 263.

Isaac Comnenus ascended the throne after a coup, and in response to a joint assault of Magyars and Pechenegs renewed the aggressive policy abandoned in 1053.[33] He achieved no substantive success. In one of his

---

[28] Trojanos 1969: 39–57; Lemerle 1979: 224.

[29] Theophylact, *Letters*: 237, 324. See below at pp. 150–2.

[30] Zacos and Nesbitt 1984: ii, 300; Iordanov 1993a: 143–4, favours an otherwise unattested Michael in the 1060s. Michael may also have held the office (or used the title) *katepano* of Mesopotamia (141–2).   [31] Iordanov 1993a: 143–4.   [32] Iordanov 1988: 89–92; Barnea 1987: 84–5.

[33] Attaleiates: 66; Scylitzes Continuatus: 106–7.

rare literary excursions beyond the walls of Constantinople, Michael Psellus provides a vivid account of Isaac's confrontation with the 'Mysians . . . [who had] emigrated to our side of the river'.

Determined to drive these people beyond the Roman [Byzantine] frontiers (*Rhomaikon horion*), Isaac set out against them with a strong force. He was particularly confident before an enemy that was so scattered and had such a different conception of war. He led his army in an attack on the strongest enemy concentration. It was difficult to fight them and no less difficult to take them captive. As he drew near . . . and when they saw the unbroken line of Roman shields, they abandoned the idea of fighting in mass and attacked in isolated groups, howling their war cries. But they found the Romans too compact for them, and having discovered that they could neither catch them by ambush nor face them in open battle . . . [they] dispersed in the inaccessible regions of that country. (*Chronographia*: ii, 127; trans.: 317–19)

The campaign was thus indecisive; Isaac I had failed to learn from Constantine IX's experiences, and vainly hoped to crush the fragmented nomad forces in a pitched battle. He had to be content to return to Constantinople having destroyed some nomad tents and bearing booty, although he granted himself a triumph of sorts, and entered the city with 'his head crowned with the garlands of victory'.

If the Pechenegs proved unwilling to relinquish territory in Paristrion it had much to do with their old adversaries, the Ouzes, who had occupied their former lands north of the lower Danube. Ominously for both the Pechenegs and Byzantines, in 1064 the Ouzes cast their gaze across the river, and set off in search of new wealth and territory. Attaleiates records the episode thus:

In the third indiction when the commanders of the towns of the Danube were the *magistros* Basil Apocapes and the illustrious *magistros* Nicephorus Botaneiates, the entire tribe of Ouzes, bringing their possessions, crossed the frozen river Danube in long wooden boats and sharp-prowed vessels made of branches lashed together. They defeated the Bulgarians and other soldiers who attempted to block their passage. (Attaleiates: 83)[34]

Both Byzantine commanders were captured, and lands were despoiled as far south as Thessalonica and the Greek lands beyond. Fortunately for the Byzantines the Ouzes fell victim to a disease similar to that which had decimated Tyrach's Pechenegs in winter 1047. Some survivors were recruited into the Byzantine army and served as ethnic mercenary units. (Their notorious defection contributed to the Byzantine defeat at

[34] See also Scylitzes Continuatus: 113–14.

Mantzikert in 1071.) Others returned north, and were employed either
as border guards by the ruler of Kiev, or as *Grenzwächter* by the ruler of
Hungary. They were certainly not eliminated, and their migration only
drew further attention to the continued dynamism and turbulence north
of the Black Sea. The spectre of a further nomadic people, the Cumans,
loomed large, and Byzantine agents in Cherson would have monitored
their advance across the south Russian steppe.

The persistent threat posed by the various nomadic peoples
confirmed the new emperor Constantine X (1059–67) in his decision
that there could be no effective military solution to the problems in
Paristrion. It had been demonstrated consistently that the Pechenegs
could not be eradicated by pitched battle, and that security and stability
were better achieved by appeasement. Moreover, although the menace
of the Ouzes was apparently over, experience demanded that the
emperor take precautions against further invasions. The best way to do
this was to regard the Pechenegs' settlement as permanent and to
harness their interests to those of the empire. 'Patzinakia' had been
established in the face of Byzantine opposition, but it could now be organized into an effective buffer against further attacks on the empire.
Control over the rich trading cities remained paramount. Păcuiul lui
Soare, Dinogetia, Noviodunum and Presthlavitza served as outposts of
civilization, as centres for the dissemination of influence and the dis-
persement of wealth, and as headquarters for those charged with monitoring the lands to the north and south. Their strong walls could resist
land and sea attacks, and they could be reached swiftly by sea. We should
reiterate that Byzantium retained control of the Black Sea ports *en route*.
Thus, the same Cyril Phileotes who had spent his youth sailing to the
phrouria of the lower Danube could send a friend to Anchialus with goods
to exchange for wheat; and he warned an Armenian against his decision
to travel by land from Dercus in Thrace to the port of Varna, urging him
to 'take a boat to return to Varna along with sailors we know and trust'.
The Armenian chose to cross the Haemus, and was killed by brigands.[35]

A further major advantage of maintaining peaceful relations with the
nomads was that it allowed for the advancement of a powerful force for
stability between the Haemus and lower Danube: the Orthodox faith.
Baptism was a precondition of settlement within the *oikoumene*. A monk
was charged by Constantine IX with performing mass baptisms of
nomads in the Danube's waters, and in a series of panegyrical orations

---

[35] *The Life of St Cyril the Phileote*: 117, 126–7, 343, 352–3.

presented at the time of the Pecheneg wars John Mauropous com-
mended the baptisms, and praised the emperor for saving so many
souls.[36] Cyril Phileotes spent his later years dodging Pechenegs. His hag-
iographer has Cyril praise Alexius I for ending the nomad threat,
announding: 'If now I would want to recount the peoples of all languages that you led to Christ by your divinely-inspired teaching and holy
baptism I would run out of time. Above all the Scythians [Pechenegs]
who were otherwise wolves you transformed with God's aid and favour
into lambs and gathered them to God's flock with the bath of regener-
ation'.[37] Quite how effective the act of immersion was in soothing the
nomadic wolves must be questioned, but their frequent exposure to the
faith was to be guaranteed by the reappointment of a metropolitan in
Dristra with responsibility for at least five suffragan sees in Paristrion.
The exact sites of these is uncertain; a diocese of Axiopolis existed until
1092 when its incumbent was transferred to Abydos, and bishops may
also have been present at Noviodunum, Dinogetia, Troesmis and
Lovech.[38]

In a century Byzantine frontier policy north of the Haemus mountains had come full circle. After frequent recourse to battle during the
eleventh century by 'civilian' emperors like Constantine IX, and 'military' emperors like Isaac I, the tenth-century Byzantine strategy for
dealing with their 'barbarian' neighbours was restored: stability and
security were to be guaranteed by the controlled disbursement of titles,
tribute and access to trade. Coin finds at the 'paristrian' emporia remain
high for the period after Isaac I's reign (see figure 3.1). For example there
have been *c.* 280 finds of bronze *folles* at Păcuiul lui Soare which were
struck between 1060 and 1071, compared with *c.* 300 struck between 1042
and 1060, and *c.* 275 struck between 1025 and 1042; thus the number of
coins found per year actually increases. At other sites the numbers of
Byzantine coins found remain high, if fewer than between 1025 and
1045, and sherds of Constantinopolitan pottery are still abundant.
Furthermore, a series of copper coins appears which was significantly
thinner than regular issues from Constantinople, with a more sharply
defined relief. It has been suggested that these coins were struck at a
regional mint, originally situated in Dristra. Finds are too abundant for
them to be 'counterfeits' or a local initiative, accounting for more than
60 per cent of coins dating from the reign of Romanus IV (1068–71), and

[36] Mauropous: 142–7. For further discussion see below at pp. 111–12.
[37] *The Life of St Cyril the Phileote*: 230.
[38] Darrouzès 1984: 186; Diaconu 1991: 82–7; Georgiev 1987: 153–4; Dimitrov 1992: 82–91.

between 75 per cent and 90 per cent for the distinct issues of Michael VII (1071–8).[39] This does not mean that coins from the capital were no longer reaching the lower Danube, for according to a fundamental and universal numismatic principle, the higher bullion content of the Constantinopolitan issues would have led to their rapid withdrawal from general circulation. They would, therefore, not occur as stray losses. However, it does suggest strongly that the imperial government was having difficulty meeting the demands for abundant cash to service the 'paristrian' emporia. This was part of a general cash crisis in Byzantium which resulted in rapid debasement of the gold currency after 1067. Further efforts to recoup bullion for the imperial fisc had serious repercussions in Paristrion.[40]

THE LOSS OF PARADOUNAVON

In 1072, soon after the accession of Michael VII, rebellion erupted in Paristrion. The turmoil resulted from a decision by Michael VII's chief minister, the notorious Nicephoritzes (a diminutive form of his given name, Nicephorus), to stop both the annual subsidies paid to the *mixobarbaroi* dwelling beside the Danube and the 'gifts' despatched to the Pechenegs.[41] The emperor despatched his confidant, the *vestarches* Nestor, who was a native of the northern Balkans, to calm the locals.[42] However, Nestor was condemned in his absence by Nicephoritzes, prompting him to join the rebellion and lead an allied force across the Haemus to the walls of Constantinople. He demanded the removal of his accuser, but while the emperor dithered tensions rose between his forces and his Pecheneg allies. Therefore, Nestor withdrew beyond the Haemus and engineered an independent solution in Paristrion.[43]

The turmoil in Paradounavon can be discerned in the numismatic profile of the 'paristrian' sites. A remarkable series of coin hoards have been discovered which were concealed between 1072 and 1074 (or shortly thereafter). A parcel of coins discovered at Păcuiul lui Soare in 1978 comprised thirty-three copper coins dating from the reigns of Michael IV (four coins), Constantine IX (nine), Constantine X (five), Romanus IV (eleven) and Michael IV (one). The chronological range of the coins

---

[39] Oberländer-Târnoveanu 1983: 261–70. Figures do not include anonymous *folles*.

[40] Morrisson 1976: 3–47.

[41] Attaleiates: 204–5. On Nicephoritzes see Angold 1997: 121–4. On *mixobarbaroi* see below at pp. 109–10.

[42] For the various, inevitably inconclusive, discussions of Nestor's ethnicity see Diaconu 1970: 102–3; Cheynet 1990: 390.   [43] Attaleiates: 205–9.

suggest that this may have been the savings of a person of very modest means. However, it is more likely to reflect the fact that copper coins remained in circulation for many years. That the greatest number of coins date from the brief period 1068–71, and the terminal coin is of Michael VII's first issue, suggest concealment early in that emperor's reign.[44] Two hoards from Dristra also terminate with Michael VII's early issues. The first, a copper parcel, contained a range of anonymous *folles*. The most common type was class G, with two contemporary initialled *folles* of Romanus IV, and one of Michael VII. The second, Gyurgendzhik hoard consisted of twenty-one *nomismata* of Michael's second issue, and one *tetarteron* of his third. A fourth hoard, discovered at Ishirkovo in Bulgaria, consisted mainly of gold from the reign of Constantine IX, but was concealed during or after the reign of Romanus IV. A fifth hoard of fifteen *nomismata* struck by Romanus IV (six coins) and Michael VII (nine) was unearthed in 1959.[45]

Nicephoritzes' decision to withdraw the annual subsidies is remarkable when one considers what sustained efforts had been made to ensure the loyalty of the local elites and the effective functioning of the emporia. It seems impossible that so much would be risked by mere shortsighted and short-term money-grubbing, and we might conjecture that the withdrawal of the *philotimiai* payments were part of a general shift in imperial policy towards Paristrion which fitted into the chief minister's grand design. Nicephoritzes was the architect of a series of initiatives designed to reestablish central control over the empire's resources and finances. For this reason alone he would not have jeopardized control of the rich markets on the lower Danube. Might Nicephoritzes have intended in the longer term that the markets themselves rather than direct subsidies from Constantinople would support the local elites and their retinues who defended the frontier? We have already seen that a regional mint had been established which supplied the majority of coins used in everyday transactions, and that coins struck at that mint by Michael VII's moneyers swiftly came to replace regular Constantinopolitan issues. To my knowledge no gold coins were ever struck in the region, but the capability was there. Furthermore, the chief minister had devised a new method for privileging individuals who engaged in trade which simultaneously generated greater taxation revenue for the imperial treasury: the *phoundax*.

Nicephoritzes had established an imperial monopoly over the sale and

---

[44] Conovici and Lungu 1980: 397–402.   [45] Metcalf 1979: 75; Barnea 1960: 245–54.

purchase of grain at Rhaidestus, a port on the Sea of Marmara which supplied Constantinople. All producers were obliged to sell their grain to traders in the imperial depot (*phoundax*), whence it would then be sold on at considerably inflated prices. Magdalino (1995: 44–5) has pointed out that the intention was not to eliminate the market or to take over the infrastructure, but to tax the process of exchange more efficiently, and to privilege those merchants established within the *phoundax*. He also noted that the '*phoundax* at Rhaidestus was not the only one, or the last one of its kind in Byzantium'. It seems certain that Nicephoritzes would have sought to establish closer imperial control over the rich markets on the lower Danube, and his preferred method may thus have been by the imposition of a *phoundax* (or even several *phoundakes*). While no documentary proof for this supposition exists, Attaleiates (204) did begin his account of the rebellion of the *mixobarbaroi* by noting that they were aware of the developments at Rhaidestus. Is it not possible that Nicephoritzes intended to return with one hand what he had taken with the other? Many of those who had lost out by the withdrawal of their annual stipends could have been recompensed with privileged trading rights within the *phoundax*. Where hitherto imperial coin had been minted and despatched to facilitate trade and benefit traders indiscriminately, the supply of cash and goods would be closely monitored, and certain individuals granted exclusive rights to charge inflated prices and extract inflated profits. Both the imperial government and the local elite would benefit economically, and the emporia would continue to flourish. The obvious flaw in Nicephoritzes' plan – if this was his plan – is that it was immensely unpopular. Even at Rhaidestus, in the heart of the empire, the *phoundax* inspired outrage, and was subsequently destroyed in a popular revolt.[46] If Nicephoritzes had determined to establish a *phoundax* as far away as the lower Danube his judgement was doubly flawed, and responsibility for the loss of Paradounavon was his.

THE RECOVERY OF PARADOUNAVON

The debacle of 1072–4 left the Pechenegs in charge of key outposts on the Danube. It also saw the end of the distribution of stipends and subsidized trade, forcing the nomads to look elsewhere for booty. Once again they set their sights on the lands south of the Haemus, and in 1077 launched a devastating raid into Thrace.[47] In the following year their

---

[46] Attaleiates: 248–9.   [47] Bryennius: 236.

support was secured by the pretender Nicephorus Basilaces with the promise of imperial gold. Indeed, Pechenegs seem to have played a role, as 'hired guns' (or bows) in many revolts and attempted coups during this brief but turbulent period.[48] Ominously, they also began to forge connections with the Paulicians, a heretical sect who had been settled as imperial federates near Philippopolis by John Tzimisces, but who had since taken control of the surrounding lands and several passes through the Haemus.

From his stronghold at Beliatoba, which dominated a pass of the same name through the Haemus, the Paulicians' leader Traulos controlled access between Paristrion and Thrace. When he sought to ally himself with the Pechenegs and married the daughter of one of their chieftains, the new emperor Alexius I Comnenus (1081–118) 'foresaw the evil likely to result, and wrote conciliatory letters full of promises. He even sent a chrysobull guaranteeing Traulos an amnesty and full liberty'.[49] The emperor's efforts at conciliation were fruitless, and the Pechenegs once again crossed into Byzantine lands.

Gregory Pacourianus, the Domestic (commander-in-chief) of the imperial forces in the west, was given responsibility for the Pechenegs while the emperor personally conducted the war against the Normans in Dyrrachium (see below at pp. 171–4). In his *typikon* of December 1083 Gregory claims to have won a magnificent victory over the nomads for the most holy emperor Alexius.[50] However, the Pechenegs were undeterred and advanced through the defiles to Beliatoba, where a great battle was fought in 1086.

The Romans [Byzantines] were vastly outnumbered and the sight of the enemy filled all of them with dread. Nevertheless they attacked. Many were slain and [the Byzantine general] Branas was mortally wounded. The Domestic [of the western forces, Pacourianus], fighting furiously and charging the Scythians with great violence, crashed into an oak tree and died on the spot. After that the rest of the army dispersed in all directions. (*Alexiad*: ii, 83; trans.: 213)

Immediately a second Byzantine army under the general Taticius was sent against the Pechenegs. They fell on the nomads who were weighed down with plunder and achieved a significant victory. Taticius withdrew to Philippopolis to prepare for a third decisive confrontation. However, after feigning for three days the nomads withdrew.

---

[48] Cheynet 1990: 81–94.   [49] *Alexiad*: ii: 49 (trans.: 187).
[50] Gautier 1984: 43; Frankopan 1996: 278–81.

In spring 1087, Tzelgu, the supreme chieftain of the Pechenegs who were still settled north of the Danube, launched a devastating invasion. His route, crossing the middle Danube, suggests that he had reached an agreement with the nomads in Paristrion not to violate their territory. He had also reached an understanding with the Magyars, and a large force under the former Hungarian king Salomon accompanied him. A Byzantine force led by Nicholas Mavrocatacalon fell on them in a mountain pass and succeeded in killing Tzelgu. However, those who escaped 'returned to the Danube and made their camp there. Living alongside [Byzantine] lands they treated them as their own and plundered with complete licence.'[51] Clearly, no longer monitored or policed from the 'paristrian' *kastra*, the different groups of nomads on both sides of the Danube had made common cause. Alexius Comnenus was forced to reconsider his northern policy; he abandoned his openly aggressive stance and entered into a treaty with the nomads.

The emperor's new willingness to treat with the Pechenegs is celebrated in an oration, the *basilikos logos* delivered on 6 January 1088 by Theophylact, the future archbishop of Ohrid.[52] Theophylact spoke in praise of Alexius' 'bloodless victory' over the Pechenegs, thus referring to the treaty he had negotiated in 1087, and we will explore his sentiments in greater detail shortly. For now it suffices to note that Theophylact provides some factual information: as a condition of the treaty Alexius recovered many *poleis*, surely the 'paristrian' cities, 'as daughters returned from captivity to their mother'.[53] And the orator makes it abundantly clear that Alexius had postponed any plan to recover the land between the Haemus and lower Danube, and determined to defend Thrace and Macedonia by securing the Haemus passes, and by resorting to established diplomatic methods through the 'paristrian' emporia. However, Anna Comnena (*Alexiad*: ii, 89; trans.: 218–19) records that 'specious arguments failed to divide them and, despite the emperor's repeated efforts to win them over by all kinds of enticements, no deserter came to him, even in secret, so inflexible was their determination'. So Alexius consulted his generals. Several, notably the older men including Gregory Mavrocatacalon and Nicephorus Bryennius, maintained that the Haemus should remain the frontier. However, the impetuous young emperor was convinced by his young peers, and committed his forces to a series of arduous campaigns in the northern Balkans.

---

[51] *Alexiad*: ii, 87–9 (trans.: 217–18).
[52] Theophylact, *Discours*: 222–7. See also the discussion by Malamut 1995: 138–9.
[53] Theophylact, *Discours*: 227.13–15.

The Pecheneg wars, which are copiously documented by Anna Comnena, reached their bloody conclusion at Levunium in Thrace on Tuesday 29 April 1091. This was a magnificent victory for the imperial forces, 'hence the burlesque chanted by the Byzantines: "All because of one day, the Scythians never saw May"'.[54] *The Life of St Cyril the Phileote* (127, 135) provides a near contemporary account of the panic before the battle when 'because of the imminent danger all took refuge in citadels (*phrouria*)', and the relief afterwards when 'the insurmountable turmoil caused by the Scythians was transformed into peace with the aid of God and the perseverance of the emperor'.

ALEXIUS' REORGANIZATION OF PARADOUNAVON

Soon after Levunium a new Byzantine governor was appointed in Paristrion. Leo Nicerites was 'a eunuch [who] had from his earliest years spent his life among soldiers and was a man of proved reliability'.[55] A seal of his has been discovered at Noviodunum, and others bear the legend '*doux* of Paradounavon'.[56] So trusted was he that in 1092 the suspected conspirator George Decanus 'was sent with letters to Leo Nicerites, who was at that time *doux* of Paradounavon. Apparently he was to assist him in protecting the Danube area, but in fact he was sent so that Nicerites could keep an eye on him.'[57] Alexius' willingness to despatch seditious elements to Dristra suggests that the situation at the lower Danube was considered stable. His confidence bears eloquent testimony to the significance of the victory at Levunium, which established the Comneni in an unassailable position in Constantinople. Alexius was able, after ten years in power, to disinherit the son of Michael VII Ducas and appoint his own son John as junior emperor.

Despite the emperor's confidence, almost immediately his arrangements in Paradounavon were tested by a massive incursion of Cumans. They may have craved more than plunder, for they were encouraged and accompanied by a character who claimed to be the son of the deposed emperor Romanus IV Diogenes. With the pseudo-Diogenes in tow they set out from the lower Dnieper. However, the emperor 'was not unaware' of their movements, and he prepared for war.

The army was summoned by letters from all parts of the empire and when everything was ready he set out to fight the Cumans. At Anchialus which he had

[54] *Alexiad*: ii, 143 (trans.: 258).   [55] *Alexiad*: ii, 93 (trans.: 221).   [56] Barnea 1987: 82–3.
[57] *Alexiad*: ii, 155 (trans.: 268).

reached with all his forces he sent for his brother-in-law, the Caesar Nicephorus Melissenus, and George Palaeologus, and his nephew John Taronites. They were despatched to Berrhoia with instructions to maintain vigilant guard over that city and the neighbouring districts. The army was then divided with the other generals as separate commanders: Dabatenus, George Euphorbenus and Constantine Humbertopoulos were to protect the mountain passes through the Haemus. Alexius went on to Chortarea (itself a pass in the area) and inspected the whole range to see if his previous orders had been faithfully carried out by the officers entrusted with the task; where the fortifications were half-finished or incomplete, he insisted that things should be put right: the Cumans must be denied easy passage. (*Alexiad*: ii, 193; trans.: 298)

Only after this did Alexius return to Anchialus, which was to serve as his base for operations. Numerous seals discovered at Anchialus, and others found elsewhere bearing the town's name attest to a Byzantine ecclesiastical, commercial and administrative presence there throughout the eleventh century. Finds include two seals of a Nicephorus, archbishop of Anchialus *c.* 1080, and a seal of a contemporary metropolitan of Dristra, Christopher *protosynkellos*.[58] The value of Anchialus was twofold. First, it had an impregnable citadel. Second, and more importantly, it lay on the Black Sea, so communications could be despatched to and received from both Constantinople and the lower Danube. Indeed, Alexius soon received news that the Cumans had crossed the Danube and were headed for Adrianople.

Despite all his efforts 'the Cumans were shown the way through the passes by the Vlachs and so crossed the mountains without any trouble'.[59] Thereafter, the value of the pretender was demonstrated as the inhabitants of various citadels were persuaded to surrender to the nomads.[60] Once again battle was required to settle affairs. Alexius waited until the Cuman forces were divided and absorbed in plundering before he engaged a body of 12,000 under their chieftain Kitzes. His victory brought certain of the other chieftains to treat, but Alexius suspected that while he was thus engaged the majority would flee back across the Danube with their booty. Therefore, he secured the passes and launched an attack in the so-called 'Iron Defile', where 'many were slaughtered, but most were captured alive'.[61]

This episode reveals the key elements of imperial northern frontier policy after 1091. First, information gathering was paramount. The

---

[58] Iordanov 1993b: 36–50. [59] *Alexiad*: ii, 194 (trans.: 299).
[60] This can be compared with the activities of the Normans, considered below at pp. 165–6.
[61] *Alexiad*: ii, 203 (trans.: 306).

emperor was informed swiftly of the Cumans' advance, allowing him to raise an army and bolster the empire's defences. Second, the Haemus passes were regarded as the only secure and defensible barrier, and no efforts were made to prevent the nomads from crossing the river, nor to engage them in Paristrion. Since the Cumans were intent on plunder there was little to interest them on the uncultivated and unpopulated Mysian plain, and access to the rich lands of Thrace and Macedonia should have been barred. However, the third element, and Alexius' Achilles' heel, was the loyalty of the mountain dwellers. Just as the Pechenegs had been rewarded for their alliance with Traulos' Paulicians, the Cumans benefited from the fickleness of the Vlachs. This problem would arise again after 1180 with devastating consequences (below at pp. 288–94). However, for many decades after Alexius' victory peace prevailed in Paristrion.

For this frontier system, as outlined, to operate only a skeleton presence was required on the lower Danube. This is mostly simply illustrated by a straight comparison of the number of seals discovered in the area which date from the eleventh century (many) and from the twelfth century (very few).[62] Resources were concentrated in a few fortified emporia nearest to the Cumans, that is nearest to the mouth of the Danube, and other sites were allowed to decline. The once mighty fortress of Preslav was decommissioned, and finds of seals and coins at the excavated site end abruptly at this time.[63] The last evidence of occupation at Păcuiul lui Soare is a seal of Alexius I and several of his coins which were minted before the coinage reform of *c.* 1092 (see above at pp. 84–5). These were withdrawn from circulation rapidly, and therefore must have been lost shortly before the Cuman invasion. A destruction level dated by a precious single coin of Alexius' first post-reform issue proves that the site was razed by the Cumans.[64] At Presthlavitza (Nufărul) the last finds are copper coins struck by Alexius, three-quarters of which are of the rare pre-reform types. Although it does not appear to have been sacked in 1094, the site rapidly fell out of favour, possibly because it was served by a particularly shallow stretch of river.

PARADOUNAVON IN THE TWELFTH CENTURY

Trade flourished throughout the twelfth century both at familiar and new sites on the lower Danube. Both archaeological and documentary

[62] A representative, although not comprehensive, list of seals discovered at sites in the northern Balkans which date from the eleventh and twelfth centuries is appended to Stephenson 1996c.
[63] Iordanov 1993a: 261–2.   [64] Diaconu and Vîlceanu 1972: 161; Diaconu 1978: 53.

evidence demonstrate that the Russians were still regular visitors. Idrisi (ed. Jaubert: ii, 386), a twelfth-century traveller, observed that Dristra was full of bazaars. Leo Charsianites, who was the Orthodox metropolitan of Dristra from the later 1140s, despatched gifts to Constantinople that he purchased locally. His friend, the author John Tzetzes, received an exquisitely carved 'little box of fishbone' and a slave-boy named Vsevolod, whom, he informed Leo, was not Russian, but was in fact 'Mysian'.[65]

While the small Russian dugouts (*monoxyla*) could proceed easily to Dristra, other trading centres benefited from the deeper waters nearer the Danube's mouth. The site of Dinogetia is very rich in twelfth-century artefacts. Seventy sherds have been catalogued of high-bellied piriform amphorae with long narrow necks, some in deposits with coin of Alexius I and John II (1118–43). These originated in Constantinople (Dinogetia type 2b = Saraçhane type 61), and have also been found in Kiev (as well as Athens, Corinth and Corfu).[66] Trade intensified at Kilia, a site we have not previously noted, perhaps as a response to the decline of Presthlavitza. Kilia is on the Braţul Chilia, the northernmost arm of the Danube as it enters the Black Sea. It can almost certainly be identified as Akli or Akla, known to Idrisi (ed. Jaubert: ii, 388–9) for its manufacturers of iron. It became principal regional market for Italian merchants in later centuries, but like the other ports on the lower Danube and the Black Sea, the westerners were explicitly forbidden to trade there by the Comnenian emperors. There can be no doubt that this was principally a political decision intended to safeguard relations with the Russian and other northern peoples whom the emporia were intended to, and continued to service throughout the twelfth century.

Only occasionally did the rich trading cities with their strong defences tempt the Cumans to raid rather than trade. In 1122 the Byzantine sources record an invasion by 'Scythians'.[67] Choniates (16; trans.: 11) adds that 'as a remembrance and thanksgiving for [his victory, the emperor John II] established what we today call the festival of the Pechenegs (*Patzinakon*)'. However, the use of the emotive ethnonym, so hated and feared in his father's day, should not blind us to the fact that John was dealing with Cumans. The Priest of Duklja (*LPD*: 368) records a campaign shortly after this led by John, who bore the epithet 'Cumanus'. A further Cuman raid in 1148, the only one recorded during

[65] Shepard 1979b: 191–239. On 'Mysians' see below at pp. 109, 289.
[66] Ştefan et al. 1967: 259–64, figs. 159.4, 160–2; Hayes 1992: 76.
[67] Cinnamus: 7–8 (trans.: 16); Choniates: 13–16 (trans.: 10–11).

the long and well-documented reign of Manuel I (1143–80), succeeded in capturing (most probably) Dinogetia, which Cinnamus (93–6; trans.: 76–8) knew as 'Demnitzikos, a notable city on the shores of the Danube'. Manuel followed his grandfather's example, and coordinated his successful counterattack from Anchialus.

Once he had driven the nomads back across the river Manuel took no further direct role in the government of Paradounavon. Coins of Manuel's first issue are the last Byzantine coins to be found in any numbers on the lower Danube, suggesting a marked shift in focus. Indeed, at exactly this time the emperor directed his attention and his (finite) resources towards the north-western Balkans, where coins and seals suddenly appear in large numbers (see below at pp. 224–34). Instead of direct administration, Manuel guaranteed stability in another time-honoured way: by granting rights to interested parties in return for their loyalty. He thus presented four *kastra* in Paradounavon to successive Russian princes in the 1160s.[68] This was clearly sufficient to deter the steppe nomads from contemplating any further incursions. In the second half of the twelfth century, Eustathius of Thessalonica (*PG* 135: 938) characterized the Paristrion frontier as a peaceful region 'where the Scythian bow does not function, and his ropes are kept unused. He brandishes them only to keep his hand in'.

FRONTIERS, SCYTHIANS AND SEMI-BARBARIANS

The victory at Levunium was so magnificent, and the celebrations that ensued so glorious, because the threat of the Pechenegs had been so great and deeply felt by all sections of Byzantine society. While the farmers in Thrace endured their raids and sought shelter in local *phrouria*, the civilized elite of Constantinople suffered the Pechenegs' assaults on their sensibilities. Within the great walls of the Queen of Cities, the fierce nomads represented the universal threat of barbarism to civilization, and since Herodotus the Scythian was the archetypal barbarian.[69] The use of the term to refer to numerous northern peoples alludes both to their origins (as far as the Byzantines were concerned) in ancient Scythia, and to their way of life, which resembled that of Herodotus' Scythians. According to Michael Psellus the Pechenegs were archetypal Scythians: they had a loose social structure, fought as

[68] Kazhdan and Epstein 1985: 258, excerpt 42 is a translation of the *Hypatian Chronicle s.a.* 6670 (1162). See also Cinnamus: 236 (trans.: 178).
[69] On familiarity with Herodotus see *ODB*: ii, 922; Wilson 1994: 8, 15, 42.

individuals (not in ordered regiments), and lived as nomads with swift horses. Worse still, they observed no law, and were pagans.[70] These were also the traits Michael Attaleiates attributes to the Pechenegs who were settled south of the Danube in the 1070s, who persisted in their 'Scythian lifestyle'.[71] Whatever the reality of their preferred lifestyle, it is clear that both Psellus and Attaleiates are drawing a distinction between stereotypes, between nature and culture.[72]

Thus, the description of the Scythian is a topos, and one equally applicable to numerous nomadic peoples. Anna Comnena shows little consistency with her use of the name. She fails to differentiate consistently between the Pechenegs and the Cumans, both of whom she regards as Scythian tribes and refers to most frequently with the general ethnonym *Skythai*. A glance at the index to Leib's edition of the *Alexiad* reveals the relative infrequency with which Anna used the terms *Patzinakos* (ten times) and *Komanos* (seventy-one times; *komanikos* ten times) compared with her use of *Skythes* and related adjectives (248 times). This has caused much confusion for modern commentators, and is at the root of an academic debate about whether or not the Pechenegs were annihilated at Levunium since they (or the Cumans) appear consistently in the *Alexiad*, and in Cinnamus' (7–9; trans.: 15–16) and Choniates' (13–17; trans.: 9–11) accounts of John II's decisive battles with Scythians in 1122–3. Anna would not have anticipated this problem, for she would have regarded her treatment of the Scythians as both accurate and in keeping with established classical practice. Herodotus refers to numerous distinct peoples as Scythians, but saw no overwhelming need for Greeks to differentiate consistently between them. He records that while it was necessary for Scythians to know their own tribe, and also for those Greeks who lived as their neighbours to be aware of distinctions, even locals need not use the same name as the Scythians, nor should Greeks within the *oikoumene* trouble to differentiate at all, but should apply the general ethnonym (*Histories*: iv, 6–7 & 17–18; trans.: 244, 248).

---

[70] Psellus, *Chronographia*: ii, 125–6 (trans.: 318–19). Psellus also produced orations where he described the Pechenegs as a 'simple nomadic people, who lead an undisciplined (*automatizon*) life and do not recognize the higher rule of law'. See Psellus, *Orationes Panegyricae*: 63.

[71] Attaleiates: 30–1, 205. These show great similarities with the Magyars described in Leo VI's *Taktika*, and to the Avars in Maurice's *Strategikon*. See Malamut 1995: 121–2.

[72] Lévi-Strauss 1966: 20, 124–5, 129. See also Le Goff 1988: 107–31 for an approach to contemporary western perceptions of the distinction between nature and culture, and the representation of the 'wild man'. Scylitzes (455), whose work was not within the tradition of classicizing history, used contemporary ethnonyms, and usually refers to the Pechenegs as *Patzinakoi*. Nevertheless he presents a similar excursus on the 'Scythian Pechenegs', who favour life on the hoof and dwell in tents.

Nevertheless, we can identify some consistency in whom Anna does not consider to be Scythian: she uses 'Sarmatians' (*Sauromatai*) to refer only to the Ouzes. Her first use is in describing their migration across the Danube in 1059 (*Alexiad*: i, 127; trans.: 122), where she borrows freely from Psellus (*Chronographia*: ii, 125; trans.: 317). However, she corrects Psellus, who fails to identify the barbarians by name, noting only that they used to be known as Mysians. (Which led the English translator of the *Chronographia* to believe that Psellus was referring to the Pechenegs.) Both Psellus and Anna record that the migration was provoked by the activities of the *Getai*. Anna adds that they were inspired by the treachery of the Dacians. The latter were clearly the Hungarians; the *Getai* cannot be identified as certainly, and Anna clearly borrowed the name, for once uncritically, from Psellus' account. Anna's second reference to the *Sauromatai* (*Alexiad*: ii, 30; trans.: 172) allows a more certain association of the ethnonym with the Ouzes. She describes an encounter in 1082 when a detachment of Turks and Sarmatians confronted some Normans in a defile. Prominent in the skirmish was a certain Ouzas, so named because of his *genos*. Anna's third reference (*Alexiad*: ii, 81; trans.: 212) to the Sarmatians has them in the role of the *Getai*, driving a further group of nomads, a *genos Skythikon*, towards the Danube. Here she is describing the migration of a tribe of Pechenegs who were driven south by the Ouzes in around 1070. Sarmatians were a component of the confederate army commanded by Tzelgu and the Hungarian Salomon in 1087 (*Alexiad*: ii, 97; trans.: 224). They were confronted by a Byzantine army that included mercenaries (*ethnikoi*) commanded by the aforementioned Ouzas and a fellow Sarmatian named Karatzas. In her final reference Anna modifies this statement, identifying Ouzas once again as Sarmatian, but distinguishing him from Karatzas 'the Scyth', and Monastras 'the *mixobarbaros*' (*Alexiad*: ii, 204; trans.: 306). Once again we can identify the reason for Anna's deliberate distinction between the Scythians and Sarmatians in her knowledge of Herodotus, for according to his description the latter lived beyond the former, once 'one has left Scythia behind' (*Histories*: iv, 22; trans.: 249). This was also the case with the Pechenegs and the Ouzes before they began their migrations to the Danube, and such a happy coincidence cannot have escaped Anna, even if she did not truly believe the contemporary and ancient peoples were directly related.

As we have seen, Anna Comnena refers on numerous occasions to a further category of settlers in Paristrion: the *mixobarbaroi*, whom we should distinguish clearly from the Pechenegs (*Skythai*).[73] Thus she remarks on a *mixobarbaros* who knew the language of the Scythians, and refers several times to a *mixobarbaros* named Monastras who is distinguished from his Scythian associates.[74] Attaleiates (204) refers without further elaboration to the *mixobarbaroi* dwelling in the lands beside the lower Danube.[75] Given the region in question, Romanian and Bulgarian scholars have devoted much effort to proving the ethnicity of the *mixobarbaroi*. According to preference they were Bulgarians or Vlachs who had adopted a barbarian lifestyle, natives who had lived with, or intermarried with the Pechenegs, or even those who were a strange individual racial and linguistic mélange akin to the fourteenth-century Momicila from Macedonia, a *boulgaralbanitovlachos*.[76] In fact *mixobarbaros* was a classical term, used by Euripides (*Ph* 138), Plato (*Mx* 245d) and Xenophon (*HG* 2.1.15) to describe non-Athenian Greeks. In Euripides' tragedy Antigone wondered at the 'semi-barbarian' equipment of Tydeus, the warrior from Aetolia. In his dialogue *Menexenus*, Plato described numerous barbarians who considered themselves Greeks, but who were not pure-blooded Athenians, and thus only *mixobarbaroi*. Xenophon, similarly called the inhabitants of Cedreiae, a city in Caria (Asia Minor) allied to Athens, *mixobarbaroi*. He clearly meant those who are bound by treaties to Athens, but who are not Athenian.[77] Thus, *mixobarbaroi* is perhaps the closest equivalent that classicizing authors could find for people who lived within the frontiers of the *oikoumene* and had signed treaties with the emperor, thereby recognizing the rule of law, but who were not *Rhomaioi* (Byzantines). Their ethnicity was of less importance, for unlike in classical Athens, pure blood was not a qualification for citizenship in Byzantium. Here then we have an attempt by Byzantine authors to articulate in Attic Greek the relationship between central government and local elites who wielded power at the lower Danube. The *mixobarbaroi* were non-Romans who lived within the empire's frontiers as Christians, and were bound to the empire by treaties; therefore they were no longer entirely, but only half, barbarian.

[73] See *Alexiad*: iii, 205, 207 (trans.: 485, 487, as 'half-breeds') for *mixobarbaroi* who spoke Greek fighting for (and betraying) the Turks. Also *Alexiad*: iii, 192 (trans.: 474), where Anna refers to a *mixobarbaros*, slave, gift and namesake of the noble Styppeiotes. Choniates: 209 (trans.: 119) considered the *mixobarbaros* inferior to the pure *Rhomaios* in his martial ability.

[74] *Alexiad*: ii, 194, 204; iii, 14, 15, 41, 154 (trans.: 299, 306, 338–40, 359, 365–6, 445).

[75] A sensible approach to the *mixobarbaroi* is taken by Tanaşoca 1973: 61–82, who suggests (71) that the 'semi-barbarians' were superficially hellenized peoples with an ambivalent attitude towards the empire. See also Cheynet 1990: 380. The latest useful comments are by Ahrweiler 1998: 1–17, who ponders Byzantine acculturation by 'backward peoples', and the emergence of *Mixoellenes*. However, I disagree with her statement (13) that 'the term *Mixobarbaroi* refers to cultural issues' alone.   [76] Diaconu 1970: 103.   [77] Liddell et al. 1996: 1136.

THE FRONTIER AND THE IMPERIAL IMAGE, 1025–1100

The treatment of barbarian peoples in Byzantine sources also reveals a great deal about the imperial image and how it changed through the period of the Pecheneg wars. The orator John Mauropous praised the emperor Constantine IX's handling of the Pechenegs after they had crossed the Danube in 1046–7, and in so doing expounded most clearly the 'civilian' attitude to the barbarian threat and to the frontier lands of Paristrion. According to Mauropous the barbarians were not overcome by force of arms alone, but inspired to throw down their weapons by the appearance of a divine portent, the sign of the cross in the sky above them as it has appeared to Constantine the Great at the Milvian Bridge. Thus they demanded to be baptized, and their conversion to Christianity was regarded as the emperor's greatest victory, the transformation of wild beasts into men.[78] There is surely a parallel between John Tzimisces' defeat of the Rus by the intervention of St Theodore the Stratelate, and this second *deus ex machina*. As we have seen (at pp. 52–4), the earlier victory was widely publicized and was central to attempts to lend legitimacy to Tzimisces' usurpation. However, the articulation of a martial image for that emperor by his association with a military martyr was reversed by Constantine IX's publicists. For Mauropous the simple cross was symbol of the emperor's own divinity, for he was Christ's vicegerent on earth and heir to his namesake, the first Christian Roman emperor. And to wage war was not the goal of a good emperor, ruling in Christ's stead, but was a necessary evil. Mauropous wrote instead in praise of the 'pacific emperor' (*eirenikos basileus*) who only resorted to arms when pretenders raised armies, or when barbarians violated treaties and breached the frontiers.[79]

Jacques Lefort (1976: 286) noted with great insight that for Mauropous the frontier in Paristrion was less 'a border to defend, and more a zone where one might instil [in others] Roman values: this is the message conveyed by Mauropous' treatment of the installation of the Pechenegs within the empire.' Thus, the barbarians were allowed to remain within the frontiers of the *oikoumene* by virtue of their treaty with the emperor, and by observing the rule of law and receiving baptism they were no longer entirely barbarian. Psellus observed the same phenomenon, but he wrote about it in less welcoming terms:

---

[78] Mauropous: 145, poem 145, § 12–13; Lefort 1976: 266–7.
[79] Mauropous: 184, poem 186, §28.2; Lefort 1976: 291.

Ravines, mountains and rivers formed the natural frontiers, reinforced by towns and fortresses constructed by men. The barbarian who rode his mount as far as these was struck by the sight and restrained, not daring to advance further into our lands: the fortress was an obstacle to him. But when this barrier is broken down, all those opposite rush into our lands like the flood of a river when a dyke is breached. Now Romanity and barbarity are not kept distinct, they are intermingled and live together. For this reason the barbarians are at war with us, some at the Euphrates, others on the Danube. (Psellus, *Scripta Minora*: ii, 239)[80]

Psellus thus attacked the decision to abandon far-flung fortresses which lined the empire's 'natural' frontiers, and condemned the policy of settling barbarians in frontier region which he saw as a barbarization of Roman lands and, by implication, values. Therefore, we might expect him to have favoured the return of Roman militarism under Isaac I Comnenus (although as we have already seen he was no fan of Isaac, and criticized his campaigns against the nomads).

Isaac sought to portray himself as an aggressor, notoriously appearing on his imperial coinage with a drawn sword. Attaleiates (60) and Scylitzes Continuatus (103) both attribute this to Isaac's vanity: his intention was to demonstrate that his accession owed more to his strong right arm than to God. The abrupt shift to a militant imperial image lasted only as long as Isaac's brief reign, and thereafter martial and pacific motifs competed for precedence in the construction of the imperial image. Whereas Constantine IX was praised by Christopher of Mitylene for having distributed rivers of gold and titles, quite different fluvial imagery was employed to praise emperors who dispensed only floods of sweat and rivers of barbarian blood.[81] However, given how few sources have survived, it is difficult to identify a point at which military prowess, victory over barbarians, and the duty to extend the frontiers became the predominant imperial ideals. One of the few extant contemporary comments on Alexius' exploits, by Manuel Straboromanus, praises the emperor's martial prowess and his restoration of the empire's frontiers in east and west, but also extols Alexius' philanthropy.[82] Alexius himself advised his son and heir John not to trust all to the sword, but 'to lay up treasure which will clamp the jaws of the barbarians who breathe enmity against us'.[83]

It has been suggested that Theophylact of Ohrid 'put military prowess at the top of his list of virtues for a ruler', and his attitude reflects

---

[80] See also Cheynet 1990: 380.
[81] Christopher of Mitylene: 33, nr. 55.3–6; Kazhdan 1984: 48–51; Dennis 1997: 135. See below at pp. 236–7.   [82] Manuel Straboromanus: 190.   [83] Maas 1913: 348–59; Magdalino 1993: 28.

a wider change in Byzantine attitudes to the duty of the emperor not only to defend, but to advance the frontiers.[84] Thus he warned the *porphyrogennetos* Constantine Ducas not to think 'the purple-edged golden imperial robes will prevail over the servants of Ares, men whose appearance is as fierce as lions if they do not see you in a bronze cuirass applying yourself to war'. But Theophylact did not advocate aggressive military action, merely vigilant guard and careful preparation.

In matters of war [the emperor] concerns himself with everything, examining all and helping everyone. Above all he should not put himself in danger thoughtlessly, nor die like a simple soldier, but must reason like a general who has won many victories. In times of peace he must prepare himself for war and train himself on every occasion in all forms of war, without neglecting a single one, participating in exercises with all his troops, and taking veterans and experienced warriors as his instructors and observers at his drills. (Theophylact, *Discours*: 207)

Moreover, Theophylact was equally willing and able to extol more pacific imperial exploits. In the aforementioned oration delivered on 6 January 1088, he spoke in praise of Alexius I's 'bloodless victory' over the Pechenegs, referring to the treaty he had negotiated in 1087.[85] We have seen that at this time Alexius had suffered a significant defeat, and was obliged to recognize the Pechenegs' settlement of the lands north of the Haemus. Even Anna Comnena admitted, some time later, that her father had considered making his northern frontier that mountain range, abandoning all hopes of recovering Paristrion. Unlike Mauropous, Theophylact does not dwell on the baptism of barbarians; their brute nature was transformed, instead, by rhetoric and the emperor persuading them to recognize the force of law. For Theophylact, Alexius was a Homeric hero, now Odysseus booming, now Menelaus speaking in softer tones, briefly but fluently (*Iliad*: iii.214–22). Beguiling everyone with his rhetoric, he enchanted philosophers and orators with his sharp wit and the clarity of his speech. In this way Alexius exposed the Scythians' secret plans, and forced them to sue for peace. 'Those who previously solved their disputes by spilling blood, swore their faith in writing and with a treaty' (Theophylact, *Discours*, 225). The emphasis is on the triumph of imperial order, in the form of written law (*nomos*), over the undisciplined barbarian nature (*physis*).

So barbarism could be brought within frontiers of the empire and modified by the contacts with the civilized (or, according to Psellus,

---

[84] Kazhdan 1984: 46.   [85] Theophylact, *Discours*: 222–7.

Romanity could mix with barbarity). Even in defeat the civilized would triumph by the extension of its cherished values, its defining character-istics: by baptism, soothing the brutish nature of the barbarian; or by treaties, obliging barbarians to recognize the force of law. Both were the triumph of culture over nature, and both made the Pechenegs now settled within the *oikoumene* not entirely barbarians. It is fascinating to see how imperial rhetoric was brought to bear on a political reality: the Pechenegs had settled in the heartland of what had until so recently been the Bulgarian empire. This had to be explained, and in the context of the annual *basilikos logos* it had to be lauded. Moreover, in doing so Mauropous and Theophylact (and Psellus) modified the polarity of the civilized *Rhomaioi* and barbarian Scythians, allowing for an intermediate category, the semi-civilized world which was Byzantium's Balkan fron-tier.

CONCLUSIONS

The situation at the lower Danube seems to fit with Michael Angold's thesis that Basil II bequeathed his successors a poisoned legacy. Far from leaving them a strong, defensible and well resourced military frontier at the lower Danube, he had failed to anticipate the enduring problem of the Pecheneg migrations which commenced in the final decade of his reign. Driving the raiders back across the river was a temporary and unsatisfactory solution. The dispersed watchtowers which Basil had restored and manned proved to be no more than potential targets for determined warbands, and could offer no resistance to the sustained assaults of 1032 to 1036. Since authority in the lands beside the Danube relied on the Byzantines retaining the support of the local elites, and har-nessing their interests to those of the empire, to allow regular raids into Paristrion undermined the *status quo* in the frontier region, even while they may not penetrate very far into the empire. A more effective solu-tion was urgently needed, and one was provided shortly after 1036 by Michael IV and his brother John the Orphanotrophus.

The nature of the abundant archaeological evidence, and the few pre-cious references to trade initiatives *vis-à-vis* nomads when placed together allow us to reconstruct this policy. First, resources were concen-trated in fewer, more heavily fortified sites: Dristra, Păcuiul lui Soare, Noviodunum, Dinogetia and Presthlavitza. These sites were both mili-tary and commercial centres where nomads, and others, might converge to dispose of their wares and purchase the products they desired from within the empire in controlled conditions. To facilitate the process of exchange large numbers of low value coins were pumped into the region from Constantinople; and to make the system even more attractive, stipends were despatched to the native elites of the cities, who might use them to purchase the Pechenegs' services in the manner familiar to Chersonites known from the *DAI*. This money had to be provided from Constantinople, and therefore required the expansion of taxation and raising of cash revenues in regions of the empire deemed to be less volatile. (Therefore, John the Orphanotrophus determined to impose direct Byzantine authority in southern Dalmatia, and extend the collection of taxes in cash into Bulgaria. To raise cash quickly and guarantee a regular income rights to raise taxes in the provinces were sold off to tax-farmers, leading to corruption and extortion. The subsequent events suggest that John's decisions upset the whole balance of power in the western Balkans, where control, as far as it was exercised, was through local and regional magnates (as we will see below at pp. 130–6).)

First Kegen's invasion, and subsequently the Pecheneg wars of 1048–53 served as a brake to the trade policy in Paristrion, and as a reminder that Byzantine frontier policy had still to develop according to changing circumstances; not least the building external pressure from the north. The flexible, military approach taken by Constantine IX gives the lie to the notion, championed by Ostrogorsky, that this 'civilian' emperor allowed the frontiers to be breached by his neglect of the army. Indeed, the guerilla tactics his generals employed were remarkably effective against the nomads; far more so than the subsequent attempts at pitched battle by the 'military' emperor Isaac I. We have seen that differences in imperial rhetoric between Constantine and Isaac are equally striking. Rhetorical accounts of Constantine's encounters with the Pechenegs portray his intentions as defensive and pacific, placing greater value on religion (the baptism of barbarians), and law (the settlement of affairs by treaties) than war. Isaac favoured pitched battle, and celebrated triumphal processions where no substantial victory had been won. But behind the rhetorical facade in Constantinople peaceful processes of exchange continued to promote trading over raiding.

Material evidence suggests that trading continued at the emporia on the lower Danube for as long as the Pechenegs (and Russians) desired the empire's cash and commodities, and the empire was able to supply them in sufficient quantities. There are indications that the system of controlled exchange at the frontier emporia began to suffer later in the 1060s as a consequence of the general lack of bullion available to the imperial government. A regional mint was established which produced inferior coins which came to dominate exchange. A corollary of this, the decision to withhold the annual subsidies paid to the *mixobarbaroi*, led to the Pechenegs gaining control of Paristrion with the connivance of the local magnates. So, the issue at stake in the frontier lands of the northern Balkans was one familiar throughout the empire at this time: how the state controlled and distributed its resources. It was this, not a tension between military and civilian factions, which saw the frontier system develop and then falter in the middle years of the eleventh century. Thus, once he had reestablished Byzantine military supremacy in the region, it was to the empire's financial organization that Alexius I Comnenus turned his attentions. In the years immediately after Levunium he issued an entirely new series of Byzantine coins, with more and graduated denominations far better suited to the needs of commerce, and to the taxation system; and this he also set about reforming over the next fifteen years.

Overall, we must conclude that Basil II's successors were acutely aware of the political possibilities of promoting controlled trade at the lower Danube, but less sensitive to the economic or fiscal ramifications. While the treasury might benefit from the exaction of the *kommerkion*, this might represent only a percentage of the sum required to finance the annual payments to frontier elites, or to barbarian warlords. Indeed, the associated duties of *kommerkiarioi*, to monitor and control trade in such a sensitive area, were as important as their tax raising function. Continued sensitivity to the political nature of the trade in the region is underlined by the Byzantine decision to ban Italian merchants from trading in the Black Sea throughout the eleventh and twelfth centuries, despite their extensive privileges elsewhere. And these privileges, which allowed the Venetians, and later the Pisans and Genoans, to establish commercial dominance in the Mediterranean, were similarly conceived of and extended for purely political reasons. We will return to this later, but for now must turn to the other part of the Balkan frontier that Basil recovered for Byzantium, and explore the consequences of his expansion into the lands of the southern Slavs.

CHAPTER FOUR

Southern Slavs (1025–1100)

We have already encountered the southern Slavs, and referred to several of the distinct regions that they occupied. Unlike the Pechenegs, the Slavs had been settled within the Balkan lands for several centuries, and various groups had developed sedentary power structures in particular geographical contexts. Peoples, lands and their correct or appropriate names are matters of considerable importance in the history of the Balkans, and it is only sensible to consider some medieval perceptions. William of Tyre (97–8; trans.: i, 139–41) knew the whole region between the Danube and the Adriatic as Dalmatia, and both Anna Comnena (*Alexiad*: i, 60, 155; trans.: 72, 144) and John Cinnamus (12; trans.: 19) refer to the region's various inhabitants as Dalmatians. However, there was little unity in the region, and the fragmented nature of political authority is reflected in certain texts. The *DAI* (145) enumerates the various lands in the mid-tenth century: Duklja (also called Dalmatia Superior, and later Zeta), Zahumlje (Hum), Travunija (Trebinje), Dalmatia Inferior, and Croatia. Travelling further inland one reached the highland regions of Raška (also known as Rassa and Rascia), and Bosna (or Bosnia).

Each of the larger regions comprised many smaller districts or counties known as *župas* or *županias*, governed by *župans*. The *DAI* (144–51) also provides unique contemporary information on the northern lands, which were settled by the Croats. We have noted in chapter one that a clear distinction was drawn between the Romani settled in the maritime cities of Dalmatia, and the Slavs who settled the hinterland, who were known as Croats (above at p. 29). The region between Istria and the river Cetina was known to Constantine VII as 'Baptized Croatia', and there were found 'the inhabited cities of Nin, Biograd, Belice, Skradin, Livno, Stupin, Knin, Karin and Klaboka'. Constantine also knew of and named eleven *županias*: Livno, Cetina, Imotsko, Pliva, Pset, Primorje, Bribir, Nin, Knin, Sidraga and Nina; and three regions possessed by the

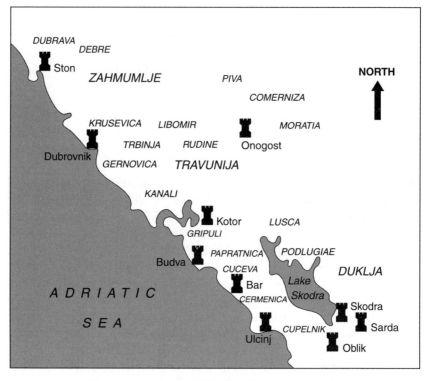

4.1 The cities and *županias* of Duklja, Travunija and Zahumlje

ban: Krbava, Lika and Gačka. No information is provided on Pannonian Croatia, which had been annexed to the southern lands by the Croatian ruler Tomislav before *c.* 950. However, later sources corroborate and supplement the *DAI*. Thomas of Split's *Historia Salonitana*, written in the mid-thirteenth century, records the regions placed under the jurisdiction of the archbishop of the Croats as the 'parishes which comprise the *comitates* [counties, thus *županias*] of Cetina, Livno, Klis, Mačva, Almisium and Krbava, and beyond the *fereas Alpes* as far as the borders of Zagreb, and the whole of Maronia [north-western Croatia]'. Two further *županias* in north-western Croatia, Vinodol and Modruše, and are first mentioned in 1163.[1]

The *Chronicle of the Priest of Duklja* (*LPD*) offers alternative names for the regions identified by Constantine VII. The coastal lands which we have called Dalmatia were also called *Maritima*, and were divided into two

---

[1] *Historia Salonitana*: 45; *Codex Diplomaticus*: ii, 96.

provinces: the northern section stretched south to the river Cetina and was known as either Croatia Alba (White Croatia), or Dalmatia Inferior; the southern section as far as Dyrrachium was known as Croatia Rubea (Red Croatia) or Dalmatia Superior. The use of *Maritima* as a synonym for Dalmatia was in use at least until the fourteenth century, for example by the Venetian doge and chronicler Andrea Dandolo. However, Dandolo uses Dalmatia far more frequently, and notes that 'today the coastline of *Maritima* is called Dalmatia, and the mountains Croatia'.[2] Daniel Farlati, who in the eighteenth century undertook the first exhaustive survey of written sources relating to the history of Dalmatia, also recognized the fundamental division between coastal and upland regions.[3] His compilation in eight volumes is fascinating for what it has preserved that would otherwise have been lost forever, although all of the material was transcribed uncritically and must be treated with the utmost caution.

It is worth dwelling briefly on the *LPD*, which will feature on numerous occasions in this chapter. The Priest of Duklja's work was written in Slavonic in the last decades of the twelfth century, although it has survived only in a sixteenth-century Latin translation. It was probably the work of Grgur (Gregory), bishop of Bar from 1172 to *c.* 1196.[4] The *LPD* draws no firm distinction between the coastal strip and the mountains, which may reflect the fact that between the tenth and late twelfth centuries a degree of intermingling had occurred between the two groups (Latins and Slavs) and regions (Dalmatia and Croatia), and we will examine some of the forms of contact between city and hinterland in chapter six (below at pp. 194–6). However, we must also be aware that the *LPD* was written to champion the rights of the bishopric of Bar to preside over all the lands south of the river Cetina, and the alternative schema for the 'Divisione Dalmatiae sub dominatu Slavorum' created a pseudo-historical precedent for the twelfth-century land claims. When the *LPD* was written Bar had lost its metropolitan status and was obliged to recognize the higher authority of the archbishop of Split. The chronicle, therefore, attributes the division of lands to the fictional King Svetopelek – probably Svetopulk of Moravia – who placed Bar on an equal footing with Split, with both superior in status to Dubrovnik.[5] The events took place in an unspecified 'Golden Age' which is intended to appeal to common folk memory, and the author attempts to bolster the impression of antiquity and continuity by the inclusion of ancient

---

[2] Dandolo: 156 (Dalmatia and Croatia), 249 ('Maritima').   [3] Farlati 1751: i, 122–7.
[4] Peričić 1991: 255–72.
[5] *LPD*: 305–6. For commentary see Havlík 1976: 87–9; Peričić 1991: 240–51.

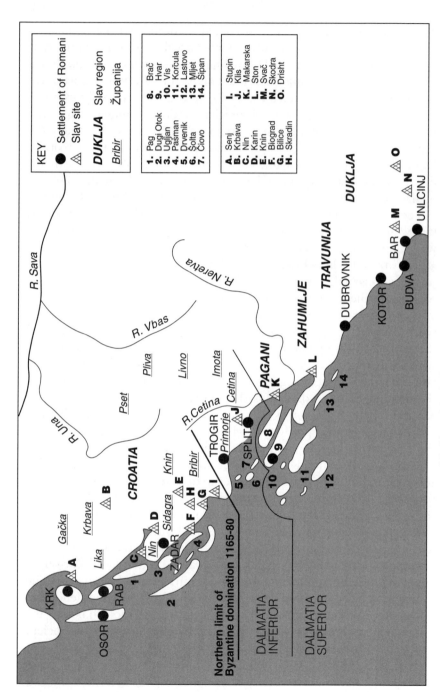

KEY

● Settlement of Romani
△ Slav site

DUKLJA Slav region
Bribir Županija

1. Pag	8. Brač
2. Dugi Otok	9. Hvar
3. Ugljan	10. Vis
4. Pašman	11. Korčula
5. Drvenik	12. Lastovo
6. Šolta	13. Mljet
7. Čiovo	14. Šipan

A. Senj	I. Stupin
B. Krbava	J. Klis
C. Nin	K. Makarska
D. Karin	L. Ston
E. Knin	M. Svač
F. Biograd	N. Skodra
G. Bilice	O. Drisht
H. Skradin	

R. Sava

R. Neretva

R. Vbas

Pliva

Pset

Livno

R. Una

Imota

CROATIA

Knin

Bribir

R. Cetina

Cetina

Primorje

Sidagra

Gačka

Lika

Krbava

Nin

KRK

OSOR

RAB

ZADAR

TROGIR

SPLIT

PAGANI

ZAHUMLJE

TRAVUNIJA

DUKLJA

DUBROVNIK

KOTOR

BUDVA

BAR

UNLCINJ

DALMATIA INFERIOR

DALMATIA SUPERIOR

Northern limit of Byzantine domination 1165-80

4.2 Maritime cities in Dalmatia and northern *županias*

placenames alongside their modern equivalents. However, if the historical account advanced by the Priest of Duklja is spurious, the tradition his story is intended to authenticate may well be valid. A large triconical church, possibly a cathedral church, has been discovered at Bar which seems to date from the eighth century. A smaller church was built on an adjacent site in the tenth century, when Bar had become subject to the metropolitan archbishopric of Dyrrachium.[6]

Later disputes over ecclesiastical authority, therefore, have coloured our picture of lands and authority in Dalmatia before 1200. Nevertheless, an approximate picture can be drawn. For around 250 years the archbishop of Dyrrachium held sway over the bishoprics in southern Dalmatia, known as Dalmatia Superior. The see of Split then acquired authority, and some time later a synod was called to which the bishops of Kotor, Bar and Ulcinj set sail in the same ship. That ship was wrecked off the coast of the island of Hvar at a date during the reign of Basil II (976–1025), and also during the reign of the Croatian king Cresimir when a certain Peter was archbishop of Split; that is between 1000 and 1022.[7] As a consequence of that tragedy the bishops of southern Dalmatia were once again granted their own metropolitan, which must have been Dubrovnik. This brings us up to date at *c.* 1025.

The *LPD* also enumerates the *županias* of the southernmost regions, and despite the mythical context in which it is found, much of the information is credible at least for the later twelfth century.

King Predimir sired four sons, who bore the following names: the first-born was called Chlavimir, the second Boleslav, the third Dragislav and the fourth Svevlad. He divided his kingdom between them in the following way. To Chlavimir he gave the region of Zeta with its towns and these *županias*: Lusca, Podlugiae, Gorsca, Cupelnik, Oblik, Papratnica, Cermenica, Budva with Cuceva and Gripuli; to Boleslav he gave these *županias* [which together comprised Travunija]: Libomir, Vetanica, Rudina, Crusceviza, Vrmo, Rissena, Draceviza, Canali, Gernoviza. To Dragislav he gave the region of Zahumlje and these *županias*: Stantania, Papava, Yabsko, Luca, Vellica, Gorimita, Vecenike, Dubrava and Debre. To Svevlad he gave the region which the Slavs calls Podgorica, in Latin 'Submontana', and these *županias*: Onogost, Moratia, Comerniza, Piva, Gerico, Netusini, Guisemo, Com, Debreca, Neretva and Rama. (*LPD*: 326–7)[8]

The authority of each prince, in this case each fictional son, over the various *županias* relied on his retaining the support of the *župans*, and

---

[6] Mijović 1970: 140–54.   [7] *Historia Salonitana*: 43–4.   [8] See also Jireček 1879: 21–7.

we will see below that this involved regular consultations and meetings. The size of the *župania* varied according to the nature of land it occupied. Hence, accessibility, density of population and degree of cultivation were key factors. The rich coastal lands of Zeta supported ten distinct *županias* in a relatively small area. The eleven *županias* of Podgorica stretched over a much larger mountainous region.

If the affairs of the coastal lands are complicated and deliberately obfuscated, the history of the highland regions is even more obscure, and we cannot even locate many of the regions for which we have names. For example, the location and extent of the region known as Rama, and later as Bosna (or Bosnia), has provoked a great deal of discussion. Much of this, of course, has been concerned with modern rather than medieval Bosnia.[9] It seems most sensible to avoid discussion of an issue than cannot be resolved from the incredibly meagre documentary, and manifestly unremarkable material evidence. However, it is less controversial, and certainly less anachronistic to venture suggestions as to the location of a neighbouring region known as Dendra. The best evidence we have is contained in John Cinnamus' account of Manuel I's encounters with the Serbs and Hungarians. He notes that the emperor summoned the *veliki župan*, Grand Count and supreme ruler of Raška – whom he calls Primislav but we know to have been Uroš II – and his brothers Beluš and Desa, to determine who should be their ruler. Desa, we are told, 'ruled the region of Dendra, a prosperous and populous area near Niš'.[10] The region then passed into Byzantine hands in exchange for Desa's being recognized as *veliki župan*. As we will see in chapter eight (pp. 239–61), from the later 1150s Manuel was most interested in securing lands which lay beyond Niš. The Greek toponym Dendra, used by Cinnamus, is the same as the word for trees, so it seems safe to conclude that Dendra was a wooded region. Forests abounded in the region to the west and north of Niš, running right up to the Danube between its confluence with the Sava and the Velika Morava. Arnold of Lübeck (118) wrote of the infamous Bulgarian forest (*Bulgarewalt*) where marshes impeded the progress of those on horseback or pulling wagons. Various chroniclers of the crusades provide vivid descriptions of the

---

[9] Even more recently electronic histories have appeared on the World Wide Web which stress the contiguity of the medieval Serbian archdiocese of Raška (including Prizren) with Kosovo. The home page of the 'Raška and Prizren Diocese' made by Fr. Sava of Dečani Monastery makes the association in a sensitive manner, calling for a peaceful solution to issues of political sovereignty (http://www.decani.yunet.com/glavna.html).   [10] Cinnamus: 204 (trans.: 155–6).

terrain.[11] Albert of Aachen (275) noted that the citizens of Belgrade, who took fright at the passage of the First Crusade, sought refuge in the neighbouring 'forests, mountains, and deserted fastnesses'. Odo of Deuil (30–2) described the Velika Morava corridor as naturally fertile, abounding in wild fruit, but wholly lacking inhabitants. (It is as well to note that the Greek plural *dendra* is used particularly to refer to fruit trees.) William of Tyre (946–7; trans.: ii, 349) described the region as 'thickly wooded and very difficult of access'. It seems safe to place Dendra in this wooded buffer region to the west and north of Niš, with Raška to the north, and Bosna to the east. Recent attempts to locate Dendra quite precisely have placed it to the west of Niš where, it has been noted, there is today an area known as Dubrava. This is the Serbian word for 'grove' (of trees), which might be considered the equivalent of Dendra.[12]

BYZANTINE AUTHORITY IN THE SLAVIC PERIPHERY AFTER 1025

A glance at any map of the middle Byzantine empire at its 'apogee' in 1025 will show that Basil II exercised authority throughout the lands of the southern Slavs, and the border of his empire ran west along the Sava and Danube from Sirmium to the Black Sea, and south the length of the Adriatic coast from Istria through Dyrrachium and into Greece.[13] However, Basil's authority did not translate into direct Byzantine control of the most peripheral regions. Instead, the various local and regional rulers swore allegiance to the emperor, but each retained power within their own lands subject to the emperor's sanction. Even in the administrative district known as Bulgaria imperial control depended on Basil's retaining the support of the *archontes* of regions and peoples or *proteuontes* in the towns where he had razed fortifications. Where fortifications had been left intact Basil installed Byzantine garrisons to monitor the activities of local magnates.

There are indications that Basil's immediate successors, Constantine VIII (1025–8) and Romanus III (1028–34), refined this policy, and archaeological evidence suggests that Byzantine troops were withdrawn from the *phrouria* on the Danube between Sirmium and Vidin soon after Basil's death. We have seen that relatively large numbers of low value

---

[11] However, we should note that these observations coincide with others identified by Le Goff 1988: 47–59, as typical of the characterization of the forest in western medieval texts.

[12] Radojčić 1970: 249–60; Blagojević 1996: 197–212.

[13] For example Angold 1997: 352–3, map 1.

coins struck by Basil appeared in several small restored forts, and that
these must be seen as evidence of a military presence in *c.* 1020. Coins
struck later in the eleventh century are very rarely found. For example,
at Belgrade twenty-one class A2 anonymous *folles* were discovered, but
thereafter only two further coins for the whole eleventh century. A saint's
life confirms that around 1030 the *kastron* at Belgrade was under the
control of a local magnate (*princeps*) who prevented the blessed Symeon
from proceeding into the Balkans on his planned pilgrimage to the Holy
Land.[14] We also know that in 1027 Constantine Diogenes had been withdrawn from Sirmium and returned to Thessalonica as *doux* with responsibility for Bulgaria.[15] From this we must conclude that soon after Basil's
death it had been determined that the frontier marches were best left in
the hands of the native *župans*; the nearest Byzantine regional commanders were stationed some way to the south and east at Niš and
Skopje.

Niš sat at the far end of the long Velika Morava river valley, and the
journey from the Danube took eight days on foot, or five on horseback.
As we have seen, William of Tyre (946–7; trans.: ii, 349) described the
journey south, and noted that the emperor did not allow cultivation or
settlement, even though the lands were well suited, in order to maintain
a buffer between the rich lands of the empire and the world beyond.
Once a traveller reached Niš he entered the rich lands of the eastern
empire. Idrisi (ii, 382–3) described Niš as 'a town remarkable for the
abundance and low prices of provisions such as meat, fish and dairy
products. It is situated on the banks of the Morava, a river which flows
from the mountains of Serbia and over which is built a great bridge for
the use of travellers and merchants.' William of Tyre (50–2; trans.:
100–1) was similarly impressed by the stone bridge and the large garrison of brave men within the city's strong walls under the command of a
Byzantine general. The first evidence for a *strategos* in Niš is the seal of a
certain Nicephorus Lykaon (or Lalakon), *protospatharios*, which can be
dated to the mid-eleventh century.[16]

The strong walls of Skopje were similarly renowned. They were built
of small stones held together with mortar, and studded with round,
square and triangular towers. In the eleventh century the lower town
outside the walls expanded greatly, and the fortifications show a tendency towards 'monumental' development.[17] Within the walls dwelt the

---

[14] *Ex Miraculis Sancti Symeonis*: 210. For the date of 1030 see Wattenbach 1939: ii, 174.
[15] Scylitzes: 376.   [16] Nesbitt and Oikonomides 1991: i, 100.
[17] Mikulčić 1982: 121–3, 149; Mikulčić 1996: 298–309.

strategos autokrator (later the *doux*) of Bulgaria, and the first was David Arianites, a patrician and general who had previously been in command of Thessalonica and played a significant role in Basil II's campaigns.[18] Between Niš and Skopje stretched the mountain chain known as the *Zygos* (or 'yoke', the modern Kapaonik which extends south into Kosovo Polje). In the later eleventh century it was regarded as the empire's frontier with Dalmatia, and its passes were studded with small watchtowers: Lipljan, Zvečan, Galič and Jeleč. Beyond the mountains stretched an area of no-man's-land before the lands occupied by the independent groups of Slavs.[19] The same system extended south from Skopje, where Byzantine territory was clearly distinguished from the lands of Duklja, Travunija and Zahumlje, all ruled by Slav *archontes*. Thus a fixed internal frontier was established within which Byzantine *strategoi* exercised direct authority, and beyond which the empire depended on the loyalty of the Slavic *župans*. The latter lived within the external frontiers of the *oikoumene*, and in the Byzantine 'world view' remained dependent *archontes* subject to imperial commands.

The task of monitoring the local rulers was entrusted to the *strategoi* in Niš, Skopje and the coastal towns of Dubrovnik (also known as Ragusa), and Dyrrachium. After 1018 Nicetas Pegonites, the vanquisher of John Vladislav, had been replaced as *strategos* of Dyrrachium by the *patrikios* Eustathius Daphnomeles. A further *strategos* of this period, otherwise unattested, was the *protospatharios* Leo Botaneiates, known from a seal in the Dumbarton Oaks collection.[20] The first recorded *strategos* of Dubrovnik, Catacalon Clazomenites, was responsible for conducting imperial relations with the Dukljan Serbs. Writing in the late eleventh century, the disgruntled Byzantine provincial named Cecaumenus (ed. Litavrin: 170–2) reported that a certain 'Vojislav, the Dukljan, who was *toparch* of the *kastra* in Dalmatia, Zeta and Ston' recognized Byzantine authority, and maintained contacts with the imperial *strategos* in Dubrovnik, from whom he frequently received gifts. As the senior man in the region Catacalon was expected to take a role in the baptism of Vojislav's young son, presumably as the godfather, and thus arranged to meet the *toparch* at an assigned spot 'between their areas of jurisdiction', that is beyond the internal frontier. Then, in an act of treachery, Vojislav ambushed the *strategos* and his party, and took them bound to Ston. Scylitzes recounts a second episode involving Stefan Vojislav, whom he calls the *archon* (or *archegos* in certain recen-

---

[18] Scylitzes: 345, 350, 354–5, 358. See above at p. 66.
[19] *Alexiad*: ii, 166–7 (trans.: 276). See below at pp. 148–50.
[20] Nesbitt and Oikonomides 1991: i, 43–4.

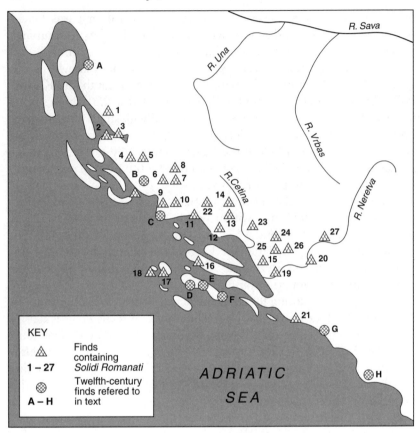

4.3 Findspots of *Solidi Romanati* and twelfth-century Byzantine coins in Dalmatia

sions of the text) of the Serbs. Vojislav seized ten *kentenaria* of Byzantine gold coins bound for the emperor in Thessalonica from a ship wrecked on 'the Illyrian coast', and ignored a letter from the emperor Michael IV demanding its return.[21] These episodes are fascinating for what they reveal about the interaction between the Byzantines and the Slavic *archontes*. The Byzantine *strategos* was the recognized superior, who would distribute gifts and supervise Christian offices in a manner similar to that performed by the emperor in Constantinople. His regular personal contact and gift-giving were essential for retaining the loyalty of the local ruler, and his participation in ceremonial was expected to forge lasting personal bonds. However, the emperor might intervene personally.

[21] Scylitzes: 408–9.

If the *archon* were willing and able to travel to Constantinople, the emperor might secure his loyalty in person.[22] Cecaumenus provides a full description of the ceremony of obeisance involving another important Dalmatian:

Dobronja (*Dobronas*), a wise and most worthy man, was the *archon* and *toparch* of the Dalmatian cities of Zadar and Salona [Split]. He travelled from there to make obeisance to (*proskyneo*) the blessed emperor, lord Romanus Argyrus, who honoured (*philotimeomai*) him with gifts and with honours (*timais*), and sent him back to his own lands with great wealth. Delighted by such favours he made a second journey, and was honoured again, although not so richly as the first time, before he returned. (Cecaumenus, ed. Litavrin: 300)

Remarkably, we can find confirmation of Romanus' policy to secure Dobronja's loyalty in the archaeological museums in Zagreb and Split, where gold coins discovered in the Dalmatian region of modern Croatia are kept (see fig. 4.3). In Zagreb there are just six *solidi* struck by Basil II and Constantine VIII (976–1028), but eighty-five for Romanus' six-year reign. In Split there are sixty-two *solidi romanati*, so-called after the emperor whose portrait they bear.[23] This is the 'great wealth' that the *toparch* took back to his lands, and seems to have financed a campaign of monumental building in Zadar.[24]

The ceremony of obeisance was a precondition for obtaining an imperial rank with an annual stipend. We are already familiar with such ceremonies involving 'barbarian' chieftains who received baptism before being invested with their honorific rank, generally becoming *patrikioi*. Dobronja was already baptized in the Latin rite, and had taken the name Gregory.[25] Moreover, we know from extant charters preserved in Zadar that he received the rank of *protospatharios* and the title *strategos* of all Dalmatia. Since the reign of Basil I (867–86) the maritime cities had paid a nominal sum annually to the *strategos* of Dalmatia as a token of their submission, although each city remained essentially autonomous. They also paid a more substantial tribute in gold, wine and other commodities to the neighbouring Slav *archontes*.[26] Dobronja's elevation to that office suggests that the practice had been revived, and as the leading man in Zadar he was granted *de iure* authority over the other maritime cities in Dalmatia Inferior. Charters issued during Dobronja's period of office are dated according to the year of the Byzantine emperor's reign,

---

[22] For imperial ceremonial involving dependent rulers see above at pp. 40–1, 53–4.
[23] Jakšić 1982: 173–84; Mirnik 1981: 31; Metcalf 1979: 176–9.   [24] Goss 1987: 48.
[25] Budak 1994: 39–40.   [26] *DAI*: 146.

Map Ref.	Location	Coin Types	References	Hoard/Stray
1-27	Various sites	*Solidi Romanati*	Metcalf 1960: 103; Mirnik 1980: 34-5; Jaksic 1982: 176-7	All Hoards?
A	Senj	*AE* (1) John II *Bn* (1), *El* (1) Manuel I *Bn* (1) Isaac II *Bn* (1) Alexius III	Matijašić 1983: 229	Hoard
B	Lepuri	*AR* (2000+) Coloman *AV* (Several) Romanus IV, Michael VII, Alexius I	Metcalf 1979: 189; Mirnik 1981: 94	Hoard
C	Rogoznica	*AR* (100s) Friesacher	Metcalf 1979: 182; Mirnik 1981: 101-2	Hoard
D	Korčula (x2)	*AV* (Several) Alexius I *AV* (4) Romanus IV Michael VII, Alexius I	Mirnik 1981: 94	Hoards (x2)
E	Korčula	*AE* (1) Manuel I *Bn* (Several) Andronicus I, Alexius III	Metcalf 1979: 182	Stray?
F	Majsan	*AE* (1) Alexius I *Bn* (1) Anon. 12th C.	Mirnik 1985: 87-96	Stray
G	Dubrovnik	*Bn* (102) Manuel I, Isaac II, Alexius III, Latin imitations	Sacher 1971: 219-20; Metcalf 1979: 193	Stray
H	Ulcinj	Various	Bošković 1965: 339	Stray

4.4 Table of *Solidi Romanati* and twelfth-century coins found in Dalmatia

reflecting his subordination (*douleia*).[27] However, subsequent events prove that the emperor had no *de facto* power in Dobronja's lands, and operated entirely through the native *strategos*.

A *sigillion* preserved in Dubrovnik demonstrates that Michael IV similarly granted imperial ranks and titles to Ljutovid, the Slav ruler of Zahumlje, in return for his obeisance and loyalty. The charter was issued by Ljutovid '*protospatharios epi tou Chrysotrikliniou, hypatos*, and *strategos* of Serbia and Zahumlje', and dated in the Byzantine fashion to 'the month of July in the seventh indiction'. The indiction was a fifteen-year period, which allows us to date the *sigillion* to July 1039.[28] We will see below that shortly after this Ljutovid received imperial gold and silver, and was placed in command of a force of Slavs who fought on behalf of the emperor against the Dukljan ruler, Stefan Vojislav. This charter contradicts the notion that a Byzantine theme of Serbia had been established. It clearly demonstrates that Byzantine authority was recognized the length of the Dalmatian coast and some way inland, but that power was exercised by the established Slavic *župans* whose people became subject-allies (*hypekoa*) of the emperor. (The term *hypekoa* is reminiscent of the *mixobarbaroi* we met in the previous chapter, for it is also an Attic Greek term used in the fifth century BC to describe non-Athenian Greeks who were bound to the Athenians by oaths and treaties.[29])

Some time between 1036 and 1041 a decision was taken to impose direct Byzantine rule in Zadar. The last charter issued by Dobronja (Gregory) is dated 13 February 1036. This is the *terminus post quem* for his third and final trip to Constantinople, recorded by Cecaumenus.

After the death of the aforementioned *basileus*, when the blessed emperor Michael the Paphlagonian ruled, Dobronja once again came to the City where he was received with contempt. When he asked permission to return [to his command] he was not deemed worthy of this, and thus aggrieved he began to complain. When they heard of his complaints the palace officials informed the emperor, and gave him the following advice: 'Since we have him in our hands, we will have control over his land without resistance'. And so it happened. They imprisoned him in the gaol of the *praitor* and thus without any trouble seized his land. His wife and son who had accompanied him were also led away to the *praitorion*, where they all remained imprisoned. Dobronja and his wife died in the *praitorion* during the reign of Constantine Monomachus. (Cecaumenus, ed. Litavrin: 302)

---

[27] *Codex Diplomaticus*: i, 66–70; Ferluga 1978: 205–6.   [28] Falkenhausen 1970: 10–23.
[29] Liddell et al. 1996: 1871–2, *hypekooi*, the opposite of *autonomoi*. For *mixobarbaroi* see above at pp. 109–10.

The dramatic change in imperial attitudes cannot be attributed solely to the vagaries of court gossip or the personalities of the emperors. Dobronja's imprisonment and the imposition of direct imperial rule in Zadar must be related to the situation in the western Balkans soon after the *toparch* issued his final extant charter. It was a period of general unrest which resulted in a reassessment of imperial policy in Bulgaria and beyond.

Between 1040 and 1042 four rebellions occurred in the various lands of the southern Slavs. The first was started by a certain Peter Deljan in Belgrade and Margum, *kastra* on the Danube from which Byzantine troops had been withdrawn some years before. The second was a direct result of the first, and involved the troops raised in the *thema* of Dyrrachium who were to be sent to fight Deljan. Instead, under their leader Tihomir (Teichomir), they joined Deljan. The third rebellion was also a response to Deljan's activities: a Bulgarian prince, Alusjan (Alusianus), observed his success with envy from Constantinople, and determined to seize control of the rebellion to further his own interests. He succeeded in dividing support for Deljan and, ultimately, replacing him at the head of the rebel army. The fourth rebellion was an entirely distinct affair which arose in Duklja under the aforementioned Stefan Vojislav.

In his account of Deljan's rebellion Scylitzes (409–11) makes much of Deljan's claim that he was the grandson of Samuel, and son of Gabriel Radomir. This lineage secured his acclamation as ruler of the Bulgarians.[30] News of his accession was spread far and wide as he pressed south through Dendra and Raška, and facilitated his entry into the Byzantine strongholds at Niš and Skopje. The *strategos* of Dyrrachium, Basil Synadenus, raised an army from the surrounding lands and marched out immediately to confront Deljan before the rebellion spread. However, the Byzantine position was undermined by one of Basil's subordinates, the *hypostrategos* of Debar, Michael Dermocaites, who complained falsely to the emperor of his commander's seditious behaviour. Basil was placed under arrest in Thessalonica, and Dermocaites took command of the conscripted army. However, he

---

[30] Cirac Estopañan 1965: 200, 401, fig. 531. Grabar and Manoussacas 1979: plate 39 and fig. 255 reproduce the illustration of Deljan's acclamation from the Madrid Scylitzes (fol. 215). He is shown being raised in the arms of several Bulgarians.

proved to be inept and lost the support of his men. Instead, they chose one of their own, 'a brave and wise man' named Tihomir, and determined to elect him as Bulgarian emperor. Thus Bulgaria was in turmoil with two pretenders to Samuel's title at the head of two armies. Deljan saw a further opportunity to augment his growing authority, and proposed an alliance if Tihomir brought his troops north. He then wrested control of the joint forces during a public meeting in Skopje, having himself acclaimed once again and the wretched Tihomir stoned to death.[31] Deljan immediately set out at the head of his mighty army for Thessalonica, where the sickly emperor had taken up residence within easy reach of the shrine of St Demetrius. Without gathering his possessions, the imperial tent, nor even his gold and robes, Michael IV fled back to Constantinople.

Deljan pressed on and captured Dyrrachium, Prespa and parts of northern Greece. He also secured the support of inhabitants of the *thema* of Nicopolis who had rebelled against a corrupt local tax collector. Cecaumenus (ed. Litavrin: 172–4) reveals that among Deljan's conquests was Demetrias, a town in the *thema* of Hellas where he installed as commander an 'aged and battle-hardened veteran' named Litovoj (Lutoboes) of Devol, who supervised repairs of the crumbling walls. Thus secure he indulged himself, not suspecting the locals whom he regarded as ignorant, and whom he had bound to himself with oaths. However, they sent word to the *doux* of Thessalonica who despatched aid by sea, overpowered Litovoj, and handed him over to the Byzantines. Meanwhile a threat to Deljan's authority in Bulgaria had emerged.

Psellus provides a full account of the activities of Alusjan, the grandson of Samuel's brother Aaron and son of John Vladislav, who had spent many years in Constantinople and the provinces in the service of the empire. However, when he learned of Deljan's rebellion, he set off for Bulgaria and 'approached certain individuals'.

He referred to his father in an impersonal way, as though he himself was a member of another family. He then spoke with pride of his father's ancestry, and made some tentative enquiries: if any of his sons turned up in the country, would the rebels choose the legitimate heir as their ruler, or the pretender? Or, now that the latter had already assumed the leadership, was the rightful heir completely forgotten? When it was obvious that the acknowledged son was universally preferred to the doubtful one, he ventured in a somewhat mysterious way to reveal his true identity . . . and little by little the story was spread abroad.

---

[31] Cirac Estopañan 1965: 200–1, 402, fig. 533; Grabar and Manoussacas 1979: fig. 256, reproduce the illustration from the Madrid Skylitzes (fol. 216) showing Tihomir being stoned.

The majority of the Bulgarians transferred their allegiance to him, the real heir, and the monarchy became a 'polyarchy' as some preferred this, and others that son, but both parties were anxious to maintain peace and they reconciled the two protagonists. Thereafter they lived on equal terms, with frequent meetings but mutual suspicion. (Psellus, *Chronographia*: i, 81–2; trans.: 113–16)

The episode recalls many of the details of Scylitzes' account of Deljan's rise to power, and his ephemeral arrangement with his rival Tihomir. We cannot tell how much of the information contained in the two accounts has been confused or conflated. However, we can identify themes central to both which deserve emphasis. First, there was a process of consultation involving important individuals in Bulgaria before each pretender secured support. Second, a prerequisite for securing this support was convincing the nobles of one's suitability to rule. Tihomir's claims, as a brave and wise veteran, were inadequate. Both Deljan and Alusjan claimed direct descent from Bulgarian tsars, and thus to be the legitimate heirs to Samuel's lands. Third, the process of election involved acclamation by the aforementioned nobles. Fourth, there was a concerted effort to make the legitimacy of the claim and of the election known far and wide by heralds sent through all the lands occupied by Samuel's subjects (not only the Byzantine district of Bulgaria). All of these measures were required to convince the Slavs to transfer their allegiance from the Byzantine emperor to a Bulgarian pretender.

Reconciled with Deljan, Alusjan led a force of 40,000 Bulgarians against Thessalonica.[32] After a brief siege the Byzantine commander in the city, the *patrikios* Constantine, rallied his forces and inflicted a crushing defeat on the attackers. Consequently, the relationship between the two Bulgarian leaders deteriorated. But unlike Tihomir, Alusjan came out on top; he had Deljan arrested, blinded, and his nose slit, thus rendering him ineligible to rule. The rebellion continued, but after a second defeat Alusjan reconsidered his position. He opened secret negotiations with the emperor, and accepted high honours in return for his submission. 'And as for his people, now torn asunder with war on all sides, and still without a leader . . . Michael again made them subject to the empire from which they had revolted.'[33]

The complete ineptitude in battle displayed by Alusjan, who had been the Byzantine *strategos* of Theodosiopolis, has raised suspicions about his motives and true intentions in 1040. Fine (1983: 206) has concluded that

---

[32] Scylitzes: 413; Cirac Estopañan 1965: 201, 402, fig. 535; Grabar and Manoussacas 1979: fig. 257.
[33] Psellus, *Chronographia*: i, 82 (trans.: 115).

he was a Byzantine agent throughout, whose only aim was to destroy the rebellion. The subsequent marriage of his daughter to the future emperor Romanus Diogenes demonstrates that if he had truly strayed, Alusjan had returned to the Byzantine fold with his position considerably improved by his adventures in Bulgaria.

The Priest of Duklja provides a fascinating account of a further, but quite distinct rebellion in Duklja by Vojislav, whom he calls Dobroslav:

Showing his wiles and ingenuity, Dobroslav [Vojislav] had subordinated himself to the Greeks [Byzantines] and rode with them through the provinces as an ally and comrade. He gave clandestine counsel to the Greeks so that they would treat the people harshly and unjustly. However, at the same time he was speaking to the people thus: 'How great is the injury you have suffered at the hands of the Greeks? They judge you unjustly and banish all that is good. They commit adultery with your wives, and they violate and rape your virginal daughters. My forefathers who were rulers before me never afflicted such evils upon you, so great and grave is their wickedness'. As he did this in each locality the people began to turn to him and desire him as passionately as they despised the Greeks. The people consulted among themselves and, exchanging messengers and messages, reached a common decision: on a certain day known to all they would rise up and kill every Greek noble that was found throughout the whole of Dalmatia. (*LPD*: 344–5)

There are clearly problems with the *LPD*, not least the attribution of the general uprising, 'throughout the whole of Dalmatia', to the Dukljan ruler 'Dobroslav'. However, much of the contextual detail rings true.[34] The account clearly implies that Byzantine authority throughout Dalmatia rested on the support of local *župans*. The accusations of rape and adultery should not be taken as evidence of a large military presence, and the 'Greek nobles' were the aforementioned Byzantine commanders and their officers operating out of Dyrrachium and Dubrovnik. They were neither so numerous nor so vigilant as to prevent the Slavs from convening public meetings, exchanging messengers, and meeting secretly with Vojislav. There are many parallels between this account and the general picture I have sought to paint, emphasizing the independence of action retained by the local Slav rulers, and the process of consultation with regional *župans* that was essential for decision-making.

Having dispensed with his recognition of the emperor's authority in his own lands, Vojislav set out to plunder and overrun the lands of other

[34] Ferluga 1980: 446–7.

imperial subjects and allies (*hypekoa*). His depredations provoked the wrath of the new emperor, Constantine IX Monomachus (1042–55), who ordered the *strategos* of Dyrrachium, Michael, *patrikios* and son of the Logothete Anastasius, to assemble his army, and also those of neighbouring *themata* and lands under his jurisdiction. His allies included the *župan* of Raška, the *ban* of Bosna and Ljutovid, the aforementioned ruler and appointed *strategos* of Zahumlje, who were recruited by imperial legates 'with piles of gold and silver'. The Priest of Duklja (*LPD*: 346–7) does not mention the *strategos* Michael, but attributes his actions to the *toparch* of Dyrrachium, Chryselius (Cursilius), a further representative of that city's leading family. We should not doubt that Chryselius accompanied Michael and the *hypostrategoi* at the head of the huge army which marched to confront Vojislav. The joint action is further evidence for the Byzantine dependence on local support, and of the continuing loyalty of Dyrrachium and the majority of highland magnates, notwithstanding the recalcitrance of the most powerful coastal *župan*.

The Dukljan ruler had no desire to engage the allied force, which was reputed to number 60,000. Therefore, he withdrew into the mountainous lands of southern Serbia, which Scylitzes, for once classicizing, calls '*Triballos*'.[35] Foolishly, the allied force followed him, marching two abreast through the long and narrow defiles into Vojislav's ambush. The Priest of Duklja provides a wonderful account of the Dukljan's clever ploy and victory. 'Summoning his five sons, Vojislav addressed them thus':

Behold, my dearest sons, how great is the army of the Greeks, and how few we are in comparison. We would achieve nothing by resisting them in battle, so we should act in the following manner. Two of you, Goyslav and Radoslav, should remain here, while you other three should take ten strong men with trumpets and horns, climb into the mountains and disperse yourselves through the lofty peaks until the Greeks seem to be encircled. My companions and I will charge into their camp in the middle of the night. When you hear our horns and trumpets you should at the same time blare forth with your own, and shriek at the tops of your voices from the surrounding ridges. Shortly afterwards, you should sweep down towards their camps, and as you approach be not afraid, for God will deliver them into our hands. (*LPD*: 348)

A double agent was then installed in the Byzantine camp, who forewarned the commander of an attack by a huge army. Thus, when they heard the trumpets from all sides they panicked and began to bolt. 'As

---

[35] Scylitzes: 424; Cirac Estopañan 1965: 206, 407, fig. 550; Grabar and Manoussacas 1979: fig. 264.

dawn approached Vojislav and his followers saw the Greeks in flight, and flooded into their camp, mutilating, slaying and slaughtering them from behind as they chased them down.' Vojislav followed up his victory by invading Zahumlje, annexing Ljutovid's territory and 'capturing all the lands of Dyrrachium as far as the river Vjossa'.[36] Fortunately for the emperor, Vojislav died shortly after this, in 1043, sparking a bitter struggle between his sons, and we will return to this shortly.

BULGARIA, 1043–1071

The general unrest in the western Balkans at this time has been attributed to changes in Byzantine policy. Much attention has been drawn to a decision by Michael IV's brother and chief minister, John the Orphanotrophus, to reverse Basil II's policy allowing the Bulgarians to pay their taxes in kind rather than cash.[37] This has been adjudged arbitrary and grasping by scholars persuaded by Scylitzes' characterization of the Orphanotrophus. Certainly, taxation was an issue in the Byzantine administrative district of Nicopolis, which bordered Bulgaria and Dyrrachium: Scylitzes expressly attributes the unrest of locals in that region to the oppression they endured at the hands of a corrupt local tax collector. Such corruption, the chronicler opines, was endemic under Michael IV because John the Orphanotrophus had sold the rights to raise provincial taxes. However, there is no evidence that similar frustrations caused the four rebellions. Indeed, there is stronger evidence against this interpretation: Psellus (*Chronographia*: i, 78; trans.: 109) states expressly that 'there were no immediate signs of open revolt' in Bulgaria before the appearance of Deljan. Moreover, Deljan's revolt gained momentum in the lands between Belgrade and Niš, where taxation was not raised, either in cash or kind; the same can be said of Vojislav's lands.

The Orphanotrophus' decision to raise taxes in cash was an element in a wider project to put Bulgaria on the same footing as other *themata*. Payments in kind had been useful for supporting a field army, and could be collected and dispersed by the local military commander. The withdrawal of troops from many watchtowers, and the greater reliance on local magnates who demanded cash stipends made this system impracticable. Moreover, after twenty years of Byzantine rule the administrative district of Bulgaria would have had access to regular supplies of coin

[36] *LPD*: 353.
[37] Ostrogorsky 1968: 325; Obolensky 1971: 277; Fine 1983: 203; Cheynet 1990: 388; Angold 1997: 32; Treadgold 1997: 588. Most recently and cautiously, Mullett 1997: 57–8.

from the mints at both Constantinople and Thessalonica. However, the most pressing need at this time was to find a solution to the Pecheneg crisis that we considered in the previous chapter (at pp. 84–9), and it is in this context that we must interpret the Orphanotrophus' actions. First, the need to direct large sums of cash to the lower Danube to support the payment of *philotimiai* to the locals, and to facilitate the exchange process that promoted trading over raiding, required that large numbers of coins were available immediately. The decision to sell taxation rights to individuals, that is to institute tax farming, would recoup much bullion for the imperial treasury quickly. Selling rights to taxation revenues in Bulgaria was a straightforward, and rather cynical, attempt to extend the tax base, enticing unscrupulous entrepreneurs to part with coin in advance. The Orphanotrophus passed on the difficulties of raising levies in cash rather than kind to the tax farmers, and must have been aware of the potential for corruption and extortion his policy entailed. However, it may have been justifiable if he had thereby devised a means to exploit the increasing wealth of the empire and to direct the resources to political ends. Since there is no evidence that the new policy contributed directly to any of the rebellions in the western Balkans between 1040 and 1042, and since the subsidized trading system at the lower Danube, despite major setbacks between 1048 and 1053, continued to function through the eleventh century and into the twelfth, we might even consider the move to have been justified, even if it earned him the approbation of Scylitzes (and his continuator).[38]

The decision taken shortly after this by Constantine IX to debase the imperial gold coinage, allowing more *solidi* to be struck from the same quantity of bullion, was also intended to supply greater quantities of ready cash.[39] Some time afterwards, probably by 1060, the financial administration of Bulgaria fell to a certain Constantine, *patrikios*, *anthypatos* and *vestes*, the *logariastes* and *anagrapheus* of all Bulgaria (*pases Boulgarias*).[40] The geographical scope of his authority (which may have reached as far as the Danube) and multiple titles suggest that

---

[38] Scylitzes Continuatus: 162, states bluntly that the Bulgarians rebelled against the 'insatiate greed' (*aplestia*) of the Orphanotrophus (see below at p. 142). It is quite probable that Scylitzes was his own continuator (*ODB*: iii, 1914). On the imperial cash crisis and the attempts to extend or reform the tax base, see now the interpretation advanced by Oikonomides 1997: 199–215.

[39] Morrisson 1976: 6–7.

[40] For seals see Laurent 1962: 94–6; Nesbitt and Oikonomides 1991: i, 93–4; Szemioth and Wasilewski 1969: ii, 35; Zacos 1984: ii, nr. 422. For the date see Oikonomides 1976: 140, 148–9; Ahrweiler 1966: 272–3. However, Guilland 1969: 104 maintains that this Constantine should be associated with the *logariastes* mentioned in two bulls issued by Alexius I in 1084 and 1089, now preserved at Athos.

Constantine was responsible for the correct measurement of lands to be taxed, the setting of taxation rates, the sale of tax-raising authority to private individuals, and overseeing the activities of tax farmers, or *praktores* in all the Bulgarian lands. The appointment of such an individual demonstrates how far the fiscalization and privatization of taxation had progressed in lands which now lay squarely within the internal frontier.

After twenty years on a military footing, where civil matters were subsumed within the military, and the *strategos autokrator* of Bulgaria in Skopje had ultimate responsibility for both, a distinct civilian administration was introduced. After 1042 an official known as the *pronoetes* of (all) Bulgaria was installed in Skopje.[41] The first known *pronoetes*, the eunuch and monk Basil, even took command of the Bulgarian expeditionary force sent against the Pechenegs in 1048.[42] Subsequently a civilian administrator known as the *praitor* operated alongside the *doux* of Bulgaria. The *praitor* John Triacontaphyllus held the elevated rank of *protoproedros*, which was introduced *c.* 1060[43], and he may well have been a contemporary of Gregory, *protoproedros* and *doux* of Bulgaria.[44] Other eleventh-century *doukes* of Bulgaria include Nicephorus Vatatzes *proedros* and Nicetas Carices.[45] There is also an unpublished seal in the Ashmolean Museum in Oxford which was struck by a certain Andronicus Philocales, *vestarches* and *katepano*, perhaps during his tenure as *katepano* of Bulgaria from *c.* 1065.[46] Subsequently military commanders were known as *doukes* of Skopje. The first man known to have held that title is Nicephorus Carantenus, followed soon afterwards by Alexander Cabasilas.[47]

The ecclesiastical administration of Bulgaria was also brought closer to Constantinople. Although the archbishop of Bulgaria was still not subject to the patriarch of Constantinople, a *Rhomaios* was installed for the first time in Ohrid; Archbishop Leo (1037–56) had been *chartophylax* of the Great Church, that is archivist and principal assistant to the

---

[41] The exact meaning of *pronoetes* in this context is unclear. For suggestions see *ODB*: iii, 1733; Oikonomides 1976: 149–50.

[42] Cecaumenus, ed. Litavrin: 164.20–1 for Basil the *protonoetes Boulgaron*; Attaleiates: 37 calls Basil the *satrapes* of Bulgaria. See also Schlumberger 1884: 740–1 for a seal of the *protonoetes pases Boulgarias*; Ahrweiler 1960: 85–6, n. 13. For the Pecheneg encounter see above at p. 92.

[43] Oikonomides 1976: 126; *ODB*: iii, 1727.　　[44] Nesbitt and Oikonomides 1991: i, 94–5.

[45] Nesbitt and Oikonomides 1991: i, 94.

[46] Cecaumenus, ed. Litavrin: 264.17–18; Bănescu 1946: 144. The seal is nr. 32 on Marlia Mundell Mango's unpublished catalogue, and I am grateful to her for providing me with a copy.

[47] Scylitzes Continuatus: 163, 185. Nesbitt and Oikonomides 1991: i, 98 are wrong to suggest that John Taroneites is the first known *doux* of Skopje.

patriarch, and was remembered in an extant list of Bulgarian archbishops as the founder of the Church of Holy Wisdom, St Sophia in Ohrid.[48] The reference is to Leo's rebuilding the cathedral church as a domed basilica modelled on the Great Church in Constantinople with elaborate fresco decoration executed by painters from the imperial capital.[49] It has been suggested that 'the program of decoration provides an explicit statement of the imperial agenda for the newly reintegrated province' (Wharton 1988: 106). This seems accurate insofar as the imperial agenda was to embrace the vitality of Bulgarian Christianity within the universal Orthodox Church without imposing direct rule from Constantinople. The ecclesiastical development stood in stark contrast to the ruins of fortifications at Ohrid razed by Basil II, which Scylitzes Continuatus (164) noted were still 'a pile of ruins' (*ereipion*) in 1073.[50] In the same vein new congregational basilica churches were constructed in Servia and Veria, both decorated with Christological narrative pictoral sequences.[51]

DUKLJA, 1043–1071

The *LPD* (354–6) provides our only account of the struggles which followed the death of Stefan Vojislav in *c.* 1043. His five sons each received a region to rule: 'Goyslav [the eldest] and Predimir, his youngest brother, received Travunija and Gri(s)puli; Michael [received] Oblik ([*mons*] *Obliquus*, [Montenegro]), Prapatn(ic)a and Cermenica; Saganek [received] the *župania* of Gorsca, Cupelnik and Barezi; and Radoslav [received] the *župania* of Lu[s]ca, and Cuccevi [with] Budva.'[52] The geographical range of Vojislav's authority at the time of his death is thus neatly delimited, and we can see that it was far less extensive than that attributed to the mythical King Predimir, encompassing only the *županias* of Duklja (including Zeta) and Travunija, but not those of Zahumlje or Podgorica (*Submontana*).[53] Moreover, his powerbase was in Duklja, and the threat to his sons came swiftly from Travunija.

While Goyslav was lying ill in bed men came from Travunija ostensibly to consult with him, but instead murdered him and his brother

[48] Gelzer 1902: 6. Subsequent archbishops were Theodoulus (1056–65), John Lampenus (1065– ?), John (*c.* 1075), and Theophylact Hephaistus (*c.* 1090– ?).   [49] Wharton 1988: 105–6.
[50] For an archaeological approach to what is now called 'Samuel's Fortress', see Mikulčić 1996: 240–6.   [51] Wharton 1988: 111–12.
[52] *LPD*: 354–5. The place-names have been amended to be consistent with earlier use, although the eleventh-century spelling may have been as changeable as in the sixteenth-century redaction.
[53] *LPD*: 326–7, and see above at pp. 120–2 for comparison.

Predimir. They then set up their own leader, Domanek, as ruler of Travunija. The three remaining brothers led an army into Travunija, captured the murderers and put them to death 'most horribly'. However, Domanek escaped, and was later able to return. There was clearly resistance to Dukljan rule in Travunija, and Saganek, who had remained in the region 'took fright, and returned to Zeta and his own *županias*'. Similarly, Radoslav refused to leave his own lands, until Michael and Saganek both promised to hand over their lands in Zeta for him to rule along with Travunija if he should triumph there. 'In return Radoslav gathered a host and set off to attack Travunija. He made war on Domanek, overcame and killed him. Then he invaded the region of Zahumlje and captured it.' While this was taking place the queen died and Michael 'acceded to the kingdom' (*accepti regnum*). 'Because he had seven sons he did not wish to carry out his promise to his brother Radoslav, and instead he took from him the *župania* of Zeta and gave it to his [eldest] son Vladimir.'[54]

There are several interesting facts embedded in this abbreviated narrative. First, the rich coastal lands of Zeta west of Lake Skodra were clearly considered the greatest prize by Vojislav's sons. The other lands of Duklja are scarcely mentioned, although this may have more to do with the fact that Bar is within Zeta, and by the time the *LPD* was written the name Zeta had replaced Duklja as the name of the region. Second, the decision to cede lands in Zeta to Radoslav was not taken by the brothers alone, but in a council of magnates summoned from throughout Duklja. This reminds us that the lands were still controlled by *župans* whose loyalty to the princely family needed to be ensured. Third, we are told that neither Michael nor Saganek marched against Travunija because 'they were scared that the Greeks, who were preparing an invasion, would attack their lands'. There is no mention of such a plan in the Greek sources, but we do have a single reference in Scylitzes to an agreement whereby Michael promised that the '*Triballoi* and Serbs . . . would be allies and friends of the Romans', and in return was honoured with the rank *protospatharios*.[55] The dating of this reference is difficult, as it suggests that Vojislav was still alive and Michael was ruling jointly with him, directly contradicting the testimony of the *LPD*. Moreover, it appears in the context of the Pecheneg wars immediately before the conflict and treaty of 1053 (see above at pp. 89–93). The most plausible solution is that Vojislav had died by 1053, but Scylitzes (if he knew) did not record

---

[54] *LPD*: 356–7.   [55] Scylitzes: 475.

it, and we can place both the Dukljan invasion of Travunija and the death of Michael's mother to between 1046 and 1053.

According to the *LPD* (355) Michael and his brothers all held the title 'prince' (*knesisus* in Latin, from the Slavonic *knez*) until the death of their mother. Thereafter, Michael is referred to as 'king' (Latin: *rex*, the Slavonic equivalent is *kralj*), as Vojislav had been before him. However, there is no indication that Michael was regarded as a king in Duklja by the Byzantines; nor is there any confirmation in Greek sources for the claim advanced in the *LPD* (357) that Michael took a Greek wife, a relative of the emperor Constantine IX, by whom he had four sons, two of whom were given Greek names (Nicephorus and Theodore).[56] It is possible, since no Greek source mentions a second treaty, that the marriage sealed the agreement we have already discussed, when Michael was given the rank of *protospatharios*. However, *protospatharios* seems a very lowly rank for such an important regional magnate – such men, as we have seen, were most often made *patrikioi* – and it seems inconceivable that a *protospatharios* would marry the emperor's niece. Therefore, we might conclude that a second treaty was negotiated after the death of Michael's first wife, which saw him receive an imperial bride and a more senior rank in the imperial hierarchy, both of which have gone unrecorded in Greek sources. Perhaps in the light of Dukljan recalcitrance in the 1070s and 1080s such information was suppressed and Michael's elevated status concealed.[57]

Without doubt his marriage to a Byzantine woman, and his receipt of an imperial court title had augmented Michael's prestige among his peers. However, his major advantage was that with his two wives he had produced eleven sons, each of whom could be expected to consolidate his father's authority in a given region, and extend it into neighbouring territories by force of arms. But producing so many sons also produced competing demands for lands which could not easily be satisfied from within the patrimony (Duklja) and recently conquered lands (Travunija and Zahumlje). A lacuna in the *LPD* deprives us of detail for much of Michael's reign, but we are informed that at an unspecified time: 'Bodin, who [afterwards] ruled the whole kingdom, Vladimir and their brothers marched into Raška and annexed it.'[58] Petrislav, the second of his sons

---

[56] *LPD*: 357; Ferluga 1980: 453.

[57] A similar marriage alliance was sealed in 1046 with Iaroslav of Kiev, in the aftermath of the Russian attack on Constantinople in 1043. See Franklin and Shepard 1996: 215; Dölger 1925: ii, nr. 875; Dölger, ed. Wirth 1977: ii, 21, nr. 879a.

[58] *LPD*: 357. Šišić, the editor of the text, interpolated 'afterwards' (*postea*), and quite correctly noted that the emphasis placed on Bodin reflects his later importance. At the time of the annexation of Raška, whenever that was, Bodin was the youngest of Michael's sons by his first wife.

by his second wife, was granted authority over Raška, and we might consider this an attempt by Michael to satisfy the demands of his second family with lands acquired by conquest, while the older sons retained Duklja, Travunija and Zahumlje. Similar demands seem to have driven the opportunistic invasion of Bulgaria by Dukljan troops.

TURMOIL IN THE WESTERN BALKANS AFTER 1071

After the Byzantine defeats at Bari and Mantzikert in 1071 imperial authority was challenged throughout the empire and from beyond the frontiers. The *Hungarian Chronicle* (369–77) relates how Belgrade came under attack from the Hungarian King Salomon, where the Bulgarian and Greek defenders used 'Greek fire' to set light to the Magyars' ships. To deflect a second assault they appealed to the Pechenegs (*Bisseni*), upon whom the Magyars inflicted great slaughter. The besieged city fell after three months, and many of the inhabitants were put to the sword before Salomon, and the dukes Géza and Ladislas marched on to Niš, seizing much plunder *en route*. The situation was resolved by negotiation soon thereafter, but it seems probable that Salomon was allowed to keep the former Byzantine outpost of Sirmium (modern Sremska Mitrovica), which sat on the northern bank of the Sava, opposite the residence of the bishop of Sirmium (at Mačvanska Mitrovica).[59] The invasion was the first of a series of crises at Byzantium's Balkan frontier, as Nicephorus Bryennius relates:

The emperor Michael [VII, 1071–8] was afflicted by a myriad troubles: the Scythians overran Thrace and Macedonia, and the Slavic people threw off the Roman yoke and laid waste Bulgaria taking plunder and leaving scorched earth. Skopje and Niš were sacked, and all the towns around the river Sava and beside the Danube between Sirmium and Vidin suffered greatly. Furthermore, the Croats and Dukljans throughout the whole of Dalmatia rose in rebellion. (Bryennius: 211)

Scylitzes Continuatus considered the catalyst for these troubles to have been the 'insatiate greed' (*aplestia*) of Nicephoritzes, whose efforts to recoup currency we considered in addressing the 'Scythian' menace (see above at pp. 98–100). Offering a potted history of Bulgaria since 1018, he compares Nicephoritzes' behaviour with that of John the Orphanotrophus, condemned so vigorously by Scylitzes – hardly surprising if, as is probable, Scylitzes was his own continuator – and contrasts the actions of both with Basil II's careful hands-off approach.[60]

---

[59] We will return to this below at pp. 188–9.   [60] Scylitzes Continuatus: 162–3.

Scylitzes Continuatus also provides an explanation for why the revolt
spread so rapidly: Michael of Duklja, we are told, was approached by
Bulgarian chieftains (*proechontes*) intent on rebellion, who demanded that
he despatch a son whom they might acclaim as emperor of Bulgaria 'to
deliver them from the oppression and exactions of the Romans'
(Scylitzes Continuatus: 163). Michael gladly sent his son Constantine
Bodin with three hundred troops to Prizren, where they were met by the
magnates and the ruler (*exarchos*) of Skopje, George Vojteh, who
acclaimed Constantine Bodin 'as emperor of the Bulgarians and gave
him the new name Peter'. Consequently, the *doux* of Skopje, Nicephorus
Carantenus, marched on Prizren with an allied force of Romans and
Bulgarians. However, before battle was engaged Carantenus was
replaced by a certain Damian Dalassenus, who destroyed the morale of
his troops with taunts and insults before sending them into a bloody rout
at the Serbs' hands. Consequently, the rest of the Bulgarians recognized
Bodin as their emperor, and acclaimed him by his new name, Peter.
They then divided into groups, the first of which accompanied Bodin-
Peter to Niš, while the latter followed his second-in-command, Petrilus,
to Kastoria via Ohrid.

Ohrid was ceded to Petrilus without a fight, for its walls still lay in
ruins. The *strategos* of Ohrid, Marianus, was by that stage holed up in
Kastoria with the *strategos* of Devol, the *patrikios* and *anthypatos*
Theognostus Bourtzes. However, the commander of Kastoria was a Slav
named Boris David, and he was without doubt in command of the
Bulgarian contingent of the allied force which launched a violent attack
on Petrilus, forcing him to flee home 'through inaccessible mountains'
(Scylitzes Continuatus: 164). Meanwhile, Bodin-Peter had set himself to
plundering lands around Niš and abusing his 'subjects'. Vojteh's opportunism in approaching the Dukljans had thus been turned against him,
for the new 'Bulgarian emperor' was greedier than Michael VII.
Moreover, when a Byzantine army led by a certain Saronites marched
on Skopje, Bodin-Peter showed no concern, obliging Vojteh to surrender without offering resistance. A garrison was installed in Skopje while
Saronites turned his attention to Niš. Subsequently, Bodin-Peter was
captured and despatched to Constantinople, and from there to Antioch
where he resided for several years.[61] Hearing of his son's capture,
Michael sent a further army under Longobardopoulos, a Byzantine
general whom he had only recently taken captive and married to one of

---

[61] *LPD*: 358.

his daughters. Longobardopoulos defected swiftly to the Byzantines, and to mark their victory the German and Varangian mercenaries in imperial service plundered the lands around Prespa.[62]

Scylitzes Continuatus' account shows many parallels with Scylitzes' treatment of the Slavic rebellions between 1040 and 1042. While we might refute his suggested catalyst for both uprisings – a eunuch chief minister's 'insatiate greed' – other factors are common to both episodes. First, Vojteh's revolt demonstrates the fragmented nature of political authority in Bulgaria. The burden of taxation caused particular offence to the local leadership in lands around Skopje, at the northern limits of direct Byzantine administration where Deljan had initially found his supporters. Such sentiments were not necessarily shared by other Bulgarians, for example those who fought alongside the Byzantine troops against Bodin, and only joined the rebellion in defeat as a consequence of Dalassenus' appalling generalship. Similarly, Kastoria was defended by both Byzantines and Bulgarians under a Bulgarian general.[63] Second, there was a process of consultation involving important individuals (*proechontes*) in Bulgaria before the standard of rebellion was raised, as there had been before each of the revolts between 1040 and 1042. Third, Bodin (like both Deljan and Alusjan) was considered suitable not only by virtue of his lineage, but also (like Tihomir) on account of his martial prowess which he demonstrated at Prizren. Fourth, Constantine Bodin's taking the name Peter was clearly intended to signify his succession to the former tsar; Peter was clearly an 'imperial name' in Bulgaria, whereas his Greek name Constantine, which had peculiar imperial resonance in Byzantium, was unacceptable. Fifth, the process of election involved acclamation by various Bulgarian nobles, and subsequently a second 'popular' acclamation by troops.

To some extent, therefore, we can establish the anatomy of a Slavic rebellion against Byzantine authority without recourse to the notion that all peoples west of the river Vardar shared a common 'ethnic consciousness' (*to sympan ethnos*) and were implacably opposed to Byzantine (Greek) rule. The self-interest of numerous magnates had to be considered, and many would serve a Byzantine master as willingly as a Bulgarian. However, it is also clear that the principal means to galvanize popular support for a secessionist movement was to appeal to the

---

[62] Scylitzes Continuatus: 165–6.
[63] Fine 1983: 214 also notes this and suggests 'other ties were at times stronger than ethnic ones'.

common memory of an independent ruler of the northern Balkans, whose authority resided in the title 'emperor of the Bulgarians'.[64]

THE BYZANTINE RECOVERY

The various Serbian defeats by Byzantine forces seem to have led to a period of instability in Duklja. The *LPD* (358) states that 'Bodin's remaining brothers rode hither and thither throughout their provinces fighting many battles, and because their father had provoked God's wrath by his sinful oath-breaking, they all died in battle while he was still alive'. It later becomes clear that this means the six elder sons of Michael's first marriage. Therefore, Michael sought other means to guarantee his control over Duklja and the neighbouring regions, and in 1077 turned to Pope Gregory VII. Already, in October 1075, Gregory had despatched a legate to convene a synod in Split, who proceeded to crown a certain Zvonimir as king of Croatia in return for his oath of fealty. Such papal intervention cut across any claims the Byzantine emperor advanced to suzerainty over the Church in Dalmatia and over the 'baptized Croats'.[65] It has also been suggested that Gregory was acting as a powerbroker in relations between the Croats and Venice, and we will return to Venetian interest in this area in later chapters.[66] As such the emperor in Constantinople had much to fear from the extension of papal influence across the Adriatic, and would have been even more disturbed by Gregory VII's despatching a crown to Michael of Duklja, whom he addressed thereafter as 'king of the Slavs'. Thus, a letter dated 9 January 1078 begins 'Gregory, slave of the slaves of God, to Michael, king of the Slavs (*Sclavorum regi*), greetings and apostolic benedictions'. The document is concerned with the disputes over ecclesiastical jurisdiction between Split and Dubrovnik, and incidentally proves that at this time Bar was still a simple bishopric (*Antibarensem episcopuum*), and not an archiepiscopal see.[67] (Subsequently in 1089, and perhaps as a consequence of the bishop of Bar's role as mediator between the two archdioceses and his personal contacts with the pope, Bar became an archbishopric.[68])

Soon after his coronation by Gregory VII's legate, Michael sought a wife for his son Bodin, now returned from Antioch. He chose Jaquinta

[64] In general see Tăpkova-Zaimova 1971: 289–95.
[65] *Codex Diplomaticus*: i, 139–41; *Historia Salonitana*: 55. For nominal Byzantine suzerainty see above at p. 29.   [66] Mandić 1973: 453–71.
[67] *Codex Diplomaticus*: i, 158–9.   [68] *Acta et diplomata res Albaniae*: 21.

(Jakvinta), the daughter of the Norman governor of Bari. The *Annales Barenses* state that this marriage took place in April 1081, although it could have taken place at any time after 1078.[69] The Dukljan-Norman alliance would have appeared ominous in Constantinople, since Byzantine relations with the Normans had recently soured (as we will see below at pp. 159–60). Much, therefore, depended on the Byzantine commanders in the western Balkans. However, at the same time relations between centre and periphery had broken down and several provincial commanders staged rebellions. The first was Nicephorus Bryennius – the grandfather of the aforementioned author with the same name – who had in *c.* 1074 been appointed as *doux* of the whole of Bulgaria. Bryennius had achieved significant early successes, and was transferred to the command of Dyrrachium. However, his success won him enemies in the capital, and in 1077 agents were sent out to investigate allegations that he was plotting to rebel. We can hardly trust his grandson's protestations of his innocence, but if he had been contemplating a coup Bryennius was pre-empted. While the investigation was taking place Michael VII was displaced by Nicephorus III Botaneiates (1078–81). The *doux* was stung into a vigorous counter-offensive, and 'using the city of Dyrrachium as his base he overran and subdued all of the western provinces'.[70] The task of putting down this latest revolt was entrusted to the young Domestic of the Schools Alexius Comnenus. The man appointed to replace Bryennius in Dyrrachium was a certain Nicephorus Basilaces, the next general to launch a concerted bid for the throne. Anna Comnena describes his advance:

The man was masterful, arrogating to himself the highest offices of state; some titles he coveted, others he usurped. When Bryennius was removed he became master of the whole revolutionary movement as his successor. He started from Dyrrachium (the capital of Illyria) and came as far as the chief city of Thessaly, crushing all opposition on the way and having himself elected and proclaimed emperor. (*Alexiad*: i, 28–9; trans.: 46–7)

Alexius Comnenus once again was charged with confronting a pretender, and once again was successful. He was soon strong enough to contemplate launching his own bid for the throne. Meanwhile, the emperor Nicephorus Botaneiates had appointed a new *doux* of Dyrrachium, George Monomachatus. Following an interview with the emperor, Monomachatus was furnished 'with written instructions with

---

[69] *Annales Barenses*: 60; *LPD*: 360; Ferluga 1980: 455.   [70] Bryennius: 215.

regard to his ducal office'.[71] This fascinating insight confirms that a confidential dossier existed which outlined the principal duties of the provincial commander. This would be all the more essential when it was not possible for the departing commander to brief his replacement.

Anna Comnena (*Alexiad*: i, 60; trans.: 72) condemned Monomachatus for exchanging letters with 'Bodin and Michael, the rulers of the Dalmatians', and despatching gifts to them 'to influence their judgement and thereby open up for himself by underhand means all kinds of doors'. In fact, as we have seen (above at pp. 125–30) the exchange of letters and gifts with the Slavic rulers was a fundamental duty of the *doux*, and Anna's description of Monomachatus' 'underhand' activity could have been applied to any number of his predecessors. Her hostility is a reflection of her father's when Monomachatus professed his loyalty to Botaneiates, and refused to support Alexius' coup of 1081. Thereafter Alexius was confronted with an entirely new threat, in the form of an invasion of Dyrrachium by Robert Guiscard, and was concerned with maintaining his suzerainty over the Serbs in the face of Norman competition. Therefore, he sent his brother-in-law George Palaeologus 'with instructions to drive Monomachatus from that place without bloodshed . . . and counteract the machinations of Robert as best he could' (*Alexiad*: i, 132; trans.: 126). A seal has survived which perhaps accompanied one of George's many despatches to the emperor, and attests to his promotion to the esteemed rank of *kouropalates* during his period of office at Dyrrachium.[72]

Faced with a Norman siege, Palaeologus was advised to reduce his opponents by skirmishing, to prevent them from foraging, and to ensure that the same policy was pursued by 'Bodin and the Dalmatians, and the other rulers (*archegois*) of the surrounding lands' (*Alexiad*: i, 155; trans.: 144). However, all was risked on a pitched battle, and there the loyalty of the Dukljans could not be guaranteed. According to Anna:

Bodin had put on armour and had drawn up his troops in battle array; throughout the day he stood by, apparently ready to help the emperor at any minute in accordance with their agreements. Really it seems he was watching anxiously to discover whether victory was going to the emperor; if it did he would join in attacking the Normans; if Alexius lost he would quietly beat a retreat. From his actions it is clear that this was his plan, for when he realized that the Normans were certain of victory, he ran off home without striking a single blow. (*Alexiad*: i, 162; trans.: 149)

---

[71] *Alexiad*: i, 58 (trans.: 70).
[72] Nesbitt and Oikonomides 1991: i, 41. For George's many letters to Alexius, see *Alexiad*: i, 143–5 (trans.: 135–8).

Such was the careful policy of 'wait and see' adopted by Bodin throughout the Byzantine-Norman war in the western Balkans. Despite Anna's accusatory tone, it is difficult to see why he should have acted otherwise: given that the empire had changed hands several times in recent years, demonstrating loyalty to an individual emperor might quickly be seen as having resisted his successor. Moreover, as we will see in the following chapter, Robert Guiscard had brought a man he claimed was the former emperor Michael Ducas, whose presence persuaded many of the locals to support his cause against Alexius Comnenus. Therefore, Bodin withdrew and played little further role in the conflicts, but used the preoccupations of others to consolidate his authority in Duklja, and restore Dukljan interests in neighbouring Slavic lands.

At the time of the Norman invasion of Dyrrachium, probably in the second part of 1081, Michael of Duklja had died, leaving Bodin as his successor. However, according to the *LPD* (359) Bodin's right to rule all his father's lands had been challenged by his uncle Radoslav, whom Michael had deprived of his lands in Zeta. Although the Priest of Duklja claims Radoslav succeeded and ruled Zeta for sixteen years, Fine (1983: 221) has suggested that we might interpret this as an instance of Zetan prejudice in the chronicle and regard Radoslav and his eight sons as rulers of the various *županias* around Bar. Thus, when 'after he obtained the kingdom, Bodin set about attacking his cousins', the bishop of Bar – wrongly, but deliberately called archbishop in the *LPD* – mediated between the two factions and negotiated a settlement. In this way, with his suzerainty recognized in Zeta, Bodin was free to turn his attention to Raška and Bosna, which no longer recognized Dukljan authority. Bodin invaded Raška 'with his [step-]brothers, secured and possessed it by waging war, and established there two *župans* from his court, Belcan [Bolkan] and Mark'. And in Bosna he established a certain Stephen as 'prince' (*knesius*). It is also claimed that Bodin 'secured his authority over the whole territory of Dyrrachium and the city of Dyrrachium itself, both of which had previously been under Frankish [Norman] dominion. However, he subsequently made peace with the emperor and returned the city to him' (*LPD*: 361). We will see below that Anna Comnena offers a different, more credible, account of the fate of Dyrrachium, but nevertheless should regard the troubles in that region as the context for the consolidation of Bodin's authority (see below at pp. 166–71).

In subsequent years Bodin proved to be a thorn in Alexius' side, as did

Bolkan his *župan* in Raška (although we hear no more of Mark).[73] Anna
Comnena makes passing references to the ongoing skirmishes at and
across the border between 'Romania' and 'Dalmatia', which we can
translate as Byzantine Bulgaria and Serbia. She describes Bodin as 'a
combative and thoroughly unprincipled rascal who refused to stay
within his own borders (*ton idion horion*) and made daily attacks on the
cities nearest Dalmatia' (*Alexiad*: ii, 115; trans.: 237). The *LPD* (362–3)
reveals that the main prize seized by Bodin was Dubrovnik, which previously was held with the emperor's blessing by Branislav, a son of
Bodin's uncle Radoslav. In defeat Branislav, his brother Gradislav, and
his eldest son Predichna were all beheaded. Branislav's other brothers
and sons fled to Constantinople via Split and Apulia, where they were
received by the emperor. Bolkan seems also to have raided Byzantine
lands, probably seizing the border fortresses between Skopje and Niš.
The Byzantine counter-offensive was led by the *doux* of Dyrrachium,
John Ducas, 'who recovered many of the watchtowers (*phrouria*) which
Bolkan had seized, and took many Dalmatian prisoners' (*Alexiad*: ii, 115;
trans.: 237). It is also stated that he captured Bodin, but this is not mentioned in the *LPD*, and if it were the case he was swiftly released since
he reappears planning to violate a treaty and invade Byzantine lands
shortly after spring 1092.[74] At this time the new Byzantine commander
of Dyrrachium, John Comnenus, was suspected of conspiring with the
Serbs against the emperor, and although the matter was resolved, in the
following year Bolkan 'crossed his own frontiers (*ton idion horion*) and
ravaged the neighbouring towns and districts. He even got as far as
Lipljan, which he deliberately burnt down'.

The emperor was informed of his actions and decided that he must be pun-
ished. Collecting a strong army he marched against the Serbs taking the direct
route to Lipljan, a small fortified post (*polychnion*) lying at the foot of the *Zygos*
which separates Dalmatia from our own lands. He intended, if he had opportunity to meet Bolkan in battle, and provided God gave him victory, to rebuild
Lipljan and all the other places; the *status quo* would be restored. Bolkan, when
he heard of the emperor's arrival, left for Zvečan, a tiny fortress north of the
Zygos lying in the disputed land (*mesaichmion*) between the Roman and Dalmatian
borders. After Alexius reached Skopje, however, Bolkan sent ambassadors to
arrange peace terms. (*Alexiad*: ii, 167; trans.: 276)[75]

---

[73] Chalandon 1900: i, 142–5, dispensed with the notion that Bodin and Bolkan were the same man.
[74] *Alexiad*: ii, 147 (trans.: 262). And see below at p. 173.
[75] *Mesaichmion* (alternatively *metaichmion*) might also be translated as 'no-man's-land', which recurs
in a frontier context at the Danube. See below at p. 235.

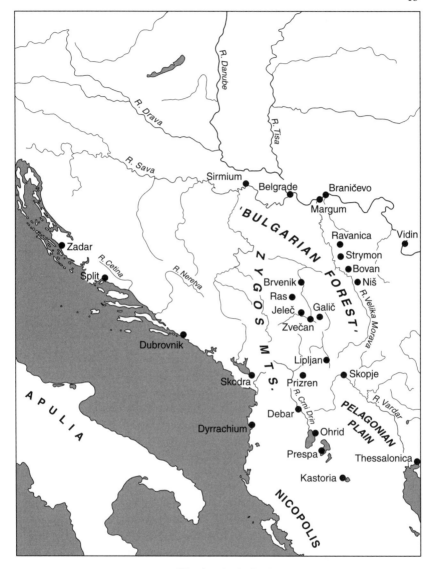

4.5 The frontier in Raška

Bolkan blamed the confrontation on the 'Roman satraps' who violated his frontiers, meaning of course the Byzantine commanders of the frontier fortresses. Thereafter he remained at peace with Byzantium for several years.

Many of the fortresses highlighted by Anna, including Lipljan and

Zvečan, have been identified by archaeologists. Zvečan was, as Anna indicated, a small fort (125×50 metres) situated high above the river Ibar on a rocky spur which controlled access to Kosovo Polje from the northwest. Marko Popović (1991: 177–8) has argued that the elongated irregular plan, the style of the walls and variety of towers, and the presence of a church dedicated to St George all suggest construction or significant rebuilding by Alexius I. North of Zvečan lay Galič, and to the northwest Jeleč. The latter was even smaller than Zvečan (45×35 metres) with a polygonal plan. Popović (1991: 178–9) maintains that the masonry style – irregular stone courses interspersed with layers of brick and occasional cloisonné – is akin to early Comnenian constructions in Asia Minor. Within the walls there is a grain silo similar to one at nearby Ras. Ras, on the outskirts of modern Novi Pazar, was first fortified in the fourth century. The antique ramparts were restored and functioned until the later eleventh century when a new curtain wall was built; this consisted primarily of reused stone *spolia* bound together with a lime mortar and has been dated by the discovery of coins struck by Alexius.[76] Ras was later destroyed by fire, probably during the 1120s, and was rebuilt with an irregular elongated plan (180×20–60 metres). North of Ras on the Ibar are the ruins of many further fortresses which we know to have been occupied at later dates, and which may have existed in the later eleventh century. Among these Brvenik is littered with twelfth-century pottery sherds.

THEOPHYLACT OF OHRID IN BULGARIA

In the face of recalcitrance first from Duklja and then from Raška, Alexius determined to reorganize the administration of the western Balkans. Like Basil II he considered the appointment of a suitable archbishop in Ohrid to be crucial, and in *c.* 1090 selected his Master of the Rhetors, Theophylact Hephaistus. Theophylact was the fifth *Rhomaios* to be appointed autocephalous archbishop of Bulgaria, and the first to leave clear indications of his principal concerns and interests in more than 130 letters, his theological treatises, and his works of hagiography. Theophylact the author, and more particularly the writer of letters, has been the subject of a ground-breaking study by Margaret Mullett (1997), and the following section should be read with that at hand.

Among Theophylact's earliest letters are two to the *doux* of

---

[76] M. Popović 1991: 179–81 does not indicate whether these were pre- or post-reform coins.

Dyrrachium, John Ducas. In the first Theophylact solicits unspecified favours for his relatives in Euboea, and in the second requests that a village near Pelagonia (Bitola) be returned to his jurisdiction. They reveal that although Ducas was primarily a general, and spent much of his time embroiled with the Dukljan Serbs, he was also expected to concern himself with everyday problems of administration throughout the vast area under his jurisdiction, or to intervene further afield where his personal authority might secure a favourable outcome for the petitioner.[77]

In spring 1092 John Ducas was promoted to the new office of Grand Duke of the Fleet, and sent against Tzachas, the Turkish emir of Smyrna.[78] His replacement in Dyrrachium was John Comnenus, the emperor's nephew and son of the *sebastokrator* Isaac. This appointment underlined the importance now attached to Dyrrachium as the senior military command in the western Balkans; a fact which was made more explicit in a lost letter from Theophylact to the emperor which revealed John's suspected sedition, and prompted a bitter confrontation between Alexius and Isaac.[79] However, perhaps because the archbishop's role in the affair was suppressed, Theophylact's relationship with John does not seem to have been damaged. Over the next couple of years he despatched at least eight letters to the *doux*, making a series of quite specific requests concerning: the taxation of monks in the Vardar valley (Theophylact, *Letters*: 166–9, 194–5); taxes imposed on the bishopric of Devol (202–5); recognition of a particular village (*chorion*) owned by the church of Ohrid but not recorded in its charter (*praktikon*) (214–17); the conscription of infantrymen from the region of Ohrid (208–11). On two occasions Theophylact makes particular mention of the wicked *kastrophylakes*, guardians of *kastra*, who were in receipt of a peculiar military levy on land, the *kastroktisia* (237, 324).[80] Theophylact's *bête noir* was the tax-collector (*praktor*) Iasites who was based at the *praitorion* in Ohrid,[81] and his letters make it plain that the *doux* of Dyrrachium had the authority to issue written instructions (*pittakia*) to empower a local official (*ex prosopou*) to overrule the *praktor*. Thus, the *ek prosopou* was to intervene if Iasites' functionaries (*mesazontes*) abusively detained monks to perform personal services.[82]

---

[77] Theophylact, *Letters*: 152–5, 186–9; Mullett 1997: 360, nr. 38. Mullett 1990: 127–8 notes that in both cases 'Theophylact appears to operate impeccably through official channels'.

[78] *Alexiad*: ii, 147 (trans.: 262). Chalandon 1900: i, 145, preferred spring 1091, but current consensus is for 1092: Mullett 1997: 84. However, for continued ambiguity see Nesbitt and Oikonomides 1991: i, 41–2, 98. [79] *Alexiad*: ii, 147 (trans.: 262); Theophylact, *Letters*: 599; Mullett 1997: 7, 86.

[80] On the introduction of the *kastroktisia* see above at pp. 93–4.

[81] Theophylact, *Letters*: 162–5, 168, 460, 486, 568; Mullett 1997: 130, 369; Obolensky 1988: 53–4.

[82] Theophylact, *Letters*: 167–9, 194.

More generally Theophylact's letters reveal that in the early years of the reign of Alexius I the *doux* of Dyrrachium was regarded as the ultimate authority in the western Balkans, who might intervene at will in civil or fiscal matters as far east as the Vardar river; lands which previously fell within the jurisdiction of the *strategos* of Bulgaria based in Skopje. Moreover, we know that before his appointment to command in Dyrrachium John Comnenus had been *doux* of Skopje, which clearly was no longer the senior command in the Bulgarian lands.[83] Theophylact was also in touch with John's replacement in Skopje, John Taroneites, whom he chastises for interfering in the appointment of bishops in the lands north of Skopje.[84] The appointment of Taroneites as *doux* of Skopje around 1091 is roughly contemporary with that of Theophylact's confidant Nicholas Anemas to a further (unspecified) command in western Bulgaria.[85] Moreover, at around the same time, and certainly before 1114, a *thema* of Niš-Braničevo was created, and a *doux* appointed with nominal authority over lands as far north as the Danube.[86] The reorganization of the provincial administration in the western Balkans should be understood in the wider context of Alexius I's innovations in government which commenced in the early 1090s.[87]

THEOPHYLACT OF OHRID ON BULGARIA: *THE BARBAROS OIKOUMENE*

Theophylact is notorious – too notorious Mullett has demonstrated – for his condescending attitude towards his barbaric Bulgarian flock, who stank of sheep- or goatskin.[88] Certainly, Bulgaria was rustic and rough, and Theophylact suffered from the *agroikia* and *amousia*, rusticity and the absence of high culture. He complained that 'having lived for years in the land of the Bulgarians, the bumpkin lifestyle is my daily companion.'[89] The phrase he uses is adapted from Euripides' *Orestes* (485) and it is fascinating that Michael Choniates used the same phrase more literally a century later to describe his 'becoming a barbarian by living a long time in Athens'.[90] The Athenians may have appeared provincial and

[83] For his seal as *doux* of Skopje see Nesbitt and Oikonomides 1991: i, 98. This must have been struck before his promotion to Dyrrachium, and not after as the editors suggest.
[84] Theophylact, *Letters*: 126–8, 190–3; Mullett 1997: 187–8, 299–300, 364.
[85] Theophylact, *Letters*: 39–40, 236–9, 242–3; Mullett 1997: 94, 183, 305, 306, 309, 349.
[86] *Alexiad*: iii, 178 (trans.: 462), for the first mention of the *thema* of Niš-Braničevo.
[87] Magdalino 1996a: 146–66.   [88] Theophylact, *Letters*: 141; Mullett 1997: 266–74.
[89] Theophylact, *Letters*: 243.17; Mullett 1997: 276; Obolensky 1988: 58.
[90] Michael Choniates: ii, 44.

parochial to their archbishop, but he certainly did not mean to imply that they were pagan and lawless. The same can be said of Theophylact's attitude to the Bulgarians, whom he regarded as somewhat barbaric, but not entirely barbarians.

We have already considered Theophylact's attitude to the Pechenegs, whom he considered Scythians, the archetypal barbarians and greatest threat to all things civilized (above at pp. 112–13). The barbarism within Bulgaria was quite different to that of the Pechenegs, for it had been modified by years of contact with the civilized world to the south. Even before its annexation Bulgaria had benefited from the greatest gifts of civilization: Christianity (through its conversion) and law (by entering into treaties with the empire). In the early years of the tenth century, Nicholas Mysticus had acknowledged to the Bulgarian tsar Symeon that, as fellow Christians, both Bulgarians and Romans were Christ's 'peculiar people, his inheritance'.[91] Shortly afterwards, in a speech to celebrate the end of hostilities between the Byzantines and Bulgarians, and to mark the marriage between Tsar Peter (927–969) and Maria Lecapena, Theodore Daphnopates declared that the Bulgarians 'are no longer called Scythian or barbarian . . . but may now be named and shown to be Christians'.[92] In his *History of the Fifteen Martyrs of Tiberiopolis* (*PG* 126: 200–1) – a work now firmly attributed to Theophylact – the archbishop expands upon this theme in considering the conversion of Bulgaria: 'What was previously not a people but a barbarian nation (*ethnos barbaron*) became and was called a people of God (*laos theou*), and the inheritance of the Bulgarians, which had not been an object of mercy, was called an object of mercy by God who calls those things which are not as though they were . . . the Bulgarian people have become, as it is written, a royal priesthood, a holy nation, a peculiar people.' Theophylact stresses the Pauline nature of the mission by using a Pauline quotation. He is more explicit in his *Vita Clementis* (xxii.66), where we find a people called into being and given a recognized identity through conversion by Clement, 'a new Paul to the new Corinthians, the Bulgarians'.[93] Thus, Theophylact demonstrates a grudging respect for distinct Bulgarian institutions in the Cyrillo-Methodian tradition, including the Slavonic language.[94] As Obolensky (1988: 67) has written: 'A language which serves as a medium for the Christian liturgy becomes

[91] Nicholas Mysticus, *Letters*: 124.66–9.
[92] Jenkins 1966a: 289, 293. See above at pp. 24–6.
[93] Quoted by Obolensky 1988: 69.
[94] Although he notoriously parodied many Slavonic terms and place-names, Theophylact knew and used them. See Mullett 1997: 272–3.

a sacred one. Hence every people which acquires a sacred tongue is raised to the status of a nation consecrated to the service of God, with its own legitimate place and particular mission within the family of Christendom.' The Bulgarians had been granted something denied other northern peoples: a distinct Christian identity.

Before Obolensky and Mullett, scholars could not believe that Theophylact, the author of letters which contained such vitriolic outbursts against the Bulgarians, was the same man who wrote so sympathetically about the Bulgarian church and its founding fathers. Now we can see that the contradictions between Theophylact's *Lives* and letters reflect the inherent contradictions of the two traditions in Byzantine thought and literature: the precepts of the Orthodox world view, which was ecumenical and hierarchical; and the heritage of classical Greece – for example in his borrowing from Euripides – which emphasized polarity. These two perspectives came together in the nether world of Bulgaria, which was at once within the frontiers of the civilized world, but also the realm of Christians who were not Romans. Theophylact's attitude to his own flock was, therefore, ambivalent, and when he wrote that he was 'a Constantinopolitan, and, strange to tell, also a Bulgarian',[95] he perhaps considered himself the most refined resident of a second barbarian, but legitimate *oikoumene* with an autonomous but inferior church with its own liturgy and hierarchy. In a letter to the caesar Nicephorus Melissenus, Theophylact even coins the phrase '*barbaros oikoumene*' to refer to Bulgaria, and although this might most accurately be translated as 'the barbarian world', it also appears to sum up the archbishop's position of grudging recognition for a region which was peripheral – geographically and culturally – to Byzantium, but also crucial to the empire's interests: a semi-barbarian hinterland which comprised Byzantium's Balkan frontier.[96]

CONCLUSIONS

The major Byzantine achievement in the western Balkans between 1025 and 1100 was the incorporation of the region known as Bulgaria into the system of provinces ruled from Constantinople. In 1100 there was a Byzantine *thema* of Bulgaria with recognizably Byzantine institutions (for example civilian and fiscal administrators) and characteristically Byzantine problems (harsh or unfair taxation, rigorous recruitment of

---

[95] Theophylact, *Letters*: 141.58–60; Mullett 1997: 274.
[96] Theophylact, *Letters*: 171; Mullett 1997: 274–5, 298.

provincial infantrymen). On occasion the process of incorporation had met with resistance, for example the murder of the Greek bishop of Sofia in 1082.[97] And there was periodic resistance from some magnates for whom greater autonomy suggested greater rewards. Psellus identified a desire for 'freedom' (*eleutheria*) among certain notables, and a wider sense of 'Bulgarian-ness' (*to sympan ethnos*) which generated popular support for their occasional rebellions.[98] However, such attempts coincided with more general 'non-Bulgarian' unrest, when central authority was facing stern challenges from foreign invaders or Byzantine magnates. Thus Peter Deljan's revolt benefited from the rebellion of Maniaces, and George Vojteh's from the turmoil which ensued from the Byzantine defeats at Bari and Mantzikert, and the Hungarian invasion across the Danube, all in 1071. Moreover, we must beware of drawing such firm distinctions between Byzantine provincial aristocrats with court titles and the southern Slav *župans*. In some instances *župans* were imperial officers, and in others they cooperated with or confronted *Rhomaioi* as equivalent peripheral potentates. As recent scholarship has shown, not least the exhaustive study of revolts by Cheynet (1990), centrifugal forces in eleventh-century Byzantium did not recognize racial or ethnic boundaries.

Throughout the period 1025–1100 Serbia (Duklja or Zeta, and Raška) lay beyond the empire's internal frontier, and was controlled by autonomous rulers, albeit men who were nominally subject to the emperor's higher authority. The internal frontier of the empire, which separated *themata* from *županias*, and *strategoi* or *doukes* from *župans*, was marked by a line of fortresses which divided Bulgaria from Serbia. It did not coincide with the external, 'natural' frontier, at the Danube, which still marked the *de iure* limits of imperial authority. Serbia now acted as a buffer of sorts between the empire and the world beyond. However, since Serbian rulers were free to conduct an independent foreign policy they might choose not to absorb or deflect potential threats to Byzantium, but instead elect to embrace alternative sources of patronage or ally with enemies of the empire. This was the case with Michael's approach to Pope Gregory VII, and with Bodin's dealings with the Normans, to which we will return shortly (below at pp. 165–6). And as the centre of power in Serbia shifted from Duklja to Raška in the last years of the century, the Hungarians, Venetians, and even the Germans, became potential patrons and allies of the southern Slavs.

---

[97] Scylitzes Continuatus: 184; Fine 1983: 220.
[98] Psellus, *Chronographia*: i, 76–7 (trans.: 109–10); Cheynet 1990: 388.

CHAPTER FIVE

The rise of the west, I: Normans and Crusaders (1081–1118)

When Alexius Comnenus came to power in 1081 the empire's frontier to the north had been breached by the Pechenegs. Eventually, as we have seen, he achieved a hard-fought victory against the nomads which secured the imperial position at the lower Danube for almost a century. However, even as the tumult to the north was calmed, several new threats emerged beyond the empire's western borders which would severely test imperial arrangements in the lands of the southern Slavs and the coastal lands of Dalmatia and Dyrrachium. The first major threat was posed by the Normans.

THE NORMANS IN SOUTHERN ITALY, 1059–1081

At the council of Melfi in 1059 Pope Nicholas II invested Robert Guiscard, the leader of a group of Normans who had settled in Italy, with legitimate title to Apulia and Sicily.[1] These regions hitherto had recognized Byzantine suzerainty. After 1051 imperial interests in Apulia had been served through a local magnate named Argyrus, who had been raised to the rank of *magistros* and given the title *doux* of Italy. However, his appointment had led indirectly to the Papal-Norman entente, for it provoked the patriarch of Constantinople, Michael Cerularius, to consider the problems of the Orthodox church in Italy. Argyrus was a Latin Christian who had clashed with the patriarch when he served as patron of the Latin churches in Constantinople between 1045 and 1051. Cerularius regarded the Latin use of unleavened bread (azymes, *azyma*) to be heretical, and undertook to regularize practices in the Latin churches, including those under Argyrus' dominion. His high-handed approach led to a clash with the papacy, and then inextricably to the schism of 1054. In the aftermath of this confrontation the papacy cast

---

[1] William of Apulia: 152–5.

around for new allies, and after some considerable hesitation formalized an arrangement with the Normans which effectively denied Byzantine claims to political authority in southern Italy. Suddenly Byzantine interests were under threat from an invigorated Robert Guiscard. After forty years of limited success the Normans captured Reggio on the toe of Italy, and Brindisi and Taranto on the heel within a single campaigning season in 1060. Guiscard then turned his sights ominously on the Byzantine stronghold of Bari.

The coordination of military efforts to halt the Normans' progress was entrusted to the *katepano* of Dyrrachium, Michael Mauricas. Several seals have survived which attest to Mauricas' progress from imperial *ostiarios* in *c.* 1050 to '*vestarches* and *katepano* of Dyrrachium' between 1065 and 1068.[2] In 1066 he prevented a Norman invasion of the western Balkans. According to Lupus Protospatharius (59) 'Count Godfrey, the son of Petronius, wanted to invade the Roman Empire (*Romania*) with a mighty host, but was hindered by a certain Greek commander named Mauricas (*Mambrita*).' In the following year Mauricas commanded the Byzantine fleet that appeared off the coast of Italy near Bari.[3] However, his activities could not prevent the setting of a Norman siege at Bari in 1068. Three years later, on 15 April 1071 the last Byzantine stronghold fell to Guiscard.[4] This coincided with the infamous Byzantine defeat at Mantzikert, and was followed by a period of turmoil in the eastern and western parts of the empire.

In the previous chapter we considered the problems in the Balkans after 1071, and noted that a possible solution considered by Michael VII was to forge an alliance with the Normans (above at pp. 144–6). Details of the negotiations are preserved in a series of letters written by the emperor Michael VII between 1072 and 1075. The first letter, written in late 1072 to Guiscard, recognizes, by implication, his conquest of lands in southern Italy which had previously pertained to the Byzantine empire, and proposes an alliance of interests to be sealed by the marriage of Guiscard's daughter Olympia to Michael's brother Constantine.[5] It places much emphasis on their common religion, stating that 'priestly books and true histories teach me that our realms have a single root and origin, that the same redeeming word was spread

---

[2] Seibt 1978: 168–71; Iordanov 1983: 106; Nesbitt and Oikonomides 1991: i, 42.
[3] William of Apulia: 331 (commentary).   [4] William of Apulia: 172–3.
[5] Sathas 1874: 208–9 also refers to an earlier offer of marriage by Romanus IV Diogenes. Michael VII points out that Romanus was a mere interloper, whereas the Ducases were the true imperial family, and Michael's brother Constantine was a *porphyrogennetos*. Kolia-Dermitzaki 1997: 251–68 has argued unconvincingly that this letter was never sent.

among both, and that the same eyewitnesses of the divine mystery and heralds of the word of the gospel resounded among them.'[6] Clearly, if certain theologians felt that a chasm had opened between eastern and western Christendom after 1054, the emperor had no desire to draw attention to it. We do not have Guiscard's reply, but a second letter sent in 1073 once again suggests the marriage alliance, so that the Norman might 'become the watchtower of our frontiers (*horion*) . . . furnish aid to the empire in all things, and fight for us against all enemies'.[7] The implication is that Guiscard would furnish troops to assist in Michael's planned campaigns against the Turks, who had since 1071 began to occupy much of the Anatolian plateau, and this is made explicit in the earliest Byzantine history to mention the episode, Scylitzes Continuatus (167–70, esp. 170). The Norman rejected the proposal, but in 1074 the emperor tried again, this time offering his infant son, the *porphyrogennetos* Constantine, as a husband for Olympia. The offer was accepted, and in a *chrysobull* issued in August 1074 Guiscard was granted the title *nobelissimos*, the right to name his son *kouropalates*, and a number of other Byzantine court titles were put at his disposal to grant to his followers.[8] He had been brought into the imperial hierarchy, and undertook to rule southern Italy as a vassal of the eastern emperor, also agreeing to supply forces for Michael's campaigns. Olympia came to Constantinople in 1076, and took the name Helena.[9]

While these negotiations proceeded slowly between 1072 and 1074, Michael Ducas had also approached Guiscard's sworn enemy, Pope Gregory VII. We know of his approaches from the pope's own letters to the German ruler Henry IV and William of Burgundy. In each case Gregory expressly states that the Greeks desired Church union, and he appeals to them both to muster an army to subdue their common enemy, Robert Guiscard, which might then proceed on to aid the Greeks against the infidel Turks. In March 1074 the pope followed these letters with a general appeal to the faithful to come in full force to the assistance of the *ecclesia orientalis*, the eastern Church. On the matter of azymes he was pragmatic, stating: 'while we defend our unleavened bread with arguments irresistible before God, we do not condemn or reject their leavened bread, following the apostle's words that to the pure all things are

---

[6] Sathas 1874: 212–15; for the date see Bibicou 1959–60: 52; also Shepard 1988a: 101 for this partial translation.   [7] Sathas 1874: 210–11; Charanis 1949: 19.

[8] Psellus, *Orationes Forenses et Acta*: 176–81; Bibicou 1959–60: 44–8, provides a French translation of the document. See also Dölger 1925: ii, nr. 1003; Dölger, ed. Wirth 1977: ii, 64–5, nr. 1003.

[9] Lupus Protospatharius: 60; Bibicou 1959–60: 48–9.

pure'. This left him room to manoeuvre, and carried the implication that the eastern Church was in need of purification. It was this sentiment which was made explicit on 2 January 1075, after Gregory had become aware of Michael Ducas' deal with Guiscard. On that date he wrote to Hugh Abbot of Cluny in the following terms: 'Great pain and universal sorrow obsess me. The eastern church is moving further from the catholic faith, and the devil, having killed it spiritually, causes its members to perish in the flesh by the swords of his henchmen lest at any time divine grace brings them to a better understanding.'[10]

What we have in the correspondence of 1072 to 1075 is an appeal to the papacy by the Byzantine emperor for armed assistance against the Turks; an offer of church union if this aid is forthcoming; an enthusiastic response by an energetic pope, who sends out appeals to the faithful to march to the defence of the *ecclesia orientalis*; and a number of theological issues fudged in the name of high politics. In effect, we have all the elements which led to the First Crusade two decades later. Moreover, Gregory had already developed the notion of remission from sins for those performing military duties under papal sanction. However, this was not put into practice in the east because Michael VII had found another avenue for acquiring the troops he required through his deal with Robert Guiscard. In fact this agreement did not come to fruition. Michael VII was deposed by the usurper Nicephorus III Botaneiates, who annulled the marriage contract, earning Guiscard's enmity. However, shortly afterwards, in 1081, Botaneiates was himself deposed by Alexius I Comnenus. Gregory VII promptly excommunicated Alexius, for by now the pope had thrown his support behind Robert Guiscard, and sanctioned a Norman assault on the Byzantine empire, ostensibly with the intention of restoring Michael Ducas.

The arena for the renewed struggle between the Byzantines and the Normans was the *thema* of Dyrrachium, and the commander entrusted with its defence was Nicephorus Bryennius. After his successes as *doux* of all Bulgaria, Bryennius was transferred to Dyrrachium with a dual portfolio: to quash the rebellious 'Dalmatians', and to monitor the Normans 'who harbored hostile designs against the Romans'.[11] He thus set about restoring order in the Adriatic where Italian vessels were harassing Byzantine and Dalmatian merchant ships. However, as we have seen (at pp. 145–6), Bryennius and his

---

[10] Gregory VII, *Registrum*: ii, 188, nr. 49; Emerton 1932: 64–5, for a full English translation. The partial translation cited here is from Charanis 1949: 23. See also Cowdrey 1988: 155.
[11] Bryennius: 213.

replacement Basilaces both used Dyrrachium as the launchpad for their bids for the imperial throne. Left unchecked, the Normans made approaches to the Dukljan Serbs, seeking their allegiance and support for a planned invasion. Anna Comnena portrays the anxiety that the Dukljan-Norman understanding generated, and stigmatizes the latest *doux* of Dyrrachium, George Monomachatus, who had been appointed by Botaneiates and showed no inclination to support the usurpation by Alexius Comnenus. Alexius' great fear, we are told, was that Monomachatus would make a deal with Robert Guiscard, and William of Apulia (216) records that he did exactly this: 'George who had been entrusted with the city [of Dyrrachium] had already and often encouraged the Duke [Robert] to hurry thither because he had heard the Nicephorus [Botaneiates] had been expelled from the throne.' Monomachatus then fled to Michael and Bodin, and awaited the Norman onslaught.

DYRRACHIUM IN THE LATER ELEVENTH CENTURY

The Norman invasion of Dyrrachium in 1081 presents us with our first opportunity to study how the frontier system in the western Balkans functioned in the face of a substantial foreign military threat. It also allows us to examine in some detail the network of fortifications which comprised the military frontier south of Serbia. We have already seen that next to Thessalonica, Dyrrachium was considered the greatest prize in the western Balkans. We know from the letters of Leo Choerosphactes that the city was surrounded by a nexus of fortifications, and have encountered several in the context of Basil II's 'Bulgarian' wars. With the development of the *thema* of Bulgaria to the east, and the emergence of Duklja as a powerful autonomous region to the north-east, the fortifications in Dyrrachium assumed additional importance. Moreover, they were the main line of defence against an invasion from the west.

In the northern reaches of the *thema* of Dyrrachium sat the fortress of Sarda, which, situated atop a steep hill above the river Drin, dominated the approach to the Dukljan capital of Skodra. The fortress comprised two circuits of walls, the lower of which was entirely rebuilt in the late eleventh or early twelfth century. This wall was punctuated by eleven towers, seven of which have been engulfed by an artificial lake created for the Mao Tsetung hydroelectric power station. Within the walls a series of dwellings have been dated to the period 1081–1195 by the discovery of several coins.[12] Heading south along the river Drin from Sarda one reaches Alessio (modern Leshë) which is referred to in both the *DAI* (145) as a fort governed from Dyrrachium, and in the *Alexiad* (iii, 84; trans.: 393) as 'small, but absolutely impregnable on its hill'. Today this site marks the point of transition between the limestone karst highlands of Montenegro, and the northern plain of Albania.

Heading south from Alessio one crosses the uninhabited plain of Mati where the rivers Drin, Mati and Ishm converge to form an enormous marsh. South of the marsh low ridges of sands and clays bisect the coast from Cape Rodoni to Cape Pali; the latter being the northern extremity of the Dyrrachium peninsula where a permanent lookout was posted to defend the approach to the city. The fortress at Dyrrachium (modern Durrës) has been subject to several excavations in the past century. Although very little of the eleventh-century structure has survived, excavations carried out on the north-east compound of the lower fortress have uncovered the foundations of three circular towers constructed in unquarried stone with irregular double brick bands and occasional vertical brickwork. This style is typical of the later eleventh and early twelfth centuries, and the structures certainly pre-date the thirteenth century when polygonal towers were built on top of them. It has recently been proven that these towers represent the eastern corner of the Byzantine citadel, from which a curtain wall ran south-west to the acropolis (phase 1 on map 5.1). The remains of further circular towers have been found which define the limits of the twelfth-century fortress, which was previously assumed to have been engulfed by phase 2 of the fortress' construction.[13] Anna Comnena provides the following description of Dyrrachium in 1106:

The city of Dyrrachium has ramparts interrupted by towers which all around the city rise to a height of eleven feet above the curtain wall. A spiral staircase leads to the top of the towers and they are strengthened by battlements. So much for the city's defensive plan. The walls are of considerable thickness, so wide indeed that more than four horsemen can ride abreast in safety. (*Alexiad*: iii, 97; trans.: 403)

South of Dyrrachium is the Gulf of Valona, which was dominated by a fortified port, Valona (modern Vlorë), which also dominated access to the Vjossa river valley. South of Valona lay Jericho and Kanina, *kastra*

---

[12] Karaiskaj 1975: 133–50; Karaiskaj 1987: 73–83. The coin types are not noted, but they are surely post-reform billon scyphates, and therefore must post-date 1092.
[13] Karaiskaj 1977: 29–53; which corrects Rey 1925: 33–48.

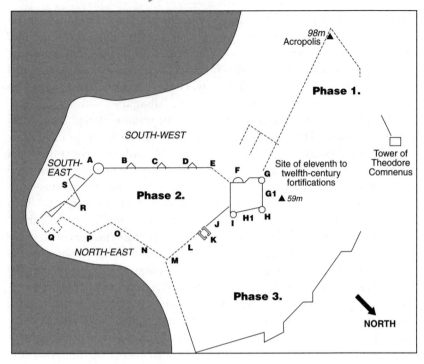

98m ▲
Acropolis

Phase 1.

SOUTH-WEST

Tower of
Theodore
Comnenus

SOUTH-
EAST
A   B   C   D   E   F   G   Site of eleventh to
twelfth-century
fortifications
S   G1 ▲ 59m
Phase 2.
R
                    H1 H
                  I
Q   P   O   J
              L   K
NORTH-EAST N
          M

Phase 3.

NORTH

5.1 Sketch plan of the fortifications at Dyrrachium

which dominated respectively the valleys of the rivers Dukat and
Shushica. We have two seals struck by *strategoi* of Jericho which date from
the tenth and eleventh centuries.[14] Kanina is mentioned in Basil II's *sigillia* as a town in the diocese of Glavinica, a further important settlement
in the region and a suffragan bishopric of Ohrid. The site can probably
be associated with modern Ballsh. The territory of Dyrrachium
stretched south as far as Butrint (or Butrinto) which is currently under
excavation by a British-led team of archaeologists.[15]

The highland passes east of Dyrrachium were dominated by small
fortresses. The *Alexiad* (iii, 93, 106, 108; trans.: 399, 409, 411) records the
pivotal role played by the fortresses of Diabolis and Mylos. The exact
locations of these strongholds are uncertain, but Diabolis is almost certainly associated with the Devol valley and lay near Lake Ohrid, and the
location of Mylos can be pinpointed from the detailed information provided by Anna Comnena. Mylos, we are told, lay beyond the river Devol.

---

[14] Nesbitt and Oikonomides 1991: i, 46; Schlumberger 1884: 733–4.
[15] Hodges et al. 1997: 207–34.

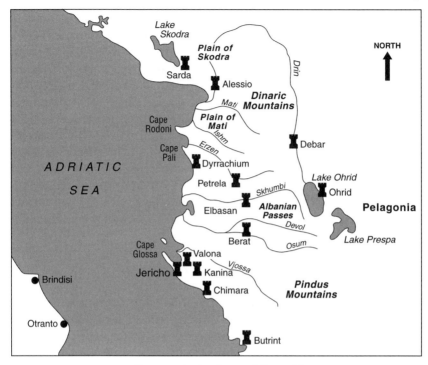

5.2 Fortresses in the theme of Dyrrachium

It was a small fortified site which Bohemond captured in 1107. When the Byzantine general Cantacuzenus besieged it, the Normans encamped on the far side of the river Vjossa saw his siege engines and rushed to assist the defenders. We can therefore surmise that the fort was close to the river Vjossa, on the northern bank, and it lay a short distance from a plain between a marsh and the river Charzanes, whither Cantacuzenus withdrew and fought a successful battle. Mylos, therefore, must be placed in the complex of forts in the vicinity of Valona. It was probably still defended by its late antique walls which would prevent its certain identification as a twelfth-century site.

The *kastron* of Debar defended a crucial transport node some twenty-five miles north of Lake Ohrid. First, it lay on the direct road to Ohrid along the Crni Drin river. Second, at this point the river Radlika, a tributary of the Crni Drin, has cut a deep gorge through the mountains. Its northern arm flows into the Vardar, and thus forms a direct route to Skopje. Its southern arm flows on to Prilep.

The *kastron* of Petrela is situated on the river Erzen immediately north of modern Tirana in Albania. It is the westernmost point mentioned, and sits on the route on the great land road, the Via Egnatia. Petrela monitored access to the Valley of Shkumbi and the adjoining passes through the south-central highlands. The small triangular fortress initially consisted only of a wall and a large circular tower, probably constructed by Anastasius I (491–518). The second phase of development, which is sixth-century, added a triangular tower within the walls enclosing a cistern. The third phase clearly dates from the eleventh or twelfth century. A second circular tower was added and the curtain wall was thickened and extended. The masonry is of irregular stone and brick bands with occasional cloisonné, similar in style to the new towers at Dyrrachium. Furthermore, a new gate complex was added which faced the steep slope down to the river Erzen, and a second accommodation block was built within the fort.[16]

Two further fortresses which lay at crucial strategic locations were Elbasan and Berat. The extant walls at Elbasan have late antique foundations, and above the first three metres the masonry is Ottoman. However, there are clear traces of Byzantine construction in the south and west walls. Similarly, the sixth-century walls of Berat were strengthened after the tenth century and before the construction of the tower of Michael Comnenus in 1205.[17] Three churches have also been excavated at Berat, the oldest of which dates from the thirteenth century.[18] However, a church must have existed before this, as Berat was included among the sees subject to Ohrid in Basil's *sigillia* (above at p. 75).[19]

Very few churches in modern Albania pre-date 1200. Meksi (1972b: 47–94), an Albanian expert in medieval church architecture, has argued that the largest and best preserved Byzantine church in his country, the monastery church of St Nicholas at Mesopotamit on the river Bistrica, which has traditionally been dated to the reign of Constantine IX (1042–55), must be redated to the end of the thirteenth century. Two exceptions are the three-naved church of St Maria at Peshkopi e Sipërme, the seat of the bishop of Drinopolis, which Meksi (1975: 103–4) has dated to between the late eleventh and mid-twelfth centuries, and the ruins of a one-naved basilica at Sarda, which has been dated to the same period by finds of jewellery.[20]

---

[16] Baće and Karaiskaj 1973: 139–60; Ducellier 1965: 163–5; Ducellier 1968: 364–6.
[17] Karaiskaj 1971: 61–77; Baće 1971: 43–62.
[18] Meksi 1972a: 59–102.
[19] It should be noted that the identification of Berat has been problematic. See Gelzer 1893: 43, 53; *Notitiae episcopatuum*: 113, n. 5.   [20] Karaiskaj 1975: 148.

THE NORMAN INVASION OF DYRRACHIUM IN 1081

The Norman invasion of Dyrrachium followed swiftly after Alexius I's accession in April 1081, and the earliest indications were not good for the new emperor. First, the citizens of Dubrovnik and other unspecified 'Dalmatians' provided transport ships for Norman troops.[21] Next, advance forces were handed the citadel at Corfu by its defenders, and proceeded to capture the ports of Vonitsa (on the Gulf of Arta in Greece), Butrint, and Valona without difficulty.[22] Control of Valona, the northernmost of these sites, was crucial to the Norman plan for a land and sea assault on Dyrrachium. First, it controlled access to the Vjossa river valley which passed through the southern highlands. Bohemond was instructed to march on Dyrrachium by land. Second, the Norman fleet setting out from Brindisi would cross the narrowest stretch of the Adriatic before landfall, minimizing the risk of catching one of the violent squalls. Third, the bay of Valona is up to twenty-eight fathoms deep, and thus eminently suited to harbouring heavy Norman transport ships.[23] Fourth, the fleet would approach Dyrrachium along the coast using the current which is permanently to the north-west.

The greatest concern for the new Byzantine *doux* in Dyrrachium, George Palaeologus, was retaining the loyalty of the native population. This is hardly surprising given how often in recent years they had pledged to support several pretenders to the imperial throne. Anna Comnena records that 'Alexius sent letters to the leaders (*hegemones*) of the coastal towns and to the islanders earnestly exhorting them not to lose heart, nor to relax their efforts in any way'. However, the news of Robert's impending invasion 'filled the islanders with consternation; and people living on the coast by Dyrrachium were equally dismayed'. And when he arrived, 'No wonder then that the inhabitants of Dyrrachium, hemmed in on either side (that is to say by land and sea) and in sight of Robert's forces, innumerable and surpassing all description, were seized with the greatest dread.'[24] In fact, Guiscard's forces were probably not all that large, insofar as they consisted of Norman knights (although there may also have been hundreds or even thousands of freebooters and pirates, such as accompanied the 1185 invasion, examined below at

---

[21] William of Apulia: 210.134–5 (Dalmatians), 220.302 (Ragusans and other Dalmatians).
[22] William of Apulia: 214–17.
[23] The British Naval Intelligence Division report on Albania (1945: 71) notes that the bay will accommodate at anchor up to twenty-five ships weighing between 5,000 and 15,000 tons.
[24] *Alexiad*: i, 132, 139, 143 (trans.: 126, 131, 135). See also William of Apulia: 218–19.

pp. 284–8). Guiscard's intention was to secure, through intimidation and persuasion, the support of the *hegemones* in the western Balkans upon whom Byzantine control depended. That he was successful is demonstrated by William of Apulia's observation (218.253–6) that the Norman camp expanded daily. Moreover, Guiscard had taken further measures to secure the defection of the locals: he had in tow a man claiming to be the deposed emperor Michael VII Ducas, whom he dressed in fine robes and paraded before the walls of the besieged city. Clearly, the Norman was aware that the population of Dyrrachium was loyal to the empire, but not necessarily to the current emperor. While the fortress itself held out, the surrounding lands rapidly went over to Guiscard.

Palaeologus kept the emperor informed of developments with regular despatches. Perhaps one of these was secured with a seal in the Dumbarton Oaks collection which bears the legend 'George Palaeologus, *kouropalates* and *doux* of Dyrrachium.'[25] From his missives 'the emperor learnt that . . . countless hosts from all directions were rallying to Robert thick as winter snowflakes, and the more frivolous folk, believing that the pseudo-Michael was in truth the emperor were joining him. Alexius saw the magnitude of his task and was afraid.'[26] He approached foreign powers for assistance: the sultan in the east, the German ruler Henry IV, and even the pope. He also summoned the Grand Domestic, Pacourianus, who left Constantinople in August 1081, and personally led the heavy infantry from their base at Adrianople. The force that Alexius constructed included Magyars who had been settled near Ohrid, 2,800 Manichaeans, regiments of Franks, and the so-called Varangian guard.[27] He also commanded Bodin to lead the Dukljans to meet him, and pressed on to Thessalonica where he received news that Palaeologus had already fought and lost a pitched battle outside Dyrrachium. The *doux* had been badly wounded and withdrew within the walls, in the shadow of Guiscard's siege engines. Palaeologus' decision to act before the emperor's arrival may be another indication that, if the Norman forces were initially small, they were expanding daily.

The emperor and his allied forces arrived near Dyrrachium on 15 October. He received Norman envoys who proposed to acknowledge Alexius' legitimate succession, abandon his support for the pseudo-Michael, and call off any hostilities in return for certain concessions. We

---

[25] Nesbitt and Oikonomides 1991: i, 41. See above at p. 146.

[26] *Alexiad*: i, 146 (trans.: 137).

[27] *Alexiad*: i, 151 (trans.: 141). William of Apulia: 222.323 refers merely to 'a huge throng of Greeks and barbarians'.

can only guess that these concesssions, considered outrageous by Anna Comnena, involved handing over control of the southern Dalmatian coast to the Normans. Alexius dismissed the embassy and committed all to battle. Anna Comnena provides a graphic description of the grim encounter on 18 October 1081, which militarily was a worse defeat for the Byzantines than the infamous rout at Mantzikert of 1071.[28] Many magnates fell, and the emperor barely escaped, leaving Dyrrachium at the mercy of the Normans. Yet the city did not pass immediately to Guiscard. Instead the citadel was entrusted to the emperor's Venetian allies, and we will return to this shortly. The rest of the city was put under the command of a certain 'Comiscortes, from Albania, to whom the emperor gave profitable advice for the future in letters'.[29] The identity of this character, who is reported to have come '*ex arbanon*', has been the subject of intense scholarly debate, because it is one of the few explicit references we have that seem to imply a distinct and recognized people known to the Byzantines as *Arbanoi*, which may be translated as Albanians. Alain Ducellier (1968: 361–4) favours the rendering offered by both Leib (in French) and Sewter (in English) that Comiscortes is the name of an individual who was 'a native of Albania'.[30] Although Comiscortes may not be a proper name, but a corruption of the title '*komes tes kortes*' ('count of the tent', for which see *Listes de préséance*: 341) it is clear enough from the context that Alexius was, like Guiscard, wholly dependent on local support, and would therefore have been most likely to have appointed a native of the region with a military background to defend Byzantine interests. However, he also required wider public support, particularly that of the leading men in Dyrrachium.

In 1082 a public assembly was convened in Dyrrachium to discuss the fate of the city. The circumstances were exceptional: the Byzantines had suffered a crushing defeat and the citadel of the city had been entrusted to their Venetian allies. However, the assembly was not exceptional. A patriarchal act issued at this time refers to certain 'leading men of Dyrrachium' (*Dyrrachitai archontes*), who represented the city.[31] We have already seen that from the later part of the tenth century until at least the middle of the eleventh authority in Dyrrachium had rested with the Chryselius family. Clearly there were other powerful families whose advice was regularly sought and support canvassed by the resident *doux*. Moreover, there is ample evidence for similar councils in other maritime

---

[28] *Alexiad*: i, 157–66 (trans.: 145–51); William of Apulia: 224–7; Angold 1997: 130.
[29] *Alexiad*: i, 168 (trans.: 153). [30] *Alexiad*: i, 153 (trans. 153).
[31] Rhalles and Potles 1852–9: v, 103–4.

cities in Dalmatia at this time, and the development of their municipal institutions through the twelfth century in the face of diverse external threats will feature in the following chapter (at pp. 200–2). Alexius could not succeed without securing the support of these municipal elites, and our sources suggest that Guiscard was winning them over with his 'carrot and stick' tactics.

In his hour of need, summer 1081, Alexius had turned to various potential allies. Only the Venetians reacted with haste and in force because they shared the imperial fear of Norman expansion across the Adriatic.[32] Some years earlier, in 1074, a Norman count named Amico of Giovinazzo had invaded Dalmatia and occupied the maritime cities as far south as Split. The citizens seem to have welcomed his arrival, and even requested assistance against the encroachments of the Croatian ruler Cresimir. However, the Venetians were less pleased, and the doge Domenico Silvio (1070–84) launched an expedition to drive the Normans out. He seems to have enjoyed tacit imperial backing for the successful campaign, and on 8 February 1075 he extracted an oath from the leading citizens of four cities that they would never again grant entry to the Normans. In the extant document which records this oath the doge styled himself 'Duke of Venice and Dalmatia and imperial *proto-proedros*'.[33] By 1081 the common Byzantine and Venetian fear of the Normans had intensified. Unlike Amico, Robert Guiscard was not, or at least was no longer, a pirate or freebooter, and Alexius approached the doge formally seeking his help in return for 'promises and gifts'.

Some rewards were pledged, others granted immediately on the condition that the Venetians equip their fleet and sail at speed to Dyrrachium to protect the city and engage in serious warfare with Robert's fleet . . . all their desires would be satisfied and confirmed by chrysobulls . . . the Venetians listened, made all their requirements known through envoys and received firm pledges. (*Alexiad*: i, 146; trans.: 137)

The Venetians sent a mighty fleet to join the inadequate Byzantine navy, still commanded by Mauricas (see above at p. 157). Their arrival brought fresh hope for those besieged in Dyrrachium, and bought the emperor time to muster a force large enough to challenge the Normans. However,

---

[32] For the Norman perspective on the Venetians see William of Apulia: 218.276–85.
[33] *Codex Diplomaticus*: i, 137–9.

it also introduced a further complication after the aforementioned Byzantine rout of 18 October 1081.

Lupus Protospatharius (61) reports 'in the month of January 1082 Duke Robert took the city of Dyrrachium which was surrendered to him by certain Venetians'. Anna Comnena provides a much fuller account of the handover:

> The people of that city, as I have said, were mostly emigrants from Amalfi and Venice. When they learnt of the misfortunes of the emperor, the enormous casualties suffered and the death of soldiers so distinguished, not to mention the withdrawal of the fleets and Robert's decision to renew the siege in the following spring, their own policy was thoroughly examined. How could they save themselves and avoid the recurrence of such perils? They met in an assembly. Each man expressed his own private opinion and when they failed to reach one common cause, they decided to resolve the impasse by submitting to Robert and surrendering the city. (*Alexiad*: ii, 7; trans.: 155)

This passage raises many questions about political authority in Dyrrachium. However, we must dismiss the claim that the city, the fulcrum for the defence of the entire western seaboard of the Byzantine empire, comprised mostly Italian emigrants. Even after the debacle of 1081 the permanent colonies of Amalfitans and Venetians cannot have comprised more than a small percentage of the total population of Dyrrachium, and there is no evidence that before 1081 the Italians had dominated municipal government. Clearly, Anna is here guilty of exaggeration. In making such a claim she was seeking to apportion blame for the loss of the city, and resorted to a familiar theme: the fickleness and greed of the Latins. (She returned to this later, revealing that Alexius tried to recover the city after 1085 'unceasingly with bribes and promises . . . for all Latins lust after money. For one obol they would sell even their nearest and dearest.'[34]) However, Anna's explanation does reveal that local economic interests might be placed above fidelity to the empire. Mercantile interests in Dyrrachium could be served best by avoiding a second protracted siege and facilitating continued trade, and some of the most important merchants were now resident aliens whose home towns lay across waters now dominated by the Normans.

While the Italian merchants' wealth was a significant factor in the influence they had come to wield, their wishes only became paramount after the appointment of a Venetian governor named Domenico.[35]

---

[34] *Alexiad*: ii, 57 (trans.: 193). We will return to the recovery of Dyrrachium below at pp. 172–3.

[35] William of Apulia: 228. William later (240–1) reveals that the Normans only had secure hold of the citadel, and the Venetians were able to spend fifteen days in the city without confrontation. See also Malaterra: 74.

Anna does not mention the Venetian commander by name, nor does she provide any details of the brief period of Venetian domination. However, she does record that Alexius later bribed certain inhabitants to put to death 'a man who had first led them to betray the city to Robert, and they killed his partisans with him' (*Alexiad*: ii, 57; trans.: 193). Placing this beside her reticence to provide any details of what the Venetians had been promised in return for their aid, we must surmise that the installation of a Venetian governor and the prioritization of Venetian mercantile interests signalled that control of Dyrrachium had been demanded by the doge, and reluctantly agreed to by the desperate emperor when he had cast around for allies in 1081. This was only part of an extensive package offered in return for naval assistance against the Normans.

The Venetian doge Domenico Silvio was granted the elevated rank of *protosebastos* and the title *doux* of Dalmatia and Croatia. So esteemed was the doge that he took fourth place in the new imperial hierarchy, behind only the *basileus* himself, his older brother Isaac the *sebastokrator*, and the *kaisar* Nicephorus Melissenus. Ranks based on the title *sebastos*, formerly applied to the imperial person, were the preserve of the emperor's relatives by blood or marriage, but an exception appears to have been made for the doge, who had much earlier married the sister of the emperor Michael VII. It seems clear that the doge's authority in 'Dalmatia and Croatia' included for the first time rights in Dyrrachium, where he received the church of St Andrew with all its property and revenues except for material stored there for the imperial navy. Other Venetian rights and privileges in that city, and throughout the empire were formalized in an imperial chrysobull, promised in 1081 and issued some time afterwards. The exact date that the chrysobull was issued has been hotly debated, and scholars have favoured 1082, 1084, and even 1092.[36] The most we can say with certainty is that the earliest known instance of the doge using the imperial rank 'protonsevasto' is on a charter issued in May 1083. However, this does not prove that the full privileges had been granted before then. The rank and title were regranted to Silvio's successor Vitale Falieri in 1084.[37]

Although the text has not survived, most of what was granted can be surmised from later documents. The privileges, usefully summed up by Nicol (1988: 60–1), greatly enhanced Venetian standing throughout the empire. In addition to the doge's honours, the Venetian patriarch of Grado was given the imperial title *hypertimos*, 'most honoured', and was

---

[36] Borsari 1969–70: 111–31; Lilie 1984: 8–16; Nicol 1988: 59–63.
[37] Dandolo: 217, who does not mention an earlier grant.

to receive an annual grant of 20 lbs of gold coin for distribution among their churches as he saw fit. And Venetian merchants were given several warehouses in Constantinople and three quays at Galata on the opposite bank of the Golden Horn from which they might trade throughout the empire free of the ubiquitous sales tax (*kommerkion*) and associated port and road duties. The markets where these privileges pertained were recorded, and the emporia on the Black Sea and lower Danube were notable exceptions: Italian interests could not be allowed to interfere with the delicate balance of trade and diplomacy with the nomad and Russian merchants at the empire's northern frontier (see above at pp. 105–7). This last point reminds us that the Venetian privileges had many precedents, and the employment as diplomatic devices of trade, tribute and court titles was far from exceptional. However, the reduced rate of taxation was an innovation, offered in the place of the customary payment in gold and forced upon the emperor by the dearth of ready cash at his disposal. The use that Venetians made of their 'most favoured' status in the course of the twelfth century proved how much more valuable were their exactions than a simple cash payment.

NORMANS IN THE WESTERN BALKANS, 1082–1084

Venetian support was instrumental in the Byzantine recovery of territory and authority in Dyrrachium after 1082. The doge maintained vigilant guard over the Adriatic sea lanes while the emperor carefully clawed back land. However, the defeat of the Normans required a radical change in Alexius' strategy, with the emphasis on diplomacy and chicanery rather than pitched battle. First, Alexius attempted to bribe the German emperor to launch an invasion of Lombardy, and succeeded in forcing Guiscard back across the sea. However, the Norman leader left his son Bohemond to proceed on into Byzantine lands, assisted by many who had defected from Alexius' defeated army. Bohemond made his base at Ioannina, whither Alexius hurried in May 1082 at the head of a new army consisting largely of mercenaries recruited with ambitious promises of large cash payments. Battle was engaged soon after the emperor's arrival, and despite his attempt to out-manoeuvre Bohemond, the Norman emerged victorious.[38] The emperor fled north to Ohrid where he mustered his scattered forces and set out for a further pitched battle, which once again ended in his flight. Cowed he returned

---

[38] William of Apulia: 236–7.

to Constantinople, while the Normans established their mastery of Skopje and set a siege at Ohrid. Matters in the western Balkans were desperate, but the emperor took some comfort from the spirited resistance of Ariebes, the commander of the citadel at Ohrid. Similar assaults on other fortresses in Bulgaria also failed, and the Grand Domestic Pacourianus swiftly razed a small fort that the Normans had erected at Moglena. However, the Normans had greater success to the south, seizing Pelagonia, Trikala and Kastoria, before laying siege to Larissa. For six months the Byzantine commander Leo Cephalas held out awaiting the emperor, but Alexius did not arrive in full force to raise the siege. Instead:

He summoned one of the old men from Larissa and questioned him on the topography of the place. Turning his eyes in different directions and at the same time pointing with his finger, he carefully inquired where the land was broken in ravines, where dense thickets lay close to such places. The reason why he asked the Larissean such questions was of course that he wished to lay an ambush there and so defeat the Latins by guile, for he had given up any idea of an open hand-to-hand conflict; after many clashes of this kind – and as many defeats – he had acquired experience of Frankish tactics in battle. (*Alexiad*: ii, 25; trans.: 168–9)

This decision was a definitive moment in the Norman wars. Alexius had great experience campaigning in the western Balkans and had achieved significant victories there when he was Grand Domestic against aspirants to the throne. Therefore, he had been inclined to regard pitched battle as the most effective means to achieve his military objectives. Even after the great defeat in October 1081 he had continued to put his faith in battle, innovating in his tactics but adhering to the overall strategy. His new strategy was less honourable, but far more effective.

The emperor did all that he could to convince Bohemond that he remained committed to battle, and ranged his troops in the familiar fashion. The Normans similarly adhered to the previous rules of engagement, launching a frontal assault straight at the imperial standard. But Alexius was elsewhere, watching as his troops turned from the fight and led the pursuing horsemen away from their entrenchment. He then fell on their camp with the bulk of his army, massacring the remaining Latins, and sent a force of archers after the Norman cavalry with instructions to fire from a distance at their horses. In this way Alexius won his first significant victory. He followed this up with a ruse to test the loyalty of Bohemond's own officers, sending envoys who encouraged the Norman counts to demand their salaries for the previous four years; if Bohemond failed to provide these they were offered alternative positions and high salaries in the imperial army. Bohemond was obliged to withdraw to Valona and prepare to sail to ask for funds from his father, and in his absence the emperor recovered Kastoria. Alexius returned to Constantinople where he celebrated his victory with a triumphal entry into the city, while Bohemond returned to meet his father at Salerno in October or November 1083.[39]

Guiscard returned in full force in 1084.[40] However, Alexius had learned not to risk his forces in pitched battle. The Norman fleet was confronted first by the Venetians, who achieved significant victories. Then, having landed and advanced again into the interior of the *thema* of Dyrrachium, Guiscard's forces were caught between the mountains, where the Byzantines vigilantly guarded the passes, and a vigorous naval blockade prosecuted by the Venetian and Greek fleets. The lands that the Normans foraged were rapidly depleted, and Guiscard withdrew to the port of Jericho where he was trapped for two months by adverse winds and the allied ships.[41] Robert's men, encamped beside the river Glykys, were in dire straits: up to 10,000 are said to have starved to death before a withdrawal was effected. Alexius had discovered how best to use the natural defences of Dyrrachium and the services of his allies.

In the year after his withdrawal from Dyrrachium, on 17 July 1085, Guiscard died. Subsequently the emperor successfully persuaded the Italians to return the city to imperial control. The conspirators who delivered the city were granted an amnesty for their previous defection, and forthwith Alexius despatched his brother-in-law John Ducas to command the citadel. The installation of a relative and *sebastos* in this sensitive command was symptomatic of a new trend in appointments which characterized the reigns of Alexius and his two successors. John's period of office is given as eleven years by Anna Comnena, who thereby incorporates the period of Venetian-Norman domination. For much of the time he was preoccupied with the Dukljans, and his successes won him promotion to the office of Grand Duke of the Fleet (see above at p. 151). His replacement in Dyrrachium was the emperor's nephew John Comnenus, the son of the *sebastokrator* Isaac. In 1093 he led an unsuccessful campaign against Bodin, suffering many casualties as a result of his inexperience and impetuousness. However, John retained his command and was therefore the Byzantine commander who first encountered an entirely new menace from the west: the First Crusade.

---

[39] *Alexiad*: ii, 32, 41–3, 50 (trans.: 173, 181–3, 188).   [40] William of Apulia: 245–9.
[41] *Alexiad*: i, 149 (trans.: 139). Anna incorrectly places these events in her account of the 1082 campaign.

THE FIRST CRUSADE

There is now little resistance from scholars of the medieval west to the notion that Alexius Comnenus played a significant role in the calling of the First Crusade. Anna Comnena states explicitly that in 1089–90, pressed by Pechenegs to the north and Turks to the east, Alexius 'did all he could to summon mercenaries from all sides as fast as possible'. Two pieces of evidence, both considered at various times by Jonathan Shepard (1988a, 1997), suggest that his appeals met with considerable success. First, we have the much disputed letter of Alexius to the count of Flanders, Robert le Frison. The version of the letter which has been preserved is generally agreed to be a forgery. However, there is every reason to believe that it was based on a real letter despatched by the emperor to request that the count send the 500 cavalry he had promised to Alexius when he passed through Constantinople some years earlier. These horsemen arrived, probably before 1090, and were swiftly sent east to defend the region of Nicomedia from Turkish raids. Attempts to dismiss the letter have focused on its use of militant Christian imagery to inspire recruits into Alexius' service. Such language, it is argued, would not be generated by the eastern emperor. But we know from a further letter that Alexius sent to the abbot of Montecassino that he was aware of the appeal of Jerusalem to western knights, and of the notion of martyrdom for those who fell in battle with the infidel. Both considerations were promoted by Pope Urban II in his preaching of the crusade. Therefore, we have no reason to dismiss the evidence of the letter, and every reason to believe that it produced the 500 horsemen Alexius had sought.[42]

The second piece of evidence, also discussed by Jonathan Shepard (1997: 107–29), is a text composed soon after 1103 which relates how certain relics were brought to Cormery, near Tours in France. Remarkably, it makes no mention of the crusade, but it does relate that the emperor Alexius, provoked by the advances of the Turks, 'sent envoys everywhere with letters full of immense complaints and tears, and weepingly sought the aid of the entire Christian people, promising very great rewards to those who would help'. Then, with the multitude he had mustered, Alexius 'and the aid of merciful God', drove the Turks back from the lands they had overrun. The implication of the text is that even before 1095 Alexius had considerable success in appealing to fellow

---

[42] Shepard 1988a: 67–118.

Christians in France who willingly entered his service, and received substantial rewards. Indeed, before 1095 both the Franks and the Normans, who made up the vast majority of participants in the First Crusade, had a history of serving the Byzantine emperor, not least Alexius himself in his wars against the Turks.[43]

It has been suggested that after twenty years campaigning Alexius would have been ready to take a break and devote himself to administrative reforms in Constantinople.[44] However, Arabic sources suggest that the situation in the Muslim world was such that he could not afford to waste an unprecedented opportunity to recover lost territory and prestige. Between 1092 and 1094 the major Islamic polities in the near east suffered political crises. In 1092, the vizier Nizām al-Mulk, the power behind the throne of the Sunni Muslim Seljuk empire, was murdered. A month later, the Seljuk sultan himself, Malikshāh died in suspicious circumstances after a twenty-eight-year reign. His death was swiftly followed by those of his wife, his grandson, and other figures who had been prominent in his regime. In the consequent power vacuum various Seljuk princes and pretenders fought each other for supremacy, and as this struggle continued crisis struck the Shi'ite Fatimid Caliphate in Egypt when, in 1094, the caliph Mustansir died. He had ruled for fifty-eight years, and had been implacably opposed to the Seljuk expansion to the north. His vizier, Badr al-Jamālī, died shortly afterwards. Also in 1094 the Abbāsid Sunni caliph, al-Muqtādi died. The fourteenth-century Mamlūk historian, Ibn-Taghribirdī recalled this as 'the year of the death of caliphs and commanders'.[45] Nor was the struggle over Muslim orthodoxy between the Sunni Seljuks and the Shi'ite Fatimids ended by the unprecedented series of deaths, as various pretenders and new rulers saw the opportunity to press their claims to legitimacy by waging war against the others whom they regarded as heretics.

So, 1092 to 1094 was the perfect time for Alexius Comnenus to attempt to recover territory to the east, and secure his frontiers for an offensive against the Turcoman bands who had occupied the Anatolian plateau. Therefore, he sent letters to all parts of western Christendom appealing for fellow Christians to join his fight against the infidel. A twelfth-century Latin author, Ekkehard of Aura (*Hierosolymitana*: 15), wrote of many letters which were sent from Constantinople. This appeal is suppressed entirely in the *Alexiad*, because Anna Comnena, writing at the time of the Second Crusade had no desire to implicate her father in

---

[43] Shepard 1993: 275–305; Magdalino 1996b: 9–13.   [44] Treadgold 1997: 620.
[45] All references are taken from Hillenbrand 1997: 132–3.

the calling of the First Crusade. More surprisingly, it is also omitted from the history of John Zonaras, who wrote a hostile account of Alexius' reign as a response to Anna's eulogy. Like Anna, Zonaras (iii, 742–3) characterized the crusade as an unexpected plague which swept across the empire from west to east. However, we do have the testimony of a thirteenth-century Greek chronicle which faithfully reproduces passages from earlier works which have survived, and from others which have not. An uncorroborated passage in the work, generally attributed to Theodore Scutariotes, states the following:

Having considered, therefore, that it was impossible for him alone to undertake the battle on which everything depended, he recognized that he would have to call in the Italians as allies, and effect this with considerable cunning, adroitness and deeply laid planning. Finding a pretext in the fact that this people considered unbearable the domination of Jerusalem and the life-giving Sepulchre of our Saviour Jesus Christ by the Persians [Seljuk Turks] and saw therein a heaven sent opportunity. He despatched ambassadors to the bishop of Old Rome and to those whom they would call kings and rulers of those parts, who, by the use of appropriate arguments, managed to prevail over not a few of them to leave their lands and directed them in every way successfully to the task. For this reason, thousands, indeed tens of thousands of them crossed the Ionian sea and reached Constantinople with all speed, and having exchanged assurances and oaths advanced towards the east. (Scutariotes: 184–5)

The appeal from Alexius, and hints at the language he employed, can be found in the most popular contemporary account of the First Crusade, by Robert the Monk which has been preserved in more than 120 manuscripts.[46] Robert put the following words into the mouth of Pope Urban II: 'From the confines of Jerusalem and from the city of Constantinople a grievous report has gone forth and has *repeatedly* been brought to our ears. Namely that a race from the kingdom of the Persians [the Seljuks], an accursed race, a race wholly alienated from God . . . violently invaded the lands of those Christians and has depopulated them by pillage and fire. . . . The kingdom of the Greeks is now dismembered by them and has been deprived of territory so vast that it would take two months to cross.'[47] And we have confirmation that Urban was responding to an appeal from the emperor in further Latin sources: Bernold of St Blaise, wrote that, 'There arrived at this council [at Piacenza] an embassy from the emperor of Constantinople which humbly beseeched our lord the pope and all the faithful of Christ to procure for him help against the

---

[46] Edgington 1997: 59.   [47] Krey 1921: 28–30.

pagans for the defence of our Holy Church which the pagans had already almost destroyed in his territories as far as the walls of Constantinople. Our lord the pope, therefore, urged many to furnish this aid, even engaging then to promise under oath to go there, with the consent of God, and to bring this same emperor, to the best of their power, their most faithful aid against the pagans.'[48] Bernold may have attended the meeting at Piacenza on 17 March 1095 that he describes. If not, his bishop Gebhard certainly did, and Bernold wrote up his account swiftly before his own death in 1100.

The response to Urban's preaching, and therefore to Alexius' appeal through the pope and directly to western lords, was far greater than Alexius had ever anticipated. Instead of self-contained cavalry units he faced the mass movement of western Christians of all social and economic levels.[49] The crusaders arrived in the western Balkans by three different routes, two of which passed through Dyrrachium. However, the first wave of armed pilgrims approached the empire through Hungary. The fullest account of their journey is provided by Albert of Aachen, who records that a certain Walter 'the Penniless' and his followers set up camp at Belgrade, 'a Bulgarian city'.

Walter sought to buy the necessaries of life from the chief (*princeps*) of the Bulgarians and the magistrate (*praesides*) of the city; but these men, thinking it a pretence and regarding them as spies forbade the sale of anything to them. Wherefore, Walter and his companions, greatly angered, began forcibly to seize and lead away cattle and sheep which were wandering here and there through the fields in search of pasture. As a result a serious strife arose between the Bulgarians and the pilgrims who were driving away the flocks and they came to blows. (Albert of Aachen: 276–7)

The conflict at the frontier was swiftly resolved when Walter arrived in flight at Niš, where he first encountered direct Byzantine authority. The *doux* immediately made reparations for the losses suffered at the hands of the 'Bulgarians', gifting Walter money and weapons, and escorting his followers peacefully through Sardica, Philippopolis and Adrianople where they were freely entitled to purchase provisions.

This episode illustrates a problem inherent in granting autonomy to the local ruler, a certain Nicetas, who was clearly not party to the imperial decision to recruit Frankish mercenaries at this time, and was uncertain how to deal with the sudden arrival of a large contingent of armed Franks.[50] Nicetas had even greater problems with the arrival

---

[48] Charanis 1949: 28–9. [49] See now Riley-Smith 1997: *passim*.
[50] France 1994: 90, although he assumes that Nicetas was 'the Byzantine governor'.

subsequently of a huge horde of pilgrims led by Peter 'the Hermit'. He 'mustered his people and took general counsel' before deciding to withdraw to Niš, obliging the Byzantine *doux* to handle the situation. Peter's followers certainly included some nobles,[51] but most were more humble, and being of little use to the emperor as mercenaries were hurried through the Balkans and into Anatolia where, disoriented and confused, they were decimated by the Turks. This second instance proved the wisdom of the frontier arrangements in the north-western Balkans. The 'Bulgarian forest' which stretched between Belgrade and Niš delayed the crusaders' passage into the empire, and gave the imperial commander five to eight days to prepare for their reception and onward journey.[52]

The duties performed by the *doux* of Niš were similarly expected of the governor in Dyrrachium. In August 1096 John Comnenus, the aforementioned *doux* of Dyrrachium, received twenty-four ambassadors from Hugh of Vermandois, brother of the French king Philip I. The count himself was caught in a squall, and his ship thrown up on the coast between Dyrrachium and Cape Pali, the northern extremity of the Dyrrachium peninsula and an established watchtower. The vigilant guards spotted the wreck and escorted Hugh immediately to the *doux*. On the emperor's instructions he was then led to Constantinople, but not by 'the direct route', the Via Egnatia, but instead via Philippopolis.[53] Hugh's maritime route was followed by several subsequent bands of westerners, most notably the Norman contingent led by the emperor's old foe Bohemond. Only Raymond St Gilles made his way by land along the Dalmatian coast, where mountains extend right to the sea, and even the narrow coastal plain is generally barren. Raymond of Aguilers (36–7; trans.: 17) recorded the treacherous crawl along rocky tracks. For forty days the crusaders were harassed by wild bands of Slavs who emerged from highland lairs to attack from behind. St Gilles was obliged to stay with his rearguard, and once even resorted to mutilating Slav prisoners and using them as a barricade to protect his weary followers and deter further ambushes. Raymond had set out with ample food supplies, but by the time he reached Skodra these had been exhausted, and he paid the Dukljan ruler handsomely for the right to buy provisions at his markets. He was sorely disappointed when no such provisions were made available by the locals, and was forced to struggle on as far as Dyrrachium where the *doux* greeted him warmly and provided supplies.

---

[51] France 1994: 88; Riley-Smith 1997: 76.   [52] Nesbitt 1963: 167–81.
[53] *Alexiad*: ii, 214 (trans.: 314).

Only after St Gilles had entered the empire – crossing the internal frontier between Dalmatia and Dyrrachium – and encountered direct Byzantine authority was he properly provisioned. Thereafter a band of Pechenegs in imperial service policed his journey on to Constantinople.

The common experience of all the crusaders in the frontier lands was a lack of provisions. Little seems to have been available for foraging in the immediate vicinity of the pilgrims' routes, and access to local markets was not readily permitted. This corresponds well with the picture we have already formed of the empire's deliberately uncultivated and sparsely settled periphery, and suggests that local elites were neither able nor prepared to deal with large bands of aliens. In marked contrast, the imperial officers in Dyrrachium and Niš offered access to regular supplies from the richly cultivated lands of the central Balkans, and guaranteed safe – although not uneventful – passage to Constantinople. The contrast was quite apparent to the crusaders themselves, who initially wrote favourably of their first experiences of the eastern empire. Clearly, the frontier arrangements were adequate to cope effectively with an enormous and unexpected influx of armed westerners who displayed no desire to settle on imperial lands. However, one of their number had a more permanent interest in the northern Balkans.

BOHEMOND RETURNS, 1104–1108

It has been convincingly demonstrated that, contrary to Anna Comnena's testimony, during the course of the First Crusade the emperor enjoyed particularly close ties with the Norman leader Bohemond.[54] In spite of their earlier conflict – indeed probably because of the familiarity that encounter engendered – Alexius had received favourably Bohemond's proposals to act as his intermediary with the crusading leaders, and may even have promised him lands and an imperial rank and title in the east. However, the agreement was abandoned outside the walls of Antioch, where the Norman maintained that the emperor had betrayed the crusaders by his failure to provide siege engines and supplies. The subsequent remarkable victory by the Latins left Bohemond in command of Antioch in breach of the agreement he had reached with Alexius. While in the following years the emperor accepted the crusaders' conquests, and acknowledged their local jurisdiction in exchange for recognition of his overlordship, he would never

---

[54] Shepard 1988b: 185–277.

accept the Norman domination of Antioch. In 1104 the Byzantine commander Cantacuzenus mounted a successful assault by sea on the Norman-held city of Laodicea, while the generals Boutoumites and Monastras pressed into Cilicia and neighbouring Edessa. Byzantine control of the sea from their bases on Cyprus, and of the lands to the north-west and south-east of Antioch forced Bohemond's hand. Leaving his nephew Tancred in command, he returned to the west in autumn 1104 to recruit new troops, and proposed a crusade directed against his foe in Constantinople, the treacherous emperor who was blocking the route of pilgrims. Bohemond's resolve and status were strengthened when he married the elder daughter of Philip I of France and arranged a second marriage for Tancred.

Alexius responded swiftly to the Norman's mission: he wrote to potentates throughout Europe denying charges levelled by Bohemond and urging against a second armed pilgrimage. He was peculiarly keen to prevent any alliance that would expose the empire's western flank to attack, and Anna emphasizes his concern over approaches to the Italian maritime cities of Venice, Pisa and Genoa.[55] Alexius had a further concern: the possibility of an aggressive Norman-Hungarian alliance. In 1097 Bohemond's cousin, Roger of Sicily, had forged a marriage alliance with the Hungarians. Alexius could not afford for Bohemond to reach a similar understanding, for this would expose the empire to a massive invasion through the northern marches. As we have seen, the preferred route of the participants in the First Crusade was through Hungary, and with the support of the Hungarian king Bohemond's recruits would meet no resistance before they reached the Danube. In such an eventuality Alexius could not hope to retain control of the lands bordering the Danube, and only Niš would stand between the westerners and the direct road to Constantinople. A simultaneous sea assault on the coast of Dalmatia and Dyrrachium would have certainly led to the loss of the whole of the western Balkans.

As a response to Bohemond's efforts, Alexius Comnenus orchestrated an extraordinary diplomatic initiative. In 1104 an embassy was despatched to the court of the Hungarian king, and it was arranged that the daughter of the late King Ladislas I would be betrothed to the heir to the Byzantine throne, John Comnenus. As early as spring 1105 the Hungarian princess Piroska was brought to Constantinople. This was a demonstration of the Byzantine commitment to the marriage, but more

---

[55] *Alexiad*: iii, 54 (trans.: 369).

importantly provided the emperor with a valuable hostage, concern for whom would encourage the Hungarian king to remain loyal to his new ally. We will see in the following chapter (at p. 199) that the Byzantine-Hungarian understanding involved tacit support for an invasion of Dalmatia which altered the whole balance of power in the northern Balkans. Bohemond was left to launch his assault on the southern Adriatic littoral, and the emperor had sufficient time to make suitable preparations. Alexius had learned from his previous encounters with the Normans, and knew that for his invasion to be successful Bohemond would have to capture the city of Dyrrachium, the bridgehead between southern Italy and Albania. Without control of that city any further acquisitions would be ephemeral, and the Normans vulnerable to Byzantine counter-offensives from the rear and from across the southern highlands. The city prepared for the inevitable siege, and Alexius prepared to besiege the besiegers. Anna Comnena provides a detailed description of this campaign, which must be considered an archetype of frontier defence.

Early in 1106 Alexius Comnenus, the emperor's nephew, replaced his brother John as *doux* of Dyrrachium. His first task, on the emperor's instructions, was to strengthen the city's fortifications against the imminent Norman assault. The emperor also took great pains to seal the mountain passes:

The emperor had anticipated the enemy in establishing a considerable force in all the passes, under picked leaders, and every route was denied to the Norman by means of the so-called *xyloklasiai* [barricades of felled timber]. Without delay Michael Cecaumenus became the vigilant defender of Valona, Jericho and Kanina; Petrela was entrusted to Alexander Casabilas, a brave soldier who had put to flight many Turks in Asia with a mixed corps of infantry; Leo Nicerites defended Debar with a suitable garrison; and Eustathius Camytzes was detailed to guard the passes of Albania (*Arbanon*). (*Alexiad*: iii, 104; trans.: 408)

While the extensive programme of reconstruction was underway, Isaac Contostephanus was appointed Grand Duke of the Fleet and despatched to Dyrrachium 'with the threat that his eyes would be gouged out if he failed to arrive before Bohemond crossed the Adriatic'.[56] Contostephanus proved ineffectual, and the Normans succeeded in crossing and capturing several key fortresses, including Valona. Moreover, despite all Alexius' efforts Bohemond managed to gain access to the highlands by securing the support of certain natives of

[56] *Alexiad*: iii, 77 (trans.: 388).

Arbanon 'who were thoroughly acquainted with the mountain tracks'; they 'came to him, explained the exact position of Debar and pointed out hidden paths'.[57] Once again the emperor was confronted with the importance of retaining the support of locals in the western Balkans.

Bohemond's advance spurred the emperor to further action. A letter from the *doux* of Dyrrachium was instrumental in the appointment of Contostephanus' replacement, Marianus Mavrocatacalon, after which 'the straits had a tireless guardian, for Marianus gave the Normans no opportunity whatever for future crossings'.[58] Imperial efforts were then focused on detaining Bohemond before the city of Dyrrachium. The emperor and the Norman both realized that he was committed to capturing the citadel without which his position in the region could not be secure and his gains rapidly recovered when he ventured further inland. Both were also aware that an effective naval blockade would prevent further troops and supplies reaching Bohemond, and oblige his large army to live off the land: something they had singularly failed to do in 1084. Thus, Alexius organized an effective guerilla strategy: Norman foraging parties were frequently ambushed and returned empty-handed, if they returned at all. And while the Normans began to suffer, those within the city enjoyed continued communications with the emperor who was determined to prevent the loss of the city through subterfuge or betrayal by the inhabitants. First, according to Anna, he encouraged the *doux* with a constant stream of letters and advice. Second, he ensured that both the soldiers and the citizens received adequate provisions. Third, he devised ingenious devices for preventing the Normans scaling the newly-strengthened walls. Fourth, he secured the highland passes and prevented the Normans from reaching cultivated lands beyond. While acknowledging the obvious bias of Anna's account, and her emphasis on the ubiquity of her father's presence and influence, we can surmise that imperial frontier strategy had matured during Alexius' reign, mirroring Alexius' own path to maturity. In this way the spirit of those besieging the city was broken, and Bohemond approached the *doux* of Dyrrachium with peace proposals.

The Treaty of Devol, arranged between the emperor and Bohemond in 1107, is recorded in full by Anna Comnena, and has consequently received much scholarly attention.[59] The legal language and concepts employed in the treaty demonstrate that the Byzantine emperor had become remarkably familiar with the principles of western feudalism,

[57] *Alexiad*: iii, 104 (trans.: 408).   [58] *Alexiad*: iii, 77, 113 (trans.: 388, 415).
[59] Most recently and completely, Lilie 1993: 75–82.

and more importantly that he was willing to employ them to secure Bohemond's adherence to the treaty's stipulations. Bohemond was granted an elevated imperial rank, *sebastos*. His incorporation into the highest echelon of the Comnenian hierarchy was associated with an office which carried specific duties in Antioch and Edessa. All would be held of the emperor, and would revert to imperial control upon Bohemond's death. In addition to his honours (*timai*), the Norman was to receive an annual 'gift' of 200 gold *solidi*, the payment of which might be considered akin to *rhogai*, the annual stipends associated with imperial office and the *philotimiai* or cash payments despatched to other frontier rulers who did the emperor's bidding. Indeed, the act of homage which bound Bohemond to his lord, the emperor, was not far removed in its objective from the act of *proskynesis* by which dependent rulers bound themselves to the emperor within the established 'hierarchy of states' (see above at pp. 35–6). There may have been crucial differences in language and ritual, but there were few differences in substance between Bohemond's act of homage and, for example, the *proskynesis* of the Dalmatian ruler Dobronja to Romanus III. Both acts of obeisance committed the individual and his followers to defend the interests of the *basileus*, and both received in exchange an elevated imperial rank, a named frontier command, and a large sum in gold.

In fact Bohemond never returned to Antioch, and the carefully constructed clauses of the Treaty of Devol were never implemented. Tancred had no reason to adhere to his uncle's agreement, despite the generosity of the terms he had received. Consequently, Alexius and his successor John were committed to an arduous military and diplomatic struggle to regain Antioch. And if Devol eliminated the Norman threat to the southern Adriatic littoral, where the efficacy of the frontier defences deterred any further invasions through Dyrrachium for most of the twelfth century, it also revealed how aspects of western and eastern policy had become entwined as a consequence of the crusade. This is a theme to which we will return in dealing with the reign of Alexius' grandson, Manuel Comnenus (below at pp. 212–17).

DYRRACHIUM IN THE TWELFTH CENTURY

The absence of foreign threats and of personal acts of valour by the emperor in the western Balkans after 1108 means that the political and administrative history of the region becomes obscure. After Alexius Comnenus our knowledge of twelfth-century *doukes* is patchy. The first, mentioned by the Priest of Duklja (*LPD*: 371), is the otherwise unattested Pirogordus. Chalandon (1912: ii, 73) draws attention to a certain Pyrrogeorgius who was active at Iconium in 1146. If he were the same man, or a relative, he would have held office in Dyrrachium early in John II's reign. His replacement was Alexius Contostephanus, very probably the brother of Stephen who married Anna, one of the emperor's daughters. He should not be confused with his younger namesake, the nephew of the emperor Manuel I (1143–1180).[60] The third known *doux* was the recipient of a letter from George Tornices, and was addressed as 'Lord Alexius, *sebastos* and grandson of the *kaisar*, being *doux* of Dyrrachium and Ohrid'. Polemis (1968: 114–15) has argued convincingly that this was a certain Alexius Ducas, the son of Anna Comnena's elder daughter Irene, and reproduces the relevant fragment of a lost inscription which refers to a certain *doux* Alexius whose maternal great-grandmother was the empress Irene, wife of Alexius I. This same man was *doux* of Cyprus in 1160, when he entertained the writer Constantine Manasses.

Other Byzantines held office in the lands of Dyrrachium. In 1155 a *doux* of Valona was responsible for seizing 400 *hyperpera* from a Genoese merchant.[61] In c.1171 Manuel I appointed a certain Constantine Ducas as *doux* of the whole Adriatic littoral, which probably included Dyrrachium (see below at p. 262). However, much power as always was in the hands of the *archontes* of Dyrrachium. The city certainly retained a degree of municipal autonomy throughout the twelfth century, and on two further occasions the fate of the city was decided not by the Byzantine *doux*, but by the *archontes*. Eustathius of Thessalonica (*Capture of Thessalonica*, trans. Melville Jones: 194) records that in 1185 the resident *doux*, a certain Romanus who was the emperor's son-in-law, had alienated the inhabitants and 'brought them from prosperity to poverty through his love of riches'. Therefore, they refused to resist the Normans and Byzantine control of the city was lost. Similarly, in 1205, certain powerful citizens determined to hand the city over to the Venetians.[62]

CONCLUSIONS

Throughout the period under scrutiny Byzantine authority in Dyrrachium operated through local power structures. Loyalty to the empire, if not individual emperors, was generally assured; certainly

---

[60] *LPD*: 372; Chalandon 1912: ii, 75, n.5.   [61] *Codice diplomatico della reppublica di Genova*: ii, 218–19.
[62] Ducellier 1981: 69, 87, reproduces the relevant section of an unpublished account by the sixteenth-century chronicler, Daniele Barbaro.

more so than in the lands immediately to the north. However, allegiance could be shifted when Byzantine power waned, or where the interests of the locals were compromised by their loyalty. Thus in 1082 the citizens favoured Norman rule, and were also willing to recognize the Venetian governor Domenico if he could guarantee peace. The interests of the *Dyrrachitai archontes* were primarily economic. As the citizens who erected a commemorative inscription after 1018 said, they rejoiced in the installation of an effective Byzantine commander after decades of inadequate rule, since poor government weakened the city's economic vitality. At other times the support of the *archontes* could also be sought against a recalcitrant *doux*. We have already noted that very soon after his appointment to the command of Dyrrachium in spring 1092 the emperor's nephew John Comnenus was suspected of sedition (see above at pp. 148, 151). The archbishop of Ohrid, Theophylact, informed the emperor of rumours by letter, and forthwith Argyrus Caratzes, the *megas hetaireiarches* (an imperial officer occasionally charged with sensitive missions) was despatched to the city. He bore two letters. The first requested that John travel to consult with the emperor, then based at Philippopolis, on how best to deal with the Dukljans. The second letter was addressed to 'leading citizens' (*logades*, later also called *hyperechontes*) of Dyrrachium. It ordered them to recognize Caratzes as *doux* in John's absence. Alternatively, they were expected to assist in his arrest if he refused to depart.[63]

A further point of considerable interest is that Alexius entrusted the command of the city of Dyrrachium and relations with his neighbouring subject-allies to members of his own kin group, the *sebastoi*. This was one of the major developments in Alexius' administration, and one which initially proved effective in the turmoil of the northern and western Balkans. No successful pretender emerged after 1081 in Dyrrachium or Bulgaria. However, it remains to be seen whether the appointment of kinsmen was a viable long-term policy, or an incitement to rebellion within the privileged ranks of the *sebastoi*, and a cause of resentment for those denied access to senior commands. Overall, the reign of Alexius Comnenus saw a new style of imperial government emerge in Byzantium. It is still a matter for debate whether this was for the better or worse, but we can be certain that the system owed much to the emperor's early confrontations with the Normans and crusaders.

The Norman advance into southern Italy and Sicily was remarkable,

---

[63] *Alexiad*: ii, 147–9 (trans.: 262–3).

and for that reason alone the Byzantine defence of the lands of Dyrrachium must be judged a considerable achievement. The unprecedented waves of armed pilgrims that passed through imperial territory after 1096 were an even more astonishing manifestation of the pressures and processes affecting the west, and the Frankish colonization of Outremer saw the Byzantine empire caught between the heartland of Latin Christendom and its expanding frontier. More than this, Constantinople now lay between the two poles of the militant western Church: Rome and Jerusalem. Byzantine eastern and western policy could no longer be regarded as entirely distinct, and this would produce new pressures on the empire.

CHAPTER SIX

The rise of the west, II: Hungarians and Venetians (1100–1143)

The expansion of the Latin Christendom took many forms and involved many peoples. The advance of the Normans and the predominantly Frankish crusades were the most remarkable of its early manifestations, but other Christian powers were expanding their interests immediately beyond Byzantium's Balkan frontier. Venice, as we have seen, was extending her political and commercial nexus, initially by allying with Alexius to thwart the Normans. However, the establishment of Latin outposts in the east, surrounded on all sides by hostile neighbours and connected with the 'civilized' world only by sea, offered many opportunities for a resourceful maritime power. A second people, whom we have already met, also emerged at this time somewhat transformed. In the period between their settlement of the Carpathian basin and the advent of the First Crusade, the nomadic Magyars had moved a significant way towards establishing a more, although not entirely, sedentary Christian kingdom. The kingdom is known to English speakers as Hungary, and we will henceforth call the Magyars Hungarians. Both Venetians and Hungarians had an interest in extending their authority to Dalmatia: the former to establish control over the northern Adriatic, dominating both coasts; the latter to gain access to the sea, and thus to establish political and commercial links with the rest of the Mediterranean world. The Hungarians also saw opportunities for expansion into Sirmium and the Slavic lands beyond, encroaching further into Byzantium's Balkan frontier.

Venetian and Hungarian activities in the northern Balkans have left a relatively large volume of written material, mostly in Latin, on which we can draw. We have three Venetian sources, several Hungarian Chronicles, and for the first time a significant number of charters preserved in the archives of various maritime cities in Dalmatia. This allows us to take a different perspective, not seeing everything as it was seen from Constantinople, and this is reflected in the tone of the chapter.

187

However, this perspective also reflects the general dearth of written material in Greek for the reign of John II. The three principal Greek historians, Anna Comnena, John Cinnamus, and Nicetas Choniates, for various (and very different) reasons have very little to say about John, and – as we will see – when they do, it cannot be regarded as objective, nor as the basis for an appraisal of his Balkan policy.

HUNGARY'S BORDER WITH BYZANTIUM IN THE LATER ELEVENTH CENTURY

The Hungarian settlement of the Carpathian basin was initially concentrated on the middle Danube around Buda.[1] Large areas to the north and south were not settled, and, lying between the Hungarians and their neighbours, acted as defensive wastelands. Even as the Hungarians began to occupy and cultivate a broader region, border wastes were maintained. As late as 1074 Hungary's northern approaches were defended by a policy of burnt earth. Lambert of Hersfeld (ed. Holder-Egger: 198) records that in preparation for an attack by Henry IV of Germany, the Hungarian King Géza I 'applied himself fully to the task of ensuring that in locations where he feared the enemy may invade there would be nothing for the troops to eat, nor even pasturage for their mounts'. Furthermore, the marches were criss-crossed with barricades and obstacles, most commonly fences of sharpened stakes with parallel trenches which hindered the passage of horsemen. The routes through the fences were controlled by fortified gateways (*clusae*), which served a second function as toll booths.[2]

Géza I pursued a more friendly policy towards Byzantium. He was married, probably in 1075, to the daughter of the Byzantine aristocrat Theodoulus Synadenus,[3] and received at that time the famous crown which bears (on the reverse) his portrait on an enamel plaque beneath that of the emperor Michael VII Ducas, and beside the image of Constantine Ducas the *porphyrogennetos*. The significance of the crown, a gift from the emperor, lies in the arrangement of the plaques, which were ordered to mirror the hierarchy of heavenly bodies portrayed on the opposite side (the front), and to illustrate the Byzantine perception of Géza's subordination to the emperor (see above at pp. 33–8). More than a century after the compilation of the *De Cerimoniis*, and after a period of

[1] Gerevich 1990: 26–50.
[2] Göckenjan 1972: 3–14; Fügedi 1986: 37.
[3] Scylitzes Continuatus: 185. See now Shepard 1999b: 72–83, for the marriage of the Synadene.

rapid expansion through military endeavour, the empire was once again on the defensive. And as an element of the more pacific, indeed defensive, ideology fostered in Constantinople in the 1070s, the notion of 'the hierarchy of states' was revived and once again central to imperial foreign policy, although the gift contravened the strict prohibition by Constantine VII on the exportation of crowns.[4] More than this, the crown represented Byzantine acknowledgement of the existence of a sovereign Christian polity north of the Danube ruled over by *Geovitzas pistos krales Tourkias*, 'Géza, the faithful king of Hungary'.[5] The gift of the crown must also have guaranteed the *status quo ante quem*, which included acknowledgement of Hungarian rights in the city and region of Sirmium.

The fortified settlement of Sirmium, modern Sremska Mitrovica, lay on the north Bank of the river Sava some fifty miles west of its confluence with the Danube. As we have seen (at pp. 65–6), the Roman fortifications were extensive, and there is evidence for the reoccupation of a small area near the southern ramparts during the reign of Basil II. Thereafter, the monastery church of St Demetrius seems to have been the only outpost of Byzantine influence, and even this is uncertain.[6] No Byzantine coins were found during the excavation of the eleventh- and twelfth-century necropolis.[7] At Mačvanska Mitrovica, on the southern bank of the Sava, there are the remains of three successive church buildings, the last of which can be dated to the early years of the eleventh century by the discovery of thirty-two class A2 anonymous *folles*. Further coins have been discovered in the adjacent Slav settlement of Zidine. The church must have been the seat of the restored bishop of Sirmium.[8] As we have noted previously, Sirmium was taken by the Hungarians in 1071, as they swept along the Morava corridor to sack Niš. King Salomon – Géza I's predecessor who reigned between 1063 and 1074 – took the arm of the martyr St Procopius, preserved in Niš, and placed it in the church of St Demetrius in Sirmium.[9] Thereafter, the domination of the city was symbolically linked with the arm. As soon as the Byzantine emperor Manuel I recaptured the city in 1165 (see below at

---

[4] *DAI*: 66–9; Cormack 1992: 230–6; Ostrogorsky 1956: 10. The prohibition must surely be related to the gift of a crown to Tsar Symeon, subsequently acknowledged as the imperial insignia of Bulgaria by Romanus I in 927.

[5] Moravcsik 1966: 578–9. On the crown, and for illustrations and comment, see now the collected papers in Bakay 1994.

[6] Györffy 1959: 22–3, glosses the political history of the region, and admits a lacuna for most of the eleventh century.   [7] Parović-Pešikan 1981: 179–91.

[8] Gelzer 1893: 43, 53–4; Ercegović-Pavlović 1980: 53; Minić 1980: 58–9.

[9] *Hungarian Chronicle*: 369–77. See above at p. 141.

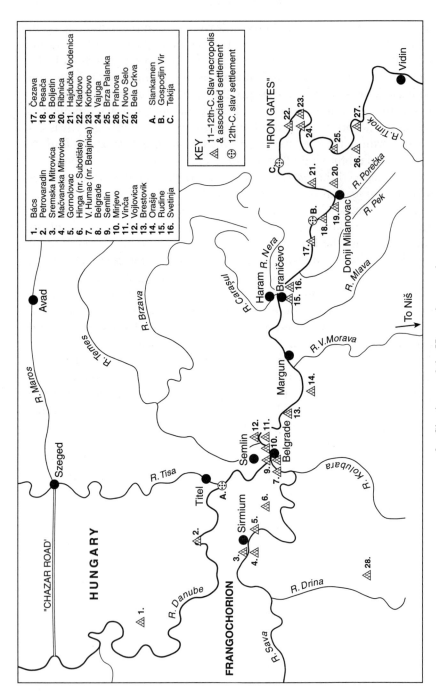

KEY

◁ 11–12th-C. Slav necropolis
   & associated settlement

⊕ 12th-C. slav settlement

1.	Bács
2.	Petrovaradin
3.	Sremska Mitrovica
4.	Mačvanska Mitrovica
5.	Gornolovac
6.	Hinga (nr. Subotište)
7.	V. Humac (nr. Batajnica)
8.	Belgrade
9.	Semlin
10.	Mirjevo
11.	Vinča
12.	Vojlovica
13.	Brestovik
14.	Orašje
15.	Rudine
16.	Svetinja
17.	Čezava
18.	Pesača
19.	Boljetin
20.	Ribnica
21.	Hajdučka Vodenica
22.	Kladovo
23.	Korbovo
24.	Vajuga
25.	Brza Palanka
26.	Prahova
27.	Novo Selo
28.	Bela Crkva
A.	Slankamen
B.	Gospodjin Vir
C.	Tekija

6.1 Sirmium and the Hungarian marches

pp. 252–3) he took the arm back to Niš, and it seems very unlikely that an earlier recovery of Sirmium would not have seen a similar action. Indeed, the historian John Cinnamus (227; trans.: 171–2) clearly implies that Sirmium was in Hungarian hands between 1071 and 1165. Certain scholars have argued that Sirmium was recovered by Byzantine forces soon after 1071, but they have relied too heavily on a single find of a seal struck by Alexius Comnenus when he was *sebastos* and *megas domestikos* (1078–81) discovered at Mačvanska Mitrovica.[10] This does not prove that Alexius recaptured the city, and may simply have been attached to a letter addressed to the Orthodox bishop who resided opposite Sirmium. Later evidence suggests that in the period of Hungarian domination a palace was built in Sirmium. Cinnamus (114; trans.: 91) claimed, rhetorically, that the destruction of the palace during Manuel's campaign of 1150 – which we will discuss in detail later – was 'a feat which can be recorded among the Romans' greatest achievements'.[11]

Hungarian political authority was recognized in the lands to the north of Sirmium, known then (in Greek) as Frangochorion, and today as Fruška Gora. A list of place names drawn up in Constantinople in the thirteenth century states categorically that 'Sirmium is now *Ouggria*' (Hungary).[12] The Latin name for the region appears to have been *Marchia*, the marches, and a Catholic archbishop of *Marchia* operated in tandem with the Orthodox metropolitan of *Tourkia* now based in Bács (Bač).[13] Both Catholic and Orthodox Christians lived in the frontier region, and ecclesiastical authority seems to have been shared. Excavations near Bács and at many other sites (listed on map 6.1) have uncovered artefacts common with those found at Slavic sites south of the Danube which were found together with contemporary Hungarian coins.[14] The principal fortified towns in the region, besides Sirmium itself, were Haram opposite Braničevo, and Semlin (modern Zemun), on the Sava's northern bank opposite Belgrade. The latter was 'Malevilla' through which the first bands of crusaders passed in 1096 (see above at pp. 176–8). When the followers of Peter 'the Hermit' arrived the governor was 'Guz, one of the Hungarian king's most esteemed men'.[15] We

---

[10] Ferjančić 1982: 47–53; Makk 1989: 125.
[11] The panegyrist Manganeius Prodromus (poem 2.115–18) has Manuel I within the palace plotting against the Hungarian *kralj*. See below at pp. 234–6.
[12] Diller 1970: 29. For the Hungarian recovery of Sirmium by Béla III, see below at pp. 281–4.
[13] Györffy 1959: 22–6; Oikonomides 1971: 527–33.
[14] Šaranik and Šulman 1954: 5–55; Veselinović 1953: 5–58; Nadj 1961: 89–115.
[15] Albert of Aachen: 276. For an alternative, and wholly unreliable account of Guz (called Kys) and his activities see *LPD*: 316–17.

are told further that Guz made a pact with his counterpart in Belgrade to oppose the crusaders' passage, and displayed arms and spoils seized from preceding pilgrims on the city's ramparts. This inspired Peter's hordes to storm the walls under a hail of arrows.

Trade between the Byzantine empire and the kingdom of Hungary continued in the later eleventh century, and we can be sure that salt was still an essential commodity (see above at pp. 42–5). The Hungarian royal clan, the Árpáds, had secured control of the tolls in the 1020s, and by the reign of Béla III (1172–96) the salt trade was the fourth most important source of revenue for the Hungarian treasury, and accounted for one-tenth of total treasury income. However, the Árpáds were not engaged personally in the trade, which seems to have been dominated by merchants of Chazar extraction. It is worth recalling that the Magyars arrived in the Carpathian basin with several confederate tribes, at least one of which (the *Kabaroi*) had Chazar origins. A second tribe of Chazar origin, the *Chalisioi*, followed later. The Hungarians of Magyar origin were Christians, the Chazars were Muslims and Jews. Legislation passed by the Hungarian king, Ladislas I, at the end of the eleventh century sought to limit the powers of 'the merchants who are called Ishmailites'. More revealing still is article xxiv of the Golden Bull issued by Andrew II in 1222 which forbids Muslims and Jews from any public office dealing with the salt trade. This represents an attempt to prevent the supervision of public revenue collection being compromised by the private interests of the Chazar merchants. Indeed, the region was so dominated by the 'Ishmailites' that the route between Szeged and the Danube was called the 'Chazar Road', a regional treasury established before the reign of Coloman (1095–1116) was known as the *Caliz*, and coins struck there bore similar designs to the Hungarian royal coinage but also bizarre inscriptions in pseudo-kufic script.[16]

The importance of trade in the southern borderlands of the Hungarian kingdom is further illustrated by the establishment of two offices responsible for the collection of royal revenues. The first was at Arad (in modern Romania), which is sixty miles from Szeged along the river Maros, the second at Titel seventy-five miles south along the Tisa, near its confluence with the Danube (in modern Vojvodina). Only three other regional chanceries served the rest of the kingdom.[17] Besides salt, other goods traded also seem to have changed little from the tenth century. As we have seen, Byzantine jewellery was a luxury much desired

---

[16] For a fuller analysis of all these points, and references to sources, see Göckenjan 1972: 60–76.
[17] Kubinyi 1980: 428.

north of the Danube.[18] Finds are far fewer at the many excavated settlements on the Danube between Vidin and Sirmium (listed on map 6.1). However, these towns appear to have been largely self-sufficient in simple jewellery and manufactured goods. Belt buckles and pectoral crosses, as well as fishhooks and arrowheads have been found in large numbers. Ceramics are by far the most abundant artefacts found at all sites, and the vast majority of pots were produced locally. Thrown on a slow wheel, they consist of a simple clay with varying amounts of added sand and crushed micaceous stone which, once fired become red-brown or red-grey. This homogeneous type is found throughout the Balkans with minor variations in design and decoration. Although many sherds have clear potters' marks, the ubiquity of a few standard forms – the cross, and the cross-in-circle being the most common – make it impossible to identify particular makers or to venture suggestions on local trade patterns. A second type of pottery, of better quality clay which turns yellow-orange when fired, has been found in small amounts the length of the Danube, but is apparently unknown in the interior of the Balkan peninsula. This suggests that it may have been produced at the lower Danube, or distributed by merchants travelling upriver. Finds represent 9 per cent of sherds discovered at Mačvanska Mitrovica, and a similar proportion at Belgrade and Prahovo, near Donji Milanovac. Excavations at Belgrade and Mačvanska Mitrovica have also turned up fragments from distinctive clay cauldrons (or kettles) of a type favoured by nomadic peoples. They consist of a clay of higher quality which turns a deep red colour once fired. Similar sherds are familiar from sites throughout modern Vojvodina and southern Hungary, and it seems very likely that the cauldrons were brought to the Danube by Hungarian traders.[19] Ceramics produced in Constantinople are rare: only in the region of the 'Iron Gates' (Djerdjap) do we find examples of Constantinopolitan green-glazed ware and the distinctive amphoroidal jugs daubed with red decoration which appear so frequently at sites throughout Paristrion and Bulgaria in the late eleventh and early twelfth centuries.

Therefore, in the last years of the eleventh century Hungarian authority over Sirmium and Frangochorion appears to have been consolidated, and recognized by Byzantium. Finds of Byzantine coins and jewellery demonstrate that trade between the empire and Hungary

---

[18] Mesterházy 1990: 87–115; Mesterházy 1991: 145–74.
[19] Minić 1980: 42–3.

continued, and passed across the Danube through Braničevo and Belgrade in the south into the Hungarian marches and the lands around Szeged. The Hungarians also sought to extend their interests, both political and economic, south of the Danube into the lands of the southern Slavs, and having integrated themselves into the trading nexus of east-central Europe, desired access to the lucrative markets of the northern Adriatic and Mediterranean.

TRADE AND THE MARITIME CITIES IN DALMATIA

Throughout the eleventh century and into the twelfth the maritime cities of Dalmatia grew wealthier through trade. The material remains of commercial activity the length of the eastern Adriatic littoral have not been explored in great detail: archaeological resources in Dalmatia have been concentrated on architectural reconstruction and renovation. Nevertheless, underwater explorations have recovered hundreds of amphorae, many of which correspond to types known throughout the Byzantine empire. A comparison can be made between Dalmatian finds, as published by Brušić (1976: 37–49) and Hayes' classification of amphorae discovered at Saraçhane in Istanbul. Notably, the popular eleventh- and twelfth-century piriform vessel, with a long narrow neck and close-set grooves and ridges across the belly (Brušić type Vb) found at many sites, including Dubrovnik, Split, Šibenik and the islet of Krapanj, appears to correspond to Saraçhane type 61. This type is also known from Athens, Corinth and Corfu, as well as Dinogetia in Paristrion (see above at pp. 84–6).

We have few contemporary indications of the volume of trade, or of goods traded, before the thirteenth century. However, later documents preserve established laws for the regulation of trade in several maritime cities, and these can shed much light on commercial activity in eleventh- and twelfth-century Dalmatia. The *Statuta Ragusii*, compiled in Dubrovnik (Ragusa) in 1272, gave considered legal form to a series of earlier – often far earlier – statutes. For this reason it bears closer examination, and while the laws of Dubrovnik cannot be considered of universal application, further documents demonstrate that similar conditions prevailed in the other trading cities. First, the barrenness of the Dalmatian coastal plain, together with the traditions of civilized Roman urbanity and the liturgical demands of the Catholic Church dictated that the principal commodity produced in the hinterland of Dubrovnik was wine. This had been the case in the ninth century, when the city paid tribute to the *župans* of both Zahumlje and Travunija because they had 'vineyards in both regions'.[20] Similarly, when he entered the city in great ceremony in 1171, the doge of Venice was presented with a supply of local wine.[21] Wine was equally important in Split, where the citizens surrendered to the Hungarians as soon as King Coloman had destroyed their vines (see below at pp. 199–200). Later in the twelfth century they surrendered to the Slav warlord Relja when he began to 'destroy vines and cut down various fruit-bearing trees', threatening 'I will not cease until all your vines are destroyed and so little wine is brought into the city that you will not be able to fill a single chalice sufficiently to perform the Eucharist.'[22]

Strict guidelines were laid down for the production and sale of wine, beginning with legally approved methods of cultivating vines. There was a restriction on the planting of vines, which must have kept the price of wine artificially high.[23] And to protect further the interests of local growers there was an embargo on the importation of 'foreign' wine, particularly that from Ston and the Pelješac peninsula.[24] Exceptions seem to have been made for foreign wine passing through Dubrovnik but not consumed there, and for that consumed by a foreign merchant and his crew while in Dubrovnik.[25] Similar guidelines applied in Kotor, where viticulture was also the principal form of agriculture.[26] In Trogir the *comes* – at this time a Venetian count, but earlier a local leader known as the prior – was allowed to import foreign wine for his own consumption and that of his family.[27] However, this was not to affect the closed domestic market, since he was forbidden to sell it or even give some away.[28]

Salt was also a serious business in Dubrovnik. The second book of the thirteenth-century statute lists the oaths that municipal functionaries were to swear to ensure loyal service to the city, and the oath of the municipal salt merchant (*salinarius*) was among the most important: it is

---

[20] *DAI*: 146. See above at pp. 28–9.   [21] *Historia Ducum Veneticorum*: 79.

[22] *Historia Salonitana*: 59, 69–70.

[23] *Liber Statutorum Civitatis Ragusii*: 115–19. The statute (p. 146) also forbids citizens of Dubrovnik from acquiring land on the islands to cultivate either trees for timber or vines, and legislates for the return of any such land previously acquired.   [24] *Liber Statutorum Civitatis Ragusii*: 216–17.

[25] *Liber Statutorum Civitatis Ragusii*: 42. Carter 1972: 36, refers to a document dated 1292 which records the importation of salt and wine from Ancona which was bound for Bosna.

[26] Sindik 1950: 57, 165–6.

[27] We will explore the office and duties of the prior (*comes civitatis*) below at pp. 200–1.

[28] *Statutum et Reformationes Civitatis Tragurii*: 7–9. The extant statute dates from 1322. However, the proem states that the text incorporates far earlier laws which have been 'examined, corrected, emended and approved by fine and wise men'.

recorded below only those of the *comes* and his advisors and the judges and other court officials, and before that of the captain of the guard and the supervisor of weights and measures.[29] All salt must have been imported, as there were no local pans.[30] Once imported, salt was sold to the municipal salt merchant, except where a licence was obtained from the *comes*. In both instances local needs would be met at a fixed price, and in the second the *comes* would also make a tidy profit. The penalty for an unlicensed transaction was severe: ten *hyperpera* (i.e. ten Byzantine gold coins or the equivalent) to be paid by both vendor and emptor, plus the confiscation of the salt. Confiscated salt joined the municipal stockpile.[31] A similar procedure operated in Trogir, although no comital licences were granted and all salt passed through the hands of the *salinarius*.[32]

The defence and prosperity of each sea-faring community depended on the production and maintenance of ships. Thus wood was a vital commodity, and demand, particularly for pine (*teda*), out-stripped local supplies.[33] It has been suggested that the earliest trade agreements between Dubrovnik and the Italian cities of Molfetta (in 1148) and Fano (in 1199) were intended to ensure a regular supply of timber.[34] Much timber must also have been acquired from the neighbouring highlands. Slaves were another lucrative commodity from the interior.[35] The Trogir statute specifies that anyone wishing to purchase a slave required a notarized certificate.[36] Also, there is evidence for the widespread use of slaves throughout Dalmatia in households (monastic and private) and on the land. The Dubrovnik statute refers to slaves cultivating the precious local vines, and rules that a slave-girl (*ancilla*) should be accepted by a creditor in lieu of a debt payment.[37] A charter from Split alludes to the maritime uses of slaves[38], and the *Chronicon Casinense* (*PL* 173: 905) records that three Italian monks were granted 'the church of St Maria in a place called Rabiata near the city of Dubrovnik, with its quay and fishing-boat, with its slaves and slave-girls (*servis et ancillis*) and everything else that fell within its remit and borders'.

---

[29] *Liber Statutorum Civitatis Ragusii*: 24–36, with the *salinarius* at 33–4.

[30] Carter 1972: 363–4 records an instance in 1215 when a shipment of salt from Dyrrachium passed through Dubrovnik for sale in Bosna, and a second in 1253 when merchants from Dubrovnik sold salt to the Raškan Serbs.   [31] *Liber Statutorum Civitatis Ragusii*: 130, 191–2.

[32] *Statutum et Reformationes Civitatis Tragurii*: 86–7.   [33] *Liber Statutorum Civitatis Ragusii*: 10–11.

[34] Abulafia 1976: 414–17. Texts of the treaties can be found at *Codex Diplomaticus*: ii, 62, 321–2.

[35] *Liber Statutorum Civitatis Ragusii*: 11, 214.   [36] *Statutum et Reformationes Civitatis Tragurii*: 121.

[37] *Liber Statutorum Civitatis Ragusii*: 10, 61–2.   [38] *Codex Diplomaticus*: ii, 141.

THE HUNGARIAN INVASION OF DALMATIA

It is not surprising, therefore that the Dalmatian cities looked attractive to various Hungarian kings. If the revenues from trade north of the Danube, particularly from slaves and salt, comprised a significant proportion of royal revenue, how much greater would be the profits from a successful annexation of the maritime cities. This certainly occurred to Coloman, the Hungarian king who had secured power after a year-long struggle in 1095. Moreover, Coloman was not concerned by the *de iure* suzerainty of the Byzantine emperor in Dalmatia. His tenuous hold on power made foreign policy initiatives, and the prestige that might be acquired thereby, extremely attractive. In a bid to secure international recognition he allied with Pope Urban II, and established a marriage alliance with the pope's ally, Roger, the Norman ruler of Sicily. This must have appeared threatening in Constantinople, and the eastern emperor's fears would have been exacerbated by Coloman's decision in 1097 to invade Croatia, where he killed the native ruler Peter and seized the coastal city of Biograd.[39] However, the immediate response was not Byzantine but Venetian. Surely acting with imperial approval, the doge Vitale Michiel (1096–1101) sailed to Trogir and Split. He extracted an oath of loyalty from the citizens, and those of Split agreed to provide him with two galleys or set aside 1,000 *solidi romanati* for military provisions.[40] Clearly, Venetian interest in Dalmatia was also inspired by the wealth of the cities. But more than this, Venice wished to gain control over potential competitors in the rapidly growing trade nexus which, via the Adriatic and Mediterranean, linked the west with Byzantium and, increasingly, the crusader principalities.

Because of the swift Venetian reaction, the Hungarian threat to Dalmatia did not materialize; instead a Venetian-Hungarian alliance, the so-called 'Conventio Amicitiae' was negotiated directed against the Normans, probably in 1098.[41] The 'Conventio Amicitiae' was essentially a pact of common aggression, and thus far it was in accordance with Byzantine interests which were implacably opposed to Norman expansion. However, the agreement was underpinned by the mutual recognition by each signatory of the other's sphere of influence in the coastal lands of the northern Adriatic: Hungary in Croatia, and Venice in the

---

[39] *SRH*: i, 182, 433; Dandolo: 224.   [40] *Codex Diplomaticus*: i, 207–9.
[41] *Codex Diplomaticus*: ii, 1. The date of the 'Conventio' has been disputed, and opinion once favoured 1101: hence its inclusion in the post-1100 volume of Dalmatian charters. Current consensus favours 1098: see Fine 1983: 284; Makk 1989: 12, 126–7, n. 49.

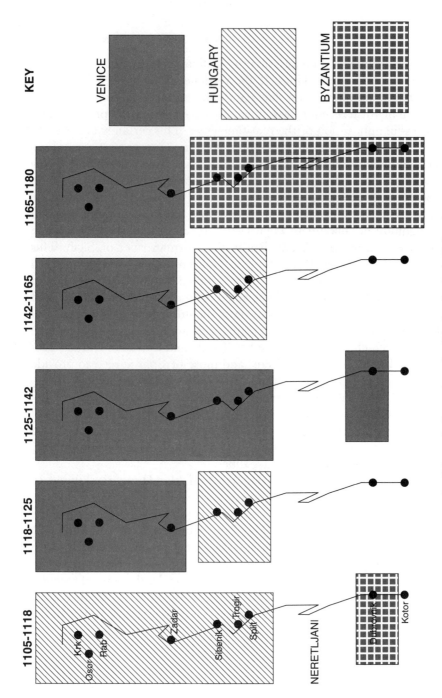

6.2 Schematic illustration of political authority in Dalmatia

maritime cities of Dalmatia. This formalization, which was not recognized by the Byzantine emperor and made no mention of his *de iure*
authority in Dalmatia, would have disturbed Alexius I. Henceforth, the
Venetians, who had received great rewards as imperial allies, were
treated with greater caution and reserve, and the emperor steered a
course between their interests and those of his occasional ally, the king
of Hungary.

In 1102 Coloman took measures to create a legal basis for his rule in
Croatia and to secure the support of the Croatian nobles who were
prone to rebellion. The so-called 'Pacta Conventa' confirmed his rule,
and shortly afterwards Coloman was crowned as king of Croatia at
Biograd. There can be little doubt that Coloman's explicit use of the title
'king of Croatia *and Dalmatia*' illustrated a desire for his authority to be
recognized throughout the northern Adriatic littoral.[42] However, there
is no explicit evidence that he attempted to rule the maritime cities, and
between 1102 and 1105 charters suggest that his dealings with the cities
involved only the confirmation of property rights in his kingdom
granted to religious foundations such as the important monastery of St
Maria in Zadar. In 1105 this was all to change.

1105 was a crucial year in Byzantine-Hungarian relations, and for the
balance of power in the northern Balkans. As we have seen (at pp.
180–3), the principal menace facing the empire at that time was the
renewed threat posed by the Normans under Bohemond. Alexius feared
the possibility that Bohemond might forge an alliance with the
Hungarians, and thus expose the empire to attack on two fronts. The
rapid negotiations and marriage of the emperor's son, junior emperor
and designated heir John, to Piroska, the daughter of the late king
Ladislas demonstrate how valuable the alliance was perceived to be in
Constantinople, and the new alliance allowed the Hungarian king to
launch an invasion of the maritime cities in Dalmatia in the same year.

Steindorff (1984: 49–50) has demonstrated that Coloman undertook
scrupulous preparations for the invasion of 1105. It can be inferred from
the *Life of St Christopher the Martyr* (Šišić 1914: i, 623) that a fleet was set sail
commanded by the *ban* Ugra who was charged with subduing the islanders in the Gulf of Kvarner. The *Life of the blessed John of Trogir* (Šišić 1914:
i, 619–22) records that Coloman was intent on personally seizing the city
of Zadar, and marched there first of all because it was the best fortified
and most powerful of the cities in northern Dalmatia. The blessed John,

---

[42] *Codex Diplomaticus*: ii, 9–10.

bishop of Trogir, negotiated a settlement which allowed Coloman to enter the city in triumph; an event which was commemorated on a triumphal inscription which can be seen on the bell-tower of the monastery of St Maria, and which confirms the date of 1105.[43] The Hungarians moved on to the fortress at Šibenik, to Trogir, and finally to Split where Coloman set a siege. Once again victory was secured by negotiation, this time through the mediation of Crescentius, the archbishop of Split.[44]

Both Andrea Dandolo and Thomas of Split record that Coloman secured the loyalty of the maritime cities by granting them certain privileges.[45] The settlement which the Hungarian agreed with the citizens of Trogir has survived in its earliest form, as a series of written notes recording the clauses to which the signatories had sworn.[46] It is peculiarly revealing about the nature of government in Trogir, and by analogy several other maritime cities in 1105 and thereafter. Six clauses in the privilege document, which are repeated in several later charters, bear closer examination:

1. *The clerics and people may continue to elect their bishop and ruler, the prior (comes), according to ancient custom, whom the king will then confirm in office.* Coloman would later relinquish his right to confirm the appointment of the bishop in return for papal recognition of his authority in secular affairs. Here we have proof that in the years before the Hungarian invasion, when the maritime cities acknowledged Byzantine suzerainty, the citizens themselves were responsible for the election of both their secular and spiritual leaders. The prior and bishop had complementary, often overlapping responsibilities for the direction of domestic and foreign policy. Charters demonstrate that the prior was charged with negotiating trade agreements with other powers, commanding a local force against an invading army, or concluding treaties with the Venetian doge or Hungarian king.[47] However, the bishop also negotiated with foreign powers. In arranging a treaty with the Venetians in 1097 the citizens of Split had been represented by their senior and junior priors, but the citizens of Trogir by their bishop John, who continued in his role as chief negotiator in 1105. As we have seen, a similar role as peacemaker was taken by the archbishop of Split. Despite the safeguards for local auton-

[43] Ferluga 1978: 247.   [44] *Historia Salonitana*: 59–60.
[45] Dandolo: 228; *Historia Salonitana*: 60.
[46] Steindorff 1984: 11–21. See now Stephenson 1999b: 127–50.
[47] *Codex Diplomaticus*: ii, 62, 124–5; *Historia Salonitana*: 61–2.

omy contained in this clause, it is clear that the Hungarian king could exploit his close relationship with the key municipal officers. In 1112 he ensured that his favoured candidate, a Hungarian named Manasses, replaced the late Crescentius as archbishop of Split.

2. *The citizens do not owe the Hungarian king or his successors tribute.* This suggests that until 1105 the cities had continued to pay tribute to the Croats in the manner arranged by the Byzantine emperor Basil I.[48] Coloman abolished this in his capacity as king of the Croats. He did so as a symbol of good faith, but also because he had devised a more profitable means to tax the rich trading cities.

3. *Duties excised from foreign traders entering the port will be divided as follows: two-thirds to the Hungarian king and one-third to the prior of the city (*comes civitatis*), of which a tithe shall go to the bishop.* The exaction of taxes on the revenues from trade must be considered the principal purpose for the Hungarian invasion, and the subsequent competition with Venice. The wealth from the taxation of trade provided the king with a means to fill his own coffers and to secure the loyalty of the native prior. Steindorff (1984: 61) uses the term *Gegenseitigkeit*, which may be translated as 'reciprocity', to describe this arrangement. Hungarian governors, or *gespans*, were installed in several cities to ensure that this, and other instructions, were carried out. However, they did not replace the local prior. A document issued in Zadar later in 1105 was witnessed by a certain *comes* Cesar, the most senior of the many Hungarians (*pluribus Ungaris*) who were present.[49] The *Life of St Christopher the Martyr* reveals that Ugra, the commander of the Hungarian fleet, remained on the island of Krk as governor (*comes*) for a year after the invasion alongside the Slav *ban*.[50] Similarly, Thomas of Split reveals that a dual administration had been established in Split before 1116, when a Hungarian officer whom Thomas calls the *dux* was in command of a large garrison based in a tower in the city's eastern ramparts. He was responsible for the collection of tribute throughout Croatia. He was not the prior, who was at that time a certain Adrian Trevisanus '*comes*, and most faithful guardian of the city'.[51] The use of the Latin term *comes* to refer in several contexts to the prior, the Hungarian nobles who accompanied Coloman, and to the Hungarian governors (also known as *gespans*) who were installed in the cities to ensure the

[48] *DAI*: 146. See above at pp. 28–9. [49] *Codex Diplomaticus*: ii, 15; Steindorff 1984: 56–9.
[50] Šišić 1914: i, 623. [51] *Historia Salonitana*: 61.

correct collection and distribution of revenue has left much scope for confusion. It had previously been imagined that Hungarian governors (*comites*) were only established in the cities after 1182.

4. *No Hungarians or other aliens may settle in the city unless the citizens see fit to allow it.* Strict controls on immigration benefited locals, who might otherwise have suffered at the hands of Hungarian nobles. Coloman also benefited, since only he and not his subjects could use political leverage for economic gain. The Hungarian king would have been at pains to prevent the emergence of a powerful rival in any of the rich coastal cities, and kept a close eye on his own *gespans*.

5. *The citizens have no duty to house and supply the king or his entourage while they are in the city, unless they choose to.* They may often have chosen to. However, the emphasis on there being no obligation was in marked, and surely deliberate, contrast to the demands of the Venetian doge who expected 1,000 *solidi* to supply his retinue.

6. *Any person whom the citizens wish to expel from the city may enter the royal domain with his family and possessions.* This was more than altruism, since exiles tended to be men of influence cast out by political or commercial rivals. Such men might be harboured by the king as sources of information or as potential replacements for recalcitrant priors.

THE VENETIAN RESPONSE

For several years the Venetians acquiesced in the Hungarian domination of Dalmatia. The excellent *Annales Venetici Breves* record that the doge was concerned principally with affairs in the Holy Land, and periodically with troubles in Italy where 'Venice stood alone against Ravenna, Padua and Treviso'. Moreover, the doge wished to maintain good relations with Byzantium, and in 1107 was an ally in the confederation which confronted Bohemond (see above at pp. 180–3). However, and finally, in 1112 Doge Ordelafo Falier took action. Andrea Dandolo relates:

Intending to recover Dalmatia, the doge sent the patriarch [of Grado, Giovanni Gradenigo] to Constantinople, along with forty galleys. As the ambassador he was to remind the emperor Alexius of his forgotten promises and treaty [with Venice] with reference to the [Hungarian] king's invasion. He also suggested that he might supply appropriate support since the Venetians had proved to be loyal agents of the empire. The emperor acknowledged the request, but sought counsel which drew out and delayed any action. (Dandolo: 229)

The emperor's procrastination reflected an obvious unwillingness to upset the balance between his two allies, both of whom had provided assistance against Bohemond. Eventually, the doge ran out of patience, and in 1115 launched an independent expedition which was a qualified success. Venetian control was restored over the Gulf of Kvarner, and possibly over several cities on the mainland. However, Biograd remained in Hungarian hands, as more significantly did Zadar where the garrison under their commander Cledin had mounted a successful defence of the citadel. It is likely that the doge would have settled for control over the northernmost section of Dalmatia if King Coloman had not died on 3 February 1116. He was succeeded by his fifteen-year-old son Stephen. In May of the same year the doge returned to Zadar, this time with the support of Alexius I. On 15 July the Venetians defeated the Hungarians in a pitched battle, seized control of the citadel, and marched on to Šibenik where they destroyed the 'impregnable fortress'.[52] Hungarian resistance was centred on Split, where Archbishop Manasses had secretly arranged for the Hungarian garrison to ride forth from their bastion in the western walls and secure control of the whole city. Manasses' betrayal was revealed to the citizens by their prior, Adrian Trevisanus, who determined that attack was the best form of defence. The swearing in of a public orator was used as a cover for an attack on the Hungarians' tower. The whole episode demonstrates the fragility of Hungarian authority and the continued vitality of municipal government. In this way, the maritime cities shifted their allegiance to Venice, and swore their loyalty to the doge and his successors, once again on their own terms.[53] An extant privilege document demonstrates that these were essentially the same terms as those negotiated with the Hungarians.[54] Despite further hostilities in 1118, the Venetians retained control of the maritime cities at the time of the death of Alexius I.

JOHN II COMNENUS AND DALMATIA

Alexius I Comnenus died 15 August 1118. He was succeeded by his son John II Comnenus (1118–43). One of John's first decisions of note was his refusal to renew the chrysobull by which his father had conferred privileges on the Venetians. The doge was concerned with affairs in the

---

[52] *Annales Venetici Breves*: 71; Dandolo: 230.   [53] *Historia Ducum Veneticorum*: 73.
[54] *Codex Diplomaticus*: ii, 393.

Holy Land, and for three years Venetian merchants continued to trade in Constantinople on considerably worse terms.[55] Only in 1122 was a response considered: a fleet was prepared which sailed for Dalmatia and laid siege to the Byzantine island stronghold of Corfu. Then, once again, concerns in the east drew the doge away, to achieve a remarkable victory at Iope and to play a crucial role in the capture of Tyre. As a reward and an incentive to remain in the east the Venetians were granted privileges in all the towns of the kingdom of Jerusalem, which included exemption from paying any taxes on all goods they traded. These concessions only reinforced the doge's desire to restore similar rights across the Byzantine empire, which lay between Venice and her newest interests. Returning from Palestine the Venetian fleet seized the Byzantine islands of Rhodes, Chios (where the body of St Isidore was found, and whence it was taken back to Venice), Samos, Lesbos and Andros.[56] John II was obliged to treat, and recovered the islands with the promise of renewed privileges.

Meanwhile, the Hungarian king Stephen II had sought to recover territory in Dalmatia. His prestige had been dented by his earlier defeats at Venetian hands, and in the intervening years he had achieved little of note in his dealings with the Russian principalities and Austria. His only success was securing the hand of the daughter of Robert, the Norman ruler of Apulia.[57] The renewal of the defunct Norman alliance must have been partly directed against the Venetians, and surely encouraged an opportunistic Hungarian invasion of Dalmatia launched in 1124. The invasion was successful, and Stephen put the seal on his conquests by granting familiar privileges to the citizens of Trogir and Split.[58] However, the Venetian response was swift and equally successful. The recovery of the maritime cities was conducted as a demonstration of the doge's might and grace: Domenico Michiel had brought the Saracens low, belittled the emperor of the Greeks, and now proceeded to drive the Hungarians from the Adriatic littoral. While the citizens of Split and Trogir swore fidelity to the doge and his successors, the fleeing Hungarians mustered at Biograd. 'Because the citizens of Biograd had dared resist the doge and his army they were deprived of all their property and possessions and their city was razed to its foundations, which is clear to see even to this day [c. 1229]' (*Historia Ducum Veneticorum*: 74). The citizens of Zadar were spared the doge's stick, and offered instead a carrot: a share in the distribution of booty. Michiel's credentials as a

[55] *Historia Ducum Veneticorum*: 73–4; Dandolo: 231–2; Nicol 1988: 77–8.
[56] *Historia Ducum Veneticorum*: 74; Dandolo: 233.   [57] *Hungarian Chronicle*: 437.
[58] *Codex Diplomaticus*: ii, 37–8. The first lay signatory was the *comes* Cledin.

suzerain were thus displayed: he was both a mighty admiral and munificent philanthropist. For the next twenty years the Venetians retained control over the whole of Dalmatia from the gulf of Kvarner to Zadar, and perhaps even Dubrovnik.

The Venetians seem initially to have been content to allow local priors to continue to govern their own cities, and there is no evidence that Venetian governors were installed as overseers. Certainly we cannot trust the testimony of three seventeenth- and eighteenth-century chronicles which maintain that the first Venetian count was installed in Dubrovnik in 1122. No contemporary documents have survived in the local archives to corroborate this claim, and such an appointment would have been completely at odds with contemporary practice in Zadar. In fact the claim is illustrative of Venetian practices in the thirteenth century, and the counts listed by the anonymous seventeenth-century author as resident in Zadar between 1122 and 1142 actually held office during the period 1260 to 1358.[59] The first attested *comes* of Zadar 'and the whole of Dalmatia' after the Venetian recovery is Peter, known from a charter dated 1134.[60] It is clear that Peter was not a Venetian, but was the native prior of Zadar. The witness list of the document states that the judges (*iudices*) of Zadar were Peter's own men. They were all native to Zadar and bore both Slavic and Latin names.[61] One of their number was Peter's own brother Bratona, and it is hard here to resist comparisons with other powerful families in trading cities, such as the Chryselioi who dominated municipal government in Dyrrachium. Further proof that Peter was a native can be found in a later charter which records that he had been *comes* before the Venetian conquest, 'under the Hungarian king'.[62] It is possible that Peter's authority, over 'the whole of Dalmatia' (*totius Dalmacie*) extended as far as Dubrovnik. In 1142 Pope Innocent II despatched a letter to a certain P[eter] *comes* of Dubrovnik.

JOHN II COMNENUS AND THE HUNGARIANS

Very little contemporary information on the reign of John Comnenus has survived. Anna Comnena, writing soon after his death, mentions her brother in only five places in the *Alexiad*.[63] Good reasons for Anna's virtually ignoring her brother have long been known to Byzantinists. Before

[59] *Annales Ragusini Anonymi*: 29–30.   [60] *Codex Diplomaticus*: ii, 44–5.
[61] For the rise of the Slav element in the urban aristocracy see Novak 1953–4: 1–29.
[62] *Codex Diplomaticus*: ii, 100. See also Steindorff 1984: 74–5.
[63] *Alexiad*: i, 5; ii, 62–3; iii, 66, 126, 127, 132, 137, 238 (trans. 19, 197–8, 379, 424–5, 429, 433, 512).

John's birth Anna had been betrothed to the *porphyrogennetos* Constantine Ducas, and she expected to succeed her father as Constantine's empress. After Alexius' death Anna and her mother plotted to replace John with Anna's husband, Nicephorus Bryennius. The consort did not comply and the coup failed. Anna was forced to become a nun, and compiled her work in exile. She expresses her hostility to John quite openly in a sentence in book fourteen of the *Alexiad*: 'Thereafter we enjoyed peace until the end of [Alexius'] life, but with him all the benefits disappeared and his efforts came to nothing through the stupidity of those who inherited the throne.'[64] Anna thus asks her reader to compare Alexius' record as she has presented it with his or her own knowledge of the reign of his son. The modern reader lacks this comparative perspective and is poorly assisted by other sources.

A rare break in the silence concerns John's dealings with the Hungarians between 1127 and 1129. Both John Cinnamus and Nicetas Choniates cover the episode, and it is worth exploring their accounts for the light this can shed on the familiar theme of 'rhetoric' and 'reality' in Byzantine literature, and so that we can dismiss the notion that John ever considered Hungary a priority or a major threat. Both Cinnamus and Choniates generally treat John's long reign as an extended preface to that of his son Manuel I. It has generally been assumed that these two historians, in contrast to Anna's silence and veiled innuendo, provide complementary, if all too brief, accounts of John's activities. In fact both seek to contrast John's deeds and achievements with Manuel's.[65] Cinnamus was Manuel's private secretary, and his work is very much the official biography. Choniates was certainly aware of Cinnamus' work, and in places he appears directly to refute the contentions of his forerunner. Since I favour Choniates' account, I will record it in full, and offer only comments on Cinnamus' alternative narrative. (Choniates' account also has the virtue of clarity, and when read beside the version contained in the *Hungarian Chronicle*, reproduced below, renders any further reportage of these events superfluous.)

Choniates provides the following summary of John's campaigns in 1127, which he portrays as an unqualified success:

During the summer season the Hungarians crossed the Danube and sacked Braničevo. They demolished the walls and transported the stones to Semlin. They also plundered Sardica, breaking and tearing up earlier peace treaties.

---

[64] *Alexiad*: iii, 159 (trans.: 448).
[65] For a fuller exposition of this thesis see Stephenson 1996b: 177–87.

The secret reason for this conflict was that Álmos, the brother of Stephen who ruled the Hungarians, had fled to the emperor and had been welcomed cordially. The professed and specious reason was the [Hungarians'] accusation that citizens of Braničevo had assaulted and robbed Hungarians who had travelled to the locality to trade, committing heinous crimes against them. Since this evil had erupted while the emperor was dwelling at Philippopolis, he considered the predicament scrupulously and resolved to expel the Hungarians. He spent some time preparing his household troops to defend against the enemy, then sailed equipped and swiftly propelled ships along the Danube from the Black Sea, falling upon the foe by both land and water. He then crossed the river in the general's trireme, ferrying the army to the far shore where the cavalry dispersed the Hungarian host with their couched lances. Demonstrating his remarkable endurance he remained in enemy lands and captured Frangochorion, the richest land of the Hungarians which lies between the rivers Sava and Danube with plains suited to driving horses. He also took Semlin and attacked Haram from which he wrested great spoils. After further struggles with this race, he offered them peace, and compelled those other barbarian peoples at the western frontier of the Roman Empire whom he had so often defeated in battle to become allies. (Choniates: 17–18; trans.: 11–12)

Choniates' emphasis on John's stamina and endurance echo twenty-two verse encomia composed by the court panegyrist Theodore Prodromus, which constantly stress the emperor's *andreia*.[66] However, there is no indication that the emperor intended for his conquest of Frangochorion to be permanent, or that he aspired to annex any lands beyond the Danube. His sights were firmly fixed on the empire's eastern frontier, and he had no desire to become embroiled in protracted conflicts with the Hungarians. Choniates glosses over the second conflict ('further struggles'), but notes that it ended in a peace accord established on John's terms. For this reason the whole episode appears as a carefully orchestrated show of strength by the Byzantine emperor.

Cinnamus provides an entirely different account of the first campaign and the 'further struggles' to which Choniates only alludes. His description is full of allusions to John's weaknesses as a commander. First, where Choniates stresses John's preparations, Cinnamus emphasizes the emperor's panic at the sudden assault, and has him marching straight to the Danube. Second, Cinnamus notes pointedly that the Hungarian king was far away when John arrived, and thus had no real foe to confront. Third, he implies that John was not personally involved in the initial decisive victory which was achieved by Lombard and Turkish mercenaries. In fact, the only martial endeavour directed by John was the capture of the

---

[66] Magdalino 1993: 419–20.

fortress of Haram 'which fell without resistance'. After this the emperor is reported to have recrossed the river into his own lands, pausing only to strengthen Braničevo with a garrison under a certain Curticius.

Cinnamus alone records a second campaign 'a short time after' initiated by a renewed Hungarian assault on Braničevo. He reports that, rather than meeting the Hungarians in battle, John's first action was to humiliate Curticius, who (we are further informed) had fought bravely to defend the fortress. At this point Cinnamus digresses to describe a similar humiliation of the commander of the fortress of Ras in Raška. Although the historian appears to allude to unrest among the Serbs at this time, the episode he describes probably took place in 1122–3,[67] and its inclusion at this later time is to invite the reader to note and condemn John's poor treatment of his generals. Moreover, in an aside, Cinnamus implies that John's actions were criticized at the time. In devoting precious time to such acts John is shown to have neglected his men and precipitated his own final humiliation. The Hungarians took heart from the fact that the Byzantine forces were stationed at the Danube with limited provisions and demoralized by the cold. They renewed their assault, and John was only saved when word of the imminent attack reached him. More shameful still, his informant was both a woman and a Latin. The emperor fled through the region known as the Evil Stairs, with the Hungarians in pursuit. Fleeing, he left behind the imperial tent, from which the barbarians stole the awnings.

The cumulative effect of Cinnamus' innuendo is to portray John II as a vengeful and spiteful coward. His reasons for doing so are not difficult to fathom. The author's true subject was John's son, Manuel I, who conducted several campaigns against the Hungarians around Braničevo and in Frangochorion. Manuel is consistently portrayed as the supreme military emperor, remarkable for his devotion to his men and for his personal bravery. We will return to Manuel's campaigns in the following chapter (at pp. 229–37), but for now must conclude that this rare well-documented episode tells us less about John II's activities in the lands bordering Hungary than we might have hoped, but more about the perspectives of our two historians than has previously been noted. Fortunately, we have a further non-Byzantine perspective on the campaigns, contained in the *Hungarian Chronicle*:

Meanwhile [before 1127] the empress in Constantinople, the daughter of King Ladislas named Piroska, sent word to King Stephen telling him that the king of

---

[67] *LPD*: 368–9; Chalandon 1912: ii, 69–73.

Hungary was her [liege]man. Even the emperor chastised her for speaking out of turn. However, when he heard this the king considered it a terrible slight and mustered an army. He launched a fierce invasion of Greek lands and devastated several Greek cities with fire and the sword, petrifying all the cities of that region. All kings were afraid of King Stephen as they would fear a bolt of lightning. In fact even squalling children were silenced by the mention of his name. The king had with him 700 Frankish troops as he ravaged Bulgaria and with whose aid he destroyed the walls of Greek fortresses. When the Greek emperor did not ride out to meet him he sent an insulting message, announcing he was not worthy to be called emperor, nor even a king, but only a wretched old midwife, since only such a crone would be so ineffectual. The emperor replied to him thus: 'Certainly the king will believe he is in the company of a midwife when I sever his manhood like an umbilical cord!' For this reason the emperor sent a mighty army against Hungary. Arriving, they crossed into Hungary at Haram. The Hungarians were unable to prevent them because the Greeks contrived to set alight their ships with sulphurous fires, burning them in their own waters. Therefore, the king sent the elite from his whole kingdom against the Greeks under the command of Setephel. On arrival they fought the Greeks on the banks of the river Karas (Caraşul), opposite Braničevo. The hand of God was with the Greeks and the Hungarians could not resist them. The slaughter that took place was so great that its like has rarely been seen. The river Karas was so infused with human blood that it appeared to flow with gore alone. The warriors began to throw corpses into the river and fled across them, crossing the river as if by a bridge. However, more Hungarians were slaughtered like cattle, for nothing could save them from the Greeks. Indeed, Count Ciz and many other fine soldiers were buried before the emperor and king consulted through trusted messengers and sailed to an island near Braničevo to negotiate. For a long time the rulers exchanged accusations and excuses before they finally agreed a firm peace and returned to their own lands. (*Hungarian Chronicle*: 439–42)

The chronicler provides a third reason for the Hungarian attack: a claim by the empress that her cousin the king was her liegeman. As we have seen (at p. 188), this was indeed the perceived relationship between the Hungarian king and the Byzantine emperor, as it was portrayed so elegantly on the Hungarian crown. However, we might question the truth, and certainly the wisdom of Piroska's claim. Other details of the campaign are entirely convincing and support Choniates' version of events. John did not rush, but delayed his response, clearly buying time for preparation. The Byzantine fleet, sent along the Danube as Choniates states, was instrumental in the initial rout by its devastating use of 'Greek Fire'. The subsequent encounter, fought on the Hungarian side of the Danube, was a great victory for the emperor, and concluded with a favourable treaty. He did not return to the Danube.

Thus, we must conclude that John's encounters with the Hungarians in 1127–29, which receive considerable attention in our sources, do not indicate that he considered Hungary a major threat. John did not consider the empire's Balkan frontier an area worthy of his concern, despite the wealth of the maritime cities, and the encroachments of both Hungary and Venice. For the remainder of John's reign the treaty signed in 1129 with the Hungarian king was honoured. Furthermore, since Hungary sat between the two great powers of twelfth-century Europe, Byzantium and Germany, stability in the northern marches was guaranteed by the good relations John Comnenus maintained with the German rulers Lothar III (1125–37) and Conrad III (1138–52). In 1136 Byzantine troops took part in Lothar's campaign which pressed into Norman-occupied southern Italy as far as Bari. Relations with Conrad were even better, and from 1140 were destined to be cemented by the marriage of John's fourth son, Manuel, to Conrad's sister-in-law, Bertha of Sulzbach. Thus, John was free to concentrate his attention and resources on his eastern campaigns, and it was in Cilicia in 1143 that he was killed in a hunting accident. By then two of his sons had also died, and the succession to his throne was disputed by the two survivors: Isaac and Manuel. Manuel succeeded.

CHAPTER SEVEN

Manuel I Comnenus confronts the West (1143–1156)

The rise of several western powers between 1081 and 1143 was clearly of significance for Byzantium's Balkan frontier, and while the Normans and crusaders were handled effectively, encroachments by both Hungary and Venice went unchecked. Alexius I's general indifference to the north-western Balkans stood in sharp contrast to his efforts to restore and retain imperial authority in Paristrion and Dyrrachium. He was willing to allow Venice and Hungary to control Dalmatia and Sirmium so long as both were his allies. His only consistent policy was to play one power against the other whenever either seemed to have gained the upper hand, often veering between positions suddenly. This did not check the independent ambitions of either the Hungarians or Venetians, and after a cooperative start both began to expand their interests without paying great attention to Byzantine concerns. John II pursued a similar hands-off policy. His priorities lay in the east, and his forays into the Balkans were brief shows of strength. They appear to have been successful, within the limits John set, but our knowledge of them is coloured by the preoccupations of Byzantine authors writing later and with different agendas. Nevertheless, by 1143 the Venetians had secured control over the whole northern Adriatic, by sea and land. The Hungarians had extended their influence further into Sirmium and the Slavic lands of the northern Balkans, and had secured recognition in the central Dalmatian cities of Šibenik, Trogir and Split. At no stage did John II take any direct action to prevent this. We can only surmise that he saw little virtue in controlling Dalmatia directly and was willing to work with both powers to ensure stability at the north-western frontier. However, it created a tangle of interests and loyalties which Manuel I had to unravel when he determined that the north-west was a region of vital strategic importance.

In the early years of his reign Manuel remained committed to his father's policies in the east. The crusader principalities, and in particular

Antioch remained priorities. He was prepared to tolerate increased Hungarian influence in Sirmium and the northern Balkans, and the Venetian domination of Dalmatia. However, his attention was drawn increasingly towards the west as affairs there threatened to undermine the delicate balance that his father had sought to maintain between the heartland and frontier of Latin Christendom. This was the period when it was realized that the grand alliance with Germany was unsuited to the changing circumstances in the west, and when German interference in the east became a reality in the form of the Second Crusade. Whereas Alexius Comnenus had considered the possibility of his actions in the west influencing policy in the east, most clearly articulated in the treaty of Devol, Manuel witnessed the encirclement of his empire by the expansion and linking of Latin interests.

MANUEL'S MARRIAGE TO BERTHA OF SULZBACH

As we have seen, John II maintained good relations with the German ruler Conrad III. Otto of Freising reproduces letters which purportedly passed between the two rulers and they reveal, beneath the mutual flattery, a meeting of minds. Both Conrad and John provided services for each other: Conrad asked for Byzantine assistance in bringing to justice certain Russians who had killed Germans and seized their money; he also sought Manuel's indulgence for the German mercenaries who lived in Constantinople, and permission for the German community to build their own church. John responded favourably, and in a letter dated 12 February 1142 he wrote, 'Of the situation which has arisen in Russia, which even as you have written to our Empire, so also have we done as it is proper for us to do in the case of a kinsman and friend' (Otto of Freising, *Gesta Friderici*: 40; trans.: 57). He did not mention the German church, but alludes to individuals whom he has treated with favour.

The mention of kinship between the rulers is an allusion to the fact that from 1140 their friendship was destined to be cemented by the marriage of John's fourth son, Manuel, to Conrad's sister-in-law, Bertha of Sulzbach. Otto of Freising states explicitly that the alliance was conceived in order to create a united front against Roger II, the Norman ruler of Sicily. However, it is clear from the text of John's letter, and from arrangements made much later in 1148 in Thessalonica – and we will return to this later – that Conrad had agreed to recognize Byzantine rights in Norman-held Apulia. In return Conrad expected his claims to Lombardy to be recognized. In effect, the German and Byzantine rulers had conceived of a plan to divide Italy between them, without reference to the papacy, and pending a joint offensive against the Normans. However, this was for the future; in the meantime both were free to concentrate on affairs in other arenas. Conrad faced serious domestic troubles, while John Comnenus chose to concentrate on his eastern campaigns. And it was in the east, in Cilicia in 1143 that John was killed in a hunting accident. Manuel, the younger of John's two surviving sons who had been with his father and thus was in command of the imperial army succeeded to the throne.

Upon his accession Manuel Comnenus was committed to his father's policy of cooperation with Germany. John II had shared the Germans' reluctance to accept Norman expansion in Italy, and Otto of Freising (*Chronicle*: 354–5) records that Manuel emulated his father in exchanging frequent embassies with the German court, the first bearing precious gifts and committed to renewing the treaty against Roger II of Sicily. However, it is also clear that Manuel was unwilling to honour the marriage brokered for him when he was the emperor's fourth son. As reigning emperor Manuel desired a more suitable partner, and we might detect in John Cinnamus' defence of Bertha's credentials (36; trans.: 36–7: 'this maiden was related to kings and inferior to no contemporary in propriety of character and spiritual worth') the suggestion that her suitability was a subject of much interest at court. Bertha had clearly been in Constantinople for some time before Manuel's accession, for she is reported to have foretold the death of his older brother John when he had mistaken her for a nun. Manuel clearly shared this view, for Choniates reveals that he was not attracted by his betrothed's plain appearance and pious habits. Bertha, we are told:

Was not much concerned with physical beauty as with inner beauty and the condition of her soul. Disdaining face powder, eyeliner and eyeshadow, she preferred nature's flush to rouge, and considered other women who needed such aids to be winsome. Instead, she was adorned by the virtues to which she was devoted. More than this, she had the natural trait of being opinionated and unbending. (Choniates: 54; trans.: 32)

The emperor was not impressed by his plain, straight-talking German wife:

For Manuel, being young and passionate, was wholly devoted to a dissolute and voluptuous lifestyle, constantly banqueting and revelling. Whatever his youthful vigor dictated, or his vulgar passions prompted, he did. Indulging in sexual intercourse willy nilly, he jumped between beds and secret liaisons, even unlawfully penetrating his niece. (Choniates: 53–4; trans.: 32)

When he could spare time between meals and sex, Manuel was simultaneously in negotiations with Roger II of Sicily, with a view to finding a suitable Norman bride. No reasons are given for his breaking off those talks, but soon after, in January 1146, Manuel married Bertha, and in some haste given her long residence in Byzantium. The reason for this was the emperor's renewed commitment to the German alliance against the Normans, and a related concern: his desire to prevent Conrad III's participation in a new and feared enterprise, the Second Crusade.

In December 1144 the city of Edessa had fallen to Zengi, the atabeg of Mosul. In the subsequent period leading up to his marriage, when Manuel was exchanging embassies with the German court, the emperor must have been aware of the possible implications of this disaster. As soon as she heard of Edessa's fate, probably in January 1145, Queen Melisende of Jerusalem had sent an embassy to Antioch to propose calling for a crusade. An embassy bound for Rome to be led by Hugh, bishop of Jabala, was prepared. At this time Raymond, prince of Antioch, who had done homage to John II in 1137 and reneged on his promises, was fighting Byzantine forces.[1] Twice defeated, Raymond set out for Constantinople to do homage to Manuel and request military assistance for the recovery of Edessa. At first Manuel would not receive him, but later accepted his oath of fealty, and with it made a commitment to defend Raymond's position in the county of Edessa. And Manuel did indeed march east, but not until 1146, and only as far as Iconium (modern Konya) which was held by the Seljuk sultan Masud. In the meantime Hugh of Jabala set out for Rome, arriving in autumn 1145. It is inconceivable that Manuel was so closely involved in these affairs and unaware of the Latins' desire for a second great armed pilgrimage to the Holy Land. Therefore, it is fascinating to have preserved details of a Byzantine embassy to the German court, also in autumn 1145, led by a certain Nicephorus. Otto of Freising provides the following record of his reception by Conrad III, preserved in a letter to Manuel:

The letter of Your Nobility, transmitted by so great and so dear a friend of ours to Our Serenity, we have gratefully received, and upon learning its contents we rejoiced greatly at your security and your exalted state. But having heard from Nicephorus, the wise delegate of Your Love, beyond the contents of the letter certain harsh words . . . Our Majesty [is] disturbed . . . For if that same messenger of yours, Nicephorus, had struck our only son Henry dead before our eyes, he could not have provoked the spirit of Our Majesty to greater anger. And

---

[1] Cinnamus: 35 (trans.: 36); Choniates: 52 (trans.: 31); Lilie 1993: 142–5.

when he had laboured in this bitterness of spirit for three days and had been unable by any ingenuity or any cleverness to bend the firmness of our resolution to his will, barely did he on the fourth day cheer Our Excellency with other, friendlier words. After quieting the fury of our indignation, he revealed to us the will of Your Nobility. And since as matters now stand – and should stand – you, the dearest of all our friends, will receive our most beloved daughter, I mean the sister of our noble consort, as your wife, we desire that there shall be herein an eternal bond of enduring friendship . . . To [our most trusted ambassadors] we have entrusted matters that are not contained in the letters to be referred to Your Zeal. You may place confidence in their words and believe what they say to you as though spoken by us. (Otto of Freising, *Gesta Friderici*: 41–3; trans.: 57–9)

We can be fairly certain that Nicephorus' demands that so vexed Conrad were for an alternative bride to be found for Manuel. He pressed the issue for three days, a familiar diplomatic tactic, before revealing Manuel's 'will' and, by agreeing to the marriage, he secured Conrad's firm undertaking. Conrad also undertook to provide Manuel not with a mere 500 knights, but two or three thousand. More than this, if necessary he undertook to come in person to Manuel's assistance. Manuel's most pressing concern, and one that might require military assistance, was the threat of a second great armed pilgrimage through Byzantine territory, and his 'will', the concession he elicited from Conrad which was to be relayed by envoys, was an undertaking that the German would remain aloof from any such enterprise. In this light we might interpret Conrad's suggestion that he personally might lead his troops as a veiled threat. Thus, both threatened and appeased, Manuel promptly married Bertha of Sulzbach. He did so – I would contend – in return for Conrad's promise not to participate in any attempt to recover Edessa, and to provide troops to help police any such enterprise. These were the 'matters not contained in the letters', and in this way Conrad undertook to remain in the west to monitor and check any Norman activity.

This contention may have a slightly hollow ring, for there is no evidence that Conrad showed any intention of heading east in 1145. Otto of Freising records that, 'At that time . . . the whirlwind of war filled the earth and involved practically the whole empire in seditious uprising' (*Gesta Friderici*: 47; trans.: 63–4). There was war in Swabia, Bavaria and Belgic Gaul. Worse still the margrave of Styria was at war with the Hungarians, and required Conrad's intervention. Thus his domestic troubles made Conrad's immediate participation in a journey to Edessa most unlikely. Moreover the pope was hostile to the idea, and alternative campaigns against the pagan Slavs to the north-east were mooted with the same spiritual rewards as those offered to those crusaders bound for Edessa and Jerusalem. Manuel may have known that Conrad had not professed his intention to march to the defence of the Franks in Edessa, and may even have figured that such an enterprise was unlikely given his situation. However, with the Norman threat to his Balkan lands revived, the Byzantine emperor could not risk losing his principal ally in the west, still less have him leading a huge army through imperial lands. Moreover, Manuel may well have been swayed by stories of the profound devotion and fervour of the participants in the First Crusade, and his knowledge of the many pilgrims who had passed through the empire since then. Manuel may also have known that Conrad had, in 1124, responded to a call by Pope Calixtus II to go to the aid of the Latins following the great defeat at the 'Field of Blood' in northern Syria. Ekkehard of Aura records that an eclipse of the moon at the beginning of February 1124 persuaded Conrad to take the crusader's vow 'to go to Jerusalem and fight for Christ'.[2] Many agreed to go with him, and his failure to fulfil the vow must have been a factor in his later decision to lead the German contingent in the Second Crusade.

Thus, Manuel considered his marriage to Bertha of Sulzbach to be a worthwhile sacrifice to prevent Conrad's participation in the proposed crusade, and the Byzantine emperor was free to set out to confront the Seljuk sultan Masud. Byzantine forces swept past Seljuk resistance as far as Philomelium, where the sultan was based. Manuel then passed on to Iconium, which he put under siege. However, the emperor was not prepared for a long siege, and his actions were mostly a show of strength cut short by the 'rumour, growing daily, that the peoples of the west, rebelling by ancestral custom, would invade the Romans' land in full force.' (Cinnamus: 45; trans.: 43). The emperor returned to Constantinople to prepare for their arrival.

We know from two letters which the emperor wrote to Pope Eugenius III, and a reference to a third sent to King Louis VII of France, that Manuel was well aware of the mustering of the Franks, and also of the role and function of the pope in calling and, it was hoped, controlling their armed pilgrimage. The first letter, written in Constantinople in August 1146, welcomed the news of a new campaign, and assured the pope that Manuel was preparing to receive the king and his followers, to facilitate their passage through Byzantine lands, and to provide provisions. But in return he demanded the same honour (in the original Greek,

---

[2] Ekkehard of Aura, *Chronicle*: 262.

time; in the Latin translation, *honor*) that had been granted his grandfather, and urged the pope to intervene to ensure this.[3] By honour Manuel must be referring to the oath sworn to Alexius I by the leaders of the First Crusade, known to Anna Comnena as the '*horkia pista*'. And this is made explicit in the second letter, dated to March 1147, which has survived only in a Latin translation, and which must have been delivered by an embassy which travelled on to France to consult with Louis VII.[4] The crusaders were now to bind themselves by oath (*certificari*) to the emperor, swearing in advance to his ambassadors that they would not harm imperial lands and would restore to him all cities which had previously pertained to his empire. A list of these places, which has not survived, was entrusted to the same ambassadors. The pope was further implored to intervene with Louis and his barons to ensure that they swore this oath, and also encouraged to appoint a cardinal as papal representative to accompany the pilgrims and check their excesses. This request confirms that the eastern emperors were well aware of papal claims to authority over the crusade, both in theory and practice. (It also suggests, incidentally, that they had recognized the role of Adhemar of Le Puy, the papal legate on the First Crusade. Both features are absent from Anna Comnena's account, where Adhemar is systematically eliminated.)

Grumel, who brought the letters to the attention of modern scholars, maintained that between the first and second approaches to the pope, Manuel had become aware of Conrad's intention to participate in the crusade. According to Otto of Freising (*Gesta Friderici:* 59; trans.: 74) this occurred at Christmas 1146. Manuel's awareness of this change of heart, Grumel suggested, explained the urgency of repeating his requests, and of extracting a close and binding commitment from the French. In fact, both can be explained without reference to the Germans, since Manuel was clearly disturbed by Eugenius' failure to respond to his first letter, and the notable absence of an embassy to Constantinople to announce and explain the armed pilgrimage. With the crusade now imminent a Byzantine embassy to Louis VII was a pressing need, and Manuel's obliging the Franks to swear an oath in advance to his representatives was intended to safeguard his Balkan territories, thus preventing the clashes that had characterized the passage of the First Crusade (see above at pp. 177–9). His arrangements were, for the most part successful, and the French journey was regarded, at least by Byzantine observers, as uneventful. However, the arrival of the Germans was not, and they came first.

---

[3] Grumel 1945: 144–5; Lemerle 1955: 604 for the significance of *time* or *honor*.
[4] Grumel 1945: 146–8, 153 (for the date).

THE PASSAGE OF THE SECOND CRUSADE THROUGH THE
NORTHERN BALKANS

Conrad's belated decision, persuaded by the preaching of Bernard of Clairvaux, to lead a large German contingent in the Second Crusade was a shock and setback for Manuel. This much is demonstrated by the tone and content of contemporary panegyrical orations, and the later account by Cinnamus to which we will turn shortly. It is also stated explicitly by Nicetas Choniates, who wrote that, 'although the emperor was taken by surprise and, naturally, thrown into a state of confusion, he did not fail to take expedient measures'. We should not disbelieve Choniates, who thus provides evidence that Manuel had continued faith in his arrangement with Conrad. Certainly, Anna Comnena portrayed the arrival of the First Crusade as a complete surprise to her father, despite – as we have seen – his calling for western support and being aware of the mustering of the Franks. But Choniates does not seek to excuse Manuel or exonerate him from any blame for the onslaught of this latest 'cloud of enemies, a dreadful and death-dealing pestilence' (Choniates: 60; trans.: 35). Indeed, he even remarks upon Manuel's duplicity in dealing with the Germans, and records accusations that the emperor allowed barley to be cut with lime before it was sold to the crusaders, a potentially fatal mixture.[5] More than that, he is said to have struck a debased coinage especially for transactions involving crusaders. Whether these allegations are true, or merely reproduced from contemporary attacks on the emperor, we will never know. But we must assume that many rumours (*phamousa*) were spread, and polemical tracts (*psogoi*) were composed by those who, like Anna Comnena, were opposed to Manuel's accession and to his policies.

Choniates' account of the passage of the crusade through Thrace is insightful. He records minor conflicts at Philippopolis and Adrianople. On the latter occasion, Duke Frederick, the future emperor Barbarossa, took revenge on some murderous Greeks by burning their monastery to the ground while they slept inside. But peace was restored before the Germans moved on to the plain of Choirobacchoi (near Baysahiyish in Thracian Turkey), where they pitched camp on a fine autumnal day, 7 September 1147:

There is a narrow and shallow river by the name of Melas which flows through this plain. In the summer a lack of water reduces it to a muddy ravine, and it

---

[5] Choniates: 66 (trans.: 39).

moves not through sandy soil but through the very fertile black earth and cuts a channel like a deep furrow made by plows pulled by oxen. With the arrival of winter, or with a downpour of torrential rains, it expands in size enormously from that trickle, and from a lifeless pond it swells into a deep eddying torrent . . . This river now contrived a wholly execrable deed . . . The Melas swollen by torrential rains . . . raced through the German camp, sweeping away weapons and horse trappings, whatever goods the mules were bearing, horses, asses, as well as the men themselves. So piteous a spectacle called forth tears as men, without even fighting, fell and were cut down without being pursued. Neither their huge stature, measured almost in stades, nor their right hands, insatiate in battle, sufficed to repel this evil, for they were mown like grass and carried away like sun-dried chaff and fleecy wool in the air. (Choniates: 64; trans.: 37–8)

Choniates, therefore, is sympathetic to the Germans, whom he regards as fellow Christians and mighty warriors. He shows grief at their misfortune, but notes that this demonstrated that the very elements obeyed the Byzantines. A very different, and far less sympathetic account of the terrible flood at Choirobacchoi is provided in a panegyrical oration delivered in Constantinople, probably in spring 1148, by the encomiast known as Manganeius Prodromus.[6] This minor court orator found favour in the thirteenth century – by his own account more than he enjoyed in his own day – when some 18,000 lines of his verse were copied into the manuscript now known as *Marcianus Graecus* XI.22, a compendium of twelfth-century court rhetoric. Two of these poems, numbers 20 and 24, are concerned expressly and exclusively with the Second Crusade. Poem 20 begins in the middle of a speech detailing the passage through Thrace of the German army under Conrad III. The earliest part, which may not be very long, has been lost. However, the poem is still among Manganeius' longest. It goes on to deal with the arrival of the crusaders before Constantinople (20.1–266), detailing the tragic flash flood at Choirobacchoi (20.131 ff.), Conrad's arrival at Pikridion (a suburb of Constantinople), and his crossing the Bosphorus (20.287–346). The second half of the poem consists of an encomium of the emperor Manuel by the poet as poet (20.347–473), and by the poet in the guise of the city of Constantinople (20.474–642).

---

[6] The author is anonymous, but is known as 'Manganeius' because, by his poetic pleading, he secured a place in the monastic complex in Constantinople called the Mangana. References are to poems as catalogued by Mioni 1973: 116–25, and reproduced with notes by Magdalino 1993: 494–500. Translations are adapted from the draft versions in the forthcoming edition by Elizabeth and Michael Jeffreys. I am grateful to the Jeffreys for encouraging me to make use of their work in progress. For Manganeius on the Second Crusade see E. Jeffreys 2000, forthcoming, which I have read in draft form.

Before he arrives at Choirobacchoi, Conrad is accused of nurturing secret designs on Constantinople, and with intending to slaughter the Byzantine troops who had escorted his army across Thrace. But the Virgin, protector of Constantinople, intervened to thwart his plans. The flooding of the Melas is compared with, and considered more fabulous than, the parting of the Red Sea; and Conrad, the Pharaoh who had threatened the 'New Israelites', suffered a similar fate.

> As the little stream began to run fiercely
> Pharaoh immediately, first on horseback
> began to flee, an adversary but no picked leader
> until the wave gathered at the head of the stream
> and whirled away many hapless victims
> who lost their lives at Choirobacchoi
> their mouths like pigs, full of mud
> that was piled up with the reeds that flowed past;
> they were washed out onto the shoals.
> For those who use urine to drink and wash their faces
> justice contrived fittingly for them
> a mud-stained banquet of pork.
>   (Manganeius Prodromus: 20.176–86)

The emphasis on pork is a less than subtle play on the name Choirobacchoi (*choiros* is a Greek word for pig). But it also fits with allusions employed elsewhere by Manganeius to the crusaders' supposed Judaistic practices, particularly their use of unleavened bread. The encomiast is far less flattering than Choniates, whose tall and mighty warriors have become urine-drinking swine. We have a further, and similarly slanted account of the disaster at Choirobacchoi in the history of John Cinnamus.

Cinnamus was clearly writing in the same vein as Manuel's panegyrists, and must have drawn on their contemporary accounts. He considered the flash flood 'a disaster beyond description', but one from which one might 'reasonably surmise that the Divinity was angry at those who had falsified their oaths and who practised great inhumanity towards people of the same religion who had done them no wrong'. We have already seen that, according to Choniates, the Byzantines had not been entirely free of blame in their dealings with fellow Christians; and the charge of oath-breaking reminds us of Manuel's demands in advance, put by his legates to the pope and Louis VII. Oaths were demanded and extracted once again before the crusaders were allowed to enter the Byzantine Empire: Cinnamus alone records a meeting at Byzantium's border with Hungary – probably on the Danube opposite Belgrade – between the leaders of the crusade, and Manuel's envoys, Demetrius Macrembolites and Alexander of Gravina. The crusade leaders met at the tent of Conrad III, 'because he possessed the principal position among the nations of the West', and stated that they would not harm Byzantine territory. According to Cinnamus they broke this promise, and thus suffered divine displeasure at Choirobacchoi.[7]

A fourth account of the flash flood, and the last that we will consider, is provided by Otto of Freising. Otto considers only two aspects of the Second Crusade worthy of prolonged coverage: the religious movement which led to it; and its failure and aftermath which provoked a long philosophical explanation. The single episode during the crusade which he considers worthy of his attention is the flash flood at Choirobacchoi, which he calls Cherevach. As was his wont, he draws attention to the fortune of his hero, Frederick Barbarossa, who alone among the Germans had pitched camp on higher ground, not in the verdant river valley. Thus 'Duke Frederick alone remained entirely unharmed by this destructive flood'.[8] Otto, like the Greek authors we have considered, attributes the flood and its consequences to God, and thus seeks to set Frederick above others, even before he ascended the imperial throne, as divinely favoured. He considers the episode a reflection of divine displeasure with the whole enterprise, and the outcome of the crusade seemed to corroborate this. Otto then turns away from the crusade and presents a detailed account of the trial of Gilbert, bishop of Poitiers. He returns to Conrad, and to his own experiences – for he was in the German contingent – only briefly, finding himself at Mid-Lent 1148 aboard a Byzantine ship bound for Jerusalem. He passes over the failed siege of Damascus and returns with Conrad to the Byzantine city of Thessalonica to meet with Manuel Comnenus, where we will also return shortly (at pp. 223–4).

The German contingent, much depleted, marched on from Choirobacchoi to encamp before the walls of Constantinople. A second poem by Manganeius Prodromus reveals the consternation felt within the city at the arrival of such a large 'barbarian' force, and provides details of the preparations Manuel Comnenus had undertaken. In poem 24, entitled 'From the city to the emperor when the kings of Alamania and Frangia arrived', the city of Constantinople is made to thank and

---

[7] Cinnamus: 73–4 (trans.: 63).
[8] Otto of Freising, *Gesta Friderici*: 67 (trans.: 81). Frederick later drowned in a fast-flowing river while leading the Third Crusade. See below at p. 300.

praise Manuel for the trouble he has taken to restore her to her former beauty, magnifying and enhancing her, and protecting her by the efficient handling of the barbarian armies from the west. At one point the city announces that those 'wild beasts [had] heard that my teeth had fallen out . . . but the young Manuel showed that I, the old woman, am young with all my teeth' (24.7–11). The reference is to the emperor's systematic renovations of the city's land walls in preparation for the arrival of the crusade. These walls were bedecked with banners and flags: the blooms – among them white lilies, red roses, golden crocuses and sky-blue hyacinths – alluded to in subsequent lines (24.40–1). These repairs actually took place on a section towards the northern limit of the Theodosian land walls, and Manuel's towers are still visible today adjoining the thirteenth-century complex known as Tekfur Sarayı, and adjacent to the site of the Palace of Blachernae, which was the favoured residence of the Comenian emperors.[9] The rebuilt walls have features similar to other fortifications erected during Manuel's reign, making use of irregular stone and antique spolia, and triple bands of flat red bricks to provide a level surface for higher levels. This technique is found at a second, contemporary fortification at Hieron of the Bosphorus, north-east of Constantinople, and it is likely that the latter was built at the same time and intended as a command post to monitor and police the passage of crusaders across to Asia Minor.[10]

Manganeius' evocation of Byzantine concerns reflect a very real fear felt within the city, which to some extent was quelled by the emperor's restoration of the northern land walls. He also reflects the relief and gratitude felt by the populace when the crusaders were transported across the Bosphorus where they might continue their march into Asia Minor. But this was not the end of Manuel's troubles.

THE NORMAN ASSAULT AND THE TREATY OF THESSALONICA, 1147–1148

While the Germans were on the march through Bulgaria and Thrace, the German-Byzantine accord was in abeyance and Byzantine resources were committed to monitoring and policing the crusade. Therefore, the Normans were able to launch a series of devastating raids on imperial lands. In summer 1147 a Norman fleet seized the island of Corfu and

[9] Magdalino 1996c: 70–6. The location is marked on map 1.2, of Constantinople.
[10] Foss and Winfield 1986: 145–50. For similar developments at Belgrade and Braničevo see below at pp. 241–5.

captured the cities of Thebes and Corinth in mainland Greece. They sailed back to Sicily with great plunder and, a greater insult to the emperor, many captives. Worse still they retained control of Corfu, a site of vital strategic importance within the Adriatic, and from which attacks on the lands south of Dyrrachium might easily be launched. The emperor 'could not tolerate a thousand pirates on his own land, or allow Corfu to become a naval base and shipyard for the Sicilian triremes to sail against the Romans' (Choniates: 87; trans.: 51). He was obliged to turn, as his grandfather had been, to the Venetians for naval assistance, and in October 1147 renewed the familiar trade privileges which hitherto he had failed to confirm. The Venetians were satisfied with such recognition, and were themselves troubled by the Norman occupation of Corfu: the island dominated access to the Adriatic, and Norman control of both sides of the southern Adriatic threatened the passage of ships between Venice and the Mediterranean.

Meanwhile things had gone badly for the crusading armies. The Germans had failed to bring sufficient provisions for the journey through Anatolia, hoping to live off the land. With winter approaching there was little to requisition and less to forage. On arriving at Dorylaium on the central plateau they were unable to break through the Turkish cordon, and retreated to Nicaea where the French and other contingents were ensconced. A second route was ventured, heading south along the coast to Ephesus near which the combined forces spent Christmas, before continuing on to Attaleia, all the time harassed by Turks. At Attaleia the leader of the French contingent, King Louis VII, was given Byzantine naval assistance and transportation to Antioch. Conrad III preferred to return to Constantinople where he was received lavishly by the emperor, and provided with sea transportation to Acre. The same fleet brought Conrad back, after his disastrous attack on Damascus, to Thessalonica, where he once again met Manuel.[11]

The treaty arranged in Thessalonica in 1148 went a long way towards restoring the trust undermined by Conrad's participation in the crusade and renewing the joint commitment to oppose the Normans in Sicily. However, whereas the earlier agreements were essentially defensive, allowing both rulers to concentrate on other matters, the arrangements of 1148 made explicit mention of a joint offensive against the Normans. It also contained draft details of how territory annexed in Italy should be divided up: Manuel pressed his claims to Apulia and Calabria, since

---

[11] Lilie 1993: 145–63.

those lands had until the previous century been Byzantine and still had a predominantly Greek-speaking, Orthodox population. Conrad agreed to this in return for Manuel's acknowledging his rights in Lombardy. Of course, both sides portrayed their side of the contract as an imperial concession, for both claimed rights in Italy by virtue of their being the legitimate Roman emperor. Thus, while Manuel emphasized his mooted recovery of Apulia, in terms of *renovatio*, Conrad represented his relinquishing *Italia* to the Byzantines as granting a territory within *his* jurisdiction a retrospective dowry for Bertha of Sulzbach, which implied no irretrievable alienation nor abandonment of his own territorial claim.[12] The revised agreement was sealed by the marriage of Manuel's niece, Theodora – the daughter of the emperor's dead brother Andronicus – to Henry Jasomirgott, the duke of Bavaria and margrave of Austria. The treaty was immediately implemented, and a strong German contingent joined the Byzantine siege of the Norman-held citadel in Corfu. On 29 July 1149 the allied forces retook the citadel, and a German garrison was installed. The emperor travelled on to Valona to formulate his plans for an attack on Sicily. However, Conrad failed to fulfil his end of the bargain because of domestic troubles. In February 1150 he despatched a letter to Manuel announcing a victory and promising an embassy after 1 May. The four letters brought by that embassy explained the delay in full. Moreover, Conrad took the opportunity to emphasize his commitment to the alliance in a further letter to Manuel's wife, Bertha, now called Irene. The letter is rather longer than a similar note addressed to the emperor personally, and suggests that the empress was expected to act as an intermediary.[13] Manuel was also facing 'domestic' troubles, for the Serbs in Raška had rebelled. More troubling still, they had reached an understanding with both the Hungarians and the Sicilian Normans.

THE EARLY YEARS OF THE REIGN OF MANUEL I COMNENUS: RAŠKA

In 1149, while preparing an assault on Norman positions in southern Italy, Manuel learned of an uprising by the Serbs of Raška. He marched north, swiftly recovering the fortress of Ras. Excavations show that around fifty metres of the western ramparts of the city were destroyed in the assault and later rebuilt of higher quality masonry.[14] Advancing

---

[12] Macrides 1992: 279.   [13] Wibald, *Letters*: 355, 363–9 (epp. 237, 243–6).
[14] M. Popović 1987: 29.

further 'he seized the region of Nikava which belonged to the *veliki župan*, and effortlessly subdued all the fortresses that he had constructed there' (Cinnamus: 102; trans.: 82). The decisive blow was struck with the storming of the fortress of Galič (see p. 150). Manuel took many captives whom he settled around Sardica and in other regions of the empire. However, he failed to capture the elusive *veliki župan*, Uroš II. The court orator and panegyrist Theodore Prodromus provides an entirely contemporary account of the imperial campaigns of 1149. At the triumphal celebrations to mark Manuel's victories he spoke, floridly, of 'the barbarous Serbs' supreme ruler, the *veliki župan* (*archiserbozoupanos*), this mountain-reared swine, thrice a slave since birth, driven by senseless audacity, [who] rose against us and our Lord, having Hungarian forces for allies and thus was misled by the Sicilian Dragon, and persuaded by his gifts to enter into treaties to distract the emperor from attacking him' (Theodore Prodromus: 354.196–202). Here we have a full explanation for the Serbian uprising, and for the deterioration after twenty years of harmony in Byzantine-Hungarian relations. Manuel determined to return to Raška the following season, for he knew that any campaigns against the Normans would first require a permanent settlement in that region.

Cinnamus provides a detailed account of the 1150 campaign which Manuel conducted against allied Serbian and Hungarian forces. He does not mention the deal struck with Roger II, but records that the Hungarian king, Géza II, committed troops at the behest of an anonymous Serb married to the sister of the *veliki župan*. The Hungarian troops were intercepted and defeated by the Byzantine army before they could join the Serbs. They fled to the river Strymon, which until recently was assumed to be an error meaning the Drina. However, it has been established that a stretch of the Velika Morava was known as Strymon, in the vicinity of modern Paraćin some seventy kilometres north-west of Niš.[15] Clearly, the Hungarians were not fleeing north, but south along the river valley deeper into Raška, and into the mountains towards their allies. Manuel pitched camp at Sečanica, twelve kilometres north-west of Niš, where he learned that the Hungarians had not yet reached the Serbs, and decided to press on to engage them immediately. The confrontation took place at Tara, where the emperor was shocked by the presence of a vast number of Serbs, and 'a countless allied force of Hungarian cavalry as well as the heterodox *Chalisioi*'.[16]

---

[15] Blagojević 1974: 65–76, associates the site of Strymon with a fourteenth-century settlement called Zastruma.   [16] Cinnamus: 107 (trans.: 86). On the *Chalisioi*, see above at p. 192.

Cinnamus describes a hard-fought battle where several prominent Byzantines performed individual acts of valour. Michael Branas, who would later command the north-western marches, and the Frank Giphardus advanced into danger. John Cantacuzenus and John Ducas accompanied the emperor; the former lost two fingers on one hand, the latter was beside Manuel who 'hurled fifteen of the foe to the floor with a thrust of his lance'.[17] The climax of the account is Manuel's duel with the commander of the Hungarian attachment, Bakchinus (Bagin), which sealed the Byzantine victory. Afterwards the *veliki župan* swore to remain loyal to the emperor, breaking off his alliance with the Hungarians and Normans. However, the battle of Tara did not end Manuel's interest in the northern Balkans.

THE EARLY YEARS OF THE REIGN OF MANUEL I COMNENUS: DALMATIA

As we have seen, during the first part of the twelfth century Venice and Hungary competed for greater influence in Dalmatia. Both Alexius I and John II had been willing to accept these developments, even if they occasionally fomented strife between the two powers, and supported the actions of one over the other. Hungarian authority was also recognized by various groups in the lands of the southern Slavs. The king of Hungary had been independently crowned as 'King of the Croats' since 1105, probably with tacit Byzantine support following the marriage of John Comnenus to Piroska-Irene. Thereafter the Hungarian king extended his authority south and east as far as Raška and Bosna. We know little of the process by which Bosna became subject to the Hungarians, apparently by spring 1137, but it may have been an element of an agreement reached between Béla II (1131–41) and the *veliki župan* of Raška, Uroš I. Béla married Uroš's daughter, Jelena, binding Serbian interests more closely to those of the Hungarians. The *ban* of Bosna demonstrated his loyalty by participating in Hungarian campaigns, including that against Byzantium in 1154 to which we will turn shortly. Then, in *c.* 1142, the Hungarians returned in force to central Dalmatia and recovered many cities, including Šibenik, Trogir, and Split (see figure 4.2, at p. 120).

Although no contemporary chronicle or history mentions it, there is a hypothesis that the Hungarian invasion of Dalmatia took place in 1133.

---

[17] Cinnamus: 110 (trans.: 88).

The hypothesis is based on two considerations. First, in 1136 the archbishop of Esztergom, in the kingdom of Hungary, oversaw the appointment of a pro-Hungarian bishop in Split. This man, Gaudius, was 'so favourably regarded by the kings of Hungary that he was a frequent visitor to their courts' (*Historia Salonitana*: 64). However, we also know that Gaudius was consecrated by the Venetian patriarch of Grado as a demonstration of his independence from the Hungarian Church. Second, there are three documents which purport to have been issued to the citizens of Split by the successive kings Béla II and Géza II in 1138, 1141 and 1142 which suggest that a policy of occupation was underway in Dalmatia and Bosna. Two of these documents have been shown to be forgeries.[18] Therefore, corroboration for the whole hypothesis rests on a charter dated 1141 in which the Hungarian king Géza II styles himself 'by grace of God, king of Hungary, Dalmatia, *Urquatie* [sic], and Rama'.[19] This is the only extant charter which dates from before 1180 in which a king of Hungary calls himself king of Rama, and is itself only preserved in a fourteenth-century copy. Therefore, the formulae, including the reference to Rama, are very likely to have been introduced by a copyist, and it is impossible to accept the Hungarian occupation of Split and Rama took place before 1142.

In 1142 Dubrovnik came under attack from the *ban* of Bosna. The Venetians sent an expeditionary force of 500 men which, rather than providing assistance, set about plundering the city. The Italians were driven out, and it remained free of Venetian authority thereafter. However, the Venetian doge, Pietro Polani (1129–48), took measures to counter the Hungarian advance north of Dubrovnik, in central Dalmatia. His principal strategy was not military, but ecclesiastical. The doge secured the support of the papacy in his endeavours, and a new bishopric was established on Hvar and Brač, the islands west of Split, to supplant the authority of the Hungarian stooge Gaudius. The archpresbyter of Split, who had been resident on the islands, was ejected by the Venetians and the *comes* of Zadar (who appears still to have been the native prior, Peter, whom we met above at p. 205). The new foundation enjoyed the support of the archbishop of Dubrovnik and the bishops of Svač and Ulcinj, who performed the consecration of the first bishop, Lampredius.[20] Thomas of Split claims that the inhabitants of Hvar and

---

[18] Steindorff 1984: 11–20, 92 on the 1142 charter; Makk 1989: 137, n. 35 for references to the literature regarding the false 1138 charter.
[19] *Codex Diplomaticus*: ii, 49. Rama was a synonym for Bosna at this time, although later a distinct region to the south.   [20] *Historia Salonitana*: 67.

Brač were determined to join with the episcopates of Osor, Rab and Krk (in the Gulf of Kvarner) which were subject to the archbishop of Zadar. In October 1154 the Venetian stooge Lampredius was transferred to Zadar, which was raised to an archbishopric and given metropolitan status over Osor, Krk, Rab and Hvar. Then, in June 1157, authority over Zadar and its suffragans was granted to the Venetian patriarch of Grado by Pope Adrian IV.

At the same time the doge sought to consolidate his authority in the northern Adriatic. A second major threat to Venetian interests was posed by the vigorous ruler of the new Norman kingdom of Sicily, Roger II, who had begun to extend his grasp northwards into Italy. Pescara had fallen in 1140, and all the surrounding lands by 1143. The doge responded by signing a treaty with Fano, situated north of Ancona on Italy's Adriatic coast.[21] In 1145 similar treaties were negotiated with the cities of Koper and Pula in Istria, which stipulated that joint action should be taken if the Venetian sphere of influence was violated. The limits of this sphere were located at Ancona in the west and Dubrovnik in the east, effectively designating the northern Adriatic as a Venetian lake. Doge Domenico Morosini (1148–55) enforced this settlement when the Istrian cities reneged on the agreement in 1150, and went further by obliging the citizens to swear an oath of fidelity and to pay an annual tribute.[22] They were no longer allies, but subjects. As if to mark the change in the doge's attitude towards both his neighbours and enemies, in 1154 he concluded an agreement with the new ruler of Norman Sicily, William I, where each acknowledged the other's sphere of influence within the Adriatic. Once again the boundary between the northern and southern sectors was placed at Dubrovnik, although the city was not in either Norman or Venetian hands.[23]

It is interesting that this agreement dates from the year after the Hungarian king had failed adequately to distract the Byzantine emperor on behalf of the Norman king, and appears to signal a break in the previously friendly relations between Hungary and Norman Sicily. The Venetian-Norman accord was symptomatic of developments in the aftermath of the Second Crusade, as patterns of alliances began to change. As we have just noted, in October 1154 Pope Anastasius IV condemned the Hungarian domination of Split and raised Zadar to metropolitan status. In response Géza II, no friend of Anastasius, determined to establish Hungarian control in Zadar. It

---

[21] *Listine*: i, 6; Dandolo: 230.   [22] *Codex Diplomaticus*: ii, 64–7; Dandolo: 244.
[23] *Urkunden der Republik Venedig*: i, 172.

would appear that he enjoyed the support of the citizens who resented their arbitrary subjection to the patriarch of Grado.[24] At the same time Venetian relations with Manuel were souring rapidly, and in 1155 the emperor granted trade privileges to the Genoese, the Venetians' commercial and political rivals. In response the doge refused to send three galleys as a token of his traditional submission to the emperor to assist in Byzantine activity in southern Italy. He went further still in northern Dalmatia.

Doge Vitale II Michiel (1155–72) determined to establish direct Venetian control for the first time in the maritime cities of northern Dalmatia. In Rab, where the appointment of the prior had remained the prerogative of the citizens subject to the doge's approval, Michiel rejected all four candidates presented to him. Instead he appointed his own son Nicholas, and installed a second son, Leonardo, as *comes* of Osor.[25] Then, in 1159, he launched a successful assault on Zadar. The commander of the fleet, Domenico Morosini (son and namesake of the former doge) was appointed as *comes* of Zadar, and received an oath from the citizens that they would be loyal to the doge and the patriarch of Grado for twenty years.[26] The oath was far more specific than earlier undertakings, and implicitly denied any Byzantine claims to suzerainty in Dalmatia.

THE EARLY YEARS OF THE REIGN OF MANUEL I COMNENUS: SIRMIUM

Scholars have long maintained that the period 1150–5 was a period of frequent and fierce hostilities between Byzantium and Hungary, and that this was due to Manuel's desire to annex Hungary to his empire. They have pointed to Géza II's commitments in the Russian principalities as evidence that the Hungarian king could not have initiated the conflicts, nor wished them to continue. A detailed analysis of events by Ferenc Makk (1989: 42–62), and his attempt to construct an accurate chronology, have shown that such assertions cannot be sustained. My own preferred chronology, which is summarized in the accompanying table (fig. 7.1), differs considerably from those that have gone before, including Makk's, and demands that we view the period as relatively harmonious, with only brief bouts of shadow-boxing.[27]

---

[24] *Historia Ducum Veneticorum*: 76.   [25] Dandolo: 248–9.
[26] *Annales Venetici Breves*: 71; *Historia Ducum Veneticorum*: 76; Dandolo: 244, 249.
[27] Stephenson 1994: 251–77.

1150	September	(1) Battle of Tara	Cinnamus: 105
	October	(2) Manuel takes round trip to Constantinople	Cinnamus: 113
		(3) Manuel launches attack in Sirmium	Cinnamus: 114
		(4) Peace is concluded at Danube	Cinnamus: 118
1151	April	(1) Géza musters troops at Danube	Cinnamus: 119
		(2) Peace concluded	Cinnamus: 120
1152		No incident	
1153	Spring	(1) Géza 'again in revolt'	Cinnamus: 121
		(2) Peace concluded at Sardica	Choniates: 100
		(3) Andronicus appointed *doux* of Niš & Braničevo	Cinnamus: 124
1154	Autumn	(1) Andronicus arrested in Pelagonia	Cinnamus: 130
		(2) Géza besieges Braničevo	Cinnamus: 131
1155	Spring	(1) Manuel launches retaliatory campaign	Cinnamus: 133
		(2) Peace concluded	Cinnamus: 134

Fig. 7.1 Chronology of Byzantine-Hungarian engagements, 1150–1155

Cinnamus and Choniates both state that the motivation for Manuel's first campaign after the battle of Tara, in October 1150, was to punish Géza II for his involvement with the Serbs. We are told further that he did this before he had 'even wiped the dust of the battlefield from his face and was still covered in warm sweat' (Choniates: 92; trans.: 54). His swift return caught Géza by surprise: the king had departed for the principality of Galich, where he received a letter from Manuel challenging him to return to the Danube to settle matters. The letter demonstrates that Manuel had no desire to seize Hungarian land, for if that had been his intention such a warning would have been counter-productive. However, he had sufficient time to devastate Frangochorion, the southern marches of Hungary between the Sava and the Danube, and lead tens of thousands of captives back into imperial lands, establishing himself in a position of considerable strength for negotiations when Géza arrived. Manuel was so encouraged by his early success that he decided, against the advice of his generals, to goad Géza into a pitched battle and therefore he despatched Boris, a Hungarian prince in his charge, repeatedly to raid Hungarian territory. However, the king saw the folly of engaging with the imperial army, for even in victory he would be forced to beg for the return of his subjects, and in defeat 'he should involve the whole remaining Hungarian force in destruction' (Cinnamus: 115; trans.: 92). He preferred to sue for terms and seek revenge later. Manuel returned to Constantinople to celebrate his extended but triumphant campaigning season.

Details of these festivities and the campaigns they honoured are provided by Manganeius Prodromus, who delivered at least three orations on this occasion.[28] The poet emphasizes the swift succession of the emperor's victories, which 'follow each other like groups of waves' (2.57), and notes that both the rivers Tara and Sava were disturbed by his filling them with corpses (27.1–7). He asks further, 'What yearly cycle ever saw so great a miracle, a terrible bloodless victory, a capturing of prisoners, herds of goats and cattle, many thousands of mares, innumerable flocks of the fattest sheep' (2.181–4), and praises the 'glory of a triple victory' (1.49) and the emperor as 'a brilliant triple victor' (1.180). Manganeius' verse encomia reflect how the emperor must have felt at Christmas 1150. In a single season he had seized thousands of hostages and head of livestock, depopulated and ravaged the Hungarian marches, and forced the Hungarian king to agree a peace. He also harboured a pretender to Géza's throne as a warning to him to honour his pledges. In fact, Géza was too humbled; so humbled indeed that he had little to lose by preparing a retaliatory attack across the Danube-Sava in April 1151. The date is known from a Russian source, the *Hypatian Chronicle* (419–20), which relates that Géza promised aid to Iziaslav of Kiev but was unable to mount his horse and set off at that time because the 'king of the Greeks' was marching against him. Similarly, Cinnamus (119–20; trans.: 95) records that Géza's plans were thwarted by Manuel's swift march north, and negotiations followed. Although the emperor still held all his cards, he agreed to Géza's demand that he return all but 10,000 of the prisoners. Manuel did so because his intention was still to direct his attention and resources to an assault on Norman Sicily, and stability at the northwestern frontier was worth the price Géza demanded.[29]

The peace of April 1151 lasted for two years. Géza had no desire to provoke a further Byzantine offensive in Frangochorion, for in 1152 he was embroiled in Russian lands. Moreover, in June of that year he must have been concerned to learn that one of the first proposals mooted by the new German ruler, Frederick I Barbarossa (1152–90), was an invasion of his kingdom. Barbarossa's accession was a compromise that ended the domestic conflicts in Germany, and in a letter to Manuel he explained that the problems which had beset Conrad had been resolved.[30] He promised that forthwith he would turn his attention to the agreed joint offensive against the Normans in the manner of a king, at

[28] For references see above at p. 219, n.6. I will return to these poems below at pp. 234–6.
[29] See Stephenson 1994: 257–65, for fuller analysis and references to sources which support the chronology preferred here. [30] Wibald, *Letters*: 549–50 (epp. 410, 411).

the head of a mighty army. He thanked Manuel for his continued commitment to the enterprise, which had been demonstrated by a Byzantine
embassy offering an imperial bride. And he urged Manuel not to delay
for this matter to be resolved, but to send Greek troops to Italy immediately. Frederick's letter was accompanied by a personal message from the
envoy, Wibald of Stablo (or Stavelot), who stressed the continuity in aims
and policy between Conrad and Frederick, and presented himself as evidence for this. Wibald confided in the emperor that he found Frederick
a very worthy successor to his former lord, and revealed that he had been
entrusted with the task of finding a suitable bride from among the
Comnenian princesses. Cinnamus (134–5; trans.: 106) suggests that
Frederick was interested in Maria, the daughter of Manuel's older
brother Isaac.

All of this suggests that in spring 1153 the Normans would have had
every reason to fear the onset of the often delayed German-Byzantine
offensive. Byzantine money had been flowing into southern Italy since
1149 through Ancona to finance native resistance to Norman rule (see
below at pp. 264–5). Frederick was massing his forces beyond the Alps,
and had secured the pope's support for the enterprise. The situation was
even more desperate than in 1149, when Roger II enlisted Serbian and
Hungarian support to deflect Manuel. Géza's commitment to the
Normans was surely the reason for his return to the Danube in spring
1153, in violation of his agreement of 1151. The Hungarian king, trapped
between two hostile and allied powers, could not afford to betray his one
firm ally. Moreover, the Normans were the only naval power to rival
Venetian domination of the Adriatic, and this alliance was therefore the
Hungarians' best hope for consolidating their interests in Dalmatia.
However, Hungary would not benefit directly from renewing hostilities
with Byzantium, and the attack was over before it had even begun.
Hungarian envoys met Manuel at Sardica before the emperor could
even reach the Danube, and agreed a renewal of the 1151 peace.[31] Géza's
volte-face makes perfect sense if the whole operation was mere postur-
ing to fulfil an obligation to the Normans, and to draw Manuel however
briefly away from his preparations. Confirmation of this can be found
in an oration delivered by the rhetor Michael of Thessalonica, who
reveals that at the time of the Hungarian operation Manuel was 'turning
his attention seaward', and Géza's intention was to create a favourable
situation for the 'Sicilian Scylla'.[32]

[31] Choniates: 100 (trans.: 58).   [32] *FRB*: 158, 162–3.

Manuel then turned his attention to the Italian campaign, and was stationed in Pelagonia until late 1153. A further letter from Wibald of Stablo (*Letters*: 561; ep. 424) dated 22 November 1153 was addressed to him at his field headquarters. The emperor would not have stationed himself so far south of Niš if he viewed Hungary as his major opponent, nor would he have appointed his cousin Andronicus to the command of the region as *doux* of Niš and Braničevo. Andronicus had used his previous posting in Cilicia to conspire against the emperor, and Manuel must have imagined that the north-western marches would not offer such opportunities. Indeed, Manuel was so confident that peace with Hungary would endure that he disbanded his Balkan army in 1154. His confidence proved misplaced, but only because he had underestimated his resourceful cousin. Andronicus made many powerful allies in Hungary, including Géza II to whom he pledged to cede the region between Braničevo and Niš in return for military aid in supplanting Manuel. The pretender intended to take advantage of his proximity to the emperor to murder him during a hunting trip in Pelagonia, but was discovered and imprisoned in Constantinople. The emperor was 'stunned at the faithlessness of the Hungarians, that they should disregard what they had so recently pledged' (Cinnamus: 131; trans.: 103), while Géza, unaware of Andronicus' capture, proceeded to besiege Braničevo.

Cinnamus' narrative treatment of the Hungarian invasion of late 1154 demonstrates that it was on a different scale to the earlier encounters, and further invaluable insights are offered in poems 7 and 31 by Manganeius Prodromus.[33] Cinnamus (130–1; trans.: 103) states that Géza had assembled allies from among 'the Czechs and Saxons and many other peoples', to which Manganeius adds 'Scythians and Celts' (7.165). Manuel was unprepared for such an army, and having hastened towards the Danube realized his forces were inadequate to lift the siege. Instead, he devised a ruse: while he encamped at Smeles in the Velika Morava corridor an archer was sent ahead with a letter which he fired towards, but beyond Braničevo. As planned, it fell into Géza's hands, who thus learned of the emperor's approach – an eventuality Andronicus was expected to have prevented – and withdrew.[34] However, Manuel determined to engage a detachment of Géza's allies, and sent the *chartoularios* Basil Tzintziluces with a force to chase Borić, the *ban* of Bosna. Instead

---

[33] I believe these poems must have been produced in spring 1155.
[34] The ruse is probably alluded to by Michael the Rhetor in an oration delivered in 1156. See *FRB*: 159; Magdalino 1993: 443.

Basil fell on the main body of Hungarian troops and lost many men in the course of the battle. In their accounts of this engagement we can once again detect the different sympathies of Cinnamus and Choniates. Cinnamus blames Basil for disobeying the emperor, and disparages the general for fleeing while many other Romans fell. Choniates counters with the affirmation that Basil 'was convinced that he had an army worthy of victory, and engaged the Hungarians in battle and prevailed against them, slaying more than half their troops'. The obvious point of disagreement is the emperor's personal role in the battle, or rather his lack of one. Whereas Choniates is content to claim a Byzantine victory, Cinnamus directs a thinly veiled attack on Tzintziluces ('he came from an undistinguished family'), absolves Manuel from any blame for the casualties, and explains that the emperor was anxious to exact revenge ('he chafed and longed to follow the Hungarians') until the counsel of his generals prevailed. Manuel wintered at Berrhoia, where he planned a major campaign for the following spring, but by early 1155 Géza's enthusiasm for the struggle had ebbed. After initial reluctance, the emperor accepted his requests for a treaty, and stability was restored to the frontier lands on the same terms as in 1151 and 1153.[35]

THE RHETORIC OF THE HUNGARIAN CONFLICTS, 1150–1155

Although the foregoing outline is based principally on the accounts of John Cinnamus and Nicetas Choniates, the fullest account of Manuel's campaigns against the Hungarians and Raškan Serbs is contained in the panegyrical orations delivered by Manuel's encomiasts. Magdalino (1993: 443) states that 'Theodore Prodromos and Michael the Rhetor both reveal, as clearly as either of the historians [Cinnamus and Choniates], that Manuel intended to follow up the recapture of Corfu with an invasion of southern Italy, and that his Balkan campaigns were essentially distractions from this goal, caused by Roger's alliance with the Serbs and the Hungarians.' It is hard to disagree simply because the two historians reveal so little about the relationship between the Italian and Balkan campaigns. Moreover, as Magdalino shows, there is an even-handedness in the presentation of certain episodes and events which could not be ignored, nor entirely subsumed beneath rhetorical artifice. Thus Manganeius Prodromus (poem 15), on the emperor's instructions, consoled Manuel after the Italian defeats of 1156. However, it would be

[35] Cinnamus: 131–4 (trans.: 103–5); Choniates: 101–2 (trans.: 58–9).

wrong to suggest that encomiasts were always so 'honest', and it is Manganeius who provides the largest dossier on the conflicts with Hungary between 1150 and 1155, presenting a rhetorical image which far outstrips their real significance.

We should not forget that Manganeius was writing to order: his orations were commissioned for, or at least intended to secure favour at, imperial celebrations arranged for the emperor. Manuel celebrated at least three triumphs between 1149 and 1155, and Manganeius spoke at each of them. What then, working to order and within certain rhetorical guidelines, did Manganeius make of the conflicts with the Hungarians? First, Manganeius provides by far the most consistent frontier imagery of any author we have encountered. He frequently uses the word *horos*, or derivations of it, and he considers the frontier as a linear border, a limit and a barrier against the non-Roman world which he places unequivocally at the Danube. Second, the Hungarians are portrayed as various ancient non-Roman peoples dwelling beyond the limits of the civilized world. Manganeius praises the emperor for his crossing of the Danube in 1150 thus:

> And then you crossed a wall made of water,
> and flew across the barrier of a liquid boundary (*horon*).
> Having crossed the stormy no man's land (*metaichmian*) of the rivers,
> you swamp the Huns by the flood of your boldness,
> devising a division (*horizon ton horizonta*) to exclude those on the other side
> so that they should not dare to cross into our land.
> You alone mark the water boundary (*horon*)
> and mark the limit (*horotheton*) for the enemy and those beyond the frontier (*hyperoriois*).   (Manganeius Prodromus: 1.93–100)

The rivers are also stated to be the empire's limits in poem 2, which is similarly full of fluvial imagery. Once again Manuel is praised for crossing this barrier and reminded that, 'The Sava and the Danube together were dividers which before walled off the wolves of the west' (2.171–2). Similarly, in poem 7, the frontier cannot stop the emperor, nor even the news of his great victory which, like perfume spilled 'at the water boundaries of Ausonians [Romans] and Paionians [Hungarians] has reached every country, the whole of Europe, and every other continent' (7. 217–18). Elsewhere the Hungarians are Dacians, Pannonians or Gepids;[36] only rarely are they Hungarians (*Ouggrikoi*).[37] They are given

---

[36] The latter is preferred by Michael the Rhetor. See *FRB*: 152–65.
[37] Manganeius Prodromus: 31.51, 83.

the names of ancient peoples, but *ethne* specifically is associated with the Carpathian basin and the middle Danube, Rome's 'natural' frontier. As such they are placed within a restrictive framework of representation; they are acquired by the 'Romans', and their threat, the universal threat of the barbarian to civilization is neutralized (see above at pp. 113–14).

Manuel's victory celebrations made maximum political capital from the conflicts at the empire's northern frontier. As Choniates' account of the 1150 triumphal procession reveals, he was not above chicanery to make his victories seem more splendid than they were:

Celebrating appropriately with a greatly extended triumph, [Manuel] led a most splendid procession through the streets of the city. Decked out in magnificent garments far beyond their wealth, the newly-captured Hungarians and seized Serbs enhanced the procession's grandeur. The emperor provided these adornments so that the victory might appear most glorious and wondrous to citizens and foreigners alike, for the captured men were of noble birth and deserving of admiration. He turned the triumphal festival into a marvel and presented the prisoners of war not in a single throng, but in groups presented at intervals to fool the spectators into believing that the prisoners parading were more numerous than they were. (Choniates: 93; trans.: 54)

Manuel was not the first to employ such tactics: as McCormick (1986: 188) has stated, 'victories and victory celebrations did not always go hand in hand, and . . . could owe as much to the political requirements of the moment as to any real military significance of the operations they honoured'. Manuel's image as a conquering emperor has much in common with that propagated by John Tzimisces, and to some extent, at this early stage in his reign when his authority was not unchallenged, the Hungarians were to Manuel what the Rus and Bulgarians had been to Tzimisces (see above at p. 54). However, Manuel's image owes more to the ideals developed by his father's image-makers than to the distant memory of earlier victories on the Danube. John Comnenus was the warrior emperor *par excellence*. It was he who revived the triumphal procession as a means to mark imperial victories, and his campaigns in the east were celebrated appropriately in Constantinople with verse *enkomia* which placed emphasis on the emperor's martial prowess. Magdalino (1993: 419) has identified four key motifs which outweigh all others: John's qualities as a leader; the glorification of bloodshed; the presentation of warfare as just; and the extension of the empire's frontiers to the ends of the earth. All feature in the glorification of Manuel's Hungarian campaigns, but Manuel surpasses John, indeed all his predecessors, and his victories are greater than his father's, greater even than his Roman or mythical forebears. His deeds are compared favourably to those of great leaders and warriors of myth and history. But unlike Agamemnon, Manuel did not need nine years to achieve his victories (2.103–6), nor like Xerxes did he need a mighty fleet (2.131–40); Manuel is not their equal, he is their superior.

Thus his military prowess, individual valour, and his victories at the edge of his empire gave much needed kudos to the young emperor, and consolidated his hold on power in Constantinople. In this regard he was similar to John Tzimisces and Basil II, and the explicit martial imagery of Manganeius' *enkomia* is reminiscent of the image propagated, briefly, by Isaac Comnenus with his infamous drawn sword; it goes much further than Theophylact Hephaistus was willing to recommend for Constantine Ducas (see above at p. 113). Manuel was no mere tactician or drill-yard general; he led from the front and risked his life in the manner of a common soldier, both activities heartily discouraged by Theophylact. Not so Manganeius Prodromus (2.139–40), for whom Manuel was 'a wonderful fighter, just like a common soldier. How incredible, frightening and wondrous a prodigy!'

1143–1156: A CHANGE IN PRIORITIES

The events of the early years of Manuel I's reign prove that his father and grandfather had been wrong to allow the Hungarians and Venetians to establish their authority unopposed in Sirmium and Dalmatia, and wrong to rely on an agreement with the Germans to secure the empire's north-western frontier. The German alliance, in which John II and, upon his succession, Manuel, had placed such faith, had proven inadequate on several counts. First, despite Manuel's grudging willingness to marry Bertha of Sulzbach, Conrad III participated in the Second Crusade. This was not only a personal betrayal for the young emperor, but allowed the Normans to ravage the Greek lands of his empire unchecked. Second, despite his assurances at Thessalonica in 1148, Conrad failed to provide the resources for a joint attack on the Normans in southern Italy. And when Manuel sought to take independent action he became embroiled with the Hungarians and Serbs, who had allied themselves with the 'Sicilian Scylla'. Although they did not amount to a prolonged war with Hungary, the campaigns he was forced to mount between 1149 and 1155 persuaded Manuel that he must urgently restore his authority in the north-western marches. Even as he did this Manuel lost the support of Venetians, who forged an alliance with Norman

Sicily; the two naval powers carved out areas of authority which threatened to extinguish any vestige of Byzantine influence on the northern Adriatic littoral.

Shortly afterwards Byzantine campaigns in southern Italy reached a juncture. Despite the lack of German assistance Manuel's agents managed to secure widespread support in Apulia, and towards the end of 1155 had even effected the surrender of Bari. The Byzantine commanders, John Ducas and Michael Palaeologus worked alongside Robert of Bassonville, the nephew of Roger II who had died in February 1154. They advanced as far as Brindisi, which was put under siege in 1156. However, the Byzantine successes were ephemeral. As we have seen, the new Sicilian king, William I, had negotiated a treaty with the Venetians which denied the Byzantines the naval assistance they would have required to launch an assault on Sicily itself, and also allowed William to launch a powerful counter-attack in Apulia. A battle was fought on 28 May 1156, the Byzantines defeated, and their commanders taken captive. They were only returned in 1158, when a treaty was signed whereby Manuel agreed to recognize William's right to the title 'King of Sicily', and to abandon his claim to southern Italy.[38] There can be no doubt that this agreement signalled the end of the Byzantine-German accord, and ushered in a new period of intensive Byzantine activity in the northern Balkans.

[38] Angold 1997: 200–4.

CHAPTER EIGHT

Advancing the frontier: the annexation of Sirmium and Dalmatia (1156–1180)

Although they were far less virulent than has hitherto been imagined, the Byzantine-Hungarian conflicts of 1150–55 unsettled the situation in Raška and the north-western marches. The instability was not just the result of opportunism by semi-autonomous *župans* who allied with whichever power was temporarily in the ascendant. Rather, it was indicative of a new balance of power that had emerged in the northern Balkans through neglect by Alexius I, John II and, in the early years of his reign, Manuel I. Both Hungary and Venice had encroached on Byzantine spheres of influence and offered alternative sources of patronage for local rulers. This seemed of secondary importance while Byzantium was allied with Germany, for the two imperial powers imagined they might control or, if necessary, crush the smaller powers that lay between them. The continued problem with the Normans must have led both emperors to question this confidence, and by the time Manuel came to realize this, his authority had more or less been eradicated in the maritime cities of Dalmatia and the Slavic lands to the north of Duklja-Zeta.

Between 1156 and 1160 the Byzantine understanding with Germany broke down. Paul Magdalino (1993: 62–6) offers a trenchant analysis of this deterioration, which I will not reproduce. However, much seems to have turned on the unexpected success Byzantine agents had enjoyed in southern Italy in 1155. Before the Norman recovery, and in spite of letters proclaiming his commitment to the joint action against the Normans, Frederick I of Germany had already reached an agreement with the pope to deny any Byzantine claims to territory in Italy.[1] In May and June 1156 Frederick stalled for several weeks before receiving a Byzantine embassy which had come to discuss his proposed marriage to Maria Comnena. In the meantime he married Beatrice of Burgundy,

---

[1] Wibald, *Letters*: 546 (ep. 407).

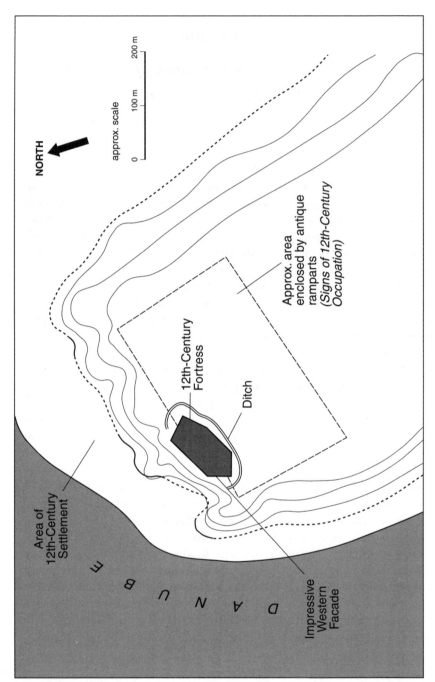

NORTH

approx. scale

0   100 m   200 m

D A N U B E

Area of
12th-Century
Settlement

Impressive
Western
Facade

12th-Century
Fortress

Ditch

Approx. area
enclosed by antique
ramparts
(Signs of 12th-Century
Occupation)

8.1 Belgrade fortress, sketch plan after M. Popović 1982

and then received news of the crushing Byzantine defeat by the Normans at Brindisi. We must place at this time the beginning of the period aptly described by Magdalino as 'cold war', when both Italy and Hungary became arenas for competition, and occasionally compromise, between the two imperial powers.

REFORTIFYING THE FRONTIER: BELGRADE AND BRANIČEVO

The developments in Germany and Italy, and the hardening of Venetian and Hungarian policy towards Dalmatia, Sirmium, Raška and Bosna forced Manuel to reconsider arrangements at the empire's north-western frontier. His concerns are reflected most clearly in his efforts to restore, rebuild and garrison fortresses at the Danube between 1156 and 1160. When, in 1154 a faction in Belgrade was intent on rebellion, John Cantacuzenus was sent to weed them out. Belgrade could not be allowed to transfer its allegiance, for that frontline fortress, together with Braničevo, was the key to the defence of the external frontier. The late antique ramparts of Belgrade had been restored in the sixth century and enclosed a settled area measuring some 200 metres by 350 metres. Such an extensive complex proved difficult to defend, and was inappropriate in an age when fortresses were built small and high. In 1096 the commander in Belgrade had despaired of his ability to defend the fort and withdrew to Niš. The Hungarian attack of 1127 must have further demonstrated the difficulties in manning the crumbling earth ramparts which inspired the so-called Ansbert (*History of Frederick's Expedition*: 26) to describe Belgrade as 'half-ruined' (*semidiruta*). Therefore, a new compact stone fortress was built in the north-west corner of the ramparts atop a steep spur carved by the Danube (see figure 8.1). The path of the river had changed slightly to expose a small floodplain below the cliff which was densely settled. Excavations have uncovered similar signs of continued occupation within the antique walls through the twelfth century. However, the new fortress was not only distinct from the associated agglomeration, it was physically separated from, indeed defended against the local community. A deep ditch – presumably a moat – ran the length of the high southern wall. The fortress' gateway did not offer access to the population, but was at the eastern end of the southern wall shielded by the ditch and defended by a large rectangular tower. It faced down the steep slope towards the river, from which the fortress was clearly intended to be approached. The river was the communication route with Braničevo and the empire beyond. Clearly, the new fortress

stood apart from the surrounding community, and did not have the traditional function of the *kastron*, as refuge for the local population in times
of crisis. Rather it served as a command post for an imperial officer to
police the local community and monitor the lands beyond. Belgrade fortress was symbolic of a new imperial attitude towards the frontier lands,
and illustrates the return to direct government with the reintroduction
of a military presence in sensitive border regions under a commander
with powers over and above the local elite.

Archaeological finds prove that the new fortress at Belgrade was constructed some time in the twelfth century. Abundant pottery sherds are
almost exclusively of twelfth-century types. Similarly, in contrast to the
few eleventh-century coins, twelfth-century issues are relatively abundant and found predominantly within the walls of the new fortress. Most
importantly, an unspecified billon scyphate was discovered in 1978
within the fabric of the western wall, which provides a *terminus post quem*
of *c.* 1100 for the construction.[2] We can, however, be more specific: the
reconstruction of Belgrade must be attributed to Manuel I on stylistic
grounds. The towers of the western walls were built in carved stone
blocks interspersed with brick bands and cloisonné. The placement of
bricks was purely decorative, and demands that we consider a similar
purpose behind the carved stonework, for there was no practical advantage in its use in that part of the fortress. The western walls were the least
exposed to attack, protected by the steepest gradient of the rock spur,
but the most visible from the plain below, from the Danube and the
Hungarian positions on the river's northern bank. The impressive
facade dominated the promontory where the river changes course and
heads south. Superior decorative construction of visible areas was a trait
of Manuel's fortifications; less visible sections were frequently built of
spoils and rubble interspersed with brick bands as a levelling device.[3]
Thus the southern wall at Belgrade consisted of unworked stones with
occasional double layers of brick to create an even base for higher levels.
All was bonded with a strong lime mortar. The result was an unimpres-
sive but solid wall between 2.6 and 2.8 metres thick. Polygonal towers,
virtually semi-circular when viewed from within, were placed at thirty-
metre intervals. In the towers the wall thickness was reduced slightly to
2.2–2.5 metres.[4]

---

[2] Bajalović-Hadži-Pešić 1979: 110. If this is the same coin identified by Bikić and Ivanišević 1996:
264 as a billon scyphate of Manuel's first issue, then we have a solid *terminus post quem* of 1143,
and a tentative *terminus ante quem* of 1160, when all coins of his first issue were withdrawn from
circulation.   [3] Foss and Winfield 1986: 149.   [4] M. Popović 1982: 49–53.

Manuel was also concerned with Braničevo, the principal Byzantine stronghold east of Belgrade, at the confluence of the Danube and the Mlava. The fortifications at Braničevo comprised two distinct but adjacent fortifications: Mali Grad and Veliki Grad. The smaller fortress, Mali Grad, occupied a position similar to Belgrade, atop a rocky spur overlooking the Danube. Excavations have uncovered Roman and late antique levels, with a considerable quantity of pottery dating from the eleventh century, but far more still from the twelfth. More Byzantine lead seals have been discovered within the walls of Mali Grad than at any other site in the region. The ramparts incorporated a semi-circular tower at each corner. The approaches from both the north and west were sheer rock faces, but the southern approach had a far gentler incline up to the peak of the spur. In the mid-twelfth century the additional fortifications which comprise Veliki Grad were constructed on this hitherto undeveloped area. With the construction of Veliki Grad the dimensions of the whole complex were increased to around 200 metres by 400 metres, and Mali Grad was provided with substantially improved defences to the south. The southern walls of Mali Grad were maintained, and access from Veliki Grad was through a fortified gateway. Thus the ground plan was very similar to Belgrade, where the compact fortress remained distinct from the outlying ramparts.

It seems likely that Veliki Grad was conceived of not as a permanent settlement, but as a mustering point for troops on active duty at the Danube frontier. A similar development on a comparable scale had been undertaken in 1130 at Lopadium on the banks of the Rhyndacus river in Asia Minor. That fortress (475 metres×150 metres) showed no peculiarities of defensive techniques that a permanent structure would require to withstand protracted assaults; excavations have uncovered variously shaped towers every thirty to forty metres and simple gateways. At Veliki Grad only a single tower has been discovered: a modest triangular structure which protrudes some four metres from the walls, which are 2.3–2.5 metres thick. It was not part of the original wall but was added some time later to improve the defences of the exposed southern approach. Besides many potsherds there is no material evidence which could be used to date the construction of Veliki Grad more accurately. Although they appear unaware of the similar construction at Lopadium, the authors of the Braničevo excavation report plump for the reign of John II, with very little explanation or justification.[5] They suggest that the campaigns of

[5] Popović and Ivanešević 1988: 125–79.

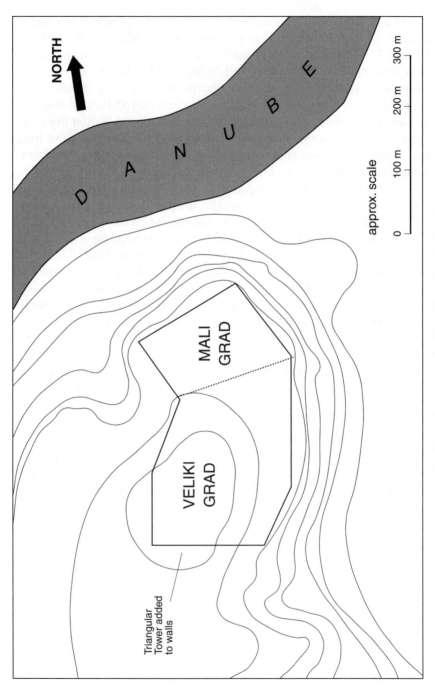

8.2 Braničevo, sketch plan after Popović and Ivanišević 1988

1127–29 would have inspired John to build a large new complex on the Danube: a suggestion we have already demonstrated has no basis (see above at pp. 205–10). They also allude to unspecified references in Greek sources for John's reign. In fact the only explicit reference to building work at Braničevo during John's reign is supplied by Choniates (17; trans.: 11) who refers to reconstruction at the site in 1128 using stones taken from the sacked Hungarian fort at Semlin. Cinnamus (10; trans.: 18) contradicts this, relating that the work was undertaken at Belgrade, and since Semlin sat opposite Belgrade his account is far more credible. We should date the construction of Veliki Grad to the same period as Belgrade fortress: certainly after 1150 and probably after 1156. The rough, towerless walls were probably thrown up at that time, and the tower added some years later. Choniates (135–6; trans.: 77) relates that in 1165 the Byzantine generals Constantine Angelus and Basil Tripsychus repaired Belgrade, built walls around Niš, and 'colonized' (*sunoikisan*) Belgrade. Thus, Veliki Grad became a more permanent settlement with improved defences during the course of a later period of Byzantine-Hungarian conflicts, to which we will turn shortly (at pp. 253–61).

MANUEL I COMNENUS AND THE SERBS OF RAŠKA

A second major concern for Manuel in restoring his authority in the north-western marches was reestablishing his authority over the Serbs of Raška. As we have seen, the *veliki župan* had developed strong links with the Hungarians in this period, and even sought to ally himself with the Norman king of Sicily. It was Manuel's task to restore Byzantine authority over his subject allies, and to do so in a manner that would impress his settlement on alternative patrons or allies to the Serbs. Before he departed the region in 1155, and probably in autumn 1154, Manuel arbitrated in a dispute between the Serbian *veliki župan* Uroš and his brother Desa; the latter had ousted the former in the turmoil of autumn 1153. Manuel's judgement in favour of his vassal Uroš was carefully orchestrated, with envoys from many foreign powers present, and afterwards was widely publicized by Manuel's panegyrists. Cinnamus (113; trans.: 90) mentions it only in the context of Manuel's dealings with the Serbs after the battle of Tara with the observation that it took place 'many years later'. Michael the Rhetor (*FRB*: 163) notes that the Hungarian king had been instrumental in Desa's promotion, contravening Manuel's earlier arrangements. Manganeius Prodromus provides further insights into the proceedings:

Desa, the usurper, false ruler of Dalmatia . . . overcome with fear, and approaching your majesty fell at your feet . . . Thus it was that Desa escaped the bond of
enslavement, by binding himself in advance to your majesty. But there with him
was a counter-witness, a counter-suppliant, a counter-pleader, the man
deprived of rule who asked that the renegade be driven away, that Desa be
imprisoned as a rebel . . . so he immediately asked your majesty for the reestab-
lishment of his previous power . . . You sat on your high seat, you took as your
colleagues knowledge, truth and just judgement, in the presence of rulers from
the western lands, men from the king of the Germans, from the king of the
Latins [of Jerusalem], from not ignoble satraps of the chief Persian satrap, from
prominent rulers wielding great power. With wise preparation and wise ground-
work you made your dais brilliant, you set up your court and you, who had
recently been the slayer of the Serbs now took the role of judge of the Serbs . . .
You returned power to the man who had lost it . . . and the rebel you persuaded
to be satisfied with his former portion, and not ever to exceed or intervene, nor
contravene those borders which were set up. Thus you bestow rulerships, thus
you divide them up, thus you measure out to your servants and your supporters
their lots. (Manganeius Prodromus: 7.271–345)

Desa threw himself before the emperor in the manner of a suppliant and
servant. When Uroš did the same he recovered his own lands and title.
We know from Cinnamus (113; trans.: 90) that Uroš had secured his position in 1150 with a similar performance. But Desa was not cast into
prison as Uroš had demanded, but instead recognized as ruler over
certain 'Dalmatian' lands.[6] Manuel fixed the borders between the
regions Uroš and Desa were henceforth to rule, and retained both as his
douloi.

The recognition of dependent rulers and their rights to lands in this
manner was unexceptional.[7] The *proskynesis* performed by both Uroš and
Desa was the same, for example, as that performed by Dobronja to
Romanus III (see above at p. 127). However, as Magdalino (1993: 56) has
pointed out, Manuel's actions were not just a reaffirmation of imperial
authority in the northern Balkans, but also 'a statement about the nature
of imperial sovereignty, calculated to impress the German, French and
Turkish emissaries who happened to be present'. More than this, it mirrored a similar judgement reached by Fredrick Barbarossa at the Diet of
Merseburg in 1152 when he arbitrated between two claimants to the
throne of Denmark.[8] The show trial in the Serbian highlands thus sig-

---

[6] Cinnamus: 204 (trans.: 155–6) makes it clear that Desa had received the region known as Dendra,
   which he later ceded to Manuel. For the location of this region see above at p. 122.
[7] *FRB*: 143 for Michael the Rhetor's account of the voluntary submission of Serbian envoys in
   1150, who similarly threw themselves to the floor before the emperor. See also Malamut and
   Cacouros 1996: 108.   [8] Otto of Freising, *Gesta Friderici*: 105–6 (trans.: 118).

nalled an early shot in what was to become a competition between two emperors advancing similar claims; a competition which soon moved north into Hungary.

FRANGOCHORION AND THE HUNGARIAN ROYAL SUCCESSION

Cinnamus (214; trans.: 163) states explicitly that 'Manuel wished to secure control of Hungary because it lay in the midst of the western realms.' More particularly, he wished to secure the loyalty of the Hungarian king and thereby retain a pliant buffer kingdom between his empire and Germany. This is the context for the Hungarian succession disputes of the 1160s. It is clear – and I have demonstrated this in greater detail elsewhere[9] – that Manuel did not seek to effect the 'feudal subjection' of Hungary at any point in this period, nor did he attempt to unite the kingdom of Hungary to his empire through a 'personal union' of crowns. However, he did wish to secure Hungarian recognition of his claims to Frangochorion, the swathe of land which stretched between the Danube-Sava and the Drava, and thus extend his frontier to the north and west.

Géza II, king of Hungary, died on 31 May 1162. He was succeeded, according to arrangements he had put in place several years before, by his fifteen-year-old son who ruled as Stephen III. Manuel Comnenus acted swiftly to replace the youth with his uncle, also named Stephen (to whom we will always refer as Stephen (IV)). In 1158 Stephen (IV) had married Maria the daughter of Isaac the *sebastokrator*, who had previously been considered a suitable bride for Frederick Barbarossa (see figure 8.3). According to Choniates, Manuel 'determined that if the rule over Hungary should pass to his niece's husband, who had an obvious and legitimate claim to the throne, glory would redound upon him, and afterwards upon the Roman empire since as partial tribute he might receive guaranteed possession of Frangochorion and [the fortress of] Semlin [opposite Belgrade]. Eagerly Manuel acted to attain his objectives' (Choniates: 127; trans.: 72).

This is not the place to explore in detail the tensions within twelfth-century Hungarian society, but a word about the widespread factionalism is essential to understand the domestic context of the succession disputes. Stephen III's election and coronation had been hurriedly arranged by a faction led by his mother Agnes, Archbishop Lucas of

---

[9] Stephenson 1996a: 33–59.

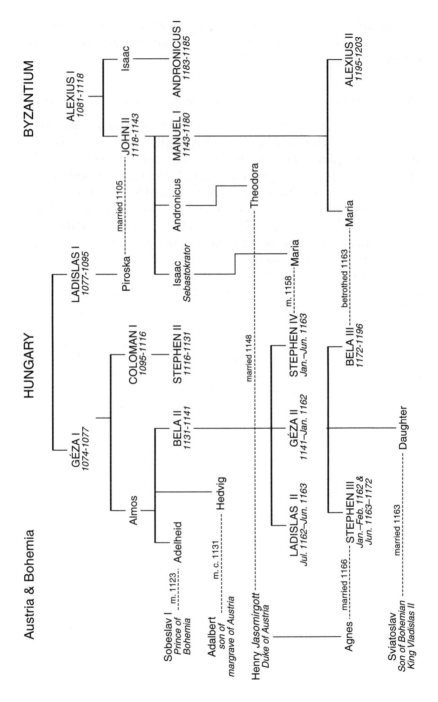

8.3 Significant dynastic connections in the twelfth century

Esztergom, and the highest ranking count called Denis. These magnates hailed principally from the northern part of the kingdom, and were staunchly in favour of closer links with the papacy. Leaders of an opposing faction were either Orthodox Christians or sympathetic to a unified Church. Many lived in southern regions of the kingdom, and looked for spiritual leadership to the Orthodox metropolitan at Bács or to the Catholic archbishop of Kalocsa. Manuel distributed bribes to many in this second group, and by their actions King Stephen III was driven from Hungary after just six weeks on the throne. But Stephen (IV) was identified too strongly with Byzantium for him to be an acceptable monarch for a great many of his nobles. Therefore, a compromise candidate was suggested who proved acceptable to both factions: Stephen (IV)'s brother Ladislas. Ladislas II was also very well connected in Constantinople, but appears not to have been Orthodox. Choniates is wrong to regard Ladislas' election as a failure for Manuel's diplomacy, for he was still inclined to honour his brother's commitments to the emperor. The historian's error is compounded by his failure to record that during the negotiations Stephen (IV) was recognized as *urum*, 'which among the Hungarians means the one who will accede to the royal office' (Cinnamus: 203; trans.: 155), the heir apparent. What *urum* signified in twelfth-century Hungary is an important and contentious issue. Makk (1989: 87) notes that it derives from *ur*, simply meaning 'lord', and maintains that the office of heir apparent did not exist at this time. However, we should not dismiss Cinnamus' explicit testimony that the institution existed in 1162, and it was as *urum* that Stephen (IV) was granted control over a large duchy in the south of Hungary; a *ducatus* larger simply than Frangochorion.[10]

Manuel Comnenus must have been satisfied with the compromise. Through Stephen (IV) he had secured a major diplomatic concession and enjoyed greatly augmented influence over a large territory beyond his north-western border. The agreement also seems to have been acceptable to the German emperor.[11] Unfortunately Ladislas II died on 14 January 1163, and was succeeded by Stephen (IV) by virtue of his designation as *urum*. Stephen IV was crowned by the archbishop of Kalocsa on 27 January 1163 (Archbishop Lucas of Esztergom refused to perform the coronation), and at the same time his southern duchy ceased to exist. Therefore, Stephen left a region where he enjoyed widespread support among the local population and proximity to his Byzantine allies, for the

---

[10] *Chronicle of Henry Mügeln*: 200.   [11] Georgi 1990: 98.

royal palace at Esztergom which was surrounded by lands pertaining to magnates who had already demonstrated their hostility to his accession. A tract by the theologian Gerhoch of Reichersberg written early in 1163 throws additional light on the repercussions of the succession crisis beyond Hungary. Géza II had followed a diplomatic course in the dispute between the papacy and the German emperor before he threw his full support behind Pope Alexander III. However, Gerhoch feared that the personal relationship between Stephen (IV) and the Greek emperor and his *sebastoi* would distance Hungary from the papacy. Indeed, he clearly implies that, following his marriage to Maria Comnena, Stephen (IV) was an adherent of the Orthodox faith.[12] Frederick Barbarossa was also unhappy. Although preoccupied with an Italian campaign he set about forging a coalition to invade Hungary and restore Stephen III. The Serbian *veliki župan*, now the aforementioned Desa, also favoured the younger candidate. He approached Frederick seeking a marriage alliance, and attacked Dendra, which he had recently ceded to the Byzantine emperor (see below at p. 267). The pressure on Stephen (IV) became too great. Just five months and five days after his accession he was defeated at the battle of Székesfehérvár and driven from Hungary.[13] Amazingly, he turned first to Frederick Barbarossa to ask for assistance. This, as much as the change in ruler, must have alarmed the Byzantine emperor: affairs in Hungary were now determined according to the will of his imperial rival. When Stephen (IV) arrived in Sardica, having received nothing from the German, Manuel 'presented him with money and sufficient forces to seize back his ancestral office' (Cinnamus: 212; trans.: 161). The encroachment from the west had to be checked.

Stephen III had recovered his throne, but his hold on power was entirely dependent on military assistance from the German ruler and his allies. His most active supporters had been Henry Jasomirgott, the duke of Austria, who had harboured him in exile, and Vladislas, the ruler of Bohemia. The Czech annalist Vincent of Prague (681) records that Stephen's mother had approached Vladislas proposing an alliance which had been sealed by the marriage of the Czech's son Sviatopluk to Agnes' daughter (see fig. 8.3). Faced with the return of Stephen (IV) at the head of a Byzantine army the young king turned to Vladislas for troops, but the Bohemian barons were reluctant to march to another

---

[12] Gerhoch of Reichersberg, *De investigatione Antichristi*: 385.
[13] *Hungarian Chronicle*: 461–2. This is also mentioned at *SRH*: i, 127, 183.

foreign war so soon after returning from Barbarossa's siege of Milan. They resented their king's obligation to sustain a weak regime in Hungary and resisted his provocative call to arms. Thus the arrival of the Byzantine army commanded by Alexius Contostephanus was enough to force Stephen III to seek terms. The agreement of 1163 demonstrated the limits of Byzantine ambitions in Hungary. Manuel was anxious not to provoke a military response from Stephen III's allies, and decided that 'it was impossible for Stephen (IV) to rule the Hungarians' (Cinnamus: 214; trans.: 163). His first concern was to secure continued control over Frangochorion. Therefore, George Palaeologus was sent to negotiate the betrothal of Stephen III's younger brother, Béla, to Manuel's daughter (see figure 8.3). Faced with Bohemian indecision, and attracted by the opportunity of a period of peace in which to consolidate his new regime, Stephen III – or more probably his mother and advisors – 'quickly handed over Béla and gladly assigned to him the territory which his father, when he was still alive, had allotted to him' (Cinnamus: 215; trans.: 163).

Where was this territory? In 1161, the year before he died, Géza II had granted Béla control over Hungarian lands in Dalmatia and Pannonia. This duchy consisted entirely of land annexed in campaigns during the preceding century, much recovered during Géza's reign (see above at p. 188). The king thereby established a distinct territory for his younger son to rule to secure the succession of his older brother. During the turbulent period after Géza's death Béla's lands had been claimed by the *ban* of Bosna. Therefore Béla would have benefited greatly by Stephen III's confirmation of his rights to the duchy, and also by the interested support of the Byzantine emperor. The status of the lands around Sirmium in these negotiations is uncertain. However, Stephen III's later actions suggest that although they did not form part of Béla's original duchy, they were added at Byzantine insistence. Thus, in theory, Manuel had found a second way to secure the same end: control over a large swathe of territory beyond the north-western frontier. Moreover, as with Stephen (IV), he did not intend to exercise direct authority in the region, but support Béla as a 'native' ruler whose interests were closely bound up with his own. The Hungarian was taken to Constantinople where he was hailed as *despotes*, a title previously reserved for the emperor himself, and was renamed Alexius.

In this way Stephen (IV) became surplus to the emperor's requirements. However, he promptly demonstrated that he could not be dismissed so easily. In spring 1164 Stephen (IV) returned to Sirmium where he secured the support of a great many of the resident population. Moreover, he turned once again to Frederick Barbarossa for aid in recovering the throne, and at the diet of Parma in March 1164 offered the German 3000 marks to recognize his claim.[14] Stephen III responded by mustering an army and marching to Sirmium. Although engaged in plans for a campaign in Cilicia, Manuel was obliged to return to the Danube, 'intending to recover Béla's ancestral domain and rescue Stephen (IV) from difficulties' (Cinnamus: 217; trans.: 164). Manuel was committed to defending Béla's *de iure* claim to rule the southern marches, and also to recognizing the *de facto* influence that Stephen (IV) still enjoyed in the region. He wrote to Stephen III explaining his intentions:

We have come, my boy, not to wage war on the Hungarians, but to recover his land for Béla, your brother, not something which we have seized by force, but which you and your father before have both granted. Also to rescue from danger your uncle Stephen (IV) who is related to our majesty by marriage. If it is according to your will that Béla should be our son-in-law, something to which you previously agreed, why do you so quickly abandon our friendship by failing to render him his land? (Cinnamus: 217–18; trans.: 165)

Manuel had promised his most valued diplomatic asset, his own daughter born in the purple chamber, to secure the lands to which he refers: the border lands around Sirmium and Frangochorion. He was now ready to take great pains to ensure that he received them. Stephen was inclined not to fight until his allies from Bohemia arrived, and for that reason the situation turned on the actions of Vladislas. According to Vincent of Prague (681–2) Manuel despatched a certain eminent Moravian named Boguta, who was held in esteem in Constantinople, to remind Vladislas of the oath he had sworn to the emperor some years before when he had participated in the Second Crusade. The Bohemian king declared that his actions were justified by the treatment of Stephen III, 'who has been unjustly injured by his paternal uncle', and he would not cooperate until it became clear, during his discussions with Boguta, that Stephen had departed the stand-off with Manuel. He then agreed to act as arbiter, and swore to restore to the emperor any land taken unjustly from Béla. Deprived of his ally, Stephen III was obliged to acquiesce in the settlement, and a little later sent envoys to Manuel to demand that he never again allow Stephen (IV) to campaign in Hungary. Manuel consented, but he left Stephen (IV) north of the Danube with a force commanded by Nicephorus Chalouphes.

[14] Georgi 1990: 99; Makk 1989: 89; Chalandon 1912: ii, 477, n.1.

Chalouphes' men occupied Sirmium and Frangochorion, which were now clearly distinguished from Hungary and together considered a protectorate of the Byzantine empire.

A case can be made, which was made by contemporary Greek historians, that the occupation of Sirmium and Frangochorion was entirely appropriate given the predisposition of the native population in that region. The aforementioned negotiations took place at Bács, which Cinnamus (222; trans.: 168) called the 'metropolitan city of the people (*ethnos*) of Sirmium . . . where the prelate (*archiereus*) of the people makes his dwelling'. A crowd of supporters are reported to have emerged to act as a guard for the emperor. The historian places great emphasis on the fond reception of the emperor by the priests and common folk of Frangochorion, and implies that the population was predominantly Orthodox and willingly subject to the metropolitan of *Tourkia*. The greater integration of *Tourkia*-Bács and Sirmium into the administrative structure of the eastern Church at this time is illustrated in *notitiae episcopatuum* 13, which is the first list of bishops subject to the patriarch of Constantinople to record that see.[15]

THE ANNEXATION OF SIRMIUM AND DALMATIA

The emperor's continued commitment to the deposed king Stephen (IV) even after his agreement of 1164 has led many to conclude that Manuel was attempting to conquer the whole of Hungary. However, it merely reflects his desire to find a satisfactory role for the powerful magnate. Cinnamus relates how easily Stephen could secure support whenever he entered Sirmium, Frangochorion and Bács, and the emperor observed that the most effective means of retaining control over that region was through him. Manuel did attempt to persuade Stephen (IV) that he did not enjoy such support north of Sirmium, and at one point he even engineered a charade involving an Árpád prince also, confusingly, called Stephen: another nephew of Stephen (IV), whom he closely resembled. The third Stephen was sent into Hungary by the emperor with a band of Hungarian mercenaries who promptly handed him over to Stephen III. But Stephen (IV) was not convinced that he had lost support in the south, and Manuel could not risk him once again turning to Frederick Barbarossa for aid in recovering his throne. Therefore, Manuel's support for Stephen (IV) was not a foolish

---

[15] *Notitiae episcopatuum*: 150, 370 (in recension *e* only).

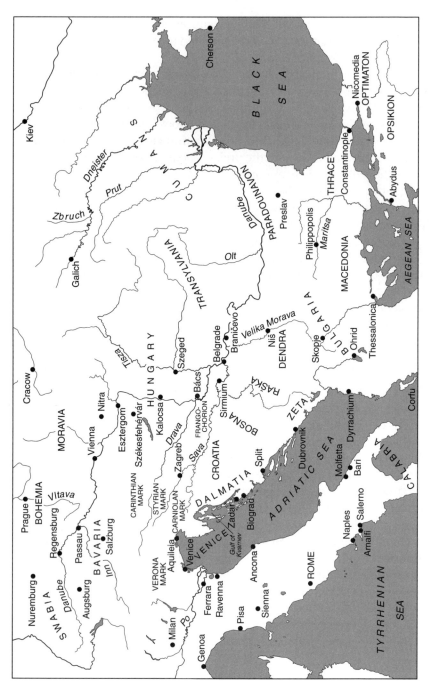

8.4 Between empires: southern east-central Europe in the mid-twelfth century

reluctance to face facts – as Makk (1989: 92) is the latest to suggest – but rather a necessary corollary of his determination to retain control over Sirmium. However, his support was the major obstacle to his reaching a lasting agreement with Stephen III, and in spring 1165 the Hungarian king launched another invasion of Sirmium. Only then did the emperor consider a novel policy, 'something he had not previously intended' (Cinnamus: 232; trans.: 175): placing Stephen (IV) back on the Hungarian throne.

Before Manuel could act on this decision he was faced with a further rebellion by his cousin, the pretender and future emperor Andronicus Comnenus. While he was thus engaged, Stephen III arrived before the fortress of Semlin, within the Byzantine protectorate of Sirmium, where his uncle had withdrawn. He secured the cooperation of a faction within the city who murdered Stephen (IV), and with him died resistance to Stephen's advance. Consequently 'the whole of Sirmium once again became subject to the Hungarians' (Cinnamus: 239; trans.: 180). Stephen had also recovered much of Dalmatia. Previously, when seeking allies against his uncle, Stephen III had 'become a friend to the [Venetian] doge', and promised to withdraw from Split, Trogir and Šibenik. He also married the daughter of his most powerful noble to the doge's son, Leonardo *comes* of Osor.[16] But Stephen had returned in force in violation of this treaty to central Dalmatia, and thus incited a rebellion in Zadar against Venetian authority. 'The rebels expelled the count Domenico Morosini, son of the late doge, and raising the [Hungarian] king's standard, they made him their master. When the doge approached Zadar with thirty armed galleys it had been fortified by the arrival of a Hungarian garrison. The doge failed to recover the city, and returned to Venice' (Dandolo: 250). Stephen III had succeeded against the odds in restoring Hungarian power to the limits established by his father, Géza II. But his success was ephemeral, for unlike his father he faced the concerted efforts of a Byzantine emperor who had prioritized the Balkan frontier in the north-west.

Manuel Comnenus despatched letters and envoys to numerous powers requesting or demanding their support for his attack on Stephen III in 1165: the military assistance of the Serbian *veliki župan* was demanded; Byzantine ambassadors in Galich and Kiev extracted pledges of support from those princes who had so recently been courted

---

[16] *Historia Ducum Veneticorum*: 76.

by Andronicus Comnenus; Henry Jasomirgott, the duke of Austria and Stephen's host during his period of exile, swore to assist Manuel, his wife's uncle (see fig. 8.3); even Frederick Barbarossa professed his agreement with Byzantine policy. Indeed, the episode smacks of the early stages of a deal between the two imperial powers to establish areas of influence in Hungary at the expense of the Hungarian king and his nobles. The Venetians were willing allies, and committed 100 ships for an attack on Hungarian positions in Dalmatia which was launched in May 1165. By the time Manuel arrived at the Danube the whole of central Dalmatia was in Byzantine hands, and the Venetians had recovered Zadar. Cinnamus described the campaign briefly, since the emperor was not involved personally:

Already, John Ducas had subdued Dalmatia and turned it over to Nicephorus Chalouphes as he had been directed by the emperor who had previously sent him there to conquer it by force of arms or negotiation. The reason for this was that the Hungarians had designated it in a treaty as Béla's patrimony. Passing by the lands of the Serbs, [John] drove into Dalmatia and in a brief spell ensured that authority over the whole region was in the emperor's hands. At that time Trogir and Šibenik came over to the Byzantines, as well as Split, and the people known as the Kačići (*Katzikoi*) who dwelt around the famous city of Dioclea which the emperor Diocletian had built, and also Skradin, Ostrovica and Solin, and whatever cities are located in Dalmatia which total fifty-seven. So the situation in Dalmatia was resolved. (Cinnamus: 248–9; trans.: 186–7)

Manuel took personal responsibility for the recovery of Sirmium, despite the serious illness which afflicted the empress. Both Cinnamus and Choniates provide detailed accounts of the assault on Semlin, which culminated in the slaughter of many of the inhabitants. The emperor proceeded on into Frangochorion, where he settled a detachment of *Chalisioi*, who were fighting as mercenaries, at an unspecified fortress.[17] In response Stephen III sent envoys promising the return of Sirmium and Dalmatia, prompting Manuel to ask which Sirmium and Dalmatia he meant since he was already in possession of two regions by those names. Departing for Constantinople the emperor left his generals Constantine Angelus and Basil Tripsychus to reconstruct the defences of Semlin. Basil also showed 'the most earnest concern for the fortifications of Belgrade, built walls around Niš, and brought Braničevo under settlement' (Choniates: 136; trans.: 77).

---

[17] Cinnamus: 247 (trans.: 186). On the *Chalisioi* see above at pp. 192, 225.

'PERSONAL UNION' AND 'FEUDAL SUBJECTION'

In autumn 1165 Manuel designated his daughter Maria and her husband-to-be Béla, now called Alexius, as his heirs, and Byzantine aristocrats, especially the *sebastoi*, were forced to swear an oath of allegiance to them both. Gyula Moravcsik, the eminent Hungarian Byzantinist, elaborated an hypothesis to explain Manuel I's plans for Béla-Alexius which, he claimed, went far beyond control over Sirmium and Dalmatia. 'In calling Béla to his court', wrote Moravcsik (1966: 583), 'and designating him as his heir, Manuel had not regarded him simply as a political pawn, like Stephen (IV) and Ladislas II, but had in mind the idea of bringing about, through him, a personal union between Hungary and the empire.' That is, it was intended that Béla-Alexius would succeed to both Hungary and Byzantium and rule them jointly from Constantinople, thus annexing Hungary. Such an hypothesis fitted well with Moravcsik's view that Manuel was striving throughout the 1150s and 1160s to effect the 'feudal subjection' of Hungary. We have already seen that this was not the case, and that Manuel had far more limited territorial ambitions. What then did he intend by the designation of Béla-Alexius as his heir?

Although the designation occurred soon after a period of intensive activity with regard to Hungary, it is important to remember that Manuel's confrontation with Stephen III was sparked by Hungarian support for the Byzantine pretender Andronicus Comnenus. Moreover, at this time Manuel had failed to produce a son, and as we have noted his second wife had fallen ill. Therefore, Andronicus' attempt on the throne obliged the emperor to consider an expedient: for the first time the possibility that Béla-Alexius might succeed as Maria's consort was made explicit. The Hungarian prince may have been considered as a possible successor as early as 1163, since his being given the name Alexius allowed for the fulfilment of the *AIMA* prophecy. Manuel had justified his own contested succession by noting that the first letter of his forename and those of his Comnenian predecessors spelled out the Greek word for blood.[18] Therefore, his own successor would have to have a name beginning with 'A'. The fact that Andronicus did was no doubt a thorn in his side. However, even as the oaths were sworn that guaranteed Béla-Alexius' succession, Manuel remained uncommitted to the

---

[18] The Greek word is *aima* (although the appropriate transliteration should be *haima*, to represent the 'rough' breathing). The forename of John II in Greek is *Ioannes*.

marriage. In 1166 he considered marrying Maria to the new Norman king of Sicily, William II. Therefore, he engineered a means to disavow the commitment to Béla-Alexius, issuing a *prostagma* which confirmed a recent patriarchal decision – dated 11 April 1166 – which prohibited marriage between kin to the seventh degree: the same degree of kinship as existed between Maria and Béla-Alexius. Although the Norman alliance failed to materialize, it was with reference to this order that the betrothal was annulled in 1169 when a son was finally born to Manuel.[19]

Clearly Manuel was never committed to the marriage between his daughter and the Hungarian prince, and the personal union of kingdom and empire is no more than a historiographical fiction. However, Béla-Alexius' position was enormously enhanced by his proximity to the emperor and the title *despotes*. He was certainly in a position to take on the mantle of Stephen (IV), and Manuel's future policy north of the Danube could be conducted with confidence through his new protégé. For the moment, however, Manuel had achieved all he had intended in that arena, as is demonstrated in an oration delivered shortly before 6 January 1166 by Michael Anchialus.[20] The speech lists the three principal conditions of the 1165 peace treaty, all of which are consistent with Manuel's limited territorial ambitions. First, it specifies that Sirmium be recognized as Byzantine territory. Second, that Croatia and Bosna be similarly recognized after John Ducas' successful campaigns. Third, that the coronation church and metropolitan see of Hungary, Esztergom, be subject to Byzantine sovereignty. Browning, the editor of the text, recognized that this did not imply subjection of the whole Hungarian Church to the patriarch of Constantinople. However, he did suggest that references to tribute and subjection are evidence that Manuel had achieved his wish to reduce Hungary to the status of an imperial vassal. A single sentence in a panegyrical poem has thus become central to the contention that Manuel intended the feudal subjection of Hungary. However, each of Anchialus' claims is an exaggeration, and while this was entirely appropriate to panegyric, we have seen often enough already that such claims do not always stand close historical scrutiny; we should not be surprised that this is once again the case.

First, Sirmium was under Byzantine control, but authority had always been exercised through a Hungarian, previously Stephen (IV) and now

---

[19] *Regestes des actes du patriarcat*: iii, 123–4, nr. 1068; Choniates: 169–170 (trans.: 96–7); Magdalino 1993: 200, 214–15; Parker 1956: 86–93.

[20] Michael Anchialus, ed. Browning 1961: 173–214. For the date see Magdalino 1993: 81; Makk 1989: 101–3.

Béla-Alexius. Second, both written and archaeological evidence prove that their supposed conquest had little impact on either Bosna or Croatia; the *župans* of each region would merely acknowledge the suzerainty of a different master. Third, the subjection of Esztergom may well have amounted only to the undertaking that the archbishop would recognize the claims of Béla-Alexius to succeed Stephen III, and if necessary perform the coronation. Therefore, it may simply reflect the concerns that were raised by the political affiliation of Archbishop Lucas, who had refused to crown either Ladislas II or Stephen (IV), and subsequently would refuse to crown Béla III (see below at p. 268). Moreover, it did not indicate any greater Byzantine authority over the Hungarian crown than had been claimed a century earlier, and represented by the act of giving the crown itself and by the iconography which it bore (see above at p. 188). The Hungarian ruler was still seen to receive his legitimate title and the symbol of his authority from the emperor in Constantinople, and the rhetorical reiteration of this fact fits well with Manuel's desire to be seen at home and abroad as 'King of Kings', a theme to which we will return at the end of this chapter (below at pp. 271–4).

THE END OF THE CONFLICTS WITH HUNGARY, 1166–1167

The settlement of 1165 was unfavourable to the Hungarian king and his closest supporters. Hence it comes as no surprise that in 1166, once the diplomatic pressure on Stephen III had relented, an expedition led by the *comes* Denis was launched to recover Sirmium. Manuel entrusted the defence of the region to Michael Gabras and Michael Branas: the former, who was a recent addition to the ranks of *sebastoi*, was appointed as *doux* of Niš and Braničevo; the latter was an experienced general who was placed in command of the region's forces. Manuel's division of authority led to problems on the field of battle. Cinnamus suggests that the gnarled general had only contempt for his young superior, and as he fled from an engagement with the Hungarians, mockingly called after him, addressing him as *sebastos*.[21] The episode reveals a practice which was a novelty of the Comnenian system where the highest commands were reserved for the emperor's kin by blood or marriage (a practice we have highlighted above at p. 170). Gabras, young and inexperienced, was promoted above Branas by virtue of his marriage to Manuel's niece

[21] Cinnamus: 258–9 (trans.: 194–5); Choniates: 132–3 (trans.: 75–6) records the episode out of sequence.

Eudocia. Branas had previously commanded the region, and had overseen the passage of the German crusaders in 1147. His loyalty was never
in question, but he had reached the ceiling of his career, and even in 1147
the *sebastos* Manuel Palaeologus had been despatched to receive King
Louis VII of France, while Branas stood conspicuously at his right hand.
Twenty years later Branas was expected to perform the same duties for
Michael Gabras, and therefore took some delight in the latter's inade-
quacies. Manuel was obliged to pick up the pieces, rapidly and pointedly.

The emperor launched a three-pronged assault on Hungary. The first
detachment of troops were stationed at the Danube under the command
of Béla-Alexius, following the formula of previous engagements. The
other two detachments, under the command of John Ducas, drove into
Hungary through Transylvania, where they seized many prisoners. It is
likely that Manuel had reflected on his previous use of a surprise attack,
which had brought him great success in 1150 (see above at p. 230). Once
again the captives must have put the emperor in a very strong bargaining position, and negotiations ensued. The peace that resulted in 1166
was mediated by Duke Henry Jasomirgott of Austria, and his wife
Theodora, who, as we have previously noted, was the emperor's niece.
Henry appears also to have wanted to reconcile Manuel with Frederick
Barbarossa, and there are strong indications that the settlement carved
out more clearly than before spheres of influence in Hungary for both
imperial powers. Moreover, the duke increased his own influence in the
kingdom considerably, and married his daughter to the Hungarian king
Stephen III (see fig. 8.3). Henry, the power-broker, was now a major
power within Hungary, and this was acceptable to both Byzantium and
Germany. However, the *status quo* was not acceptable to a powerful and
hitherto neglected party: the Hungarian warrior nobility.

Immediately an invasion of Dalmatia was launched, and in the follow-
ing spring a mighty host was led into Sirmium by the count Denis.
Stephen III had no reason to support these operations, which violated the
terms of his agreement with Manuel and his father-in-law Jasomirgott.
Therefore, although two western sources (Henry of Mügeln and Otto of
Freising) relate that Stephen III sent Denis, it is more likely that Stephen
was powerless to prevent the uprising by his disgruntled nobles.
Jasomirgott's peace represented the triumph of foreign influences in
Hungary, where eastern and western emperors were no longer compet-
ing but cooperating in their manipulation of the Hungarian crown. The
response was an unprecedented display of aristocratic resentment.
Cinnamus (270; trans.: 203) records that the force of 15,000 was com-

manded by thirty-seven generals, with Denis as commander-in-chief. Although his account is designed to add piquancy to the eventual Byzantine victory, the details he relates prove that the encounter was entirely different from those that had gone before. It was intended to be decisive, and negotiation was not a possibility. Denis ordered his 15,000 to drink the health of their Byzantine foes before arraying for battle. The encounter ended with the plains 'almost covered in the carcasses of barbarians'. Five generals were taken alive, along with 800 men and 2,000 breastplates of the fallen. 'The war on the Hungarians concluded there.' (Cinnamus: 274; trans.: 205).

BYZANTINE AUTHORITY IN DALMATIA, 1166–1180

As we have already seen, the Hungarians launched a retaliatory campaign in Dalmatia in 1166, led by the *ban* Ampud. An attack on Split failed, but Ampud managed to capture the Byzantine governor, the *sebastos* Nicephorus Chalouphes, who had ridden out from the city. Extant charters issued in the name of the Hungarian king suggest that Ampud succeeded in recovering Biograd and possibly Šibenik, forcing Manuel to consider a second grand campaign in Dalmatia. The emperor's initiative was delayed by the conspiracy in Constantinople of his confidant Alexius Axouch. But following the defeat of Denis' army later in 1167 Manuel enjoyed control of the whole of Dalmatia south of Šibenik. As imperial allies, following their invaluable assistance to John Ducas in 1166, the Venetians maintained control of the lands north of Zadar. Stephen III made peace with each of them in turn, and in December 1167 married his daughter to the doge's son, Nicholas count of Rab. This arrangement may well have been brokered by the Byzantine emperor:

In the year of the Lord 1167 in the month of December three days before the Feast of St Lucia, three legates from the emperor of the Greeks arrived with three galleys [and stayed until 16 December]. On the next day arrived legates of the Hungarian king, who brought the king's own niece named Queen Maria to be the wife of Count Nicholas the son of Doge Vitale Michiel. (*Annales Venetici Breves*: 71)

Throughout the 1170s Venetian counts ruled the cities and islands of northern Dalmatia. Domenico Morosini was restored to the command of Zadar, and Nicholas Michiel retained command of Rab.[22] A

---

[22] *Codex Diplomaticus*: ii, 134–5, 135–7, 150, 151, 168.

Byzantine governor controlled the southern sector (see fig. 6.2, above at p. 198). The first recorded successor to Chalouphes was Constantine Ducas, who had become a *sebastos* when he married another of the emperor's nieces. He was appointed as *doux* of Dalmatia in the second half of 1170 or early in 1171. Therefore, he must have presided over the general arrest of Venetians which occurred throughout the empire on 12 March 1171.[23] This is not the place to discuss the arrest which was undertaken on the orders of Manuel Comnenus, but we must consider the consequences in Dalmatia. The doge launched attacks on Trogir and Dubrovnik, which both fell to naval bombardment. The fleet then sailed on into the Aegean, but met with famine and disease. Choniates (172–3; trans.: 98) refers to the preparation of a great Byzantine fleet of 150 triremes which set sail for the islands at this time under the Grand Duke Andronicus Contostephanus, and this is surely the episode recalled in a later oration by Eustathius of Thessalonica.[24] Meanwhile, a Hungarian force had reestablished control over Zadar, probably with imperial connivance.[25] A Venetian embassy was received in Constantinople and diplomatic relations reestablished, although hostilities did not end.

Constantine Ducas retained command of Dalmatia until 1176 when a *buccarius* took temporary control. His permanent replacement was a certain Philocales, perhaps the same man who had commanded a detachment of Byzantine troops at the decisive battle in Sirmium some years earlier.[26] The final Byzantine *doux* was Roger Sclavonus, who is known from two documents issued in 1180.[27] The *doux* was regarded as the highest judicial authority in Dalmatia, and the priors of each city would refer matters to him for judgement or call upon him to arbitrate in negotiations, for example in discussions between the citizens of Split and Klis in 1171. Similarly, in 1178 Philocales made a sealed judgement in the tribute negotiations between Split and their neighbours, the Kačići – also known as the *Katzikoi*, who were the ruling family of the Neretljani who had acknowledged John Ducas in 1165 (see above at p. 256) – with the objective of defending Adriatic trade from Slav piracy. In 1180 Sclavonus was responsible for a grant in favour of Archbishop

[23] *Annales Venetici Breves*: 72; *Historia Ducum Veneticorum*: 78; Dandolo: 250; Cinnamus: 282–3 (trans.: 211); Choniates: 171–2 (trans.: 97). For further discussion see Nicol 1988: 97–103.
[24] *FRB*: 37–9. *Pace* Stone 1997: 251–8.
[25] *Codex Diplomaticus*: ii, 132–3. The town was back in Venetian hands by 1174 (ii, 134–5).
[26] *Codex Diplomaticus*: ii, 156–8; Ferluga 1978: 263. For his role in the 1167 battle see Cinnamus: 271 (trans.: 203). [27] *Codex Diplomaticus*: ii, 165–7; Ferluga 1978: 266–7.

Raynerius of Split, possibly following a direct appeal to the emperor during Raynerius' trip to Constantinople.[28]

Raynerius' trip illustrates the good relations that the priors and churchmen of southern Dalmatia enjoyed with Constantinople. Much of this must be due to Manuel Comnenus' posture towards the Latin Church. Thomas of Split, an unswerving advocate of Roman Catholicism, had nothing but praise for Manuel whom he remembered very fondly. Early in the thirteenth century, he wrote:

At that time when Manuel of illustrious memory was ruling in Constantinople almost the whole of Dalmatia and Croatia had become completely subject to his authority. However, he was very generous to all his subjects, and instead of exacting tribute he dispensed his own riches very liberally among them. He was accustomed to reward everyone who visited him, and paid their expenses from the imperial treasury. Once, when he received a calculation of the citizen population of Split he despatched a stipend for everyone, even providing gold coins for infants lying in their cradles! (*Historia Salonitana*: 73)

Unfortunately, no gold coins struck by Manuel have come to light to corroborate Thomas' story. Indeed, numismatic finds in the Dalmatian cities have been few, largely due to the nature of archaeological projects which have tended to concentrate on the restoration of surviving structures, predominantly churches. An exception was a rescue excavation which accompanied the destruction of some old houses in Dubrovnik in 1970 which uncovered 102 Byzantine and Latin billon trachea. The earliest of the four main coin types was the reduced value scyphate first issued by Manuel in *c.* 1160.[29]

Despite the rhetoric of conquest and subjection produced at his court, the emperor was content to allow Dalmatia to remain under papal jurisdiction. Indeed, his manifest tolerance was not only a guarantee of stability, but may well have been an indication to the Italian cities that Manuel, despite his Orthodoxy, was a more suitable emperor than the Catholic Barbarossa. We should also remember that Manuel was negotiating with the papacy for the union of the eastern and western churches and his recognition as sole emperor throughout the 1160s, and continued to do so at least until 1175.[30] Dalmatia was the perfect proving ground for his case, and therefore we should not be surprised that in 1167, soon after the Byzantine occupation of Split, the pope and not the emperor was responsible for the appointment of the

---

[28] *Historia Salonitana*: 73; Ferluga 1978: 277–8.
[29] Sacher 1971: 210–20; Metcalf 1979: 111.
[30] Magdalino 1993: 88. We will return to this shortly, pp. 271–4.

new archbishop, Gerard. Thomas of Split records that the citizens were
keen for Gerard to swear an oath of allegiance to Manuel, but this was
vetoed by the pope. Once again, in 1175, the pope alone appointed the
aforementioned Archbishop Raynerius, who later visited Constantinople
to be entertained lavishly, at length, and housed all at imperial expense.[31]
Several extant documents corroborate that between 1166 and 1180
Pope Alexander III remained the ultimate ecclesiastical authority in
Byzantine Dalmatia.[32] In return the pope recognized Split, the seat of
the Byzantine governor, as the primary archdiocese of Dalmatia (by
virtue of its inheritance from Salona) above Zadar, Dubrovnik and
Bar.[33] How Manuel behaved towards Dalmatia is the best indication of
his interest in the region, at which we have already hinted, and to which
we will now turn.[34]

WHAT WAS MANUEL'S INTEREST IN DALMATIA?

In seeking to explain why Manuel determined to recover political
authority in Dalmatia we need only look across the Adriatic to Italy; a
fairly narrow strait at Split. Immediately before his appointment to
command Dalmatia, Nicephorus Chalouphes had travelled to Venice to
secure the assistance of the doge in the 1165 campaigns. Chalouphes'
expertise was the politics of the Adriatic, and for this reason he took over
from the general John Ducas, who returned to the Hungarian front.
Thus, from the outset, the *doux* of Dalmatia was charged with certain
responsibilities in northern Italy. This will come as no surprise, for we
have previously seen that in the eleventh century the Byzantine governor in Dyrrachium was charged with responsibilities in southern Italy.
Manuel was no longer so concerned with the Normans, but northern
Italy, like Hungary, was an arena for competition with the German
emperor. For this reason I cannot agree with Jadran Ferluga (1978: 273),
the author of the seminal study of Byzantine Dalmatia, that that region,
although geographically marginal, remained of marginal interest to
Manuel.

As early as 1149 Manuel had seen Ancona as a potential ally and base

[31] *Historia Salonitana*: 68–73.
[32] *Codex Diplomaticus*: ii, 118–19, 127–8, 144–5. For the disputes concerning the metropolitan see, and
the production of texts in support of Split and Bar, see above at p. 119.
[33] *Codex Diplomaticus*: ii, 149, 159, 163, 170.
[34] For fuller analysis see Stephenson 1999b: 127–50. I am grateful to Ivo Goldstein for providing me with a copy of his paper, in the same volume, which supports much of what I have
said.

for campaigns in Italy, or more particularly as the point of distribution for Byzantine money. Between 1152 and 1158 agents despatched from Ancona were seeking allies throughout northern Italy. Rainald von Dassel, who was charged by Barbarossa with the siege of Ancona reported that he had encountered 300 men returning to Ravenna weighed down with gold.[35] The distributor was without doubt Alexius Axouch, who was active in Italy at that time, was responsible in 1158 for a treaty with the Normans, and had ensured the loyalty of Ancona.[36] As the Germans prepared their siege, the Anconitans demanded the attendance of the 'son of the Grand Domestic', on whom they had come to depend. Byzantium continued to use Ancona throughout the 1160s, whence agents were despatched to secure pledges of loyalty from municipal magnates across the north. Choniates (201; trans.: 114) wrote, 'there was not one of the towns of Italy, or even further afield in which the emperor did not have his own loyal agent and sympathizer'. Contemporary Latin sources confirm this claim, and although the extent of his influence can never be known, there is evidence for Byzantine money being despatched to Cremona, Ferrara, Genoa, Milan, Padua, Pisa, Ravenna, Siena and Venice.[37]

After 1165 Axouch's role was taken by Chalouphes, who during his trip to Venice also persuaded 'Cremona and Padua and many other outstanding cities in Liguria to join with the emperor . . . but not yet openly, for he still desired to conceal his hatred for Frederick' (Cinnamus: 231; trans.: 174). The secret was, however, widely known. In 1167, while Chalouphes was a captive of the Hungarians, the Germans began a second siege of Ancona with the express intention of seizing the Byzantine gold stored there. All the time imperial agents were working to improve relations and connections between the north Italian cities and their counterparts in Dalmatia. In 1169 the citizens of Split and Dubrovnik each negotiated treaties with Pisa. This was simultaneous with Byzantine negotiations which extended Pisan rights to trade throughout the empire.[38] Dealings with the Pisans ran parallel with the deterioration of Byzantine relations with Venice. Two years after the general arrest of 1171, the Venetian doge, Sebastiano Ziani (1172–8), was persuaded to send a fleet to support a third German siege of Ancona. A Pisan writer, Buoncompagno, wrote an account of the siege, revealing

---

[35] *Registrum oder merkwürdige Urkunden*: ii, 131–3.
[36] Cinnamus: 170 (trans.: 130); Choniates: 97–8 (trans.: 56); Dölger 1925: ii, nr. 1415.
[37] *Continuatio Zwetlensis altera*: 541; *Ex chronico universali anonymi Laudenensis*: 445; Classen 1983: 155–70; Hiestand 1986: 29–34.
[38] *Codex Diplomaticus*: ii, 124–5; Lilie 1984: 76–100; Abulafia 1984: 206.

that a certain Byzantine was present in the city. He names him as 'Constantine, *protosebastos* and envoy of the emperor of Constantinople'; in other words, Constantine Ducas, *doux* of Dalmatia, who was in command of a Byzantine garrison and had been distributing cash to potential allies in the north.[39] Eventually, Constantine's diplomacy secured the relief of the city as it teetered on the brink of capitulation. The only contemporary account of the siege is contained in an oration delivered in 1174 by the Byzantine bishop and rhetor, Eustathius of Thessalonica.[40] In praising the emperor's Italian policy he stresses that the nobles of Lombardy had ridden voluntarily to relieve Ancona. However, it is clear that Byzantine money played a decisive role. The *Historia Ducum Veneticorum* (82) records that 'men and provisions in Ancona were exhausted, the army was no longer able to resist and wanted freely to surrender . . . [when] certain Lombards who had accepted money from the Greek emperor mustered a mighty army which rushed to relieve Ancona'. The force was led by Aldruda, the countess of Bertinora and William Marchesella, who rode forth from Ferrara to drive away the German commander, Christian of Mainz.[41] Subsequently Marchesella was granted rights in the marches north of Ancona. He travelled to Constantinople, where he received the title *archon* and possibly suzerainty over towns which had sworn allegiance to Manuel.[42] Constantine Ducas also returned to be rewarded with the new title *doux* of the whole of Duklja, Dalmatia, Croatia, Albania and Split.[43]

MANUEL'S LAST YEARS: RAŠKA AND HUNGARY

There are indications that throughout Manuel's reign it was Hungarian policy to promote the interests of alternative Raškan magnates to those favoured in Constantinople. Thus, Desa had secured Hungarian support for this usurpation in 1153. He had then been raised to the office of *veliki župan* by Manuel some time after 1155 (probably in 1161). Some years later he was summoned to trial, convicted and imprisoned in Constantinople when the emperor learned that he had addressed the Hungarian king as 'lord'.[44] This probably took place in 1165, and we can

[39] Buoncompagno: 34; Schreiner 1971: 295–6; Abulafia 1984: 210–11.   [40] *FRB*: 92–125.
[41] Carile 1974: 3–31; Lamma 1953: 52–72.   [42] Buoncompagno: 46–7.
[43] *Palaeographica Graeca*: 47; cited at Polemis 1968: 191.
[44] Cinnamus: 213–14 (trans.: 162) addresses the episode in the context of the 1162 settlement, but notes that it took place 'later'. I would associate it with the account of Desa's duplicity by Choniates: 136 (trans.: 77–8).

date to this time the installation of a new *veliki župan*, Tihomir, who ruled with his three brothers; the youngest of these was named Stefan Nemanja. In his oration delivered in January 1166 Michael Anchialus (ed. Browning: 201.496–7) notes the Serbs had accepted the ruler (*archegos*) whom the emperor had given them.[45] Each of the four brothers received a region to rule, probably apportioned and delimited in the same manner as lands had been to Desa and Uroš at the stage-managed tribunal of 1154 (see above, p. 246). Nemanja received Dubočica (probably Dendra).[46]

If he were the emperor's creation Nemanja did not remain loyal. He took advantage of the 1166–7 Hungarian wars to expand his territories, and even seized the maritime city of Kotor. He then turned against Tihomir, and before 1168 had expelled his brother and assumed the title *veliki župan*.[47] His activities elicited a Byzantine response in autumn 1168.

> To make trial of Nemanja's intent, the emperor despatched Theodore Padyates with a military force. The toparch Nemanja was in such a hostile temper that he fell upon the Romans and immediately launched an undeclared war. When he saw the emperor was in pursuit, he showed himself in battle only briefly and then hid in the cover of mountain caves which he sealed with stones. At last, his pride shattered, he prostrated himself at Manuel's feet. Lying outstretched, 'mighty in his mightiness', he pleaded that he not be made to suffer cruelly, and he feared lest he be removed as ruler of the Serbs and political power be transferred to those who were more fit to rule, those whom he had pulled down so that he might seize power. (Choniates: 159; trans.: 90)

The last sentence is clearly an allusion to Tihomir. We might regard Nemanja's *proskynesis* as unexceptional given how frequently we have made reference to Slavic *župans* performing ritual obeisance. Similarly, Nemanja's subsequent unwillingness to observe his pledge had a familiarity that was not lost on contemporaries: the fickleness of the Serbs was something of a topos.[48] Cinnamus (287; trans.: 214) states that it was Nemanja's conspiring with the Venetians, in the aftermath of the general arrest of 1171, which inspired Manuel's last great counteroffensive in Serbia. This was launched to coincide with the installation of Béla-Alexius as the new king of Hungary.

Stephen III of Hungary died on 4 March 1172, aged only twenty-five. Arnold of Lübeck, who was in Esztergom at the time as a member of

---

[45] Fine 1987: 3; Malamut and Cacouros 1996: 111.

[46] Fine 1987: 2–7. Like Fine, I cannot agree with Chalandon: 1912: ii, 391–2 (or Magdalino 1993: 79) that Desa and Stefan Nemanja were the same person. Nemanja was probably the son of Desa's brother Zavid.   [47] Fine 1987: 4.

[48] Chalandon 1912: ii, 396–7.

Henry Jasomirgott's retinue, reports rumours that Stephen was poisoned at the behest of 'his brother [Béla-Alexius] who had been expelled from the country'.[49] It is impossible to judge whether the rumours were true, but Stephen's death allowed Manuel at last to install his protégé on the Hungarian throne, and extracted from him a pledge that he would never interfere in Raška except by the emperor's instruction.[50] Moreover, although he was no longer co-heir in Constantinople and had relinquished the title *despotes*, Béla-Alexius had married the emperor's sister-in-law and received the rank of *kaisar*. Therefore, he was within the imperial hierarchy and recognized the sovereignty of his superior, the emperor. Although it does not amount to the 'feudal subjection' of his kingdom, which would require quite specific oaths and undertakings, Béla III's relationship with the emperor implied that his kingdom was among the empire's subject allies. Béla was treated in the same manner as the various Slavic potentates who received court titles, although he was honoured with a significantly higher rank even than the *veliki župan* of Raška. Magdalino (1993: 81) suggests that Hungary was 'enrolled among the empire's client states on a similar basis to Jerusalem', which seems about right.

Manuel was then free to turn his attention to the troubles in Raška, leading a small expeditionary force into the mountains. Nemanja baulked at battle, and once again threw himself at the emperor's mercy. Cinnamus (287–8; trans.: 215) claims he approached the emperor 'with his head uncovered and arms bare to the elbow, his feet unshod; a rope haltered his neck, and a sword was in his hand'. The suppliant then accompanied the emperor back to Constantinople where he was paraded as a defeated barbarian in a triumphal procession through the city. Nemanja was shown the series of wall paintings that the emperor had commissioned to commemorate his victories over the Serbs; his alleged reaction is recorded in an oration by Eustathius of Thessalonica: 'Seeing these paintings, he agrees with everything and approves of the visual feast. In one respect only does he chide the painter, namely that the latter has not called him a slave (*doulos*) in all the scenes of the triumph' (*FRB*: 43).[51] *Douleia*, 'slavery', was the relationship expressed by the act of *proskynesis*.

So, in 1172, both the king of Hungary and the *veliki župan* of the Serbs

[49] Makk 1989: 107.
[50] Makk 1989: 108 suggests convincingly that Béla-Alexius' installation was more problematic than sources suggest. *Pace* Choniates: 170 (trans.: 96): '[He was] crowned without any trouble'.
[51] The translation is from Mango 1986 [1972]: 225. See also Malamut and Cacouros 1996: 111.

had pledged their allegiance to the Byzantine emperor, and appear to have remained loyal. In 1176 both provided allied troops for Manuel's grand offensive against Kilij Arslan,[52] where the emperor suffered a crushing defeat at the battle of Myriocephalon (near Iconium). The disaster was widely interpreted as divine retribution for his past excesses, and his own clergy were not slow in drawing attention to his failings. Nevertheless, it did not signal a collapse of Byzantium's eastern frontier – as is often said – nor did it herald the end of Manuel's ambitious foreign policy. The account of Manuel's eulogistic biographer, John Cinnamus, breaks off before the battle of Myriocepahlon, so we must rely entirely on Nicetas Choniates for the last four years of his reign. He is less than fair in his appraisal, claiming that the emperor lost his nerve during the battle and was never to recover it. But we know that Manuel fought on in the east between 1177 and 1180, and even negotiated a treaty in 1179 which was not entirely favourable to Kilij Arslan. Indeed, one German writer, Otto of St Blaisen, maintained that the sultan was so pressed that he was willing to convert to Christianity in order to secure a marriage alliance with Barbarossa against Byzantium.[53] And in the west both the Hungarian king and Serbian *veliki župan* remained loyal to Manuel, thanks to his continued vigilance lest they make common cause against the empire, or worse yet 'enter into an alliance with the king of the Germans' (Choniates: 159; trans.: 90).

SERBS, HUNGARIANS AND THE 'HIERARCHY OF STATES' AFTER 1160

Manganeius Prodromus delivered his last encomium in 1159 and thereafter 'the surviving panegyrical coverage . . . is provided principally in a series of prose orations written mostly by eminent churchmen.'[54] These still place much emphasis on Manuel's foreign policy and martial prowess, and still have something to tell us about Byzantium's Balkan frontier. Magdalino has established the framework for discussion of rhetoric and the imperial image, and Malamut and Cacouros (1996: 97–122) have lately demonstrated the centrality of the Raškan Serbs to the construction of the imperial image. Although few orations are addressed principally to the Serbs, they are mentioned in more than twenty works by several authors. The Serbian *veliki župan* is portrayed consistently as

---

[52] Cinnamus: 299 (trans.: 224).   [53] Cited by Magdalino 1993: 100.
[54] Magdalino: 1993: 454.

the emperor's counterpoint: the vanquished to his victor; the shade to
his light; the coward to his hero. However, the central motif of all portraits, literary and graphic, is that of the *veliki župan* as the emperor's
doulos, his political subordinate in the hierarchy of rulers.

The role which the Raškan *veliki župan* fulfilled for Manuel's panegyrists is akin to that of the deposed Bulgarian tsar in the construction of
John Tzmisces' image. His *proskynesis*, portrayed on wall paintings and
commemorated in prose orations, echoes that performed by the
Bulgarians to Basil II which featured in his famous psalter in the
Library of St Mark, Venice (see above at pp. 54–5, 62). Martial prowess
and military conquest remained important in the construction of the
imperial image in Manuel's later years. In the *intitulatio* of a conciliar
edict issued in 1166 Manuel claimed for himself the victory epithets
'*Dalmatikos, Ouggrikos, Bosthnikos, Chrobatikos*', styling himself thus in the
manner of much earlier Roman emperors as conqueror of Dalmatia,
Hungary, Bosna and Croatia.[55] However, as the emperor aged, so his
ability to impress as 'a common soldier' decreased, and the language of
praise altered. Manuel might still sit astride the white steed in triumphal
processions, but his generals enjoyed an increasingly prominent position in the parade.

Increasingly, therefore, Manuel was a 'peacemaker', and his dealings with the Serbs saw their fierce nature transformed by contact
with superior Roman culture.[56] And if his efforts in this direction
made him the successor to Constantine IX, who similarly transformed the Pechenegs (see above at pp. 111–14), Manuel's world view
was not entirely different to that of the irenic Constantine VII who
articulated his vision in the *De Cerimoniis* and implemented it in the
Great Palace and St Sophia. Manuel made similar use of ceremonial
in the capital to bolster his regime, and his triumphal processions and
the escalating hyperbole of panegyric which accompanied them,
demonstrate the importance of foreign and frontier policy for domestic consumption. Much of this was directed at impressing his own
magnates, and most of all the increasingly divisive ranks of the *sebastoi*. Thus he made full use of his palaces, particularly the development
at Blachernae where the walls were decorated with frescoes of his
vanquished foes and prostrate subjects. The walls of his subordinates'
houses were similarly decorated, and one whom we have met, Alexius
Axouch (see above at pp. 261, 265) was condemned for choosing

[55] Mango, 'The Conciliar edict': 317–30; McCormick 1986: 112–13.
[56] Malamut and Cacouros 1996: 104.

instead to decorate his residence with pictures detailing the exploits of the sultan.[57]

Manuel also had to project his image beyond Constantinople, to confront the wider world with his imperial vision in their own courts: the papal curia in Rome, the Hungarian royal court at Esztergom, or even improvised tribunals in the Serbian highlands. The ideological foundation for Manuel's foreign policy in the second part of his reign was his claim to be 'King of Kings', the sole Roman emperor recognized by the papacy and by subordinate rulers within and beyond his borders. He backed his claims with actions, and demonstrated his suitability to preside over a hierarchy of Christian rulers by his tolerance and philanthropy in Dalmatia and Italy, and by a moderate policy towards Hungary which never amounted to an attempt to achieve its 'feudal subjection'. Manuel's claims to Hungary were no more extreme than those advanced by Constantine IX or Constantine X when they despatched crowns, and by his settlement of 1172 he finally achieved the *status quo* across the Danube that he had desired since his first confrontation with the Serbs and Hungarians in 1148.

MISGUIDED IMPERIALISM?

Manuel Comnenus died in 1180, and his achievements proved so ephemeral that we are obliged to question the wisdom of his overtly imperialist policy. Manuel's activities in the northern Balkans and beyond were based on a false premise: his purpose in advancing his frontier across the Danube was to consolidate his defences against a perceived threat of German expansion into Hungary and Italy. He did so in the aftermath of the Second Crusade, and therefore in response to the encirclement of his empire by Germans and Latins to the west and east. Certainly, western and eastern concerns were now intimately linked, and the rhetoric produced at the court of Frederick Barbarossa promoted the notion of a unified Latin Christendom which recognized the suzerainty of the German 'Holy Roman' emperor. However, we now know that the rhetoric of German expansionism was as far from reality as Manuel's own propaganda. But if we no longer believe that either Barbarossa or Manuel fully intended to live up to their own imperialist propaganda, we must still concede that they believed each other's, and this fuelled the 'cold war' which prevailed for most of the period 1156–80.

[57] Cinnamus: 266 (trans.: 199). See also Mango 1986 [1972]: 224–5; Magdalino and Nelson 1982: 135–7.

In the period of 'cold war' Manuel may have believed he had the upper hand by virtue of his relationship with Pope Alexander III. We have touched upon this relationship in the context of Byzantine policy in Italy, Hungary and Dalmatia, and it bears further scrutiny by way of a conclusion. Manuel's special relationship with Alexander was something of an illusion. Alexander's accession had been challenged by Barbarossa, who raised his own pontiff, Victor IV, initiating a schism which lasted until 1177. Casting around for allies, Alexander wrote to Manuel and, according to one German source offered him the 'vanity of vanities': recognition as the sole and universal Roman emperor. Thereafter, frequent embassies were exchanged, and doctrinal discussions abounded at the imperial court, where Hugh Eteriano, a Latin theologian who was close to the pope, found favour with the emperor. Hugh was commissioned to write a treatise on the procession of the Holy Spirit, and Manuel called a synod in 1166 primarily to vindicate the position contained therein. Clearly, the eastern emperor was intent upon effecting church union in order to assure his recognition as sole Roman emperor, and he offered in return recognition of papal primacy and a resolution of doctrinal differences between the eastern and western churches. Such a resolution would have had enormous theoretical advantages for Manuel: it would allow him to establish as of right his authority in southern Italy, the regions which he had sought to conquer by arrangement with Conrad III. Beyond Italy, it would mean that Manuel need fear no challenge to his jurisdiction in the Christian lands of the east. In particular, the German emperor could not challenge his suzerainty over the Crusader states, as Conrad had envisaged during the Second Crusade. However, Manuel's theoretical aims were never likely to be achieved. There is no indication that Alexander III ever intended to deprive Frederick Barbarossa of his imperial title, even when he was excommunicated, and despite his negotiating on exactly that issue with Manuel at least until 1175, and possibly until 1180.[58]

Meanwhile, as the 'superpowers' vied for supremacy and recognition, smaller powers gained ground in the Adriatic and Mediterranean.

[58] Magdalino 1993: 89–91. Eustathius, *Capture of Thessalonica*: 35, 179–80 records that a papal legate, Cardinal John, was still in Constantinople in 1182, when he was murdered during Andronicus' massacre of Latins (see below at pp. 277–8). Further details are provided in *The Chronicles of Robert de Monte*, trans. Stevenson: 147, which record that 'as the Latins were being murdered . . . [so was] a certain cardinal of the church of Rome named John, whom the Roman pontiff had despatched to Constantinople at the petition of the emperor Manuel'. He did not flee because, he stated '"I stand here for the unity of the church, by the command of the lord Pope Alexander."'

[59] Chalandon 1912: ii, 607; Magdalino 1988: 172.

Already we have seen how Hungary had made much progress in the northern Balkans in the first half of the twelfth century, and questioned the wisdom of John II's hands-off policy. After 1160 the Hungarians were caught between the competing empires and endured the manipulation of their ruling family by eastern and western emperors. However, other interests already firmly established were not so firmly checked. The Venetians were able more freely to switch allegiance and profit from the imperial competition, benefiting both from the extension of Byzantine authority into Dalmatia, and from supporting the German campaigns against Ancona. The Normans did not ever suffer the feared joint Byzantine-German assault on southern Italy, and the shift of attention after 1160 allowed William I and William II further to consolidate their authority in Sicily and Apulia. And within the northern Balkans regional and municipal potentates benefited from the emperor's preoccupations which encouraged his policy of 'cheque-book diplomacy'.[59]

Nevertheless, Manuel's foreign policy cannot be judged solely on what he failed to achieve or prevent in and beyond the Balkans. It seems now to be commonly agreed that the most successful medieval political systems were those which redistributed resources most effectively, linking the peripheries to the centre in relationships of mutual advantage, whatever rhetorical facade of rulership was propagated.[60] By this criterion Manuel's regime was a success. It is of great significance that Manuel was remembered fondly in both Italy and Dalmatia as a fine Christian emperor, a powerful general and liberal distributor of largesse. The citizens of the Dalmatian cities spent his money gratefully, as no doubt did the Russian princeling Vasilko who was granted authority over four major trading cities in Paristrion (see above at p. 107). And his reputation for generosity spread further afield: Robert of Clari, a participant in the Fourth Crusade, heard it told that Manuel was 'a most worthy man and the richest of all Christians who have ever lived, and the most generous. Never did anyone ask him for anything of his . . . but that he would give him a hundred marks' (McNeal 1936: 46). Manuel's fine reputation lived on as a contrast to those of his successors, and the wealth that he had been able to amass from his extensive empire was soon to pass into the hands of others.

Although he failed to achieve his professed aim of a unified Christian

---

[60] For example, see comments on Charlemagne's achievements, and the rapid deterioration afterwards, in Collins 1998: 172–3. Compare this with an equally insightful exploration of medieval Germany, in Arnold 1997: 180–92.

empire, therefore, Manuel's imperialism was a qualified success. He advanced the empire's frontier across the Danube, and made inroads into Italy and Hungary through strategic use of force and aggressive diplomacy. He exploited the resources of his rich empire, with an economy expanding throughout his reign, to generate and distribute cash and valuable commodities within and beyond his borders, and bind disparate potentates and peoples to him. Moreover, he quashed rebellions effectively and efficiently, neutralizing all threats to his rule including, eventually, the recurrent challenge of his cousin Andronicus. Manuel's successors failed to impose their authority in this way, and rebellions in the outlying provinces were not effectively checked. One such rebellion in the northern Balkans could not be quashed, despite years of campaigning and diplomacy, and led to the foundation of what is now called the 'Second Bulgarian Empire'. At the same time the Serbs rebelled under Stefan Nemanja, and did not recognize Byzantine suzerainty thereafter. Nemanja's son, also called Stefan, became the first crowned king of the Serbs. Similarly, alliances which Manuel established overseas, such as those in northern Italy, were neglected and allowed to perish, to the detriment of the empire which ultimately found itself starved of aid in the face of an assault from the west.

CHAPTER NINE

Casting off the 'Byzantine Yoke' (1180–1204)

The period from the death of Manuel I Comnenus in 1180 to the cataclysmic sack of Constantinople by the forces of the Fourth Crusade in 1204 has attracted much comment from, but far less careful analysis by, Byzantine historians. As Michael Angold (1997: 173) recently noted, we have merely asked the same question to which Charles Brand offered a convincing answer in 1968: was the fall of Constantinople just an accident or did the Byzantines bring it on themselves?[1] More recently a second question, initially posed by Nicetas Choniates soon after 1204, has been asked again by Paul Magdalino: can the origins of decline be traced to the reign of Manuel Comnenus? Angold prefers Choniates' positive over Magdalino's negative response:

> The expansion of the west presented Manuel Comnenus with problems that he dealt with ingeniously, but it involved him in an increasingly grandiose foreign policy. There is no doubt that he conducted it with skill and aplomb, but it was hugely expensive and the returns were limited. It placed all kinds of strains on his empire. His rapprochement with the west produced an anti-Latin backlash that added to the difficulties facing his successors. The financial costs were enormous . . . Manuel Comnenus' reign . . . saw both the apogee of the Comnenian achievement and the beginning of its decline. (Angold 1997: 180)

Angold sees great similarities between Manuel's reign and that of Basil II, who similarly left his successors a poisoned legacy.[2] To some extent I have followed Angold's line on Basil's legacy, although I have sought to demonstrate that the apparent apogee before 1025 was something of a rhetorical artifice constructed in a period of expansion, which in turn was made possible by the conditions beyond Byzantium's frontiers. Manuel faced an entirely different situation: a multitude of external

---

[1] The most provocative restatement of this question has been by Cheynet 1990: 427–58, who sees the period as the culmination of two centuries of power struggles in Byzantium. For a survey of literature relating to the Byzantine backgound to the Fourth Crusade see now Angold 1999: 257–78.

[2] Magdalino 1993: 226–7 also draws interesting comparisons between Manuel and Basil.

threats, distinct but often allied, rhetorical and real, had massed beyond his frontiers, and he had deflected them by a combination of his own rhetoric and *Realpolitik*. Therefore, I have concluded – in agreement with Magdalino – that Manuel's imperialism was not misguided, but was justified and, for the most part, effective. Rather than blame or exonerate Manuel for what came after, it may be fairer to pose different questions. Was it possible for an individual emperor, however powerful, to check the expansionary forces from the west? Were the centrifugal pressures within Byzantium too great for the centralized imperial system to endure? How did the strands of domestic and foreign policy, which Manuel had kept gathered together, begin to unravel? And, most importantly here, how was this manifested in the lands which Manuel had reconstituted as Byzantium's Balkan frontier?

The greater part of this chapter will identify and explore the factors which, in the period 1180–1204, saw the peoples of the northern Balkans cast off the 'Byzantine Yoke'. However, by way of an introduction we will glance at the internal pressures, regional separatism and faction in the capital, which threatened to sunder links between centre and periphery, and between distinct groups in the centre. This will provide the necessary context for a fuller exploration of the actions of external powers, with which Manuel had competed and compromised; and it will help us understand how Byzantium's Balkan frontier became, within three decades of Manuel's death, a number of distinct and autonomous polities.

POLITICAL CULTURE AND FACTION IN CONSTANTINOPLE, 1180–1204

Within the Byzantine political system, as we have seen, rank and office, and associated wealth and prestige, all emanated from the person of the emperor, who sat at the top of a closely defined hierarchy. After the reign of Alexius I Comnenus all emanated from the person of the emperor as head of an extended family. Within the Comnenian political system only members of the imperial kin group could hold the highest offices of state, and bear the elevated rank of *sebastos*. Moreover, imperial ranks and offices were now often associated with lands granted free of taxes and levies. The Comnenian system created wealthy and powerful individuals who shared in the governance of the empire by virtue of birth or marriage. Whereas initially this was a force for stability, binding together the interests of a small group of potentates in capital and provinces, in the longer term it was a cause of greater factionalism at the heart of government. Any one of the *sebastoi*, given an opportunity, might make a bid for the throne itself, and by virtue of his lineage and resources secure widespread support for his claims.[3]

Very early in his reign Manuel survived at least three challenges to his authority by *sebastoi*. Thereafter these were rare, or at least rarely reported.[4] The most notorious threats to have been reported were that of his confidant Alexius Axouch in 1167, and those of his cousin Andronicus in the 1150s and 1160s. It is clear that Manuel was not convinced that Andronicus had entirely despaired of donning the purple buskins. Andronicus was recalled to Constantinople shortly before Manuel's death and obliged to swear an oath to the emperor's son and designated successor, Alexius. He received in return a large appanage in Paphlagonia. By his actions Manuel revealed that he was acutely aware of the major problem facing his son, and perhaps also aware of the potential ramifications for his empire of a struggle for the throne. But despite his best efforts, indeed almost because of them as potentates competed to 'protect' Alexius' interests, Manuel's plans faltered immediately upon his death.[5]

Upon his succession, Manuel's young son Alexius II fell under the sway of his mother's lover, the *protosebastos*, also called Alexius. This alienated Maria, Manuel's daughter by his first wife, who, as we have seen, was previously the designated heir to the throne. It was a situation analogous to that involving Anna Comnena in 1118 (see above at pp. 205–6), and like Anna, Maria became the focus of opposition to the new regime. Eventually Maria made a bid to depose her younger half-brother, and like Anna she failed. But her attempt underlined the weakness of Alexius II; weakness which his uncle, Andronicus, was able to exploit. Seeing his final opportunity to wear the purple, Andronicus marched on Constantinople with an army raised from his Paphlagonian lands in spring 1182. He met little resistance, and when he arrived before the walls he was offered assistance by the commander of the fleet detailed to prevent his crossing the Bosphorus. The city was his for the taking, but before he entered he sent an elite force to murder western settlers. According to Eustathius of Thessalonica (*Capture of Thessalonica*: 35) rumours abounded that Alexius II and his mother had intended to hand

---

[3] Magdalino 1993: 217–27.
[4] Magdalino 1993: 217–20 suggests that we have probably underestimated the prevalence of faction among the *sebastoi* during Manuel's reign. For documentation and analysis see Cheynet 1990: 106–10, 413–25.   [5] Angold 1997: 175.

over the city to the Latins. Andronicus calculated, therefore, that an effective way to secure the support of the urban populace was to target aliens, and thus inspire a sense of community through hatred. He was correct, and citizens of Constantinople joined the troops who set upon the Latins settled in the city.[6]

Andronicus swiftly established himself as regent, and in the following year the young emperor was secretly strangled, and his body thrown into the Bosphorus. Choniates claims that Alexius' demise was preordained. He states that the young emperor had been thrown from his horse on his coronation day, and 'when another horse was brought forwards, Alexius paraded with a broken crown. This was deemed an inauspicious portent for the future: that he would be unable to preserve the empire intact, but would fall from his lofty throne and be ill-treated by his enemies.'[7] However, Choniates is more convincing elsewhere when he offers a more mundane explanation for the rapid decline in imperial fortunes after 1180:

It was the Comnenus family that was the major cause of the destruction of the empire. Because of their ambitions and their rebellions, she suffered the subjugation of provinces and cities and finally fell to her knees. These Comneni, who sojourned among barbarian peoples hostile to the Byzantines were the utter ruin of their empire, and whenever they attempted to seize and hold sway over public affairs, they were the most inept, unfit and stupid of men. (Choniates: 529; trans.: 290)

Here Choniates highlights the major problem with the Comnenian system: reliance on kinship ties led, over time, to internecine competition between powerful rivals with equally acceptable claims to rule. Andronicus Comnenus was the first of these men to ascend the throne, and having done so opened the way for others. Just two years later Andronicus himself was deposed by one of the many cousins in his extended kingroup, Isaac Angelus: the great grandson of Alexius I Comnenus, and grandson of Theodora, the sister of John II Comnenus. But Isaac, who had represented the interests of a group of aristocratic families opposed to Andronicus fell victim to factionalism himself. He endured numerous coups during his ten-year reign, many of which, as we will see, scuppered his attempts to restore imperial authority in the northern Balkans. Eventually, in 1195, Isaac was overthrown by those in Constantinople who objected to his concentration of power in the hands of a small clique. He was replaced by his own brother, Alexius III

---

[6] Choniates: 20–1 (trans.: 140–1).   [7] Choniates: 458 (trans.: 251).

Angelus, who also suffered a series of coups. An attempt which nearly succeeded was engineered in 1200 by a certain John Comnenus 'the Fat', who was the grandson of John II Comnenus by his daughter Maria. His father was the now familiar, apparently seditious confidant of Manuel I, the *sebastos* Alexius Axouch.

Leaping forward another three years, the Venetian fleet that ferried the forces of the Fourth Crusade to Constantinople in 1203 carried the blinded Isaac II and his son, also named Alexius. We know from western sources that Alexius offered the Venetians full payment of the sum specified in their contract with the leaders of the Fourth Crusade. Therefore, instead of ferrying the Latins directly to the Holy Land, the fleet sailed via Zadar to Constantinople in order to install Alexius IV on the imperial throne. Alexius IV was the archetypal Comnenian princeling so loathed by Choniates: nurtured among barbarians, an inept and stupid man who brought utter ruin to the empire.

REGIONAL SEPARATISM

Rebellion was a regular feature in, and contributing factor to, the development of medieval Byzantium. As we have seen, the tendency to rebel reached unprecedented levels in the later eleventh century, when divisive forces at the centre allowed or encouraged fragmentation at the periphery of the empire. Moreover, the later eleventh century was punctuated by coups which originated at the periphery; several were successful, including that of Alexius Comnenus. Alexius, like Nicephorus Botaneiates before him, could aspire to the imperial throne because no definite hereditary principle had been established, despite the best efforts of the Ducas clan. Even if one had been, ancestry was no obstacle: within living memory Alexius' own uncle Isaac had worn the purple. Therefore, before Alexius' accession, and for several years thereafter, the stated aim of many Byzantine rebellions was to establish a new man on the imperial throne in Constantinople. This changed once Alexius had established not only his own authority in Constantinople, but that of his extended family throughout the empire, by the two-tier hierarchy of commands based on the rank of *sebastos*. After *c.* 1100 only *sebastoi* seem to have marched on Constantinople seeking to seize the throne. Lesser regional magnates, recognizing their limitations, aspired instead to establish their own autonomous principalities.[8]

---

[8] Cheynet 1990: 90–110 for revolts between the accession of Alexius I and the death of Manuel I. Very few are noted after 1100, when Alexius was well established.

The increased centrifugalism of the twelfth century was exacerbated by the extension of the empire's frontiers. John and Manuel Comnenus brought additional semi-autonomous regions within the empire, and were able, by their charisma as much as their actions, to persuade those who held power in the periphery to stay loyal to the centre. As we have seen, Manuel was at pains to establish his reputation in newly conquered territories, and was remembered in Dalmatia and Italy as a mighty warrior, a generous distributor of largesse, and the most powerful ruler in Christendom. While we have sought to draw a distinction between the rhetoric and reality of rulership, the two cannot be regarded as wholly distinct. Manuel's reputation was not mere rhetoric: it informed reality insofar as it was generally considered politically and economically advantageous to remain loyal to such a celebrated and powerful emperor. This was a most, if not the most, effective way to govern a sprawling, multi-ethnic, and increasingly decentralized empire.

Alexius II was not a celebrated and powerful emperor, and his reign was, accordingly, brief and unfortunate. His successor, Andronicus, did have a powerbase within the upper echelons of the aristocracy, and he also had popular support. Moreover, it has been claimed that he initiated reforms intended to reestablish central authority in the provinces, appointing his own men over certain members of his extended family. Alexander Kazhdan went so far as to suggest that Andronicus wished to displace the hereditary aristocracy in favour of a meritocratic bureaucracy. However, as Cheynet (1990: 427–34) has demonstrated, Andronicus merely favoured alternative members of his extended kin group, and there is no evidence that his mooted reforms were ever implemented. Ultimately, his regime was too cruel to secure widespread support, and too brief to implement substantial reform in the central administration, still less in the periphery.[9] Thereafter, under the Angeli, regional separatism increased exponentially.

According to Angold (1997: 177), 'there were now important local interests to protect. Their defence was increasingly in the hands of local ascendancies, often referred to as *archontes*. There was always a tendency at times of weak government or political crisis for each town to come under the control of a dynast or city boss, who was normally a representative of local interests.' In fact, as we have seen, this had been the case throughout the northern Balkans long before the Angeli came to power. But now the *archontes* were aiming not for elevated court titles with their

[9] Angold 1997: 302–3.

associated stipends. They were increasingly reluctant to become the *douloi* of weak and ineffectual rulers, and looked elsewhere for alternative patrons or symbols of power and prestige. Thus, as we will see (below at pp. 295, 299–300) in 1189 the rulers of Serbia and Bulgaria sought an alliance with Frederick Barbarossa not to defend their own interests, as had several pretenders to the Hungarian throne during Manuel's reign, but to launch an attack on Constantinople itself. And after 1202, Kalojan (Ioannitsa), the ruler of the restored Bulgarian realm, rejected an offer by the Byzantine emperor, Alexius III Angelus, to recognize his imperial title and grant Bulgaria a patriarch. He preferred to negotiate with Pope Innocent III, and to receive his insignia of regnal and archiepiscopal – not imperial and patriarchal – office from Rome (see below at pp. 311–12).

Under the Comneni local interests had been tied to imperial interests through style of leadership, projection of imperial image, by the emperors' charisma. Under their successors local interests came to the fore over and above imperial interests, and none were able to reassert central authority. Moreover, numerous alternative patrons appeared beyond, and began once again to encroach upon, Byzantium's Balkan frontier.

THE HUNGARIAN ANNEXATION OF DALMATIA AND SIRMIUM, 1180–1185

Immediately that news of Manuel's death reached Hungary, King Béla III marched across the Danube. We have no narrative account of the Hungarian annexation of Dalmatia and Sirmium, which must be pieced together from asides in our few histories and from references in Dalmatian charters. Archdeacon Thomas of Split relates that, after the death of Manuel Comnenus, his city once again became subject to the king of Hungary, and a Hungarian called Peter was elected as archbishop at the end of 1180, or early in 1181.[10] Zadar was also in Hungarian hands, and by 1182 the Hungarian Maurus (Mor) had become 'the *comes* and industrious overseer of the whole maritime province'.[11] Before May 1183 he had been replaced by Damian Desinus.[12] Clearly, the Hungarian system which had operated sporadically before Manuel's settlement of

---

[10] *Historia Salonitana*: 75.
[11] *Codex Diplomaticus*: ii, 179–81. Makk 1989: 116, 175, n. 113 dispenses with the claim, advanced only by Dandolo, that Venice captured Zadar in 1180. Charters prove that the Venetian campaign led by Doge Orio Malipiero, took place late in 1187. See *Codex Diplomaticus*: ii, 212–16, where the doge appeals for funds for the siege of Zadar against the king of Hungary. He uses the familiar title 'dux Venetiarum, Dalmatie atque Chroacie'. [12] *Codex Diplomaticus*: ii, 181–2.

1165 had been rapidly restored, after his death by Béla III. By the end of 1181 Hungarian control was also restored over the region of Sirmium, although not yet Belgrade and Braničevo. An oblique reference by Choniates to the machinations of Manuel's widow, Maria-Xena, reveal that Béla ravaged the lands around those cities only at her instigation in 1182.[13] Maria's conniving with the Hungarian king is presented as the reason, or justification, for Maria's imprisonment by Andronicus, and this provided further motivation and opportunity for Béla to advance along the Velika Morava, deep into the *thema* of Niš-Braničevo. Thus it was late in 1183 that, 'the news of Andronicus' accession and emperor Alexius' murder reached Andronicus Lapardas [the husband of Manuel's sister Theodora Comnena] and Alexius Branas, the commanders of the divisions which were engaged in resisting Béla, the king of Hungary, in Niš and Braničevo.'[14] Immediately the Byzantine resistance was undermined: Lapardas declared himself against Andronicus, but was captured as he fled to the east and put to death; Branas supported Andronicus, and accordingly was transferred, along with his troops, from the north-west to Asia Minor in order to crush local resistance to the new regime. Béla was able, therefore, to establish unopposed his control across the whole of Niš-Braničevo, from Belgrade as far as Sardica – whence the body of St John of Rila was taken and returned only after 1185[15] – and to justify his occupation by virtue of Andronicus' usurpation. In the absence of evidence to the contrary we must assume that Béla held these lands until 1185.[16] The fact that the next Byzantine coins to be found in significant numbers in the vicinity of Belgrade and Braničevo were struck by Isaac II Angelus may be held, albeit tentatively, to support this.[17]

The fact that Béla did not challenge Byzantine authority in Niš-Braničevo before the second part of 1182 suggests that he did not wish

---

[13] Choniates: 267 (trans.: 149). [14] Choniates: 277 (trans.: 154).
[15] Moravcsik 1966: 585; Makk 1989: 117.
[16] This is an assumption shared by Fine 1987: 7, but disputed by Makk 1989: 118, who states that Alexius Branas drove the Hungarians back to Belgrade and Braničevo. His reference, to Choniates: 280 (trans.: 155–6), does not support this. Moreover, Makk is obliged to invent a further unattested Hungarian invasion of Niš-Braničevo in 1185 to explain how Béla had possession of several strongholds which he subsequently returned to Isaac Angelus.
[17] Popović and Ivanišević 1988: 174 (Braničevo); Ivanešević 1987: 90, 103–4 (Belgrade). Ivanešević 1991: 58, 61–4 records that two coins struck by Andronicus were found near Braničevo, compared to twenty of Manuel I and fifteen of Isaac II. This is a significant discrepancy, even allowing for the different lengths of their reigns. Cf. V. Popović 1978: 192, who records that two coins of Andronicus were discovered at Sirmium, which was certainly in Hungarian hands during his reign. Byzantine control was not a precondition for coins to have reached a site, but a Byzantine military presence ensured that larger numbers did (see above at pp. 15–16).

to challenge Alexius II's suzerainty in the north-western marches, and
restricted his ambitions to regaining Dalmatia and Sirmium. Indeed,
given the silence of sources, it seems certain that no blood was shed
during the first Hungarian advance. The most plausible explanation,
therefore, for the swift and bloodless transferral of suzerainty in
Dalmatia and Sirmium, but not Niš-Braničevo, is that the latter region
was regarded truly as Byzantine, whereas the former were Hungarian.
We should remember that Dalmatia and Sirmium formed Béla's patrimony in 1165, which Manuel had defended from the depredations of
Stephen III in Béla's name (see above at pp. 255–6). And upon Manuel's
death, when his personal oath of fidelity lapsed, Béla felt entitled to
recover his patrimonial lands and to govern them free from Byzantine
interference. This much may even have been agreed by Manuel in
exchange for Béla's undertaking to defend the interests of his son and
heir, Alexius. Without additional evidence this must remain conjecture,
but it is clear that, before 1182, Béla had reestablished Hungarian rule in
Dalmatia and Sirmium without resistance from Constantinople, exploiting the turmoil which had accompanied Alexius' accession, but at the
same time fulfilling his obligations to the young emperor. Moreover, his
further campaigns in the northern Balkans were undertaken at the instigation of one faction in Constantinople, and against the usurper
Andronicus. They ended soon after Andronicus' deposition by Isaac
Angelus, who became Béla's son-in-law.

In September 1185, Isaac Angelus and his family engineered the assas-
sination of Andronicus. By the end of November the new emperor, Isaac
II, had agreed to marry Béla's nine-year-old daughter Margaret – who
took the name Maria – and to receive as her dowry the region of Niš-
Braničevo.[18] Isaac almost certainly agreed to Béla's retaining Sirmium
and Dalmatia, although this cannot have been open to negotiation. Béla,
like Isaac a widower, also sought a young bride for himself. He asked for
the hand of Theodora Comnena, once thought to be Manuel's aged
sister, the widow of Andronicus Lapardas, but almost certainly her
granddaughter and namesake. However, Theodora – like her grandmother – had entered a nunnery. Béla, therefore, acquiesced in the decision of the Constantinopolitan synod which forbade his marriage. Isaac
was permitted to marry so young a girl only because the situation was so
pressing. Moreover, an approximate legal precedent existed, according
to a law issued probably in 1105. 'If on the basis of great necessity, such

---

[18] Choniates: 368 (trans.: 203).

as a powerful people overrunning Byzantine lands, so as not to go to war, or so that Byzantine lands will not be destroyed, the emperor is obliged to marry to his own son the daughter of the leader of the warring people, even if she is only eight or ten years old.'[19] Consequently, the Hungarian troops occupying Niš-Braničevo withdrew across the Danube and abandoned Roman lands.[20] By the end of 1185 Isaac had dealt effectively with the threat to Byzantium's north-western frontier, albeit by relinquishing to Hungary all the territory annexed by Manuel. However, this was the price of stability, and stability was all the more pressing since to the south the Normans had, after almost a century, once again invaded Dyrrachium.

THE NORMAN INVASION, 1185–1186

The Norman invasion of Dyrrachium and Thessalonica in 1185 was provoked by Andronicus' usurpation, and by the subsequent flight to Sicily of several Byzantine potentates. Greek sources single out the *sebastos* Alexius Comnenus, a nephew of Manuel I and first cousin to Alexius II.[21] Andronicus' treatment of the Latins in 1182 was, of course, cited as a principal reason for the invasion, but the justification advanced was the desire to reinstall Alexius II on the imperial throne. This was quite impossible, since Andronicus had murdered the boy and was heard to comment that he would have to be a fine swimmer to make it from the bottom of the Bosphorus to Sicily without drawing breath. However, as Guiscard had produced a pseudo-Michael Ducas in 1081 (see above at p. 166), so William II found a pseudo-Alexius, and in June 1185 set out for Dyrrachium. The pseudo-Alexius convinced many of the Dalmatian *ethnikoi* – presumably the regional *hegemones* – to support the Norman cause, and his reception was thus similar to that of the Pseudo-Michael a century earlier.[22] Furthermore, unlike Guiscard, William captured Dyrrachium without resistance: the Byzantine governor John Branas

---

[19] See *Ecloga Basilicorum*: 147, nr. B.2.3.162=D.50.17.162. This is a collection of laws compiled between 1118 and 1166. This ruling most likely refers to the marriage of John Comnenus and Piroska-Irene (see above at pp. 180–1, 199). For the decision of the synod see *Regestes des actes du patriarcat*: iii, 176, nr. 1166.

[20] Moravcsik 1966: 584–5, followed by Obolensky 1971: 215–16, suggested that Béla's stance in 1180–5 was a last attempt to effect the 'personal union' of the empire and Hungary under his rule. Having dispensed with this theory above (pp. 257–9), I cannot countenance this contention, which in any case runs contrary to Béla's willingness to negotiate with Isaac and to accept without demurral the decision to refuse his request to marry Theodora. Cf. Makk 1989: 119.

[21] Eustathius, *Capture of Thessalonica*: 56–9; Choniates: 296 (trans.: 164).

[22] Eustathius, *Capture of Thessalonica*: 60–3.

preferred comfortable captivity in Sicily to facing Andronicus' retribution, and surrendered forthwith. Such a swift capitulation left no time to man the mountain passes, still less to launch a naval counter-offensive. Norman forces were able to advance by both land and sea, and converged upon Thessalonica.

We are fortunate in having an exhaustive and emotive account of the siege and capture of Thessalonica written shortly afterwards by the city's archbishop, Eustathius. Parts of it were composed and delivered as an extended lament to his congregation, probably during Lent 1186.[23] Eustathius is in no doubt that blame for the disaster must be laid squarely on two men: first, on the emperor Andronicus for his misrule which inspired the hatred of his enemies and the fear of his officers; second, on the *doux* of Thessalonica, the *sebastos* David Comnenus. 'Because of the personal hatred which existed between the emperor Andronicus and the *doux* David', Eustathius concludes, 'a general disaster struck us, and this was in direct contrast to the generally accepted maxim that often a state is advantaged by the rivalries of its citizens.'[24] As we have seen, and will see again, this maxim was increasingly inappropriate to Byzantium after 1180.

The struggle for control of the city was brief but bloody: tens of thousands died. Eustathius devotes long passages to the deaths of citizens, some by the sword, others trampled underfoot in vain attempts to seek the security of Thessalonica's citadel or churches. Choniates (302; trans.: 167), who drew on Eustathius' account, was wrong to claim that the Normans suffered no casualties. The archbishop notes that more than 3,000 Latins died in the city of disease, besides those who died in the battles, possibly another 3,000. However this was a small percentage of the Sicilian forces. From Normans who wished to discuss religion, Eustathius learned that their army had numbered 80,000, including 5,000 cavalry, and a large number of *rizico*, freebooters, who fought without payment from the king in the hope of acquiring plunder and glory. The Norman fleet numbered 200 royal ships, and numerous pirate vessels.[25]

Eustathius provides many additional insights of great value. For example, it is noted that people from Constantinople were obliged to

---

[23] Eustathius, *Capture of Thessalonica*: 162–3; Angold 1995: 181, 183.
[24] Eustathius, *Capture of Thessalonica*: 144–5, 225 (commentary) identifies this as a quotation from Aeschines' 'Against Timarchus'. As Angold 1995: 181 notes, Eustathius had every reason to wish to distance himself from Andronicus whose accession he had supported initially, and David Comnenus, with whom he had liaised closely until the *doux*'s flight.
[25] Eustathius, *Capture of Thessalonica*: 148–51.

leave the city before the siege commenced, implying that the citizens of
Thessalonica were left to face the enemy alone.[26] However, this did not
signal a lack of interest on the part of central authorities: Andronicus
was clearly in regular contact with the governor of the city, David
Comnenus, and, according to Eustathius, it was the emperor's missives
that provoked David's fear and self-interest. Neither Andronicus nor
David was a Thessalonian, but Thessalonica was not a city with an easily
defined local identity. The closest one might come to a local identity is a
common identification with the cult of St Demetrius, and as Eustathius
(*Capture of Thessalonica*: 94–5) informs us, among the local devotees was a
band of Serbians who took the fight to the Normans. While these were
clerics, not soldiers, the city was defended by a remarkably multi-ethnic
garrison: Eustathius (88–9, 92–3, 120–1) refers to Alans and Iberians,
Chounavitai (from the *thema* of Dyrrachium), Germans and Bulgarians.
The archbishop is careful to distinguish between soldiers and citizens
(102–3), and also to note the presence of a large and prosperous Jewish
community, and of many heretical Armenians, who lived outside the city
at nearby Krania and Zemenikos, and for whom he nurtured a particular loathing (112–13, 124–5).

Besides the clashing of swords, Eustathius also portrays in vignettes a
terrible clash of cultures and values. The Normans from Sicily engaged
in all manner of grotesque and sordid acts. They performed impromptu
barbering with their swords for effeminate Greeks with their long hair
and flowing beards.[27] The refined archbishop was also offended because:

Like children the [Normans] foolishly sold things of great value for very little
. . . the streets of the city were flooded with perfumed oils, aromatic distillations,
powders for the treatment of diseases, for dainty adornment, or for dyeing, and
other things needed for a life of cleanliness. If they found a piece of sweet smelling wood they burned it like kindling, and the noble raisin appeared to them as
only a nugget of charred charcoal. Rose water was nothing more than slop . . .
but they marvelled at iron rings, little nails, and small knives, tinder boxes and
needles as if they were objects of great value, while they allowed other fine
objects to be trampled underfoot. (Eustathius, *Capture of Thessalonica*:150–3)

The clash of values which so offended Eustathius – which is a clash of
interests considered appropriate for men – cannot have been so apparent or offensive to all resident in Thessalonica. It is hard to believe that
the mercenary forces from Alania or Iberia, who most likely also sported

---

[26] Eustathius, *Capture of Thessalonica*: 66–7. However, it is later noted (pp. 88–9) that many of
Thessalonica's own nobles had also fled the city before the siege began.

[27] Eustathius, *Capture of Thessalonica*: 131–3.

long hair under their red felt hats,[28] did not value knives above raisins, or that practical implements or tools had no appeal to the fishermen and harbourmen of Thessalonica. Eustathius' comments, therefore, may reveal most clearly how far removed were his own Constantinopolitan values from those of his flock. And by extension we might consider whether the real clash of cultures was not between Norman and Thessalonian, but between Constantinopolitan and provincial, refined and unrefined, centre and periphery. If they had not inflicted such atrocities upon the locals (and not just the local rose water), perhaps the seafaring, tool-loving Normans would have seemed acceptable patrons or governors for the majority of residents of Byzantium's second city.[29]

The fall of Thessalonica sent shockwaves throughout the Balkans, and Constantinople became the Normans' next stated target, provoking panic within the imperial capital. Despite his best efforts to shore up the city's defences, demolishing all houses which adhered to the land walls and preparing a fleet of one hundred longships, Andronicus had lost the support of the urban populace, and was vulnerable to attacks by his relatives and enemies.[30] He determined to crush opposition before it might crush him, but encountered greater resistance from the leading families. The Angeli acted most decisively, and the stand off between Andronicus and Isaac Angelus at Hagia Sophia saw the emperor apprehended, vilified and mutilated by an angry mob. Isaac was installed on the imperial throne by their command.[31]

Isaac immediately showed his mettle, launching a counter-offensive against the Normans. The change of regime seems initially to have inspired great popular support, allowing Isaac to despatch a large scratch army under the command of Alexius Branas. However, a greater boon was the fact that William II had yet to learn of Andronicus' overthrow, and had kept his forces divided into three sections. The first part garrisoned Thessalonica, the second occupied the lands around Serres, on the eastern bank of the Strymon, blocking passage between Constantinople and Thessalonica. Only the third part had advanced towards the capital, and these troops were defeated by the Byzantine scratch army at Mosynopolis in Thrace. With his forces inspired by their victory and the bloody sack of the Norman camp, Branas pressed on to the Strymon. Battle was engaged on 7 November

---

[28] Eustathius, *Capture of Thessalonica*: 82–3.
[29] See Angold 1995: 183–8 for comments on the peoples of Thessalonica and their relations with Eustathius. Compare with comments by, and on, Theophylact and his Bulgarian flock, above at pp. 152–4.   [30] Choniates: 320 (trans.: 176).
[31] Choniates: 342–54 (trans.: 188–95); Garland 1992: 39–40.

1185, after tentative negotiations were abandoned, and Branas achieved a notable victory. Those Normans who escaped the battle fled to Thessalonica, and bringing news of their defeat they joined the general Norman withdrawal by sea. Those who arrived later had no means of escape, and were put to death as they wandered in the city's streets. Choniates (360; trans.: 199–200) singles out the Alan mercenaries for their ingenuity in devising cruel deaths for the Sicilians.[32] Other Normans who escaped to Dyrrachium fared better, and William was able to hold on to the city for some time before, eventually, he was driven out by lack of provisions.

We have no details of how long William retained control of Dyrrachium, nor of the protracted skirmishing which must have accompanied the Norman withdrawal. However, it is clear that they retained a foothold on the eastern littoral of the Adriatic for some time. In September 1186 the ruler of the Raškan Serbs, Stefan Nemanja, and his brothers Miroslav and Strasimir, made peace with the city of Dubrovnik which was, it is stated, 'in the hands of the most glorious King W[illiam]'.[33] By then, as we have seen, Isaac had forged an alliance with King Béla III of Hungary which secured his possession of Niš and Braničevo, and provided a solid platform to restore Byzantine authority in various parts of the northern Balkans. However, this would require the submission of the various Slavic peoples, not least of the Raškan Serbs who were dealing independently with the Normans in Dubrovnik and the Hungarian king, of the Bulgarians, and of non-Slavic peoples, in particular the Vlachs.

THE VLACH-BULGAR REBELLION, 1185–1187

The Vlach-Bulgar rebellion, which broke out at the turn of the year 1185–6, and subsequently the rise of the 'Second Bulgarian Empire', has inspired a copious literature. As Robert Lee Wolff noted in 1947, much of this scholarship has started from particular premises which have, or have had, little to do with the northern Balkans in 1185–6, and much to do with Bulgaria and Romania in the twentieth century.[34] This trend has continued, and the discussions are fascinating. However, we cannot dwell on them here, and for that reason will limit references to secondary literature, excepting that of Wolff and other neutral commentators.

---

[32] Choniates: 356–63 (trans.: 197–201) for a full account of the Byzantine counter-offensive.
[33] *Codex Diplomaticus*: ii, 201–2; Fine 1987: 9.
[34] Wolff 1947: 196–7; Wolff 1949: 174–5; Fine 1987: 13. Cf. Ostrogorsky 1968: 404, n.1.

In his analysis of the origins and development of the 'Second Bulgarian Empire', Wolff went as far as is possible with the historical sources, basing his own narrative on Choniates', which he supplemented, for the period 1189–90, with information from the so-called Ansbert, and for *c.* 1197–1204 from papal correspondence with Kalojan (Ioannitsa). Wolff recognized the value of 'hitherto little-used "rhetorical" sources', but made no obvious use of them. Subsequent research has allowed us to date several orations more accurately, and to use them to supplement or correct Choniates, although we must beware not to privilege panegyric over history on certain points, particularly of chronology. The orations are best read as evidence for the increasing gulf between the rhetoric and reality of Byzantine imperial government between 1180 and 1204, and we will return to this later. Naturally, Wolff did not have access to much archaeological and numismatic evidence, which offers further valuable insights.

The Vlach-Bulgar rebellion was provoked by an arbitrary imperial decision to levy taxes. Choniates (368; trans.: 203–4) relates that, in order to raise money to celebrate his marriage to the daughter of Béla III, Isaac levied an extraordinary tax. This fell most heavily on the settlements in the vicinity of Anchialus and the Haemus mountains where the 'barbarians . . . . formerly called Mysians (*Mysoi*), and now named Vlachs (*Vlachoi*)', were provoked to rebel. Isaac must have considered Anchialus to be a staunchly loyal region: the city had remained in Byzantine hands throughout the Pecheneg wars of the later eleventh century, and had served as Alexius I's base for operations against the nomads who had established themselves in the so-called 'Hundred Hills' (see above at pp. 103–5). However, it seems likely that the itinerant Vlachs were used to paying only the sales taxes on goods traded at Anchialus. They baulked at the new levy, which was presumably on their flocks rather than lands, and sent two of their leaders, the brothers Peter and Asen, to negotiate with the emperor, who was encamped at Kypsella in southern Thrace. The brothers requested that Isaac grant them an imperial estate in the vicinity of the Haemus 'which would provide them with a little revenue'. However, their request was denied, and consequently 'they spat out heated words, hinting at rebellion and the destruction they would wreak on their way home. Asen, the more insolent and savage of the two, was struck across the face and rebuked for his insolence at the command of the *sebastokrator* John.'[35]

---

[35] Choniates: 369 (trans.: 204).

Initially the Vlachs were reluctant to embrace open revolt, 'looking
askance at the magnitude of the undertaking. Therefore, to overcome
their fellows' timidity the brothers built a house of prayer in the name
of the good martyr St Demetrius.'[36] In this way they convinced both the
Vlachs and Bulgarians around Anchialus that St Demetrius had abandoned the Byzantines at Thessalonica, and henceforth he would support
their cause. Remarkably Eustathius (*Capture of Thessalonica*: 140–1) had a
premonition of this. Adapting Psalms 79:10, he wrote: 'Then again we
cried aloud, "come to save us, so the *ethne* may never say, "where is the
protector of their city?" But he [St Demetrius] did not listen to our
prayers, and removed himself from us.' With Demetrius as their inspiration the Vlachs and Bulgars launched an assault on Byzantine settlements, seizing captives and cattle in abundance. Isaac launched a
counter-offensive in spring 1186, but the Vlachs remained in 'rough
ground and inaccessible places', so he could not force an encounter.[37]
However, a solar eclipse, which has been dated to 21 April 1186,[38] provided cover for the Byzantine troops to fall upon the rebels, who fled to
the Danube, and across to make contact with the Cumans. It is probably
on this occasion that Isaac entered Peter's house and from there recovered an icon of St Demetrius, symbolically reclaiming the martyr for the
Byzantines. This was celebrated in a poem by Theodore Balsamon, who
addresses Peter as 'the rebel Slavopetros (*apostatou Sthlabopetrou*)'.[39] We
also have, probably from late in 1187, an oration by John Syropoulus.
The date of this oration has been disputed (several scholars prefer to
date it to 1193 so that it might be contemporary with orations by George
Tornicius and Sergius Colybas, discussed below at pp. 301–2). However,
as Kazhdan has shown, an earlier dating is likely because of what
Syropoulus does, and does not, say. In particular, the revolt of Peter and

[36] Choniates: 371 (trans.: 205).
[37] Brand 1968a: 89–91 places Isaac's first campaign immediately before his second, contradicting
Nicetas Choniates' explicit testimony. Brand does so (as he explains at p. 338, n. 38) on the basis
of an oration by Michael Choniates, given in late summer 1187, in which Michael states that
Isaac launched his first campaign against the Vlach-Bulgars immediately after he had quashed
Branas' revolt. However, as Van Dieten 1971: 71–3 has demonstrated, we cannot favour Michael's
panegyric over his brother Nicetas' history on points of chronology; history and panegyric are
written according to quite different rules. Moreover, unlike Michael, Nicetas was an eye-witness
to much that he described: we have the victory despatch he drafted during Isaac's second campaign. Finally, Nicetas had his brother's works to hand when writing his history, and clearly
rejected Michael's chronology. We must follow his example.
[38] Choniates: 372 (trans.: 206); Van Dieten 1971: 73.
[39] Horna 1903: 192; Wolff 1947: ii, 1118, n. 119; Wolff 1949: 183, n. 40. Brand 1968a: 338, n. 38
prefers to date the events described to 1187 or 1188. This is required by his redating of Isaac's
first campaign.

Asen is considered a recent problem, but one which will soon be resolved. The rebellion is referred to as 'the western evil' which is destroying the region of the Balkan mountains (*Zygos*). Peter and Asen are an ox and an ass: the first will soon bow his neck (*kampseie*: future tense) beneath the imperial yoke (*zygos*), the second will be restrained by the bridle (*chalinos*) of his subjection.[40] There is no reference to the rift between Peter and Asen which emerged later, and to which Tornicius and Colybas allude.

So, at least initially, Isaac's strategy seemed to have worked: he had driven the rebels from the Haemus and reestablished Byzantine control around Anchialus. Moreover, he had gained a personal victory, leading his troops into the defiles during the eclipse. He withdrew promptly to celebrate fittingly in Constantinople. According to Choniates (373; trans.: 206), upon arriving in the capital, Isaac made much of his victory, only to earn the opprobrium – which was in hindsight, Choniates implies, well-founded – of the judge Leo Monasteriotes, who warned that the emperor had failed to heed the advice of Basil 'the Bulgar-slayer'. The *Boulgaroktonos* had predicted a Vlach rebellion, but Isaac had failed to heed both his warning and his example by withdrawing his forces too promptly. So, when the Vlachs returned across the Danube, bringing with them Cuman allies, they found the plains 'swept clean and emptied of Byzantine troops . . . [Therefore] they were not content merely to preserve their own possessions and to assume control over Mysia, but also were compelled to wreak havoc against Byzantine lands and unite the political power of the Mysians and Bulgarians (*ton Myson kai ton Boulgaron*) into one polity (*dynasteian*) as of old.'[41]

Just as the Norman assault on Dyrrachium signalled the return of a familiar menace to the south-western Balkan frontier after a century, so the seizure of Paristrion and the Mysian plains by the local population allied with a force of steppe nomads recalled the crisis at the north-eastern frontier, which had escalated in the 1070s, and had been ended by Alexius I only after a decade of campaigning on both sides of the Haemus (see above, Chapter 3). However, rather than take the field himself – as Choniates implies he should have – Isaac II entrusted the fight against the allied Vlach, Bulgar and Cuman forces first to his pater-nal uncle, the *sebastokrator* John. Adopting suitable tactics, John launched attacks only when the rebels formed into units and descended from the mountains to the plains. The waiting game may have paid off had John

---

[40] Syropoulus: 17.15–32, 18.1–4; Kazhdan 1965: 167.   [41] Choniates: 374 (trans.: 206).

not aspired to the throne himself. John rebelled, and thus he continued the series of successful generals and *sebastoi* who placed personal ambition above the greater good. The rebellion was swiftly quashed, and John was removed from his command, and replaced by the emperor's brother-in-law, the loyal but much less successful *kaisar* John Cantacuzenus. Although an experienced general, Cantacuzenus was evidently not familiar with guerilla warfare. Rather than await their descent, he sought to carry the war to his enemies in the mountains, losing not only many men, but also his standards, and 'the soft tunics and elegant cloaks of the *kaisar* which were snatched and worn by the companions of Peter and Asen. The victors, with the standards at their head, once more occupied the plains.'[42]

Isaac's third general was Alexius Branas, a commander with extensive experience of Balkan warfare, but who had already been suspected of plotting to usurp the throne when he commanded imperial forces against the Normans in autumn 1185. In spring 1187 he gained the support of his family, in Adrianople, and the troops stationed there. Then, having put on red buskins, Branas marched on Constantinople. Isaac was only able to deflect the assault with the aid of Conrad of Montferrat, once a close ally of Manuel, and to whose brother Isaac had recently married his sister.[43] Naturally, while the struggle for power took place around the capital, all momentum in the war against the 'barbarians' was lost. Thus, only in September 1187, did Isaac once again lead an army against the rebels.

Fortuitously, we have the text of a despatch to the patriarch and synod in Constantinople, drafted by none other than Nicetas Choniates, which reports on Isaac's 'victorious' campaign of 1187.[44] It is clear that Nicetas made use of this in compiling his history, and presents his account as an eye-witness – 'for I myself followed along as the emperor's under-secretary' – to a running battle which saw fortunes and captives change hands between Berrhoia, Adrianople and Philippopolis. The allied forces of Cumans and Vlachs employed familiar nomad tactics, withdrawing as if in retreat, but returning swiftly to vacated lands, and frequently falling on their pursuers. The emperor achieved some minor successes before winter closed in, but Choniates' historical account offers a broader context for interpreting his victory despatch: the Vlachs and Cumans retained the upper hand.[45]

---

[42] Choniates: 376 (trans.: 207).   [43] Choniates: 377–88 (trans.: 207–13).
[44] Choniates, *Orations*: 6–12; Van Dieten 1971: 65–79, for the date and discussion. Cf. Wolff 1947: ii, 1119–20, n. 122; Wolff 1949: 184, n. 43.   [45] Choniates: 397–8 (trans.: 218–19).

With the advent of spring 1188 Isaac returned to the field, but failed during a three-month siege to capture Lovech. Therefore he returned to Constantinople, earning Choniates' censure for his inconstancy. Isaac, he maintained, preferred 'the delights of the Propontis' to his military duties.[46] Thus, the lands north of the Haemus remained in the control of various Vlachs, Bulgars and Cumans, who acknowledged the supreme authority of the brothers, Peter and Asen.[47]

Peter and Asen came to Kypsella in spring 1186 in search of concessions. They hoped to be granted privileges by a new emperor, and their hope was well founded, since Byzantine emperors regularly granted local rulers in the northern Balkans such concessions. However, they were insulted and dismissed. Isaac Angelus had decided to make an example of the upstart Vlachs. He must have imagined he could control the pastoralists, and determined that crushing their uprising would gain him much needed military credibility. However, and in spite of his attempt to prove otherwise by announcing false victories to the faithful in Constantinople, Isaac had miscalculated, and it proved to be costly. Nevertheless, the escalation of the Vlach rebellion was not inevitable, nor was it based on an ethnic, still less a 'national', grievance against Byzantine rule. Both Vlachs and Bulgarians played a major role in the escalation of the rebellion, but others fought on the Byzantine side. The Cumans, a Turkic people, played an indispensable role in progressing the rebellion from civil unrest to military confrontation. And further escalation was the result of the actions of various Byzantine generals who placed personal ambition above the good of the empire.

So, it was not the cherished aspirations for independence of powerful magnates which served as the catalyst for rebellion, it was poor judgement by a new emperor in dealing with subject peoples who were long used to tax concessions, tribute and titles. And the galvanizing force employed by the rebels was not a common ethnic identity long suppressed under the 'Byzantine Yoke', it was a belief borrowed directly from Byzantium: the cult of St Demetrius. However, having established control in the lands north of the Haemus, and resisted Byzantine attempts to bring them to heel, Peter and Asen saw the possibility of a permanent settlement free from Byzantine interference or suzerainty. Naturally, they sought to draw on traditions of independent – which had

---

[46] Choniates: 399 (trans.: 219).
[47] I can find no evidence in support of the claim, often advanced, that Isaac signed a treaty which recognized Bulgarian independence at this time. *Pace*, for example, Fine 1987: 26. Cf. Dölger 1925: ii, 1580; Dölger, ed. Wirth 1977: ii, 297, nr. 1584a.

been called, and therefore was once again called, Bulgarian – rule in the northern Balkans. Furthermore, while Isaac Angelus would not recognize the foundation of an autonomous polity, other powerful patrons might. It was not long before both the papacy and the German emperor began to take a direct interest in the north-eastern Balkans.

THE PASSAGE OF THE THIRD CRUSADE THROUGH THE NORTHERN BALKANS[48]

Inspired by the reconquest of Syria and Palestine by Saladin, the Third Crusade is the name given to a series of independent expeditions to the Holy Land by western rulers, including the emperor of Germany, and the kings of France and England. The German forces were among the first to set off, by land, under the command of their aged emperor, Frederick Barbarossa, sometime participant in the Second Crusade, and thereafter Manuel I's competitor for the style 'emperor of the Romans'. Now aged seventy, Barbarossa saw his final opportunity to remedy the failure of the last great armed pilgrimage. But from the moment his forces reached Braničevo it was clear that the journey to Constantinople would be far more arduous even than the last enterprise. Moreover, it was in marked contrast to the five-week march through Hungary, where Béla III had himself contributed a large contingent to the crusade, and had entertained Barbarossa for two days at his private hunting lands on an island in the Danube. Elsewhere, the emperor was received with great ceremony, and his followers quartered and fed, and provided with transport and pack animals, including three camels![49] Having crossed the Danube, however, the Germans found the *doux* of Braničevo far less hospitable. By Frederick's own account, 'as soon as we reached the borders of our imperial brother, the emperor of Constantinople, we suffered no small loss by robbery of goods and killing of our men; and this is known without doubt to have been instigated by the emperor himself.'[50]

---

[48] Brand 1968a: 176–88 has covered the passage of the crusade in far greater detail than I am able here. See also Johnson 1969: 89–109, who quotes extensively from an unpublished translation of Ansbert, and the even fuller account in Eickhoff 1977: 41–82. I will focus on Frederick Barbarossa's relations with the Balkan peoples during his passage through the northern Balkans; on the notion of Barbarossa as an alternative to Isaac Angelus as patron or suzerain; and on Isaac's response to the German advance, in order to compare this with Manuel I's handling of Second Crusade.

[49] Ansbert, *History of Frederick's Expedition*: 25–7; Johnson 1969: 94.

[50] Ansbert, *History of Frederick's Expedition*: 40, which interpolates a letter dated 16 November 1189 from Frederick to his son Henry.

If the passage across the Balkans of the German contingent of the Second Crusade was coloured by mistrust and punctuated with skirmishing (see above at pp. 218–22), that of the Germans on the Third Crusade was a tale of diplomatic duplicity and open warfare. Immediately, the *doux* of Braničevo led the crusaders away from the established route into the empire, and instead directed them along a second rough track which he had previously blocked. Then, as the army of the cross struggled through the 'Bulgarian forest', which lined the Velika Morava, they were ambushed by 'puny Greeks (*Greculos*), Bulgars (*Bulgares*), Serbs (*Servigios*) and semi-barbarian Vlachs (*Flachos semibarbaros*) . . . Many of them, when seized, confessed that they had been forced to do these things by command of the *doux* of Braničevo, who was himself under orders from the emperor of the Greeks.'[51]

Upon reaching Niš, Frederick was met by a Byzantine embassy led, according to Ansbert, by Alexius, Isaac Angelus' paternal uncle; or, according to Choniates, by the Logothete of the *dromos* John Ducas accompanied by Andronicus Cantzcuzenus.[52] The Byzantine legation condemned the 'independent' actions of the *doux* of Braničevo, and promised safe conduct through imperial lands on the condition that the Germans advanced peacefully. The Byzantine army which guarded the passes, Frederick was informed, was stationed thus to monitor the recalcitrant Serbs, not to threaten the Germans. And Frederick had good reason to believe this, since as he dwelt at Niš he was approached by the *veliki župan* (*magnus comes*) Stefan Nemanja, and his brothers. The Serbs offered to support Frederick's march and provide aid against the Byzantines, and in return sought Frederick's promise to act as guarantor of recent Serbian conquests. Ansbert states that Nemanja and his brothers had 'occupied by sword and bow the city of Niš and surrounding lands as far as Sardica (*Straliz*)', and wished to 'receive that very land from the hand of the emperor of the Romans [Frederick] himself'.[53] Clearly, and not for the first time, the Serbs saw the advantage of securing an alternative, and more distant, patron and suzerain. But Barbarossa was in no position to promise such guarantees, nor did he wish to interfere in the Serbs' disputes with his 'imperial brother'. It is clear that the explanations, and the deal offered by the Byzantine delegation, were acceptable to the German emperor, who thus hoped still to

[51] Ansbert, *History of Frederick's Expedition*: 28; Johnson 1969: 98.
[52] Ansbert, *History of Frederick's Expedition*: 33; Choniates: 402 (trans.: 221).
[53] Ansbert, *History of Frederick's Expedition*: 30. Frederick also received envoys from Peter and Asen, and I will return to this shortly.

proceed rapidly through the Balkans and into Asia Minor. A German embassy led by the bishop of Münster was escorted back to Constantinople to supervise the reception of the crusading army.

Barbarossa retained his hopes of swift progress because he trusted Isaac's envoys; not just those he had received at Niš, but also those who had visited his court at Nuremburg in December 1188. That first legation may be compared with that despatched by Manuel I to Louis VII of France (discussed above at pp. 216–17). Isaac's ambassador, the Logothete (*cancellarius*) John Ducas, wished to extract oaths from the Germans because 'from the time when the idea of an expedition to Jerusalem became generally known, the emperor of Constantinople feared that the emperor [Frederick], and also the king of France, would lead an invasion of his realm'. Without firm undertakings that this was not their intention, Isaac would block the passes and deny them passage through Bulgaria. Barbarossa had travelled through the northern Balkans before, and therefore knew that without free passage through the mountains his journey would be considerably delayed, if not altogether prevented. Therefore, he concurred and had his son, the duke of Swabia, Leopold duke of Austria, and the bishop of Würzburg, all swear on his behalf, and that of 'the whole army of Christ', that he would not harm Byzantine lands.[54] In return, Ducas promised that the crusaders would be guided through the eastern empire, provided with passage across the Hellespont, and given access to markets along their route.[55] All of these are familiar undertakings: they had been offered by Manuel in 1146 in return for Louis VII's promise to return all cities and lands he might conquer which had previously pertained to the Byzantine empire. There is no indication in Ansbert's account that Isaac was able to extract such a promise from Frederick. However, the fact that a modification of this demand – half of the lands acquired to be returned – was advanced later, when Frederick was encamped at Philippopolis and putting Isaac under considerable pressure, suggests that this would have been among Ducas' initial demands.

Despite the guarantees advanced by Byzantine ambassadors at both Nuremburg and Niš, the Germans' onward journey was increasingly difficult. Both emperors took precautions against the other's potential transgressions. Isaac ordered the restoration of fortifications in the passes and cities through which the Germans would pass; Frederick divided his army into four divisions – a fifth was added at Philippopolis – and each division consisted of units of fifty men, over each of which was appointed

---

[54] Ansbert, *History of Frederick's Expedition*: 16; Johnson 1969: 91–2.
[55] Choniates: 402 (trans.: 221).

a judge. Clearly, Frederick was intent on maintaining good order in his ranks, but also on punishing those who erred. To some extent this may have been an effort to allay Isaac's fears about indiscriminate foraging and plundering. The Germans' search for adequate provisions was clearly a major stumbling block: Isaac had undertaken to provide access to well stocked markets, but had failed to do so because, he claimed, he did not have sufficient forewarning of Frederick's arrival; Frederick had undertaken to maintain good order in his ranks as they crossed Byzantine lands, but instead 'Germans sallied forth in bands in search of provisions, and poured out hither and thither like scattered flocks.'[56] Therefore, the emperor took his own measures: 'he commanded his cousin Michael Camytzes, the *protostrator*, and the domestic of the west, Alexius Gidus, to follow close behind their troops and stealthily attack the Germans as they collected fodder and searched for food.'[57]

Nicetas Choniates is well informed on these events since, at that time, he was governor of the city of Philippopolis. He notes that he was first commanded to restore the city's walls in preparation for Frederick's arrival, but later instructed to demolish them to prevent the Germans using the city as a fortified encampment.[58] Clearly, between the Germans' departure from Niš and arrival in Philippopolis, relations with the Byzantines had deteriorated dramatically. It is hard to avoid the conclusion that Isaac's policing measures were counter-productive. Frederick himself complained that he had spent 'six weeks in a rather toilsome traverse of Bulgaria'.[59] He blamed Isaac for breaking his vow to allow the exchange of money, and the opportunity to buy and sell. Moreover, his blocking of the passes and associated skirmishing merely delayed the already protracted German advance, creating a greater need for provisions. Worse still, upon arriving at Philippopolis, Barbarossa learned that Isaac had arrested his envoys in Constantinople and seized their possessions. According to Ansbert, this was because Isaac wished 'to dishonour the army of the holy cross and all Christians, since he desired to offer this favour to his friend and confederate Saladin . . . The whole army was enraged because of this and thenceforth freely pillaged the property of the Greeks and ruined what was left.'[60]

---

[56] Choniates: 404 (trans.: 222).
[57] Choniates: 403 (trans.: 221); Ansbert, *History of Frederick's Expedition*: 37, 41.
[58] Choniates: 402 (trans.: 221).
[59] Ansbert, *History of Frederick's Expedition*: 41; Johnson 1969: 95.
[60] Ansbert, *History of Frederick's Expedition*: 39; Johnson 1969: 101. Choniates: 409 (trans.: 225) also reports the German belief that Isaac had broken his oaths in favour of undertakings to Saladin.

Thereafter, the Germans ravaged widely, seizing control of several *kastra* and occupying cities, including both Berrhoia and Adrianople.[61] Isaac instructed his general, Camytzes, to pin the Germans down. According to Choniates (409; trans.: 224–5) Camytzes attacked the Germans as they foraged for firewood and supplies. But local supplies were so thin that the Byzantines themselves were obliged to look further afield. As they returned from one such trip they encountered a German force, which put all but the Alan mercenaries to flight. The Byzantine flight, in which Choniates was involved, took them as far as Ohrid. After this defeat, Isaac was obliged to enter into negotiations. But even as he did, Frederick began to accumulate still more bargaining chips. In a letter dated 16 November 1189, which is reproduced by Ansbert, Frederick instructed his son Henry to send envoys to Genoa, Venice, Pisa and Ancona to secure naval support for a siege of Constantinople. It is unlikely, despite Ansbert's claims, that such envoys would have been successful.[62] Nevertheless the prospect of an assault would have inspired great fear and panic within the city, as our accounts of the Second Crusade have shown (above at pp. 221–2). As a precaution Isaac blocked up the Xylocercus Gate – part of the Golden Gate at the southern end of the land walls – and contemplated confronting enemy forces outside Blachernae, where Manuel I had built a second tier of walls.[63] However, eventually, with Thrace trampled under German boots, and Constantinople in their sights, Isaac was obliged to meet Frederick's demands. First he returned the German hostages, then relinquished his futile claims for compensation for German depradations, and, eventually, agreed to ferry the crusading army across the Hellespont. In March 1190, after spending the winter months in Philippopolis and Adrianople, Barbarossa and his forces were transported across the narrow straits at Gallipoli.[64]

Ansbert and Choniates, our principal sources for the passage of the Third Crusade through the Balkans, both give the impression that Isaac was fickle and provocative, testing the patience and resolve of faithful Frederick. We must beware of believing this characterization too readily. Choniates portrayed the Third Crusade as a precursor to the Fourth, and Frederick as the counterpoint to inconsistent Isaac, from whom he had personally received contradictory instructions. Ansbert, similarly,

---

[61] Ansbert, *History of Frederick's Expedition*: 52–4; Johnson 1969: 104–5.

[62] Ansbert, *History of Frederick's Expedition*: 42 (for the appeal to Henry to send envoys to Italy), 68 (for news of assembled 'ships and galleys from Italy, Apulia and the maritime lands' preparing to besiege Constantinople).   [63] Choniates: 404 (trans.: 222).

[64] Ansbert, *History of Frederick's Expedition*: 71; Choniates: 42 (trans.: 226).

wrote with the benefit of hindsight, and his narrative of the earliest encounters in the Balkans is coloured by the ultimate failure of Frederick's enterprise. He began his account of the trek through the Balkans describing the Greeks as puny and duplicitous, and interpreted all subsequent actions through that prism. A third eye-witness account which we have not so far noted, supposedly a series of authentic letters incorporated into the Chronicle of Magnus of Reichersberg, have been shown to be derivative and full of *topoi*.[65] Similarly, the charge of oath-breaking levelled frequently by Ansbert was itself a *topos*, used during both the First and Second Crusades to condemn the 'double-dealing Greeks' (see above at pp. 218–22). This does not, of course, allow us to conclude that Isaac was not duplicitous. However, we must be more circumspect about the reasons for his extreme caution. We cannot, therefore, attribute the escalation from mutual suspicion to open hostility solely to Isaac's actions in general. However, we must consider further why Isaac acted in such a manner.[66]

Ansbert and other Latin authors suggested that Isaac's behaviour was due to an alliance he had forged before the onset of the crusade with Saladin. This line has been followed in many modern interpretations of the Third Crusade. However, as Lilie had demonstrated, attributing Isaac's actions in the Balkans to his deal with Saladin is not convincing. Lilie attributes far greater weight to the fact that 'before setting out [Barbarossa] had made contacts with Serbs and Seljuks . . . and the close connection of the Germans with the Sicilian Normans . . . could hardly have been calculated to placate Isaac Angelus.'[67] Once he had reached Niš, as we have seen, Frederick met with Stefan Nemanja and his brothers, and had received envoys from Peter and Asen. Moreover, once the German emperor had arrived at Adrianople, he once again approached 'Kalopetrus' who offered 40,000 Vlach and Cuman archers for an assault on Constantinople, and once the city was taken, requested that the emperor present him 'with the imperial crown of the realm of Greece (*coronam imperialem regni Grecie*)'.[68] It was surely Barbarossa's ongoing negotiations with the Balkan peoples which provoked Isaac's unease. The German emperor was regarded as an authority who might lend legitimacy to the regimes of autonomous rulers who had until

---

[65] The letters of Dietmar, bishop of Passau, worked into the Chronicle of Magnus of Reichersberg, are used enthusiastically by Brand 1968a: 178–9, 358, n. 10; but treated more cautiously by Lilie 1993: 230–6, who sees the obvious signs of Latin propaganda.
[66] Brand 1968a: 362, n. 55 lists many additional Latin sources which give accounts more or less favourable to Isaac.   [67] Lilie 1993: 236.
[68] Ansbert, *History of Frederick's Expedition*: 58; Wolff 1947: ii, 1121; Wolff 1949: 185, n. 44.

recently owed loyalty to the Byzantine emperor, effectively recognizing their permanent detachment from the eastern empire. When this is considered alongside the perceived threat of a grand alliance of German, Slavs, Vlachs and Cumans, and their professed intention of launching an assault on Constantinople itself – a threat which grew greater as the Germans approached the city – surely we have explanation enough for Isaac's actions without reference to a treaty with Saladin. Nevertheless, whatever their inspiration, we must still regard Isaac's actions, following Choniates and Ansbert, as duplicitous and counter-productive.

SERBS, VLACHS AND BULGARS, 1190–1196

If Frederick Barbarossa gained the upper hand in his dealings with Isaac Angelus, his advantage was short lived. The German emperor died before he reached the Holy Land, on 10 June 1190. It is somewhat ironic that, given his escape from the torrential flood of the river Melas during the Second Crusade, Frederick died in the fast-flowing river Saleph (Calycadnus) during the course of the Third. However, his passage through the Balkans had raised the awareness of several peoples who were intent on casting off the 'Byzantine Yoke' that powerful, but encouragingly distant, patrons and suzerains existed to the west who might be more willing to recognize their independent existence.[69]

In the aftermath of the crusade Isaac was obliged to return to the highlands of the Haemus. Choniates notes that the Vlachs, together with their Cuman allies, launched unremitting assaults on imperial lands from newly fortified strongholds in the mountains. Isaac was unable to engage them in pitched battle, and withdrew after two months for fear that the Cumans were about to cross the Danube. Withdrawing in haste he chose the shorter route through the mountains rather than the longer passage bypassing Anchialus. In this way Isaac led his army into an ambush in a narrow defile. Many of his troops, and as many of his pack animals, were crushed by rocks thrown down upon them. The emperor barely escaped to Berrhoia, and rumours of his death circulated widely. These were countered with equally false rumours of an imperial victory, spread from Berrhoia where Isaac dwelt a while before his return to Constantinople.[70] The defeat seems to have affected Isaac deeply: he

---

[69] I would agree in general with Duichev 1975: 115–18 that prolonged contact with the participants on the Third Crusade would raise awareness in Bulgaria of western military prowess and power. But that contact surely involved more displacement of local inhabitants and the plundering of their fields, and less awed gazing as the flower of western knighthood passed through the rich and fertile Bulgarian lands.　　[70] Choniates: 429–32 (trans.: 236–7).

brooded at the loss of so many men, and made wild predictions of future triumphs. Meanwhile, however, the Vlachs and Bulgars made unprecedented advances. Whereas previously their assaults had been concentrated on villages and fields, now they advanced against 'lofty-towered cities. They sacked Anchialus, took Varna by force, and advanced on Triaditza, the ancient Sardica, where they razed the greater part of the city. They also emptied Stoumbion [south-west of Sardica on the upper Strymon] of its inhabitants, and carried away large numbers of men and animals from Niš.'[71] Isaac was forced to take prompt action.

The Byzantine campaigns of autumn 1191 were, by all extant accounts, successful. Forces despatched to the north-east recovered Varna and Anchialus, and the latter was reinforced with towers and a garrison.[72] Isaac himself led a campaign against the Vlachs and Cumans from Philippopolis, and from there continued on to confront Stefan Nemanja. Apparently, the Byzantines won a considerable victory at the Velika Morava which was celebrated in an oration by Nicetas Choniates. However, Choniates integrates few of the details into his history.[73] Indeed, Choniates omits many important features of this period of Isaac's reign. He does not record that, before marching north to the Sava where he met with his father-in-law Béla III, Isaac concluded a peace treaty with the *veliki župan*. A contemporary reference to this can be found in an oration by George Tornicius, or Tornices, delivered probably at the Epiphany celebrations in 1193.[74] Tornicius alludes to a marriage between Eudocia, Isaac's niece, and the son of Stefan Nemanja, the *archizoupanos*, which restored Serbian servitude, or Dalmatian *douleia*.[75] The unprecedented offer of an imperial princess to the son of a lowly *doulos*, and the recognition that Nemanja might retain a substantial portion of the territory he had conquered, suggests that Isaac's victory over the Serbs was not so complete as Choniates' oration suggests.[76] Moreover, the Serbian treaty, and Isaac's subsequent meeting with Béla, demonstrate that Isaac was committed to a settlement in the north-western Balkans so that he would be free to concentrate on his struggle with the Vlachs and Bulgars.

---

[71] Choniates: 434 (trans.: 238).
[72] Choniates: 434 (trans.: 238). For the date, 1191, see Van Dieten 1971: 83–6. Others have preferred 1190: Brand 1968a: 93–4, or 1192: Wolff 1949: 186.
[73] Choniates, *Orations*: 26–34; Choniates: 434 (trans.: 239).   [74] Kazhdan 1965: 172–4.
[75] *FRB*: 277.20–5.
[76] A point also made by Brand: 1968a: 94, and Fine 1987: 26, who provide complementary lists of lands held by both parties. Brand notes further that Dubrovnik voluntarily recognized Byzantine suzerainty once again in 1192.

At exactly this time, to consolidate his position in the western Balkans still further, Isaac negotiated a second marriage alliance, with Tancred, the new ruler of Norman Sicily. Choniates, once again, fails to record that the Normans, who had so recently been enemies, became imperial allies when Isaac's daughter Irene was betrothed to Tancred's son Roger. This second arrangement is mentioned in the first of two contemporary orations delivered by Sergius Colybas. These orations, which must be treated as a pair, can be dated on internal evidence to 1193.[77] Colybas relates that, where previously the Sicilian arrows had been of Ares, now they are of Eros, and that Isaac no longer raises his standard against so many foreign peoples, but concludes alliances with them.[78]

Not only does Choniates fail to record the Serbian and Norman marriage arrangements, he also omits to mention that shortly afterwards, probably late in 1192, a dispute broke out between Peter and Asen. Peter, at this time, had chosen to reside in Preslav, the imperial capital of his chosen namesake, Tsar Peter of Bulgaria.[79] Asen was based in Trnovo, which was, according to Choniates, 'the best fortified and most excellent of all cities along the Haemus, encompassed by mighty walls, divided by a river, and built on a mountain ridge'.[80] Once again, we must rely for information on the orations delivered by Tornicius and Colybas in 1193. The clearest references are to be found in the second of Colybas' orations, where he refers clearly to the rupture between Peter and Asen: Peter has become a stumbling block (*petran scandalou*) to his brother, an adverse wind and an enemy to his own family.[81] Addressing Asen directly, Colybas asks 'what then do you have a mind to do, most reckless and obdurate rebel, when surrounding you are imperial traps . . . and snares have been laid for you within.'[82] And if the Scythians should mass beyond the paristrian frontier like a dense hail-bearing cloud, threatening destruction, Colybas is sure that the emperor will appear as the sun, dissipating the pall with his rays.[83] In fact, Isaac seems to have determined to disperse his enemies by negotiation. Given that Isaac had so recently met with Béla of Hungary, and negotiated treaties with the

---

[77] Kazhdan 1965: 168–70. Both Tancred and Roger died unexpectedly at the beginning of 1194, providing a *terminus ante quem* for the negotiations, and for Colybas' orations.

[78] *FRB*: 289.6–12; Kazhdan 1965: 168–70.

[79] Peter had formerly been called Theodore, and had taken the name Peter because of its imperial connotations.   [80] Choniates: 470 (trans.: 258).

[81] *FRB*: 293.20–2; Kazhdan 1965: 168, draws attention to the obvious pun on *petran* (Peter and stone).   [82] *FRB*: 294.1–2.

[83] *FRB*: 294.7–13. Cf. Manganeius Prodromus: 1.61–70, 2.61–70, 3.1–125, for the dissipating rays of sun-like Manuel. Such rhetorical allusions were often associated with the *prokypsis* ceremony, which was performed at Epiphany.

Serbs and Normans, it seems highly likely that he had also come to an understanding with Peter, and this was the reason for Peter's disagreement with Asen. Spring 1193, therefore, was the perfect time for Isaac to press his advantage, and campaign aggressively against Asen. Here, Choniates once again takes up the story.

Isaac, we are told, did not take the field himself. He preferred to remain in Constantinople where 'he delighted in ribaldries and lewd songs and consorted with laughter-stirring dwarfs'.[84] The campaigns against Asen were entrusted to the emperor's young cousin, Constantine Angelus, who was appointed *doux* of Philippopolis and admiral of the fleet, and to Basil Vatatzes, the domestic of the west based in Adrianople. With Peter neutralized and Asen isolated, Vlach-Bulgar attacks on lands around Philippopolis and Berrhoia became less frequent. And those which were undertaken met with staunch resistance from Constantine Angelus. 'But whereas Constantine should have pursued these successes for the benefit of the fatherland (*patrida*) and its cities, he did just the opposite.' Constantine secured the support of local commanders and troops, and 'chose the imperial robe instead of that of the general and put on his feet the purple-dyed boots in readiness to take the throne by force'.[85] Constantine's planned march on the capital did not make it as far as Adrianople: the pretender failed to secure the support of Vatatzes, and his followers handed him over to the emperor's men. Constantine was blinded, and the Vlach-Bulgars rejoiced at their great good fortune. They immediately set out with their Cuman allies against Philippopolis, Sardica, and even Adrianople, laying waste the lands *en route*. Once again the Byzantines had lost the initiative because of the independent ambitions of a *sebastos*.

In 1194, the domestic of the east, Alexius Gidus, was transferred from Asia Minor with a considerable number of troops to bolster defences in Thrace. Choniates' coverage of what followed is brief and damning: 'Alexius Gidus and Basil Vatatzes, the commanders of the eastern and western divisions, on engaging the [Vlachs and Cumans] near the city of Arcadiopolis, achieved nothing useful. Moreover, Gidus fled in disarray, losing the better part of his army, while Vatatzes perished with his troops.'[86] Isaac appealed immediately to his father-in-law, Béla III, for assistance, and raised conscript and mercenary forces for a grand cam-

[84] Choniates: 441 (trans.: 242).
[85] Choniates: 435 (trans.: 239), who still refers to assaults by both Peter and Asen. Brand 1968a: 95 suggests Peter had quickly returned to rebellion. However, Choniates seems to have chosen to ignore or suppress Isaac's arrangement with Peter. [86] Choniates: 446 (trans.: 245).

paign to crush the Vlach-Bulgars. Setting out from Constantinople, Isaac arrived at Kypsella on 8 April 1195. There he divided his forces into companies and awaited the arrival of additional troops. However, his brother Alexius, and others of the emperor's kinsmen, had determined that Isaac was no longer fit to rule. While Isaac was out hunting, Alexius Angelus was acclaimed emperor in the imperial tent, and on his return, following a brief chase, Isaac was blinded. Alexius withdrew his forces, and despatched envoys to Asen to propose peace. These terms were, however, rejected, and Asen launched a series of assaults on fortresses along the river Strymon in the vicinity of Serres. The Byzantine commander, Alexius Aspietes, was taken prisoner, and many of the *kastra* were occupied and strengthened. Although the majority of the Vlachs and Bulgars returned to the lands beyond the Haemus with great plunder, for the first time garrisons were installed to secure possession of fortresses in southern Thrace.[87] Moreover, a Byzantine relief force led by the *sebastokrator* Isaac Comnenus, Alexius' son-in-law, encountered a Cuman raiding party at the Strymon. Isaac was seized, and died shortly after in captivity.[88]

The period 1190–6 was one of lost or scorned opportunities for the Byzantines. Although much of the blame has been attributed to the emperor Isaac Angelus, it is clear that the independent ambitions of Isaac's relatives were as great a problem. Our only account of Isaac's reign, by Choniates, is coloured by the author's personal dealings with Isaac, and by his desire to apportion blame for the spiral of misfortune that followed. However, allusions in contemporary orations allow us to modify Choniates' historical account. Isaac seems to have acted rationally in the aftermath of the Third Crusade, accepting that the empire had, for a time at least, to abandon claims to lands beyond the Velika Morava. His alliance with Béla III of Hungary, and consequent negotiations with the rulers of the Serbs and Sicilian Normans, allowed Isaac to concentrate his limited resources on combatting the Vlachs and Bulgars in and beyond the Haemus. Raiding from that quarter posed the greatest threat to his diminished empire, and was therefore his priority. In 1193, by winning over Peter, Isaac isolated Asen and weakened considerably his ability to launch raids south of the mountains. However, Byzantium lost the initiative because of the actions of Isaac's own commanders and kin, and, having pinned his reputation on the defeat of the Vlach-Bulgars, Isaac suffered the consequences of Byzantine failures.

---

[87] Choniates: 465 (trans.: 255).   [88] Choniates: 465–9 (trans.: 255–7).

More threatening for the empire was the fact that, after Isaac's demise, the nature of Vlach-Bulgar raids changed. Whereas before 1195 they were content to plunder lands south of the Haemus and around the Black Sea ports, which remained in Byzantine hands, from 1196 the Vlach-Bulgars began to contemplate permanent possession of both *kastra* and cities. Moreover, at the same time, and for the first time, the new rulers of northern Thrace and 'Mysia' began to strike their own coins. These, the so-called 'Bulgarian Imitative' coins, have been found in considerable numbers north of the Haemus in hoards buried between 1195 and 1204. They are exclusively billon trachea, and are of three types. Type A is modelled on Manuel I's fourth issue, type B on Isaac II's first issue, and type C on the second variant of Alexius III's billon scyphate. Hendy has suggested that production would have been concentrated at Berrhoia, where a Byzantine mint may have fallen into Vlach-Bulgar hands.[89]

BYZANTIUM'S DECLINING PRESTIGE AND RETREATING FRONTIERS, 1196–1200

Before his death in Asen' gaol in Trnovo, Isaac Comnenus, the Byzantine commander captured at the Strymon by Cumans, is said to have persuaded a certain Ivanko to murder the Vlach-Bulgar ruler. A more romantic tale, also recorded by Choniates, has Asen and Ivanko quarrelling over Ivanko's illicit affair with Asen's sister-in-law. Whatever was the the true catalyst for their dispute, Ivanko murdered Asen, and was able to secure local support for his usurpation because he undertook 'to rule Mysia more justly and equitably than had Asen and would not govern everything by the sword as the fallen man had done'.[90] This is our only real insight into the nature of Asen's regime, and suggests that his power rested not only with his ability to secure and distribute booty through regular raids south of the Haemus, but also to intimidate the natives of Trnovo and its environs. His intimate association with the Cumans must have contributed to this 'reign of terror', if that is what it was. And this would explain why, rather than flee in secret, Ivanko had news of Asen's murder trumpeted from the walls and spread far and wide.

[89] Hendy 1969: 218–22.
[90] Choniates: 470 (trans.: 258). It would not be helpful here to consider whether Asen, as a Vlach, ruled local Bulgarians by intimidation. There is no indication in any source that perceived ethnicity was a source of tension between Vlachs and Bulgarians.

The announcement of Asen's murder provoked an immediate response from Peter, who marched out from Preslav with an army to besiege Trnovo. Even as he did, Ivanko's agents made for Constantinople to seek Byzantine assistance. Forthwith, Alexius III sent an army under the command of the *protostrator* Michael Camytzes, who, as we have seen, had gained experience, but not much success, in previous Balkan campaigns. Far from securing control of Trnovo, and with it the greater part of 'Mysia', Camytzes was not even able to convince his troops to enter the Haemus passes. The army mutinied not just because they feared for their lives in the narrow defiles, but because for most of them the lands north of the Haemus were no longer considered Byzantine. So much is conveyed by the words Choniates puts into their mouths: "'Where are you taking us? Whom are we to engage in battle? Have we not traversed these mountain passes many times, and not only did we accomplish nothing worthwhile, but we very nearly perished. Turn back, therefore, turn back, and lead us back to our own land (*ta sphetera*)".'[91] Without Byzantine aid Ivanko was forced to flee, and he made his way covertly to Constantinople, leaving Peter with a considerable victory. Peter entrusted command of Trnovo to the second of his younger brothers, Kalojan (Ioannitsa), and when Peter died shortly afterwards, Kalojan ruled alone.[92]

From that moment on no serious effort was ever made by the Byzantine administration to effect the recovery of lands north of the Haemus. Rather, much energy was devoted to resisting the ever more regular invasions of Thrace by Vlachs and Cumans, and increasing use was made of Vlachs and Bulgars who, unlike the Byzantine forces, were willing to fight for the emperor in the mountains. Ivanko, who had fled to Constantinople, was betrothed to Alexius III's granddaughter, an exceptional prize for the pretender to a realm the autonomy of which was not recognized. Subsequently, he played a crucial role in defending the environs of Philippopolis, serving as 'a precious bulwark against his own countrymen'. Even so, 'the devastation of the lands towards the Haemus and the despoiling of the inscribed monuments and pillars of Macedonia and Thrace give a more accurate picture of the damage wrought than any detailed historical account.'[93]

While Ivanko served the emperor, at least for a time, loyally from the

[91] Choniates: 471 (trans.: 258).
[92] Choniates: 472 (trans.: 259). In the light of Asen's demise, it is interesting to note that Peter also died at the hands of his own men, and perhaps for similar reasons.
[93] Choniates: 473 (trans.: 259–60). On the setting up of boundary stones, see above at p. 18.

lands he had been granted, a certain Dobromir (also known as Chrysus) had determined to claim autonomy for the lands he held around Strumica. Dobromir-Chrysus, Choniates reports, was, despite his Slavic name, 'a Vlach by birth (*Vlachos to genos*) . . . but had not conspired with Peter and Asen in their rebellion'. He had been rewarded with command of Strumica, but by the end of 1196, had begun to raid neighbouring lands between the rivers Strymon and Vardar. The emperor Alexius launched an abortive campaign in spring 1197, but after two months withdrew to Constantinople, leaving the locals to fend for themselves.[94] Dobromir-Chrysus remained a thorn in Alexius' side, but, after a further unsuccessful campaign in autumn 1197, the emperor sued for peace and recognized Dobromir-Chrysus' rights to lands between the Strymon and Vardar, including Strumica and the fortress of Prosek. A Byzantine bride, the daughter of the *protostrator* Michael Camytzes, was provided for the Vlach, and the marriage overseen by the *sebastos* Constantine Radenus early in 1198.[95]

In the following year, 1199, Ivanko, who had taken the name Alexius on marrying the emperor's granddaughter, rebelled. A Byzantine army was despatched, once again led by the *protostrator* Michael Camytzes. After some initial success, Camytzes once again suffered a crushing defeat, and was himself taken captive. Thereafter, Ivanko-Alexius extended his authority as far as Mosynopolis and Abdera, on the Thracian Aegean coast, and began to wear imperial garb. The emperor, for his part, 'reckoned the *protostrator*'s capture a delightful and excellent piece of good luck, and laid his hands on the man's immense riches which befitted a monarch'.[96] Consequently, dispossessed and unransomed, Camytzes was freed by Ivanko-Alexius and proceeded to fight independently against the emperor. The following spring, 1200, Alexius set out for Kypsella, whence he despatched envoys to Ivanko-Alexius to sue for peace. However, in the meantime Byzantine forces had successfully laid siege to Steinmachus (modern Asenovgrad). Taking heart, Alexius Angelus duped Ivanko-Alexius with a false agreement, and managed to seize and execute him. Apparently, Ivanko-Alexius' regime had been brutal – Choniates relates that he was 'far worse than earlier rebels, and driven to such cruelty that most barbarians deem to be

---

[94] Choniates: 487 (trans.: 267).
[95] These events are treated in some detail by Choniates: 502–8 (trans.: 277–80), and following him by Brand 1968a: 127–30. Dobromir presumably took the name Chrysus at the time of his marriage. For references to the treaty see Dölger, ed. Wirth 1977: ii, 331, nr. 1653, which dates the arrangement to summer 1199.   [96] Choniates: 513 (trans.: 283).

manliness'[97] – and Angelus was able to win back central Thrace for the empire. The obvious consequence of this significant victory, however, was that once again Alexius was responsible for the defence of imperial lands against the depredation of the Cumans, and the Vlachs and Bulgars who followed Kalojan.

The employment of Ivanko and Dobromir-Chrysus against their fellow Vlachs and Bulgars was not exceptional. As we have seen, it was a standard Byzantine strategy for dealing with recalcitrant peoples to employ divide and rule tactics; and nobody knew better how to deal with highly mobile Vlach raiding parties than Vlachs. Moreover, it was standard policy to rely on local potentates to effect imperial policy beyond what we have called the internal frontier, and where necessary to install new potentates and ethnic groups in the lands between the empire's internal and external frontiers. Ivanko and Dobromir-Chrysus, therefore, are familiar characters, and their decisions to rebel against imperial authority neither more nor less remarkable than those of Alusjan or Vojteh, John Chryselius or Stefan Vojislav, in the eleventh century (see above at pp. 130–5). However, by the end of the twelfth century, the Byzantine emperor had apparently lost all ability to persuade such recalcitrants back into line. Neither the carrot nor the stick, wielded so effectively by Manuel I in extending the Balkan frontier, had any effect: military campaigns were for the most part ineffectual and abortive, commanders inept or disloyal; and, even more troubling, among the Balkan peoples the patronage of the eastern emperor was no longer considered preferable to his enmity, his gifts of tribute and titles no longer sufficiently attractive as alternatives to the kudos and booty which might be gained by rebellion or invasion.

By 1200 the external frontier of the empire, so recently the Danube in both conceptual and administrative terms, had retreated dramatically. Byzantine forces were no longer willing to march through the Haemus passes, and that range had, for all practical purposes, become the northern limit of the empire. The empire's internal and external frontiers now followed the same, ill defined course, roughly across the Haemus as far as the Vardar, or in places the Strymon, and the Velika Morava, which together marked the effective western limit of Byzantine authority. And beyond that limit, in Serbia and Bulgaria, the emperor was regarded increasingly with contempt. This is nowhere better illustrated than in the case of Eudocia, the daughter of Alexius III Angelus. Eudocia was

[97] Choniates: 513 (trans.: 283).

married in the early 1190s to Stefan, the son of Stefan Nemanja, while she was the niece of the reigning emperor, Isaac II.[98] This should have been a coveted prize for the son of such a lowly 'barbarian' ruler, and the younger Stefan was consequently received within the ranks of the *sebastoi* with the most elevated title *sebastokrator*. By 1198 Eudocia's father, Alexius, was emperor, and the younger Stefan, 'The First Crowned', had become *veliki župan*. Yet so far and so rapidly had Serbian sentiment shifted that Stefan felt able to dismiss Eudocia from his presence. No longer a symbol of prestige for the Raškan ruler, he 'accused his wife of itching with scabby incontinence . . . stripped her of her woman's robe, leaving her only with her undergarment, which was cut around so that it barely covered her private parts, and dismissed her thus to go forth as if she were a harlot'.[99] The Byzantine emperor was held in similar disdain to the east of Serbia, where Kalojan sought recognition for his realm not from Constantinople, but from Rome. Drawing as he did on the traditions of the earlier Bulgarian Empire of Symeon and Peter, the realm of Kalojan and his successors has become known as the 'Second Bulgarian Empire'.

RECOGNITION FOR THE 'SECOND BULGARIAN EMPIRE'

In December 1199 Pope Innocent III replied to a letter from Kalojan, whom he addressed as 'the noble man Ioannitsa'.[100] Although we do not possess Kalojan's original message, we can surmise from the papal response that some time earlier, perhaps soon after his accession in 1197, Kalojan had professed his devotion to Rome, and requested an embassy to consider a certain proposal. We can also surmise, given the content of subsequent letters, that Kalojan had proposed that he would acknowledge papal authority over Christians in lands under his control if he were, in turn, recognized as legitimate sovereign – he claimed the title emperor – of an independent realm, and granted a patriarch for the church at Trnovo. Kalojan did not reply to the papal letter until some time in 1202. By that time he had conducted further campaigns against

---

[98] An approximate date can be inferred from an oration by Tornicius, *FRB*: 277.20–5. See above at p. 301. [99] Choniates: 531 (trans.: 292).
[100] Hurmuzaki and Densuşianu: 1, nr. 1. Wolff 1949: 190–8 presents an excellent analysis of this correspondence, including full quotations in Latin and references to various editions. I have limited my references to the edition by the Romanian scholars Hurmuzaki and Densuşianu, which is the only version besides Migne's to which I have had access. All references given by Wolff, and here, will be superseded upon publication of the new critical edition of Innocent III's letters, currently in progress.

Byzantium, and had entered into negotiations with the emperor Alexius III which reinforced his desire to distance himself from the eastern empire.

In spring 1201 Kalojan had marched against and captured the last Byzantine strongholds north-east of the Haemus, the Black Sea ports of Constantia and Varna.[101] The loss of these cities was of vital importance, for it dramatically undermined Byzantine ability to recover control of Paristrion. More than this, the sea route between Constantinople and the cities on the lower Danube was sundered. Not only did this hamper the use of the imperial fleet in campaigns north of the Haemus, it threatened control over trade between the centre and periphery, which, I have argued, was crucial in monitoring and controlling northern peoples. In the longer term control of the ports allowed Bulgarian merchants to export produce from the rich interior of the 'Second Bulgarian Empire', and forge closer links with the Italian maritime cities.[102] In the short term, despite convincing victories against Dobromir-Chrysus and Camytzes, Alexius Angelus was obliged to come to terms with Kalojan. In 1202, according to Kalojan, he was promised an imperial coronation should he come to Constantinople, and a patriarch for the church in Trnovo.[103] However, Kalojan continued his correspondence with the pope.

Early in 1202, probably before the conclusion of his negotiations with Alexius III, Kalojan wrote once more to Innocent III.[104] Styling himself 'Kalojan, emperor of the Bulgarians and Vlachs (*imperator Bulgarorum et Blachorum*)', Kalojan asked that papal ecclesiastical authority be extended over his realm, and that a crown be despatched to him as crowns had been despatched to Tsars Symeon, Peter and Samuel. Moreover, Kalojan claimed to be descended directly from these earlier emperors of the Bulgarians (and Vlachs). Innocent replied cautiously to 'Kalojan, the noble man and lord of the Bulgarians and Vlachs (*dominus Bulgarorum et Blachorum*)'. He noted that he was aware of previous kings (*reges*) in the region, but had been made aware also that these men had preferred to follow the instruction of the Greeks. Therefore, he proposed

---

[101] Choniates: 532–4 (trans.: 292–3); Brand 1968a: 132.   [102] Koledarov 1982: 19–38.

[103] Byzantine sources allude to this treaty, but do not provide details. See Choniates, *Orations*: 106–12; Van Dieten 1971: 129–36; Brand 1968a: 134–5. For an alternative date (the end of 1201), see Dölger 1925: ii, 1661; Dölger, ed. Wirth 1977: ii, 335, nr. 1661b.

[104] Hurmuzaki and Densuşianu: 2–3, nr. 2; Wolff 1949: 192. The fact that Kalojan mentions Alexius III's offer of a patriarch and recognition of his imperial title for the first time in a subsequent letter suggests that this offer had not yet been made. The pope's reply to this first extant letter is dated 27 November 1202.

to send his chaplain to consider Kalojan's claims, and in the meantime to bring an archbishop's pallium for Basil of Trnovo.[105] However, before the chaplain arrived, Kalojan wrote once more to the pope, in August 1203, to inform him that the eastern emperor had heard of the papal mission to Trnovo, and had said 'Come to us and we will crown you emperor and make a patriarch for you, because there can be no emperor without a patriarch'. However, this offer had not been taken up because, Kalojan maintained, he remained loyal to the papacy.[106] Clearly, Kalojan was attempting to use the Byzantine concessions as bargaining chips in his ongoing negotiations with Innocent.

In September 1203 Archbishop Basil received his pallium from the pope's chaplain, John, in Trnovo. At the same time Kalojan issued a chrysobull which recounted how he had consulted ancient texts and laws where it was recorded that previous 'emperors of the Bulgarians and Vlachs', Symeon, Peter and Samuel, had all received their imperial title, crown and benediction from the pope. Now, it was stated, Kalojan had requested and secured the same from the pope.[107] There was no veracity to these claims: Tsar Symeon had received a coronation, of sorts, from Patriarch Nicholas Mysticus, and later gained recognition as 'spiritual brother' by Emperor Romanus I; Tsar Peter had received the title emperor with the hand of Romanus' granddaughter in 927; Samuel, as far as we know, was never formally recognized as 'emperor', except possibly by Emperor Basil II in 1005 (see above at pp. 70–1). Moreover, if claims implicit in his chrysobull were false, so were those he made explicit. Kalojan failed to acknowledge that Boris was granted only the rights of an archbishop, referring to him as patriarch, and he claimed for himself the title *Dominus et Imperator*. Nevertheless, the conscious rewriting in this document of Bulgaria's 'imperial' past signalled a decisive move away from Byzantium. Kalojan had selected an alternative patron and authority to lend legitimacy to his claims to sovereignty, and, on 25 February 1204, Pope Innocent III responded with a series of letters which, up to a point, fulfilled his requests.

Innocent's letters now addressed Kalojan as 'Dearest son in Christ . . . king of the Bulgarians and Vlachs *(Bulgarorum et Blachorum regi)*'. They informed him of a king's duties, and sent him a king's sceptre, and a crown to be placed on his head by the papal legate, Cardinal Leo. Innocent also granted Kalojan's request, otherwise unrecorded, to be

---

[105] Hurmuzaki and Densuşianu: 3–5, nr. 3; Wolff 1949: 193.
[106] Hurmuzaki and Densuşianu: 1–11, nr. 10; Wolff 1949: 194.
[107] Hurmuzaki and Densuşianu: 26–7, nr. 18; Wolff 1949: 195.

permitted to mint coins bearing his own image. Archbishop Basil, it was noted, was primate, which amounted to being a patriarch. And in any case he could 'anoint, bless and crown future kings of the Bulgarians and Vlachs'.[108] Kalojan replied using the title 'King of the whole of Bulgaria and Vlachia (*rex totius Bulgarie et Vlachie*)'.[109] He had determined that it was better to be a king by papal authority than an emperor by Byzantine.

A NOTE ON THE FOURTH CRUSADE

Papal recognition of an independent realm ruled by Kalojan, king of the Bulgarians and Vlachs, was accorded in 1204. In the same year the papacy sanctioned an enterprise that had a more potent and direct impact on the eastern empire: an assault on Constantinople by the forces of the Fourth Crusade. The Fourth Crusade largely bypassed Byzantium's Balkan frontier, and for that reason, although it must serve as a rather obvious denouement, I will not examine it in detail.[110] Instead, I will merely note that the expedition was the culmination of the so-called 'rise of the west', with which we have been concerned in this and earlier chapters; and that factionalism within the Byzantine aristocracy was a major factor in diverting the crusade to Constantinople, and in provoking an assault on the city in 1204.

Historians seeking turning points in relations between east and west which led to the cataclysm of 1204 have focused on several episodes. The general arrest of Venetians in 1171, it is claimed, permanently alienated the empire's longtime allies. Similarly, the battle of Myriokephalon in 1176 was not only a crushing defeat from which imperial forces could not easily recover, but it undermined the Byzantine image of invincibility created by Manuel I through many long years of warfare and diplomacy. But the most popular turning point has been the Latin massacre of 1182, which led, allegedly inevitably, to the vengeful atrocities of the Fourth Crusade. Certainly, such episodes cannot be ignored, and they must all have involved individuals who suffered and bore grudges through many years. But the evidence simply does not support the notion that relations between east and west deteriorated 'inevitably' after 1171, 1176 or

[108] Hurmuzaki and Densuşianu: 20–1, nr. 16; Wolff 1949: 197. Hendy 1969: 221 has suggested that this letter marked the end of the series of so-called 'Bulgarian Imitative' coins.
[109] Hurmuzaki and Densuşianu: 48–9, nr. 34; Wolff 1949: 198.
[110] For a full appraisal of the crusade from a Byzantine perspective see Angold 1997: 316–28; Angold 1999: 257–78.

1182. Alliances between the eastern empire and various western powers were forged thereafter according to the same cocktail of political expediency and economic advantage that had featured in the shifting web of affiliations since the Second Crusade. The true significance of the episodes of 1171, 1176 and 1182 is that they highlight the nature of politics and political culture in Byzantium in the later twelfth century, and it is in this sense that they are but precursors to the events of 1204.

In stating this, I do not mean to suggest that the fate of the empire rested on court intrigues, nor blame individual emperors for decisions which may, or may not, have led to the cataclysm of 1204. Instead I wish to return to the discussion with which this chapter began: the problems inherent within the Byzantine political system instituted by Alexius I Comnenus, and developed by his son John, and grandson Manuel. The Comnenian political system, which was inherited by the Angeli, was based on ties of kinship. Whereas in the eleventh century in particular, but also for centuries before, access to positions of authority within the imperial hierarchy were based on merit as well as lineage, under the Comneni and Angeli the highest positions were reserved for the *sebastoi*, who were by definition related to the emperor himself by blood or marriage. This policy created resentment among other aristocratic houses, who were now by definition the lesser nobility. But it also led to a greater degree of faction within the ranks of the *sebastoi*, who competed for the imperial throne, placing personal ambition above the greater good of the empire. Thus, all the men of note who took command of imperial forces in the northern Balkans between 1180 and 1204, many of whom placed their own interests above those of the empire, were *sebastoi*. Similarly, the diversion of the Fourth Crusade to Constantinople was the result of the individual ambitions of a pretender, and its success was the result of faction among the *sebastoi*.

An oration delivered by Nicephorus Chrysoberges in January 1204 reveals that the latest Byzantine pretender, Alexius, son of the blinded and deposed Isaac II, was willing to receive praise for using the Venetian doge and his fleet to effect his usurpation.

How often have their cargo ships and naval triremes undertaken voyages hither . . .? How often has [the doge] who presides with great arrogance over Aquileia blackened his oared boats and ships with caulking pitch and, having crossed the Ionian Sea and weathered Cape Malea, dashed his oars in naval fashion in our own seas? But because he was not then serving the Lord Christ for your sake [Alexius], with all speed he was repulsed and crushed on the deeps and the shallows. But since you [Alexius], the mighty one, approved in lordly fashion all the Latin ships, and they undertook to furnish services to you, they cut the unmoved tide. (Chrysoberges: 26–7)[111]

The practice of bringing a pretender to secure local support for an invasion was, as we have seen, well-established among the western powers. However, on this occasion the pretender was exactly who he claimed to be. Moreover, for a while at least, the Venetians seemed satisfied that Alexius IV would deliver what he had promised. That is, they were confident that he would pay them a substantial sum, equal to that agreed in April 1201 as payment for transportation of the crusaders to Egypt. However, within a year of his installation, in February 1204, Alexius IV was murdered by a faction opposed to his succession, provoking an assault on the walls of Constantinople in April 1204.

Despite their failure effectively to breach the city's fortifications in 1204, the crusaders were able to enter the city in full force. As Donald Queller, the doyen of the academic industry dedicated to the Fourth Crusade, has expounded, the crusading army was inadequate to capture Constantinople, which had the most impressive fortifications in Christendom. This was not least because to make full use of their fleet the Latins were obliged to coordinate an attack on the sea walls and northern land walls: the very area that Manuel Comnenus had rebuilt to combat the Second Crusade (see above at pp. 221–2). We can dismiss Queller's bizarre suggestion, repeating a comment by the thirteenth-century Spanish traveller Benjamin of Tudela, that the Greeks were too effeminate to resist the assault.[112] The reason that the city was thrown open to the crusaders was the inability of those in power in the city to stand together and launch a solid counter-offensive. And the reason for that was factionalism within the ruling elite in Constantinople.

THE 'BYZANTINE YOKE'

The oration by Chrysoberges delivered to a usurper even as a hostile fleet was anchored outside Constantinople highlights the growing disparity between the rhetoric and reality of Byzantine power between 1180 and 1204.[113] The notion of the 'Byzantine Yoke' was similarly subject to reinterpretation in this period. The burden of the 'yoke' (*zygos*)

---

[111] The translation is taken from Brand 1968b: 466–7.
[112] Queller and Madden 1992: 467.
[113] Angold 1997: 315: 'Never had the rhetoric of of imperial ideology been made to work so hard as under the Angeli and never had it appeared so hollow.'

or the 'choking bridle' (*chalinos*) was articulated more closely so that, where it had been cast off, it might be replaced. However, in the years before 1180, I have argued, the 'yoke' rested only lightly on the shoulders of many local and regional potentates in the northern Balkans, who willingly shouldered the burden. Often the burden comprised sacks of imperial *nomismata*, and the silken robes of lofty imperial ranks. After 1180, the same potentates were offered ever greater rewards: the reigning emperor, Isaac II, married the daughter of the Hungarian king, and thereafter it was clear that the father-in-law was the senior partner; the recalcitrant Serbian *veliki župan* received the emperor's niece for his son; rebels like Dobromir-Chrysus and Ivanko were rewarded with Byzantine princesses. But even as the rewards increased, regard for Byzantium decreased dramatically.

Furthermore, in marked contrast to Manuel I Comnenus, who was remembered as a powerful and generous *basileus* throughout Byzantium's Balkan frontier, the charisma of the office of emperor was undermined by the succession of ineffectual, ephemeral rulers. Faction in the capital ensured that foreign and frontier policy took a secondary role, and the conduct of Balkan campaigns was delegated to a succession of *sebastoi*. Successful generals, like Alexius Branas and Constantine Angelus, launched bids for the throne; unsuccessful generals, for example Michael Camytzes, retained their commands. By the beginning of the thirteenth century Byzantine prestige was so low that the peoples of the northern Balkans considered the patronage of any western potentate superior to that of the eastern emperor. Indeed, according to Choniates, the only successful transmission was the politics of faction which emanated from Constantinople, so that 'fratricide spread as a pattern, model and general law from the queen of cities to the far corners of the earth'.[114]

---

[114] Choniates: 532 (trans.: 292).

Conclusions

Byzantium's Balkan frontier advanced and retreated in the period 900–1204 in such a way that, ostensibly, it supports the picture of imperial 'Apogee and Disintegration' painted by George Ostrogorsky. In the early tenth century the empire experienced a period of consolidation in the northern Balkans, striking a compromise with an independent Bulgarian realm. Then began a period of expansion, punctuated by warfare but characterized by diplomacy, as regions were conquered and local power structures were absorbed and utilized. A rapid deterioration in Byzantine fortunes at the end of the eleventh century signalled that tensions within the Balkan lands, as elsewhere, were increasing. At the same time forces beyond the frontier began to encroach upon the empire from the north, and, more significantly, from the west. This put an end to further substantial territorial expansion, which, in any case would have extended the empire beyond its 'natural' frontier at the Danube. Therefore, the empire entered a second period of consolidation, with piecemeal expansion to the east under the first Comnenian emperors. The reign of Manuel Comnenus signalled a return to limited expansion in the west, directed against the perceived threat of western, and particularly German, encroachment. Finally came a rapid contraction of the frontier, akin to the crisis of the later eleventh century, but from which the empire did not recover.

This story of advancing and retreating frontiers takes no account of the nature of political authority in the northern Balkans. It treats the position of the frontier as a simple reflection of political fortunes. It implies that when the frontier is advanced Byzantine government with all its trappings – the imposition of a developed provincial bureaucracy with powers to judge, tax and conscript, and with a duty to defend or administer the sacrament to all individuals as subjects of the emperor – is imposed upon the various peoples who had been brought within the *oikoumene*. And when the frontier retreats, various subject peoples are

316

held to have cast off this 'Byzantine Yoke', obeying and elevating their own potentates whose sole ambition, indeed ethnically determined duty, is to resist imperial government. This is not the story recounted in the preceding narrative.

The 'Byzantine Yoke' was a literary and rhetorical device which cannot serve to describe, only to mask, the nature of imperial rule in the northern Balkans. There was no single method of government applied throughout three centuries across the whole peninsula, but a complex of methods and devices which operated through and across internal and external frontiers. By my reckoning, we should not seek to establish how far direct Byzantine political authority was extended across the northern Balkans, because, given the nature of surviving evidence, we cannot measure it accurately. Nor should we imagine that this accurately reflects the degree of imperial success or failure, because the imposition of a fully functioning administration across the whole Balkan peninsula was never imperial policy. A better measure of imperial success in the northern Balkans is whether, and at what cost, those based in Constantinople were able to ensure the integrity of the empire's core lands in the face of diverse internal and external threats.

Between 900 and 1204, Byzantine emperors desired stability and security in the peripheral regions of the empire so that they might continue to control and exploit the productive lands which provisioned the principal cities, most importantly Constantinople, and supported state institutions. In the Balkans the vital regions were the rich lands of Thrace and the hinterland of Constantinople in the east, and Thessaly and the lands around Thessalonica in the west. To achieve this required direct control of major communication routes, by land and sea, and of strategic cities across the peninsula, but only a stabilizing influence in the mountainous interior, the north-eastern plains and the north-western littoral. Control of the Black Sea ports between Constantinople and the lower Danube, and Cherson beyond, was a priority. Control of the Via Egnatia, the principal land route between Constantinople and Thessalonica, which ran on to the Adriatic coast at Valona and Dyrrachium, was a priority. Control of the main land road to the north, which followed the course of the Velika Morava, was a priority, requiring close supervision of such cities as Niš, Belgrade and Braničevo. However, which of these was the greater priority changed with the direction and nature of perceived threats through time. Thus, great pains were taken to ensure control of Anchialus and Varna so long as the Bulgarians posed a threat to Constantinople in the tenth century, and later, so long as northern nomads posed a threat in the eleventh century, or the Vlach-Bulgars in the late twelfth. In the early eleventh century, Samuel's threat to the Dyrrachium–Thessalonica axis gained Basil II's attention, and Alexius I's when the region suffered successive Norman invasions. From the middle of the twelfth century the encroachments of western powers increasingly drew Manuel I's gaze along the Velika Morava, into Sirmium, Frangochorion and northern Dalmatia.

In the foregoing chapters I have explored the efforts of successive regimes to secure and maintain the loyalty of a multiplicity of potentates who dominated cities and highland strongholds, ports and passes throughout the northern Balkans. These were potentates who might otherwise seek to benefit from assaults on imperial lands or from forging alliances with external powers. (I have not explored the political or social systems which functioned in the periphery, except insofar as these affected relations between the centre and periphery. So, for example, there is no analysis of how a *župan* administered his *župania*, nor of the relationship between a prior and his municipal council, still less of the relationships between *župans* or priors and their subjects or citizens.)

The principal external threat to the security and stability of the empire in the tenth century was the Bulgarian empire. Therefore efforts were made to secure the services of sedentary and nomadic peoples beyond Bulgaria who might act in concert with the Byzantines if Bulgaria should confront the empire. At the same time concessions were offered to the rulers of Bulgaria to ensure that they preferred peaceful relations with Constantinople: these have been characterized as trade, tribute and titles. In the last years of the tenth century, the situation changed dramatically, leading to the annexation of Bulgaria through the absorption of local power structures and the imposition of military officials and garrisons between the Haemus and lower Danube. This created a frontier between Byzantium and the turbulent lands beyond the Danube.

In the mid-eleventh century the principal threat to the empire was posed by the Pechenegs, nomads who dwelt beyond the Danube. The most effective method for neutralizing the threat of nomad raids to the north-eastern Balkans was to offer them opportunities to acquire through peaceful trading what they would otherwise have sought to seize by raiding. Furthermore, the services of the nomads might be secured to defend rather than assail the frontiers of the empire by cash payments. A further element of this frontier system was the maintenance of small garrisons and administrators in several important *kastra* or *phrouria*, who might monitor both the locals and the nomads. Crucial to the maintenance of frontier stability were the regional elites, whose loyalty was required for the system to function, and through whom payments to the nomads were made. It was only when this loyalty was lost in the early 1070s that the frontier was breached. Thereafter, with the support of the so-called *mixobarbaroi*, the Pechenegs were able to raid south of the Haemus from bases in Paristrion.

A similar series of strategies were implemented to secure the loyalty of the various Slav potentates who dominated the mountainous interior of the north-western Balkans and the northern Adriatic littoral. Their loyalty was required to prevent independent Slav incursions into Byzantine Thrace, Macedonia and Thessaly. Moreover, by the end of the eleventh century their loyalty was required to prevent encroachments by external powers: Hungary, Norman Sicily and Venice, and later, Germany. We have evidence that oaths of loyalty were extracted from the various potentates by the emperor in person. For example, the Dalmatian *archon* Dobronja travelled several times in the 1030s, the last time mistakenly, to Constantinople to perform *proskynesis* before the emperor. This ritual act, which symbolized the subordination of the slave to his master, was performed similarly by Stefan Nemanja to Manuel Comnenus in the 1160s and by numerous lesser *župans* in the intervening period. Once the bond was formed, monitoring and maintaining the relationship became the responsibility of the emperor's representative in the periphery, the *strategos*, later the *katepano* or *doux*. For example, we have seen that Catacalon Clazominites, *strategos* in Dubrovnik was charged with courting Stefan Vojislav, the ruler of Duklja. Clazominites regularly despatched gifts, and agreed to act as godfather to Vojislav's son. There is no indication that this was exceptional behaviour, and, although we know of this episode only because Vojislav reneged on his promises and seized Clazominites, we can assume that for the most part Slav *župans* received imperial gifts and patronage gratefully, and willingly did the emperor's bidding. Thus the efforts to put down Vojislav's rebellion in 1042 involved the *župan* of Raška, the *ban* of Bosna, and the Slav *strategos* of Zahumlje, who all received imperial titles and tribute, and followed the imperial commander, Michael, *strategos* of Dyrrachium.

The carrot was employed more frequently than the stick in securing the allegiance of municipal and regional potentates, and thus in achieving the imperial aim of security and stability. Material benefits took the form of grants of imperial titles with associated stipends and silks, privileged trade, tribute payments or largesse. Certainly Byzantine officials were despatched from the centre to the periphery, but they came to effect accommodation with, not domination of, regional potentates, and to work through, not destroy, local power structures. Anthropologists and theoretical archaeologists have developed models for exploring such relationships of mutual benefit, and these suggest that it may be possible to conduct a fuller analysis of centre-periphery interaction, and prestige goods exchange in the medieval Balkans. Such an analysis is beyond the scope of this study, but it may be stated with some conviction that a form of dependency had been established between core and peripheral elites, and that social status in the periphery had come, to a great extent, to depend on access to prestige goods and honours from the centre. Imperial ranks and titles granted by the emperor augmented the status of regional potentates. The receipt of status-enhancing silks and stipends was deeply significant, in that they would thereafter serve as recognized symbols of authority.

My analysis of Byzantium's Balkan frontier rejects the notion that the various Balkan peoples were struggling constantly to cast off the despised 'Byzantine Yoke'. The peoples of the northern Balkan lands seem to have worn their political allegiances lightly. This is not to say that they did not feel intense personal loyalty to local or regional rulers: it is clear they did. However, there is no indication that this was translated into a higher loyalty, and certainly not to a sense of belonging to any abstract entity like a 'nation'. While sources reveal that a Slavic literary culture developed in this period, which drew heavily on, but was distinct from the culture of Constantinople, this was not developed for political reasons, nor did it bolster a movement for pan-Slavic independence from the Byzantine 'Greeks'. Similarly, while it is clear that Slavic and non-Slavic peoples, including Bulgarians, Serbs and Croats, Albanians and Vlachs, were aware of, indeed actively constructed, their own distinct identities, sources do not support the notion that such an ethnic awareness, still less a national consciousness, motivated rebellions. The most we can say is that a sense of *Wirgefühl* was exploited as a galvanizing force by rebels seeking to extend their support base. In the case of Samuel Cometopulos the appeal was to a common sense of 'Bulgarianness', drawing on the political traditions of the realm ruled by Symeon and Peter. Subsequently rebels, including Peter Deljan in the mideleventh century, and Kalojan in the late twelfth, added Samuel to Symeon and Peter.

It was not ethnic awareness that led various Balkan peoples eventu-

ally to reject Byzantine suzerainty, but rather the emergence of powerful polities in the west whose rulers became alternative patrons and suzerains for the rulers of various groups, regions and cities. Increasingly,
from the end of the eleventh century, peripheral potentates were
seduced or obliged to switch their allegiance to the Sicilian Norman
king, the Venetian doge and the Hungarian king. Each of these rulers
competed against the others as much as he did the Byzantine emperor,
in seeking to secure control of the maritime cities in Dalmatia, of the
north-western marches between Sirmium and Niš, of Bosna and Raška,
and of Dyrrachium. Moreover, each did so by offering economic and
political incentives to Balkan potentates. For example, the Dalmatian
charters reveal that the priors and bishops of the maritime cities
benefited from their association with their new suzerains, and each
received a share in the revenue raised from taxation of trade by either
the Hungarian king or Venetian doge.

Alexius Comnenus was the first emperor obliged to defend the interests of his Balkan *douloi* against encroachments from the west. Although
Alexius was ostensibly successful, defeating the Normans in two protracted campaigns, thereafter western powers played an increasingly
large role in Byzantine foreign, frontier and domestic policy. It is
hard to avoid the conclusion that Alexius was largely responsible for
this, because he secured strategic alliances with both Venetians and
Hungarians, and, moreover, was instrumental in provoking the First
Crusade. Each of the crusades launched between 1095 and 1204 had a
profound effect on Byzantium's Balkan frontier. For the most part the
contingents of Latin pilgrims who crossed the northern Balkans endured
hardship and hunger. This was inevitable, despite the promises, and best
efforts, of various emperors to ensure that sufficient provisions and
appropriate escorts were made available. The numbers involved in the
great armed pilgrimages were simply too great to feed or control.
Moreover, the mass movements inspired great mutual fear and suspicion
on both sides, which is clearly reflected in both Latin and Greek sources.
In particular, Greek sources reveal that the Byzantines believed the true
aim of each enterprise was to capture Constantinople. On the fourth
occasion this was indeed the result. However, this was not inevitable, but
the result of the rapid deterioration of Byzantine fortunes between 1180
and 1204.

The rapid decline in Byzantine fortunes after 1180 was all the more
dramatic given that, for the preceding four decades, the empire's frontiers had been advanced beyond the Danube, and imperial agents and

troops had been active in northern Italy for the first time in centuries. Manuel Comnenus had driven the frontiers forward by controlled demonstrations of force, but had secured them with treaties and by the generous distribution of largesse. In this way, he reestablished imperial suzerainty over peripheral potentates whose allegiance had been lost to the Venetians and Hungarians by his father and grandfather. He did so, however, because he feared the imperial pretensions of the German emperor. The competition between Manuel and Frederick Barbarossa has been characterized as a 'cold war'. It was fought in Italy and Hungary, over which both emperors sought to extend influence and authority, and in Outremer. In competing with each other the two men who claimed the style 'emperor of the Romans' were able temporarily to harness, but ultimately were unable to check the growing ascendancy of smaller powers: namely, the Normans, Venetians and Hungarians, who harboured their own independent ambitions for the northern Balkan lands and peoples.

From the mid-twelfth century the Balkan peoples, courted and threatened from both sides, were offered unprecedented choices. While the Dalmatians continued to enjoy Byzantine patronage, which became ever more lavish, the Raškan Serbs began to make overtures to the German emperor, as well as, on various occasions, to the Hungarian and Sicilian Norman kings, showing an informed preference for a more distant suzerain. It was for this reason that Manuel staged, and stage-managed, trials in the Raškan highlands with envoys of numerous foreign rulers in attendance. After 1160 Byzantine efforts to maintain authority in the Balkan periphery involved balancing a multitude of internal and external interests, forces and factors. Manuel Comnenus' frontier policy became ever more elaborate and expensive; his image was lauded and projected ever more ambitiously, and his agents roamed ever more widely. After Manuel's death in 1180, the empire was without an emperor able to maintain this delicate balance, and unwilling, at least initially, to commit substantial resources to the periphery. Attention was focused on the centre, where the independent ambitions of the emperor's kin, the *sebastoi*, led to a succession of coups. The empire endured a series of ephemeral reigns which were punctuated by rebellions. Increasingly, Balkan potentates saw no reason to tie their own interests to those of a series of eastern emperors who were unable even to control their own kin. A rapid escalation in the value of prizes offered from Constantinople did not change this trend. The daughter of a reigning Byzantine emperor was rejected by the Serbian *veliki župan*, and the ruler of the Bulgarians and Vlachs rejected a patriarch and imperial diadem from Constantinople, preferring to receive symbols of his regnal status from Rome. Ultimately, such encroachment by western powers in the northern Balkans, which I have dubbed the 'rise of the west', led to sovereignty being sought by, and granted to, Balkan potentates whose lands had for most of the period 900–1204 constituted Byzantium's Balkan frontier.

Bibliography

References to both primary and secondary works are presented according to the conventions used in *The New Cambridge Medieval History*. Primary sources are listed alphabetically by author or title, or following the abbreviation which has been used in the text and notes. Secondary works are listed alphabetically by author.

PRIMARY SOURCES

Acta et diplomata res Albaniae mediae aetatis illustrantia, ed. L. Thalloczy, K. Jireček and M. Šufflay, Vienna (1913)

Actes de Lavra, première partie des origines à 1204, ed. P. Lemerle, A. Guillou, N. Svoronos and D. Papachryssanthou, Archives de l'Athos V, Paris (1970)

Albert of Aachen. *Historia Hierosolymitana*, RHC, Historiens Occidentaux IV, Paris (1879), pp. 265–713

Alexiad. Anne Comnène, Alexiade, ed. B. Leib, 3 vols., Paris (1937–45); English trans. E. R. A. Sewter, *The Alexiad of Anna Comnena*. Harmondsworth (1969)

Annales Barenses, ed. G. Waitz, MGH SS V, Hanover (1864), pp. 51–6

Annales Ragusini Anonymi, ed. S. Nodilo, Monumenta Spectantia Historiam Slavorum Meridionalium XIV, Scriptores I, Zagreb (1883)

Annales Venetici Breves, ed. H. Simonsfeld, MGH SS XIV, Hanover (1883), pp. 69–72

Ansbert, *History of Frederick's Expedition. Historia de Expeditione Friderici Imperatoris*, ed. A. Chroust, MGH SS, New Series V, Berlin (1928), pp. 1–115

Attaleiates, Michael. *Michaelis Attaliotae Historia*, ed. I. Bekker, CSHB, Bonn (1853)

Borsari, S., 'Il crisobullo di Alessio I per Venezia', *Annali dell'Instituto Italiano pere gli studi storici* 2 (1969–70), pp. 111–31

Browning, R., 'A new source on Byzantine–Hungarian relations in the twelfth century,' *Balkan Studies* 2 (1961), 173–214

Bryennius, Nicephorus. *Nicéphore Bryennios Histoire*, ed. and trans. P. Gautier, CFHB IX, Brussels (1979)

Buoncompagno. *Buoncompagni liber de obsidione Anconae (a. 1173)*, ed. G. C. Zimolo, Rerum Italicarum Scriptores VII:3, Bologna (1937)

Cecaumenus. *Sovety i Rasskazy Kekavmena. Sochinenie Vizantiiskogo polkovodtsa XI veka*, ed. G. G. Litavrin, Moscow (1972)

Choerosphactes, Leo. *Léon Choirosphactès magistre, proconsul et patrice*, G. Kolias, Athens (1939)

Choniates, Michael. *Michael Akominatou tou Choniatou ta Sozomena*, ed. S. Lampros, 2 vols., Athens (1879–80)

Choniates, Nicetas. *Nicetae Choniatae Orationes et Epistolae*, ed. J.-L. Van Dieten, CFHB III, Berlin and New York (1972)

Choniates, Nicetas. *Nicetae Choniatae historiae*, ed. J.-L. Van Dieten, CFHB XI:I, Berlin (1975); English trans. H. J. Magoulias, *O City of Byzantium, Annals of Nicetas Choniates*. Detroit (1984)

Christopher of Mitylene. *Die Gedichte des Christophoros Mitylenaios*, ed. E. Kurtz, Leipzig (1903)

Chronicle of Henry Mügeln, ed. E. Travnik, SRH II, pp. 87–223

The Chronicles of Robert de Monte, trans. J. Stevenson. London (1856)

Chronicon Casinense, Leo Marsicanus et Petrus Diaconus, PL 173, cols. 439–978

Chrysoberges. *Nicephori Chrysobergae ad Angelos orationes tres*, ed. M. Treu, Breslau (1892)

Cinnamus, John. *Ioannis Cinnami epitome rerum ab Ioanne et Manuelo Comnenis gestarum*, ed. A. Meinecke, CSHB, Bonn (1836); English trans. C. M. Brand, *Deeds of John and Manuel Comnenus*. New York (1976)

Codex Diplomaticus regni Croatiae, Dalmatiae et Slavoniae, I, ed. M. Kostrenčic, Zagreb (1967); II, ed. T. Smičiklas, Zagreb (1904)

Codice diplomatico della reppublica di Genova, ed. C. Imperiale de Sant'Angelo, Fonti per la Storia d'Italia LXXIX, 3 vols. Rome (1936–42)

Continuatio Zwetlensis altera, ed. W. Wattenbach, MGH SS IX, Hanover (1851), pp. 541–4

The Life of St Cyril the Phileote. La vie de Sainte Cyrille le Philéote moine byzantin (†1110), ed. and trans. E. Sargologos, Subsidia Hagiographica XXXIX, Brussels (1964)

Dandolo, Andrea. *Chronicon Venetum. Andreae Danduli ducis Venetiarum chronica per extensum descriptum aa. 46–1280*, ed. E. Pastorello, Rerum Italicarum Scriptores XII:1, Bologna (1938)

Daphnopates, Theodore. *Théodore Daphnopatès Correspondance*, ed. and trans. J. Darrouzès and L. G. Westerink, Paris (1976)

Darrouzès, J. 'De traité de transferts. Édition critique et commentaire', *REB* 42 (1984), pp. 147–214

DAI. Constantine Porphyrogenitus De Administrando Imperio, ed. G. Moravcsik, trans. R. J. H. Jenkins, CFHB I. Washington, DC (1967)

De Cerimoniis. Constantini Porphyrogeniti De Cerimoniis Aulae Byzantinae, 2 vols., ed. J. Reiske, CSHB, Bonn (1829)

Ecloga Basilicorum, ed. L. Burgmann, Forschungen zur byzantinischen Rechtsgeschichte 15, Frankfurt am Main (1988)

Einhard. *Einhard and Notker the Stammerer: Two Lives of Charlemagne*, trans. L. Thorpe, Harmondsworth (1969)

Ekkehard of Aura, *Hierosolymitana*, RCH, Historiens Occidentaux V, Paris (1895), pp. 1–40

Ekkehard of Aura, *Chronicle*, ed. G. Waitz, MGH SS VI, Hanover (1844)

Eustathius of Thessalonica. *Eustathius Thessalonicensis metropolita, allocutio ad imperatorem Manuelem Comnenum*, PG 135, cols. 933–74

Eustathius of Thessalonica, *The Capture of Thessalonica*, trans. R. Melville Jones, Byzantina Australiensia VIII, Canberra (1988)

Ex chronico universali anonymi Laudenensis, ed. O. Holder-Egger, MGH SS XXVI, Hanover (1882), pp. 442–57

Ex Miraculis Sancti Symeonis Auctore Ebervino, ed. G. Waitz, MGH SS VIII, Hanover (1868), 209–11

FRB. Fontes Rerum Byzantinarum: Rhetorum saeculi XII orationes politicae, 2 vols., ed. V. E. Regel and N. I. Novosadskij, St. Petersburg (1892–1917), reprinted Leipzig (1982)

Gautier, P., 'Le typikon du sébaste Grégoire Pakourianos', *REB* 42 (1984), pp. 5–146

Gelzer, H., 'Ungedruckte und wenig bekannte Bistümerverzeichnisse der orientalischen Kirche', *BZ* 2 (1893), pp. 22–72

Geometres, John. *Joannes Geometra*, PG 106, cols. 806–1002

Gerhoch of Reichersberg, *De investigatione Antichristi: Gerhohi praepositi Reichersbergensis libelli selecti*, ed. L. Sackur, MGH Libelli de Lite III, Hanover (1897)

Gregory VII, *Gregorii VII Registrum*, ed. E. Caspar, 2 vols. MGH epistolae selectae II, Berlin (1920–3); Selected letters are translated in E. Emerton, *The Correspondence of Pope Gregory VII. Selected Letters from the Registrum*. New York (1932)

Grumel, V., 'Au seuil de la IIe Croisade: deux lettres de Manuel Comnène au pape', *REB* 3 (1945), pp. 143–67

Herodotus. *The Histories*, trans. A de Selincourt. Harmondsworth 1954.

Historia Ducum Veneticorum, ed. H. Simonsfeld, MGH SS XIV, Hanover (1883), pp. 72–97

Historia Salonitana. Thomae archidiaconi Spalatensis historia Salonitanorum pontificum atque Spalatensium a S. Domnio usque ad Rogerium, ed. F. Rački, Monumenta Spectantia Historiam Slavorum Meridionalium XXVI, Zagreb (1894)

History of the Fifteen Martyrs of Tiberiopolis. Historia martyrii XV martyrum, PG 126, cols. 152–221

Horna, K., 'Die Epigramme des Theodoros Balsamon', *Wiener Studien* 25 (1903), pp. 164–210

Hungarian Chronicle. Chronici Hungarici composito saeculi XIV, ed. A. Domanovszky, SRH I, pp. 217–505

Hurmuzaki, E. and N. Densusianu, *Documente privitore la Istoria Românilor*, I, Bucharest (1887)

Hypatian Chronicle. Ipat'evskaia Letopis', Polnoe Sobranie Russkikh Letopisei II, 2nd edn., Moscow (1962)

Ibn Rusteh, *Les atours précieux*, trans. G. Wiet, Cairo (1955)

Idrisi. *Géographie d'Edrisi*, ed. and trans. P. Amédée Jaubert, 4 vols., Paris (1936–40)

Ignatius the Deacon. *The correspondence of Ignatios the Deacon*, ed. and trans. C. Mango, CFHB XXXIX, Washington, DC (1997)

The Itinerary of Benjamin of Tudela, ed. and trans. A. Adler, London (1907)

John the Exarch. *Das Hexameron des Exarchen Johannes*, ed. R. Aitzmüller, 7 vols., Graz (1958–75)

Krey, A. C., *The First Crusade: the Accounts of Eyewitnesses and Participants*, Princeton, NJ (1921)

Lambert of Hersfeld. *Lamperti monachi Hersfeldensis Opera*, ed. O. Holder-Egger, MGH Scriptores in usum scholarum, Hanover and Leipzig (1894)

Lastivert, Aristakes. *Aristakïs Lastiverc'i's History*, trans. R. Bedrosian, New York (1985)

Leo the Deacon. *Leonis Diaconi Caloensis Historiae Libri Decem*, ed. C. B. Hase, CSHB, Bonn (1828)

Liber Statutorum Civitatis Ragusii, compositus anno 1272, ed. V. Bogišić and K. Jireček, Monumenta Historico-Juridica Slavorum Meridionalium IX, Zagreb (1904)

Les listes de préséance byzantines des IXe–Xe siècles, ed. N. Oikonomides, Paris (1972)

Listine, I, ed. S. Ljubić, Monumenta Spectantia Historiam Slavorum Meridionalium I, Zagreb (1868)

Liutprand of Cremona, *Legatio. Opera*, ed. I. Bekker, MGH Scriptores in usum scholarum, Hanover and Leipzig (1915); English trans. F. A. Wright, *The Works of Liutprand of Cremona*. London (1930)

LPD. Letopis Popa Dukljanina, ed. F. Šišić, Belgrade and Zagreb (1928)

Lupus Protospatharius. *Lupi Protospatarii annali*, ed. G. Waitz, MGH SS V, Hanover (1844), pp. 52–63

Maas, P,. 'Die Musen des Kaisers Alexios I.', *BZ* 22 (1913), 348–59

Malaterra, Geoffrey. *De rebus gestis Rogerii Calabriae et Siciliae comitis*, ed. E. Pontieri, Rerum Italicarum Scriptores V:1, Bologna (1927)

Manganeius Prodromus. Unpublished edition and translation of certain poems by Elizabeth & Michael Jeffreys

Mango, C., 'The conciliar edict of 1166', *DOP* 17 (1966), 317–30

Mango, C., *The Art of the Byzantine Empire 312–1453. Sources and Documents*, Englewood Cliffs, NJ (1972); reprinted Toronto (1986)

Maragone, Bernardo. *Annales Pisani*, ed. M. L. Gentile, Rerum Italicarum Scriptores VI:2, Bologna (1936)

Marvazi. *Marvazi on China, the Turks and India*, ed. and trans. V. Minorsky, London (1942)

Mauropous, John. *Ioannis Euchaitorum metropolitae quae in cod. Vat. gr. 676 supersunt*, ed. P. de Lagarde, Göttingen (1882)

Mercati, S. G., *Collecteana Byzantina*, 2 vols., Bari (1970)

Mioni, E., *Bibilothecae Divi Marci Venetiarum Codices Graeci Manuscripti* III, Rome (1973)

Nicephorus, *Short History. Nikephoros Patriarch of Constantinople Short History*, ed. & trans. C. Mango, CFHB X, Washington, DC (1990)

Nicholas Mysticus. *Nicholas I Patriarch of Constantinople, Letters*, ed. L. G. Westerink, trans. R. J. H. Jenkins, CFHB VI, Washington, DC (1973)

The Life of St Nikon. Text, translation and commentary, D. F. Sullivan, Brookline 1987

Notitiae episcopatuum ecclesiae Constantinopolitanae, ed. J. Darrouzès, Paris (1981)

Otto of Freising. *Gesta Friderici. Ottonis et Rahewini Gesta Friderici I. Imperatoris*, ed. G. Waitz, MGH Scriptores in usum scholarum, Hanover and Leipzig (1912); English trans. C. C. Mierow, *The Deeds of Frederick Barbarossa*. New York (1953); reprinted Toronto (1994)

Otto of Freising. *Chronicle. Ottonis episcopi Frisingensis chronica sive historia de duabus civitatibus*, ed. A. Hofmeister, MGH Scriptores in usum scholarum, Hanover and Leipzig (1912)

Palaeographica Graeca, ed. B. de Montfaucon, Paris (1708)

Prodromus, Theodore. *Theodoros Prodromos: Historische Gedichte*, ed. W. Hörandner, Wiener Byzantinische Studien XI, Vienna (1974)

Psellus, Michael. *Michaelis Pselli Scripta Minora*, ed. E. Kurtz and F. Drexl, 2 vols., Milan (1936–41)

Psellus, Michael. *Chronographie, ou histoire d'un siècle de Byzance (976–1077)*, ed. E. Renauld, 2 vols., Paris (1926–8); English trans. E. R. A. Sewter, *Fourteen Byzantine Rulers*. Harmondsworth (1966)

Psellus, Michael. *Michaeli Pselli Orationes Panegyricae*, ed. G. T. Dennis, Stuttgart and Leipzig (1994)

Psellus, Michael. *Michaeli Pselli Orationes Forenses et Acta*, ed. G. T. Dennis, Stuttgart and Leipzig (1994)

PVL. Povest' Vremennynkh Let, ed. D. S. Likhachev and V. P. Adrianova-Perrets, 2 vols., Moscow and Leningrad (1950); English trans. S. H. Cross and O. P. Sherbowitz-Wetzor, *The Russian Primary Chronicle*. Cambridge, MA (1953)

Raymond of Aguilers. *Le "Liber" de Raymond d'Aguilers*, ed. J. H. Hill and L. L. Hill, Paris (1969); English trans. J. H. Hill and L. L. Hill, *Historia Francorum qui ceperunt Iherusalem*. Philadelphia (1968)

Les regestes des actes du patriarcat de Constantinople, I: *Les actes des patriarches, fasc, iii*, ed. V. Grumel, Bucharest (1947)

Registrum oder merkwürdige Urkunden für deutsche Geschichte, ed. H. Sudendorf, 3 vols., Jena (1849–54)

Rhalles, G. A. and M. Potles, ed., *Syntagma to theion kai hieron kanonon*, 6 vols., Athens (1852–9)

Robert of Clari. *The Conquest of Constantinople*, trans. E. H. McNeal, New York (1936)

Sathas, C., 'Deux letters inédites de l'empereur Michel Ducas Parapinace à Robert Guiscard rédigées par Michel Psellus', *Annuaire de l'association pour l'encouragement des études Grecques en France*, 8 (1874), pp. 193–221

Scutariotes, Theodore. *Mesaionike Bibiliotheke* VII, ed. K. N. Sathas, Venice and Paris (1894)

Scylitzes Continuatus. *He Synecheia tes Chronographias tou Ioannou Skylitze*, ed. E. T. Tsolakes, Hetaireia Makedonikon Spoudon 105, Thessaloniki (1968)

Scylitzes, John. *Ioannis Scylitzes Synopsis Historiarum*, ed. J. Thurn, CFHB V, Berlin and New York (1973)

Short Life of St Clement. 'Dimitar Homitian: "On the same day, June 27, in memory of our holy father Kliment, first prelate and miracle-worker, bishop of Bulgaria in Okhrid"', ed. I. Duichev, trans. S. Nikolov, in I.

Duichev, ed., *Kiril and Methodius: Founders of Slavonic Writing: a Collection of Sources and Critical Studies*, Boulder and New York (1985), pp. 127–30
Šišić, F., ed. *Enchiridion Fontium Historiae Croaticae* I, Zagreb (1914)
SRH. Scriptores Rerum Hungaricarum, ed. E. Szentpétery, 2 vols., Budapest 1937–8
Straboromanus, Manuel. P. Gautier, 'Le dossier d'un haut fonctionaire d'Alexis Ier Comnène, Manuel Straboromanos', *REB* 23 (1965), pp. 168–204
Statutum et Reformationes Civitatis Tragurii, ed. I. Strohal, Monumenta Historico-Juridica Slavorum Meridionalium X, Zagreb (1915)
Suidae Lexicon, ed. A. Adler, 5 vols., Leipzig (1928–38)
Syropoulus, John. *Die Rede des Johannes Syropulos an den Kaiser Isaak II. Angelos (1185–1195)*, ed. M. Bachmann, Munich (1935)
Theophanes Continuatus. *Theophanes continuatus, Ioannes Caminiata, Symeon Magister, Georgius Monachus continuatus*, ed. I. Bekker, CSHB, Bonn (1825)
Theophylact. *Théophylacte d'Achrida*, I, *Discours, traités, poésies*, ed. and trans. P. Gautier, CFHB XVI:1, Thessaloniki (1980); II, *Lettres*, ed. and trans. P. Gautier, CFHB XVI:2, Thessaloniki (1986)
Urkunden zur älteren Handels- und Staatsgeschichte der Republik Venedig, ed., T. L. F. Tafel and G. M. Thomas, 3 vols., Vienna (1856–7)
Vincent of Prague. *Vincenti Pragensis Annales*, ed. W. Wattenbach, MGH SS XVII, Hanover (1861), pp. 658–83
Vita Gerardi Maioris: Legenda Sancti Gerhardi Episcopi, ed. I. Madzsar, SRH II, 461–506
Wibald, *Letters. Bibliotheca rerum Germanicarum* I: *Monumenta Corbeiensia*, ed. P. Jaffé, Berlin (1864)
William of Apulia. *Guillaume de Pouille, La Geste de Robert Guiscard*, ed. M. Mathieu, Instituto Siciliano di Studi Bizantini e Neoellenici, Testi IV, Palermo (1961)
William of Tyre. *Historia rerum in partibus transmarinis gestarum*, RHC, Historiens Occidentaux I, Paris (1844); English trans. E. A. Babcock and A. C. Krey, *History of Deeds done beyond the Sea*, 2 vols., London (1943)
Yahya of Antioch. *Histoire de Yahya-Ibn-Sa'id d'Antioche, continateur de Sa'id-Ibn-Bitriq*, ed. and trans. I. Kratchovsky and A. Vasiliev, Patrologia Orientalis 18, Paris (1924), pp. 699–833
Zepos, J. and P. Zepos, ed., *Ius Graecoromanum*, 8 vols., Athens (1931–62)
Zonaras, John. *Ioannis Zonarae epitome historiarum*, ed. M. Pinder and T. Büttner-Wobst, 3 vols., Bonn (1841–97)
Zosimus. *Zosime histoire nouvelle*, ed. and trans. F. Paschoud, 5 vols., Paris (1971–89)

SECONDARY LITERATURE

Abulafia, D. (1976), 'Dalmatian Ragusa and the Norman Kingdom of Sicily', *SEER* 54: 412–28
Abulafia, D. (1984), 'Ancona, Byzantium and the Adriatic, 1155–1173', *Papers of the British School at Rome* 52: 195–216
Adontz, N. (1938), *Samuel l'Arménien, roi des Bulgares*, Brussels, reprinted in N. Adontz, *Études Arméno-Byzantines*, Lisbon 1965, pp. 347–407

Ahrweiler, H. (1960), *Recherches sur l'administration de l'empire byzantin aux IXe–XIe siècles*, Athens and Paris

Ahrweiler, H. (1966), *Byzance et la Mer*, Paris

Ahrweiler, H. (1998), 'Byzantine Concepts of the Foreigner: the Case of the Nomads', in H. Ahrweiler and A. Laiou (eds.), *Studies on the Internal Diaspora of the Byzantine Empire*, Washington, DC, pp. 1–15

Alchermes, J. D. (1997), 'The Bulgarians', in Evans and Wixom (eds.), *The Glory of Byzantium*, pp. 320–35

Anderson, P. (1974), *Passages from Antiquity to Feudalism*, London and New York

Angelova, S. (1987), 'Sur la caracteristique de céramique du haut Moyen Age provenant de Drastar (Silistra)', in D. Ovcharov (ed.), *Dobrudža – études ethno-culturelles*, Sofia, pp. 93–114

Angold, A. (1995), *Church and Society in Byzantium under the Comneni, 1081–1261*, Cambridge

Angold, M. (1997), *The Byzantine Empire, 1025–1204: a Political History*, 2nd edn, London and New York

Angold, M. (1999), 'The state of research: the road to 1204: the Byzantine background to the Fourth crusade,' *Journal of Medieval History* 25: 257–78

Antoljak, S. (1985), *Samuel and his State*, Skopje

Antonopoulos, P. T. (1993), 'Byzantium, the Magyar raids, and their consequences', *BS* 54: 254–67

Arnold, B. (1997), *Medieval Germany, 500–1300: a Political Interpretation*, London

Baçe, A. (1971), 'Qyteti i fortifikuar i Beratit' [The fortified town at Berat], *Monumentet* 2: 43–62

Baçe, A. (1976), 'Fortifikimet e anikitetit të vonë në vendin tonë' [Late antique fortifications in Albania], *Monumentet* 11: 45–74

Baçe, A. and G. Karaiskaj (1973), 'Kështjella e Petrelës' [The fortress at Petrela], *Monumentet* 5–6: 139–60

Bajalović-Hadži-Pešić, G. (1979), 'Beograd – srednjovekovni grad' [Belgrade – medieval fortified town], *Arheološki Pregled* 20: 109–11

Bakay, K. (1994), *Sacra Corona Hungariae*, Köszeg

Baraschi, S. and O. Damian (1993), 'Considérations sur la céramique émaillée de Nufăru', *Dacia* 37: 237–77

Barnea, I. (1960), 'Ait tezaur de monede bizantine de la Dinogetia' [A hoard of Byzantine coins from Dinogetia], *Studii şi Cercetări de Numismatică (Bucaresti)* 3: 245–54

Barnea, I. (1964), 'Sceaux de deux gouverneurs inconnus du thème de Paristrion', *Dacia* 8: 239–47

Barnea, I. (1971), 'Dinogetia et Noviodunum, deux villes byzantines du Bas-Danube', *RESEE* 9: 343–62

Barnea, I. (1983), 'Sigilii bizantine inedite din Dobrogea, I' [Unpublished Byzantine seals from the Dobrudja, I], *Pontica* 16: 263–72

Barnea, I. (1985), 'Byzantinischen Bleisiegel aus Rumanien', *Vyzantina* 13: 295–312

Barnea, I. (1987), 'Sceaux byzantins de Dobroudja', in N. Oikonomides (ed.), *SBS* 1, pp. 77–88

Bănescu, N. (1946), *Les duchés byzantins de Paristrion (Paradounavon) et de Bulgarie*, Bucharest

Bănescu, N. and P. Papahagi (1935), 'Plombs byzantins découverts à Silistra', *B* 10: 601–6

Beshevliev, V. (1963), *Die protobulgarischen Inschriften*, Berlin

Bibicou, H. (1959–60), 'Une page d'histoire diplomatique de Byzance au XIᵉ siècle: Michel VII Doukas, Robert Guiscard et la pension des dignitaires', *B* 29–30: 43–75

Bikić, V. and V. Ivanišević (1996), 'Prostor oko južne kapije Gornjeg grada Beogradske Tvrdjave' [The south gate area in the upper town of Belgrade Fortress], *Starinar* 47: 253–71

Blagojević, M. (1974), 'Sečenica (*Setzenica*) Strymon (*Strymon*) i Tara (*Tara*) u delu Jovana Kinama' [Sečenica, Strymon and Tara in the account of John Cinnamus], *ŽRVI* 17: 65–76

Blagojević, M. (1996), 'Îupa Reke i "Dendra" Jovana Kinama' [The *županias* of Reke and Dendra in John Cinnamus], *ŽRVI* 35: 197–212

Bozhilov, I. (1986), 'L'idéologie politique du Tsar Symeon: Pax Symeonica', *Byzantinobulgarica* 8: 73–88

Brand, C. M. (1968a), *Byzantium Confronts the West, 1180–1204*, Cambridge, MA

Brand, C. M. (1968b), 'A Byzantine plan for the Fourth Crusade', *Speculum* 43: 462–75

Brehier, L. (1949), *Le Monde Byzantin*, II: *Les Institutions de l'Empire Byzantin*, Paris

[British] Naval Intelligence Division (1945), *Albania*, London

Browning, R. (1975), *Byzantium and Bulgaria: a Comparative Study across the Early Medieval Frontier*, London

Brušić, Z. (1976), 'Byzantine amphorae (9th to 12th century) from eastern Adriatic underwater sites', *Archaeologia Jugoslavica* 5: 31–9

Budak, N. (1994), *Prva Stoljeća Hrvatske* [The First Croatian Centuries], Zagreb

Bulgaru, V. (1977), 'Inceputurile navigaţiei commerciale antice la gurile Dunării' [The antique origins of commercial navigation on the Lower Danube], *Peuce* 6: 87–101

Bury, J. B. (1907), 'The ceremonial book of Constantine Porphyrogennetos', *English Historical Review* 22: 209–27, 417–39

Cameron, A. M. (1987), 'The construction of court ritual: the Byzantine Book of Ceremonies', in D. Cannadine and S. Price (eds.), *Rituals of Royalty. Power and Ceremonial in Traditional Societies*, Cambridge, pp. 106–36

Carile, A. (1974), 'Frederico Barbarossa, i Veneziani e l'assedio di Ancona del 1173. Contributo alla storia politica e sociale della città nel secolo XII', *Studi Veneziani* 16: 3–31

Carter, F. W. (1972), *Dubrovnik (Ragusa), a Classic City-State*, New York

Chalandon, F. (1900; 1912), *Les Comnène*, I: *Essai sur le règne d'Alexis I Comnène (1081–1118)*; II: *Jean II Comnène (1118–1143) et Manuel I Comnène (1143–1180)*, Paris

Charanis, P. (1949), 'Byzantium, the West and the origin of the First Crusade', *B* 19: 17–36

Charanis, P. (1961), 'The transfer of population as policy in the Byzantine Empire', *Comparative Studies in Society and History* 3: 140–54

Cheynet, J.-C. (1990), *Pouvoir et contestations à Byzance (963–1210)*, Paris

Cheynet, J.-C. and C. Morrisson (1990), 'Lieux de trouvaille et circulation des sceaux', in N. Oikonomides (ed.), *SBS* 2, pp. 105–36

Cirac Estopañan, S. (1965), *Skyllitzes Maritensis*, I. *Reproducciones et Minituras*, Barcelona and Madrid

Classen, P. (1970), 'La politica di Manuele Comneno tra Frederico Barbarossa e le città italiane', in *Popolo e stato in Italia nell'età di Frederico Barbarossa. Relazioni e communicazioni al 330 congreso storico subalpino*, Turin, pp. 265–79; reprinted in his *Ausgewählte Aufsätze*, Sigmaringen 1983, pp. 155–70

CMH. The Cambridge Medieval History, IV, ed. J. M. Hussey, Cambridge 1966

Collins, R. (1998), *Charlemagne*, London

Conovici, N. and N. Lungu (1980), 'Un nou tezaur de monede bizantine descoperit la Păcuiul lui Soare' [A new hoard of Byzantine coins found at the Island of the Sun], *Studii şi Cercetari de Istorie Veche şi Arheologie (Bucaresti)* 31: 397–402

Cormack, R. (1992), 'But is it art ?', in Shepard and Franklin (eds.), *Byzantine Diplomacy*, pp. 219–36

Cowdrey, H. E. J. (1988), 'The Gregorian papacy, Byzantium and the First Crusade', *BF* 13: 145–69

Crostini, B. (1996), 'The emperor Basil II's cultural life' *B* 66: 55–80

Dennis, G. T. (1997), 'Imperial Panegyric: rhetoric and reality', in H. Maguire (ed.), *Byzantine Court Culture from 829 to 1204*, Washington, DC, pp. 131–40

Diaconu, P. (1970), *Les Petchénègues au Bas-Danube*, Bibliotheca Historica Romaniae 27, Bucharest

Diaconu, P. (1978), *Les Coumans au Bas-Danube au XIᵉ et XIIᵉ siècles*, Bibliotheca Historica Romaniae 56, Bucharest

Diaconu, P. (1991), 'Sur l'organisation ecclésiastique dans le région du Bas-Danube (derniers tiers du Xᵉ–XIIᵉ siècle)', *Études byzantines et post byzantines* 2: 73–89

Diaconu, P. (1994–5), 'Point de vue sur l'organisation ecclésiastique au bas-Danube (Xᵉ–XIᵉ siècles)', *Dacia* 38–9: 449–52

Diaconu, P. and D. Vîlceanu (1972), *Păcuiul lui Soare, cetatea bizantină*, I, Bucharest

Diaconu, P. and E. Zah (1971), 'Les carrières de pierre de Păcuiul lui Soare', *Dacia* 15: 289–306

Dilke, O. A. W. (1985), *Greek and Roman Maps*, Baltimore, MD and London

Diller, A. (1970), 'Byzantine lists of old and new geographical names', *BZ* 63: 27–42

Dimitrov, H. (1992), 'The medieval town of Lovech', *Istoricheski Pregled* 1992 (iii): 82–91

Dölger, F. (1925), *Regesten der Kaiserurkunden des Oströmischen Reiches*, II: *Regesten von 1025–1204*, Munich and Berlin. Revised edition, ed. P. Wirth (1977)

Ducellier, A. (1965), 'Observations sur quelques monuments de l'Albanie', *Revue Archéologique* 1965 (ii): 153–207

Ducellier, A. (1968), 'L'Arbanon et les Albanais au XI⁰ siècle', *TM* 3: 358–63

Ducellier, A. (1981), *La façade maritime de l'Albanie au Moyen Age. Durazzo et Valona du XI⁰ au XV⁰ siècles*, Thessaloniki

Duichev (Dujčev), I. (1949), 'Recherches sur le Moyen Age bulgare [sommaire par V. Grumel]', *REB* 7: 129–32

Duichev (Dujčev), I. (1975), 'Influences orientales et occidentales dans les Balkans aux X⁰–XII⁰ siècles', *Byzantine Studies / Études Byzantines* 2: 103–21

Edgington, S. (1997), 'The First Crusade: reviewing the evidence', in Phillips (ed.), *The First Crusade: Origins and Impact*, pp. 57–77

Eickhoff, E. (1977), *Friedrich Barbarossa im Orient. Kreuzzug und Tod Freidrichs I.*, Istanbuler Mitteilungen 17, Tübingen

Ercegović-Pavlović, S. (1980), *Les nécropoles romains et médiévales de Mačvanska Mitrovica*, Sirmium 12, Belgrade

Evans, H. C. and W. D. Wixom (eds.) (1997), *The Glory of Byzantium: Art and Culture in the Middle Byzantine Era, AD 843–1261*, New York

Falkenhausen, V. von (1970), 'Eine byzantinische Beamtenurkunde aus Dubrownik', *BZ* 63: 10–23

Falkenhausen, V. von (1997), 'Bishops', in G. Cavallo (ed.), *The Byzantines*, Chicago, pp. 172–96

Farlati, D. (1751), *Illyricum Sacrum*, I, Venice

Febvre, L. (1973), 'Frontière: the word and the concept', in P. Burke (ed.), *A New Kind of History from the Writings of Febvre*, London, pp. 208–18

Ferjančić, B. (1982), 'Vizantijski pečat ot Sirmijuma' [A Byzantine seal from Sirmium], *ZRVI* 21: 47–53

Ferluga, J. (1978), *L'Amministrazione Bizantina in Dalmazia*, Venice

Ferluga, J. (1980), 'Die Chronik des Priesters von Diokleia als Quelle für byzantinische Geschichte', *Vyzantina* 10: 429–60

Fine, jr., J. V. A. (1978), 'A fresh look at Bulgaria under Tsar Peter (927–69)', *Byzantine Studies / Études Byzantines* 5: 88–95

Fine, jr., J. V. A. (1983), *The Early Medieval Balkans: a Critical Survey from the Sixth to the Late Twelfth Century*, Ann Arbor, MI

Fine, jr., J. V. A. (1987), *The Late Medieval Balkans: a Critical Survey from the Late Twelfth Century to the Ottoman Conquest*, Ann Arbor, MI

Foss, C. and D. Winfield (1986), *Byzantine Fortifications, an Introduction*, Pretoria

France, J. (1994), *Victory in the East. A Military History of the First Crusade*, Cambridge

Franklin, S. and J. Shepard (1996), *The Emergence of Rus 750–1200*, London and New York

Frankopan, P. Doimi de (1996), 'A victory of Gregory Pakourianos against the Pechenegs', *BS* 57: 278–81

Fügedi, E. (1986), *Castle and Society in Medieval Hungary (1000–1437)*, Budapest

Garland, L. (1992), 'Political power and the populace in Byzantium prior to the Fourth Crusade', *BS* 53: 17–52

Gelzer, H. (1902), *Der Patriarchat von Achrida. Geschichte und Urkundun*, Leipzig

Gerevich, L. (1990), 'The rise of Hungarian towns along the Danube', in L. Gerevich (ed.), *Towns in Medieval Hungary*, Budapest and Boulder, CO, pp. 26–50

Georgi, W. (1990), *Friedrich Barbarossa und die auswärtigen Machte. Studien zur Außenpolitik 1159–80*, Frankfurt am Main

Georgiev, P. (1987), 'L'organisation religieuse dans les terres bulgares du nord-est après l'an 971', in D. Ovcharov (ed.), *Dobrudža – études ethno-culturelles*, Sofia, pp. 146–58

Gerasimov, T. (1934), 'Tri starobulgarski molivdovula' [Three Old Bulgarian lead seals], *Bulletin de l'Institut d'archéologie (Bulgarie)* 8: 350–60

Gerasimov, T. (1938), 'Olovni pechati na Bulgarskit tsare Simeon i Petur' [Lead seals of the Bulgarian tsars Symeon and Peter], *Bulletin de l'Institut d'archéologie (Bulgarie)* 12: 354–64

Gerasimov, T. (1960), 'Novootkrit oloven pechat na Tsar Simeon' [A newly discovered lead seal of Tsar Symeon], *Bulletin de l'Institut d'archéologie (Bulgarie)* 23: 67–70

Göckenjan, H. (1972), *Hilfsvölker und Grenzwächter in mittelalterlichen Ungarn*, Wiesbaden

Goldstein, I. (1995), *Hrvatski Rani Srednji Vijek* [The Croatian Early Middle Ages], Zagreb

Goss, V. P. (1987), *Early Croatian Architecture. A Study of the Pre-Romanesque*, London

Grabar, O. and M. Manoussacas (1979), *L'illustration du manuscrit de Skylitzès de la Bibliothèque Nationale de Madrid*, Venice

Guilland, R. (1969), 'Logariaste', *JÖB* 18: 101–13

Györffy, G. (1959), 'Das Güterverzeichnis des Klosters zu Szávaszentdemeter (Sremska Mitrovica) aus dem 12. Jahrhundert', *Studia Slavica* 5: 9–74

Györffy, G. (1975), *The Original Landtaking of the Hungarians*, Budapest

Haldon, J. and H. Kennedy (1980), 'The Arab–Byzantine frontier in the eighth and ninth centuries: military organisation and society in the borderlands', *ZRVI* 19: 79–116

Hanak, W. (1995), 'The Infamous Svjatoslav: master of duplicity in war and peace', in Miller and Nesbitt (eds.), *Peace and War in Byzantium*, pp. 138–51

Havlík, L. E. (1976), *Dukljanská kronika a Dalmatinská legenda* [The Chronicle of Duklja and the Dalmatian Legend], Rozpravy Československé Akademie Věd-Řada Společenských Věd 86, Prague

Hayes, J. (1992), *Excavations at Saraçhane in Istanbul*, II: *The Pottery*, Princeton

Hendy, M. (1969), *Coinage and Money in the Byzantine Empire, 1081–1261*, Washington DC

Hendy, M. (1985), *Studies in the Byzantine Monetary Economy, c. 300–1450*, Cambridge

Hendy, M. (1989), *The Economy, Fiscal Administration and Coinage of Byzantium*, Northampton

Hiestand, R. (1986), 'Manuel I. Komnenos und Siena', *BZ* 79: 29–34

Hillenbrand, C. (1997), 'The First Crusade: the Muslim perspective', in Phillips (ed.), *The First Crusade: Origins and Impact*, pp. 130–41

Hodges, R. et al. (1997), 'Late antique and Byzantine Butrint: interim report on the port and its hinterland (1994–95)', *Journal of Roman Archaeology* 10: 207–34.

Hrbek, I. (1955), 'Ein arabischer Bericht über Ungarn (Abū Hāmid al-Andalusī al Garnātī, 1080–1170)', *Acta Orientalia* 5: 205–30

Iordanov, I. (1983; 1985; 1988; 1992), 'Neizdadeni vizantiiski olovni pechati ot Silistra' [Unpublished Byzantine lead seals from Silistra (Dristra)], (I) *Izvestiia na Narodniia Muzei Varna* 19 (34): 97–110; (II) *Izvestiia na Narodniia Muzei Varna* 21 (36): 98–107; (III) *Izvestiia na Narodniia Muzei Varna* 24 (39): 88–103; (IV) *Izvestiia na Narodniia Muzei Varna* 28 (43): 229–45

Iordanov, I. (1993a), *Pechatite ot strategiiata v Preslav (971–1088)* [Seals from the Strategate at Preslav, 971–1088], Sofia

Iordanov, I. (1993b), 'Ankhialo – spored dannite na sfragistikata' [Anchialus – the sigillographical evidence], *Arkheologiia* 1993 (iii): 36–50

Isaac, B. (1988), 'The meaning of the terms *limes* and *limitanei*', *Journal of Roman Studies* 78: 125–47

Ivanešević, V. (1987), 'Vizantijski novac sa Beogradkse tvrdjave' [Byzantine coins from Belgrade fortress], *Numizmatičar* 10: 88–107

Ivanešević, V. (1988), 'Vizantijski novac (491–1092) iz zbirke narodnog muzeja u Požarevcu' [Byzantine coins (491–1092) from the collection of the national museum in Požarevac], *Numizmatičar* 11: 87–99

Ivanešević, V. (1991), 'Vizantijski novac (1092–1261) iz zbirke narodnog muzeja u Požarevcu' [Byzantine coins (1092–1261) from the collection of the national museum in Požarevac], *Numizmatičar* 14: 57–72

Ivanešević, V. (1993), 'Optičaj Vizantijski folisa XI. veka na prostoru centralnog Balkana' [The circulation of eleventh-century Byzantine folles in the central Balkan region], *Numizmatičar* 16: 79–92

Ivanov, I. (1981), 'Vizantiiski-Bolgarskie otnosheniia v 966–969 gg' [Byzantine-Bulgarian relations, 966–969], *VV* 42: 88–101

Jakšić, N. (1982), 'Solidus Romanatus na istočnoj Jadranskoj obali' [The *Solidus Romanatus* on the eastern Adriatic coast], *Starohrvatska Prosvjeta* 12: 173–84

Janković, M. (1981), *Srednjovekovno naselje na Velikom Gradcu u X-XI veku* [The medieval settlement at Veliki Gradac in the 10th and 11th centuries], Belgrade

Jeffreys, E. (2000), 'The wild beast from the West: some literary perceptions in Byzantium of the Crusades', in A. Laiou and R. Mottahedeh (eds.), *The Crusades from the Perspective of Byzantium and the Muslim World*, forthcoming

Jenkins, R. J. H. (1966a), 'The peace with Bulgaria (927) celebrated by Theodore Daphnopates', in *Polychronion. Festschrift F. Dölger*, Heidelberg, pp. 287–303

Jenkins, R. J. H. (1966b), *Byzantium: the Imperial Centuries, AD 610–1071*, London

Jireček, K. (1879), *Die Handelsstrasse und Bergwerke von Serbien und Bosnien während des Mittelalters*, Prague

Johnson, E. N. (1969), 'The Crusades of Frederick Barbarossa and Henry VI', in R. L. Wolff and H. W. Hazard (eds.), *A History of the Crusades, II: The Later Crusades, 1189–1311*, Madison WI, pp. 87–122

Kaegi, W. (1986), 'The frontier: barrier or bridge ?', in *Seventeenth International Byzantine Congress, Major Papers*, New York, pp. 279–305

Karaiskaj, G. (1971), 'Kalaja e Elbasanit' [The citadel of Elbasan], *Monumentet* 1: 61–77

Karaiskaj, G. (1975), 'Të dhëna mbi arkitekturën dhe punimet e konservimit në kalanë e Shurdhahut (Sarda)' [Data on the architecture of the fortress of Shurdhah (Sarda)], *Monumentet* 10: 133–50

Karaiskaj, G. (1977), 'Kalaja Durrësit në mesjetë' [The medieval fortress at Dyrrachium], *Monumentet* 13: 29–53

Karaiskaj, G. (1987), 'Qyeti Shqiptar i Sardës' [The Albanian town of Sarda]', *Monumentet* 23: 73–83

Kazhdan, A. (1965) 'La date de la rupture entre Pierre et Asen (vers 1193)', *B* 35: 167–74

Kazhdan, A. (1977), 'Once more the "alleged" Russo-Byzantine treaty (*c.* 1047) and the Pecheneg crossing of the Danube', *JÖB* 26: 65–77

Kazhdan, A. (1984), 'The aristocracy and the imperial ideal', in M. Angold (ed.), *The Byzantine Aristocracy IX to XIII Centuries*, Oxford, pp. 43–57

Kazhdan, A. (1992), 'Ignatios the Deacon's letters on the Byzantine economy', *BS* 53: 197–201

Kazhdan, A. and Anne Wharton Epstein (1985), *Change in Byzantine Culture in the Eleventh and Twelfth Centuries*, Berkeley, Los Angeles and London

Klaić, N. (1971), *Povijest Hrvata u ranom srednjem vijeku* [History of Croatia in the Early Middle Ages], Zagreb

Koledarov, P. (1982) 'Bulgarskata srednovekovna durzhava i Chernomorskiiat briag' [The medieval Bulgarian realm and the Black sea coast], *Srednovekovna Bulgariia I Chernomorieto* [Medieval Bulgaria and the Black Sea region], Varna, pp. 19–38

Kolia-Dermitzaki, A. (1997), 'Michael VII Doukas, Robert Guiscard and the Byzantine-Norman marriage negotiations', *BS* 58: 251–68

Kovács, L. (1989), *Münzen aus der ungarischen Landnahmezeit*, Fontes Archaeologici Hungariae, Budapest

Kristó, G. (1981), 'Ajtony and Vidin', in G. Káldy-Nagy (ed.), *Turkic-Bulgarian-Hungarian Relations (VIth-XIth Centuries)*, Studia Turco-Hungarica 5, Budapest, pp. 129–35

Kristó, G. (1996), *Hungarian history in the Ninth Century*, Szeged

Kubinyi, A. (1980), 'Handel und Entwicklung der Städte in der ungarischen Tiefebene im Mittelalter', in K. D. Grothusen and K. Zernack (eds.), *Europa Slavica – Europa Orientalis. Festschrift für K. Ludat*, Berlin, pp. 423–44

Lamma, P. (1953), 'Aldruda, Contessa di Bertinovo in un panegyrico di Eustazio di Tessalonica', *Atti e memorie della deputazione di storia patria per le provincie di Romagna*, New Series 3: 57–72

Laurent, V. (1962), *Les sceaux byzantins de médailler Vatican*, Vatican

Lefort, J. (1976), 'Rhétorique et politique: trois discours de Jean Mauropous en 1047', *TM* 6: 265–303

Le Goff, J. (1988), 'The Wilderness in the Medieval West', in J. Le Goff, *The Medieval Imagination*, trans. A. Goldhammer, Chicago, pp. 47–59

Lemerle, P. (1955), 'Byzance et la Croisade', in *Relazioni del X Congresso Internazionale di Scienze Storiche*, III: *Storia del Medievo*, Florence, pp. 595–620

Lemerle, P. (1977), *Cinq études sur le XIe siècle byzantin*, Paris

Lemerle, P. (1979), *The Agrarian History of Byzantium from the Origins to the Twelfth Century*, Galway

Lemerle, P. (1986), *Byzantine Humanism*, trans. H. Lindsay and A. Moffatt, Byzantina Australiensia 3, Canberra

Lévi-Strauss, C. (1966), *The Savage Mind*, London

Liddell, H. G. and R. Scott (1996), *A Greek-English Lexicon*, 9th edn. with revised supplement, H. Stuart Jones and R. McKenzie (eds.), Oxford

Lilie, R.-J. (1984), *Handel und Politik zwischen dem byzantinischen Reich und den italienischen Kommunen Venedig, Pisa und Genua in der Epoche der Komnenen und der Angeloi (1081–1204)*, Amsterdam

Lilie, R.-J. (1993), *Byzantium and the Crusader States, 1096–1204*, trans. J. C. Morris and J. E. Ridings, Oxford

Macrides, R. (1992), 'Dynastic marriages and political kinship', in Shepard and Franklin (eds.), *Byzantine Diplomacy*, pp. 263–80

Magdalino, P. (1988), 'The phenomenon of Manuel I Komnenos', *BF* 13: 171–99

Magdalino, P. (1993), *The Empire of Manuel I Komnenos, 1143–1180*, Cambridge

Magdalino, P. (1995), 'The grain supply of Constantinople, ninth–twelfth centuries', in Mango and Dagron (eds.), *Constantinople and its Hinterland*, pp. 35–47

Magdalino, P. (1996a), 'Innovations in government', in Mullett and Smythe (eds.), *Alexios I Komnenos*, I: *Papers*, pp. 146–66

Magdalino, P. (1996b), *The Byzantine Background to the First Crusade*, Toronto

Magdalino, P. (1996c), *Constantinople Médiévale. Études sur l'évolution des structures urbaines*, Paris

Magdalino, P. and R. Nelson (1982), 'The emperor in Byzantine art of the twelfth century', *BF* 8: 123–83

Makk, F. (1989), *The Árpáds and the Comneni. Political Relations between Hungary and Byzantium in the 12th Century*, Budapest

Malamut, E. (1995), 'L'image byzantine des Petchénègues', *BZ* 88, 105–47

[Blangez-] Malamut, E. and M. Cacouros (1996), 'L'image des Serbes dans le rhétorique byzantine de la seconde moitié du XIIe siècle', in K. Fledelius (ed.), *Byzantium. Identity, Image, Influence. XIX International Congress of Byzantine Studies*, 2 vols., Copenhagen, I, pp. 97–122

Mandić, D (1973), 'Gregorio VII e l'occupazione Veneta della Dalmazia nell'anno 1076', in A. Pertusi (ed.), *Venezia e il Levante fino al secolo XV*, 2 vols., Florence, II, pp. 453–71

Mango, C. (1966), 'A Byzantine inscription relating to Dyrrhachium', *Archäologischer Anzeiger* 3: 410–14

Mango, C. (1975), *Byzantine Literature as a Distorting Mirror. An Inaugural Lecture Delivered before the University of Oxford on 21 May 1974*, Oxford

Mango, C. (1980), *Byzantium. The Empire of the New Rome*, London

Mango, C. and G. Dagron (eds.) (1995), *Constantinople and its Hinterland: Papers of the Twenty-seventh Spring symposium of Byzantine Studies, April 1993*, Aldershot

Mason, R. B. and M. Mundell Mango (1995), 'Glazed "Tiles of Nicomedia" in Bithynia, Constantinople, and elsewhere', in Mango and Dagron (eds.), *Constantinople and its Hinterland*, pp. 313–31

Mathisen, R. W. and H. S. Sivan (eds.) (1996), *Shifting Frontiers in Late Antiquity*, Aldershot

Matijašić, R. (1983), 'Zbirka Vizantskog novca u arheološkom muzeju Istre u Puli' [The collection of Byzantine coins in the Istrian Archaeological Museum in Pula], *Starohrvatska Prosvjeta* 13: 217–33

Mănucu-Adameşteanu, G. (1991), 'Circulaţia monetară la Nufăru în secolele X–XIV' [Monetary circulation in Nufărul in the 10th–14th centuries], *Peuce* 10: 497–554

McCormick, M. (1986), *Eternal Victory. Triumphal Rulership in Late Antiquity, Byzantium and the Early Medieval West*, Cambridge and Paris

McGeer, E. (1995), *Sowing the Dragon's Teeth: Byzantine Warfare in the Tenth Century*, Washington, DC

McGrath, S. (1995), 'The battles of Dorostolon (971): Rhetoric and Reality', in Miller and Nesbitt (eds.), *Peace and War in Byzantium*, pp. 152–64

Meksi, A. (1972a), 'Tri kisha bizantine të Beratit' [Three Byzantine churches at Berat], *Monumentet* 4: 59–102

Meksi, A. (1972b), 'Arkitektura e kishës se Mesopotamit' [The architecture of the church at Mesopotamit], *Monumentet* 3: 47–94

Mesterházy, K. (1990; 1991), 'Bizánci Balkáni eredetű tárgyak a 10–11. századi Magyar sírleletekben, I' [Objects of Byzantine and Balkan origin in Hungarian cemeteries of the 10th and 11th centuries], *Folia Archaeologica* 41: 87–115; II, *Folia Archaeologica* 42: 145–77

Metcalf, D. M. (1960), 'A shipwreck on the Dalmatian coast and some gold coins of Romanus III Argyrus', *Greek, Roman and Byzantine Studies* 3: 101–6

Metcalf, D. M. (1979), *Coinage in South-Eastern Europe, 820–1396*, London

Mijović, P. (1970), 'Bar (Antibaris), est-elle l'héretier direct de Duklja ?', *I Między-narodowy Kongres Arheologii Słowanski* [International Congress of Slavic Archaeology], Warsaw, V, pp. 140–54

Mikulčić, I. (1982), *Staro Skopje so okolnite tverdini* [Ancient Skopje and surrounding fortifications], Skopje

Mikulčić, I. (1996), *Srednovekovni Gradovi i Tvrdini vo Makedonija* [Medieval towns and castles in the Republic of Macedonia], Skopje

Miller, T. S. and J. Nesbitt (eds.) (1995), *Peace and War in Byzantium: Essays in Honor of George T. Dennis, S. J.*, Washington DC

Minić, D. (1980), *Le site d'habitation médiéval de Mačvanska Mitrovica*, Sirmium 11, Belgrade

Mirnik, I. (1980), 'O skupnom nalazu Vizantskog novca 10.- 11. stoljéća iz Mataka kod Nina' [A hoard of Byzantine coins of the 10th and 11th centuries from Matak near Nin], *Numizmatičke Vijesti (Zagreb)* 24: 29–31

Mirnik, I. (1981), *Coin Hoards in Yugoslavia*, Oxford

Mirnik, I. (1985), 'Nalazi novca s Majsana' [Coin finds at Majsan], *Vjestnik Arheološkog Muzeja u Zagrebu* 18: 87–96

Moravcsik, G. (1966), 'Hungary and Byzantium in the Middle Ages', in *CMH* IV.1, pp. 566–92

Morrisson, C. (1976), 'La dévaluation de la monnaie byzantine au XIe siècle: essai d'interpretation', *TM* 6: 3–47

Mullett, M. (1990), 'Patronage in action: the problems of an eleventh-century archbishop', in R. Morris (ed.), *Church and People in Byzantium*, Birmingham, pp. 125–47

Mullett, M. (1997), *Theophylact of Ohrid. Reading the Letters of a Byzantine Archbishop*, Birmingham Byzantine and Ottoman Monographs 2, Birmingham

Mullett, M. and D. Smythe (eds.) (1996), *Alexios I Komnenos*, I: *Papers*, Belfast Byzantine Texts and Translations 4.1, Belfast

Nadj, Š. (1961), 'Tvrdjava Bač' [The fortress at Bač/Bács], *Rad Vojvodjanskikh Muzeja (Novi Sad)* 10: 89–115

Nesbitt, J. (1963), 'The rate of march of crusading armies in Europe: a study and computation', *Traditio* 19: 167–81

Nesbitt, J. and N. Oikonomides (1991), *Catalogue of Byzantine Seals at Dumbarton Oaks and in the Fogg Museum of Art*, I: *Italy, North of the Balkans, North of the Black Sea*, Washington, DC

Nicol, D. M. (1988), *Byzantium and Venice. A Study in Diplomatic and Cultural Relations*, Cambridge

Nikolić, M. (1982–3), 'Karta balkanskog poluostva iz prve polovine XV veka' [A map of the Balkan peninsula from the first part of the 15th century], *Istoriiski Chasopis* 29–30: 63–75

Noonan, T. (1985), 'Khazaria as an intermediary between Islam and Eastern Europe in the second half of the ninth century: the numismatic perspective', *Archivum Eurasiae Medii Aevi* 5 [1987]: 179–204

Novak, V. (1953–4), 'The Slavonic-Latin symbiosis in Dalmatia during the Middle Ages', *SEER* 32: 1–29

Oberländer-Târnoveanu, E. (1983), 'Un atelier monétaire byzantin inconnu de la deuxième moitié du XIe siècle dans le thème de Paristrion', *RESEE* 21: 261–70

Obolensky, D. (1971), *The Byzantine Commonwealth. Eastern Europe 500–1453*, London

Obolensky, D. (1988), *Six Byzantine Portraits*, Oxford

Obolensky, D. (1994), *Byzantium and the Slavs*, New York

ODB. The Oxford Dictionary of Byzantium, ed. A. Kazhdan, A.-M. Talbot, A. Cutler, T. E. Gregory and N. P. Ševčenko, 3 vols., Oxford & New York 1991

Oikonomides, N. (1965), 'Recherches sur l'histoire du Bas–Danube au Xe–XIIe siècles: la Mésopotamie d'Occident', *RESEE* 3: 57–79

Oikonomides, N. (1966), 'The donations of castles in the last quarter of the eleventh century', in *Polychronion. Festschrift F. Dölger*, Heidelberg, pp. 413–17

Oikonomides, N. (1971), 'À propos des relations ecclésiastiques entre Byzance et la Hongrie au XIe siècle: le Métropole de Turquie', *RESEE* 9: 527–33

Oikonomides, N. (1976), 'L'évolution de l'organisation administrative de l'empire byzantin au XIe siècle (1025–1118),', *TM* 6: 125–52

Oikonomides, N. (1983), 'Presthlavitza, the Little Preslav', *Südost-Forschungen* 42: 1–9

Oikonomides, N. (1997), 'Title and income at the Byzantine Court', in H. Maguire (ed.), *Byzantine Court Culture from 829 to 1204*, Washington, DC, pp. 199–215

Olster, D. (1996), 'From periphery to center: the transformation of Late Roman self-definition in the seventh century', in R. W. Mathisen and H. S. Sivan (eds.) (1996), pp. 93–101

Ostojić, I. (1973), 'Relations entre la Venise médiévale et les monastères Bénédictines en Croatie', in A. Pertusi (ed.), *Venezia e il Levante fino al secolo XV*, 2 vols., Florence, II, pp. 583–98

Ostrogorsky, G. (1949), 'Une ambassade Serbe auprès de l'empereur Basile II', *B* 19: 187–94

Ostrogorsky, G. (1956), 'The Byzantine emperor and the hierarchical world order', *SEER* 35: 1–14

Ostrogorsky, G. (1968), *History of the Byzantine State*, trans. J. Hussey. 2nd edn., Oxford; translation of G. Ostrogorky (1963), *Geschichte des byzantinischen Staates*, 3rd edn, Munich

Parker, J. (1956), 'The attempted Byzantine alliance with the Sicilian Norman kingdom, 1166–1167', *Papers of the British School at Rome* 24: 86–93

Parović-Pešikan, M. (1981), 'Srednjovekovna nekropola u Sremskoj Mitrovici' [The medieval cemetery at Sremska Mitrovica], *Starinar* 31: 179–91

Peričić, E. (1991), Sclavorum Regnum *Grgura Barskog. Ljetopis Popa Dukljanina* [Grgur of Bar's *Sclavorum Regnum*. The Chronicle of the Priest of Duklja], Zagreb

Phillips, J. (ed.), *The First Crusade: Origins and Impact*, Manchester

Polemis, D. (1968), *The Doukai: a Contribution to Byzantine Prosopography*, London

Popescu, E. (1986), 'The city of Tomis as an autocephalous archbishopric of Scythia Minor (Dobrudja). Remarks on the chronology of Epiphanios' notitia', *Vyzantiaka* 6: 121–48

Popović, M. (1982), *Beogradska Tvrdjava* [Belgrade Fortress], Belgrade

Popović, M. (1987), *Stari Grad Ras* [The Old City of Ras], Belgrade

Popović, M. (1991), 'Les fortresses du system défensif byzantin en Serbie au XIe–XIIe siècle', *Starinar* 42: 169–85

Popović, M. (1996), 'La fortresse de Slankamen', *Starinar* 47: 155–68

Popović, M. and V. Ivanišević (1988), 'Grad Braničevo u srednjem veku' [The town of Braničevo in the Middle Ages], *Starinar* 39: 125–79

Popović, V. (1978), 'Catalogue des monnaies byzantines du musée de Srem', in C. Brenot, N. Duval and V. Popović (eds.), *Etudes de numismatique danubienne: trésors, l'ingots, imitations, monnaies de fouilles, IVe au XIIe siècle*, Sirmium 8, Rome and Belgrade, pp. 179–93

Popović, V. (1980), 'L'évêché de Sirmium', in S. Ercegović-Pavlović (ed.), *Les nécropoles romains et médiévales de Mačvanska Mitrovica*, Sirmium 12, Belgrade, pp. i–vi

Prinzing, G. & M. Salamon (eds.) (1999), *Byzanz und Ostmitteleuropa: Beiträge zu einer table-ronde des XIX International Congress of Byzantine Studies, Copenhagen 1996*, Mainzer Veröffentlichungen zur Byzantinistik 3, Wiesbaden

Queller, D. and T. F. Madden (1992), 'Some further arguments in defense of the Venetians on the Fourth Crusade', *B* 62: 433–72

Radojčić, B. (1970), 'La région de Dendra de la Serbie au XIe siècle', *Balkan Studies* 11: 249–60

Rey, L. (1925), 'Les ramparts de Durrazo', *Albania* 1: 33–48

Riley-Smith, J. (1997), *The First Crusaders, 1095–1131*, Cambridge

Runciman, S. (1929; 1963), *The Emperor Romanus Lecapenus and his Reign: a Study of Tenth-Century Byzantium*, Cambridge

Runciman, S. (1930), *A History of the First Bulgarian Empire*, London

Runciman, S. (1951), *A History of the Crusades*, I: *the First Crusade*, Cambridge

Sacher, H. (1971), 'Münzfunde: Dubrownik/Jugoslawien', *Numismatisches Nachrichtenblätt* 20: 210–20

Salamon, M. (1971), 'Some notes on a medieval inscription from Silistra (*c.* 976)', *RESEE* 9: 487–96

Šaranik, O. and M. Šulman (1954), 'Srednjovekovna nekropola kod Subotice' [A medieval cemetery near Subotica], *Rad Vojvodjanskikh Muzeja (Novi Sad)* 3: 5–55

Schlumberger, G. (1884), *Sigillographie de l'empire byzantin*, Paris

Schreiner, P. (1971), 'Der Dux von Dalmatien und die Belagerung Aconas im Jahre 1173', *B* 41: 285–311

Schwarz, E. (1982), 'Medieval ceramic decoration in Bulgaria', *BS* 43: 45–50

Seibt, W. (1975), '*Georgios Archiepiskopos Boulgarias*. Zur Identifizierung des bulgarischen Erzbischof während der Herrschaft des Johannes Tzimiskes mit Hilf zweier Siegeltypen', *JÖB* 24: 55–9

Seibt, W. (1978), *Die byzantinischen Bleisiegel in Österreich*, I: *Kaiserhof*, Vienna

Ševčenko, I. (1969), 'A Byzantine inscription from Silistra reinterpreted', *RESEE* 7: 591–8

Shandrovskaia [Šandrovskaya], V. (1981), 'Iz istorii Bolgarii X–XII vv. po dannym sfragistiki' [The evidence of seals for the history of Bulgaria, tenth to eleventh centuries], *Byzantinobulgarica* 7: 455–67

Shandrovskaia [Šandrovskaya], V. (1982), 'Die Bedeutung der Bleisiegel für das Studium einiger Aspekte der byzantinischen Geschichte', *JÖB* 32: 165–73

Shepard, J. (1975), 'John Mauropous, Leo Tornicius and an alleged Russian army: the chronology of the Pecheneg crisis of 1048–1049', *JÖB* 24: 61–89

Shepard, J. (1979a), 'The Russian steppe frontier and the Black Sea zone', *Archeion Pontou* 35: 218–37

Shepard, J. (1979b), 'Tzetzes' letters to Leo at Dristra', *BF* 6: 191–239

Shepard, J. (1988a), 'Aspects of Byzantine attitudes and policy toward the west in the tenth and eleventh centuries', *BF* 13: 67–118

Shepard, J. (1988b), 'When Greek meets Greek: Alexios Comnenos and Bohemond in 1097–1098', *BMGS* 12: 185–277

Shepard, J. (1989), 'Symeon of Bulgaria – Peacemaker', *Annuaire de l'Université de Sofia 'St Kliment Ohridski'* 83 [1994]: 9–48

Shepard, J. (1992a), 'Byzantine diplomacy, AD 800–1204: means and ends', in Shepard and Franklin (eds.), *Byzantine Diplomacy*, pp. 41–71

Shepard, J. (1992b), 'A suspected source of Skylitzes' *Synopsis Historion*: the great Catacalon Cecaumenus', *BMGS* 16: 171–81

Shepard, J. (1993), 'The uses of the Franks in eleventh-century Byzantium', *Anglo-Norman Studies* 15: 275–305

Shepard, J. (1995a), 'A marriage too far ? Maria Lekapena and Peter of Bulgaria', in A. Davids (ed.), *The Empress Theophano. Byzantium and the West at the Turn of the First Millennium*, Cambridge, pp. 121–49

Shepard, J. (1995b), 'Constantinople – gateway to the north: the Russians', in C. Mango and G. Dagron (eds.), *Constantinople and its Hinterland*, pp. 243–60

Shepard, J. (1996), '"Father" or "scorpion" ? Style and substance in Alexios's diplomacy', in Mullett and Smythe (eds.), *Alexios I Komnenos*, I: *Papers*, pp. 68–132

Shepard, J. (1997), 'Cross-purposes: Alexius Comnenus and the First Crusade', in Phillips (ed.), *The First Crusade: Origins and Impact*, pp. 107–29

Shepard, J. (1999a), 'Bulgaria: the other Balkan "empire"', in T. Reuter (ed.), *New Cambridge Medieval History* III, Cambridge, forthcoming

Shepard, J. (1999b), 'Byzantium and the Steppe Nomads: the Hungarian dimension', in Prinzing and Salamon (eds.), *Byzanz und Ostmitteleuropa*, pp. 55–83

Shepard, J. and S. Franklin (eds.) (1992), *Byzantine Diplomacy: papers from the Twenty-fourth Spring Symposium of Byzantine Studies, Cambridge, March 1990*, Aldershot

Sindik, I. (1950), *Komunalno uredjenje Kotora od druge polovine XII. do početka XV. stoljeća* [The municipality of Kotor from the second half of the 12th to the beginning of the 15th century], Belgrade

Ştefan, G., I. Barnea, M. Comşa and E. Comşa (1967), *Dinogetia*, 2 vols., I, Bucharest

Steindorff, L. (1984), *Die dalmatinischen Städte im 12. Jahrhundert. Studien zur ihren politischen Stellung und gesellschaftlichen Entwicklung*, Cologne and Vienna

Stephenson, P. (1994), 'Manuel I Comnenus and Geza II: a revised context and chronology for Hungaro-Byzantine relations, 1148–1155', *BS* 55: 251–77

Stephenson, P. (1996a), 'Manuel I Comnenus, the Hungarian crown and the "feudal subjection" of Hungary, 1162–1167', *BS* 57: 33–59

Stephenson, P. (1996b), 'John Cinnamus, John II Comnenus and the Hungarian campaign of 1127–1129', *B* 66: 177–87

Stephenson, P. (1996c), *The Byzantine Frontier in the Balkans in the Eleventh and Twelfth Centuries*, Ph.D. thesis, University of Cambridge

Stephenson, P. (1999a), 'Byzantine policy towards Paristrion in the mid-eleventh century: another interpretation', *BMGS* 23: 43–66

Stephenson, P. (1999b), 'Political authority in Dalmatia during the reign of Manuel I Comnenus (1143–1180)', in Prinzing & Salomon (eds.), *Byzanz und Ostmitteleuropa*, pp. 127–50

Stone, A. (1997), 'The amphibious serpent: Manuel I and the Venetians', *BF* 24: 251–8

Szabó, C. (1993/4), 'Die militärischen Aspekte der deutsche-ungarischen Beziehungen während der Salierzeit', *Ungarn-Jahrbuch* 21: 1–18

Szemioth, A. and T. Wasilewski (1966; 1969), 'Sceaux byzantins du Musée National de Varsovie, I', *Studia Źródłoznawcze Commentationes* 11: 1–38; II, *Studia Źródłoznawcze Commentationes* 14: 63–89

Tanaşoca, N.-Ş. (1973), 'Les mixobarbares et les formations politiques paristriennes du XIᵉ siècle', *Revue Roumaine d'Histoire* 12: 61–82

Tăpkova-Zaimova, V (1971), 'L'idée impériale à Byzance et la tradition étatique bulgare', *Vyzantina* 3: 289–95

Todorova, M. (1997), *Imagining the Balkans*, Oxford and New York

Totev, T. (1979), 'Icôns peintes en céramique de "Tuzlalaka" à Preslav', in D. Angelov (ed.), *Culture et art en Bulgarie médiévale (VIIIᵉ-XIVᵉ siècles)*, Sofia, pp. 65–73

Totev, T. (1987), 'L'atelier de céramique peinte du monastère royal de Preslav', *Cahiers archéologiques* 35: 65–80

Tóth, S. László (1999), 'The territories of the Hungarian tribal federation around 950 (some observations on Constantine VII's "Tourkia")', in Prinzing and Salamon (eds.), *Byzanz und Ostmitteleuropa*, pp. 23–33

Tougher, S. (1997), *The Reign of Leo VI (886–912): Politics and People*, Leiden

Treadgold, W. (1997), *A History of the Byzantine State and Society*, Stanford

Trojanos, S. (1969), 'Einige Bemerkungen über die finanziellen Grundlagen des Festungsbauen im byzantinischen Reich', *Vyzantina* 1: 39–57

Turner, F. J. (1920), 'The significance of the frontier in American history', in F. J. Turner, *The Frontier in American History*, New York, pp. 1–38

Van Dieten, J.-L. (1971), *Niketas Choniates. Erläuterungen zu Reden und Briefen nebst einer Biographie*, Supplementa Byzantina 2, Berlin and New York

Veselinović, R. L. (1953), 'Starosrpske naselje na Bostaništu kod Mošorina u Bačkoj' [An old Serbian settlement at Bostaništa near Mošorin in Bačko], *Rad Vojvodjanskikh Muzeja (Novi Sad)* 2: 5–58

Vogt, C. and A. Bouquillon (1996), 'Technologie du plaque murales décorées de Preslav et de Constantinople (IXᵉ – XIᵉ siècles)', *Cahiers archéologiques* 44: 105–16

Wasilewski, T. (1964), 'Le thème de Sirmium–Serbie au XIᵉ et XIIᵉ siècles', *ŻRVI* 8: 465–82

Wasilewski, T. (1975), 'Le katepanikion et le duché de Paristrion au XIᵉ siècle', in *XIVᵉ congrès internationale des études byzantines*, 4 vols., Bucharest, II, pp. 641–5

Wattenbach, W. (1939), *Deutschland Geschichtsquellen im Mittelalter*, 2 vols., Berlin

Wharton, A. J. (1988), *Art of Empire: Painting and Architecture of the Byzantine Periphery: a Comparative Study of Four Provinces*, University Park, MD and London

Bibliography

Whittow, M. (1996), *The Making of Orthodox Byzantium, 600–1025*, London

Wilkes, J. J. (1969), *Dalmatia,* History of the Provinces of the Roman Empire, London

Wilson, N. G. (1994), *Photius: the Bibliotheca,* London

Wolff, R. L. (1947), *The Latin Empire of Constantinople (1204–1261),* Ph.D. thesis, Harvard University, Cambridge, MA

Wolff, R. L. (1949), 'The "Second Bulgarian Empire." Its origin and history to 1204', *Speculum* 24: 167–206

Zacos, G. and A. Veglery (1972), *Byzantine Lead Seals* I, Basel

Zacos, G. and J. Nesbitt (1984), *Byzantine Lead Seals* II, Berne

Zafiropoulou, D. (ed.) (1997), *Journeys on the Seas of Byzantium,* Athens

Index